ZAGAT SURVEY

Back in 1979, we never imagined that an idea born during a wine-fueled dinner with friends would take us on an adventure that's lasted three decades – and counting.

The idea – that the collective opinions of avid consumers can be more accurate than the judgments of an individual critic – led to a hobby involving friends rating NYC restaurants. And that hobby grew into Zagat Survey, which today has over 350,000 participants worldwide weighing in on everything from airlines, bars, dining and golf to hotels, movies, shopping, tourist attractions and more.

By giving consumers a voice, we – and our surveyors – had unwittingly joined a revolution whose concepts (user-generated content, social networking) were largely unknown 30 years ago. However, those concepts caught fire with the rise of the Internet and have since transformed not only restaurant criticism but also virtually every aspect of the media, and we feel lucky to have been at the start of it all.

And that wasn't the only revolution we happily stumbled into. Our first survey was published as a revolution began to reshape the culinary landscape. Thanks to a host of converging trends – the declining supremacy of old-school formal restaurants; the growing sophistication of diners; the availability of ever-more diverse cuisines and techniques; the improved range and quality of ingredients; the rise of chefs as rock stars – dining out has never been better or more exciting, and we've been privileged to witness its progress through the eyes of our surveyors. And it's still going strong.

As we celebrate Zagat's 30th year, we'd like to thank everyone who has participated in our surveys. We've enjoyed hearing and sharing your frank opinions and look forward to doing so for many years to come. As we always say, our guides and online content are really "yours."

We'd also like to express our gratitude by supporting **Action Against Hunger,** an organization that works to meet the needs of the hungry in over 40 countries. To find out more, visit www.zagat.com/action.

Nina and Tim

Nina and Tim Zagat

ZAGAT®
CELEBRATING 30 YEARS

World's Top Restaurants

2009/10

Covering 1,268 Restaurants in 58 Cities.
From the Diner's Point of View.

Published and distributed by
Zagat Survey, LLC
4 Columbus Circle
New York, NY 10019
T: 212.977.6000
E: world@zagat.com
www.zagat.com

The reviews in this guide are based on public opinion surveys. The ratings reflect the average scores given by the survey participants who voted on each establishment. The text is based on quotes from, or paraphrasings of, the surveyors' comments. Phone numbers, addresses and other factual data were correct to the best of our knowledge when published in this guide.

ISBN-13: 978-1-60478-146-5
ISBN-10: 1-60478-146-7
Printed in the
United States of America

Contents

Ratings & Symbols

Name | Symbols | Cuisine | Zagat Ratings (FOOD, DECOR, SERVICE, COST)

Area, Address & Contact

Tim & Nina's ◐ *Chinese* ▽ 23 | 9 | 13 | I

W 50s | 4 Columbus Circle (8th Ave.) | 212-977-6000 | www.zagat.com

Review, surveyor comments in quotes

"You're the tapas" croon connoisseurs of the "cheap" cart-circulated Chinese-Castilian cuisine channeled by this "cramped" concrete Columbus Circle compound; to the contrary, critics claim Tim and Nina "push the concept too far" with dishes such as sweet-and-sour sardines, Sichuan ceviche and Beijing-Barcelona bouillabaisse, with service a la Spain in the '30s and China in the '60s.

Ratings

Food, Decor and **Service** are rated on the Zagat 0 to 30 scale.

0 - 9 poor to fair

10 - 15 fair to good

16 - 19 good to very good

20 - 25 very good to excellent

26 - 30 extraordinary to perfection

▽ low response | less reliable

Cost

Cost is estimated by the following symbols:

I Inexpensive

M Moderate

E Expensive

VE Very Expensive

A restaurant review listed without ratings is too new to have been surveyed.

Symbols

◐ serves after 11 PM

Ⓢ closed on Sunday

Ⓜ closed on Monday

₵ no credit cards accepted

About This Survey

This **2009/10 World's Top Restaurants Survey** covers 1,268 outstanding eateries in 58 major markets across Asia, Europe and North America. Like all our guides, it's based on the collective opinions of thousands of consumers who have been there before you. As the guide's coverage illustrates, dining throughout the world just keeps getting better and better.

WHO PARTICIPATED: Input from over 150,000 frequent diners forms the basis for the ratings and reviews in this guide (their comments are shown in quotation marks within the reviews). Of these surveyors, 46% are women, 54% men; the breakdown by age is 10% in their 20s; 27%, 30s; 23%, 40s; 22%, 50s; and 18%, 60s or above. Collectively they bring roughly 26 million annual meals worth of experience to this Survey. We sincerely thank each of these participants - in whatever language we put it, this book is really "theirs."

HELPFUL LISTS: While all the restaurants in this guide were chosen for their high quality, we have prepared two separate sets of lists to facilitate your search: see Top Food by City (pages 7-10) and Most Popular by City (pages 11-14).

ABOUT ZAGAT: This marks our 30th year reporting on the shared experiences of consumers like you. What started in 1979 as a hobby has come a long way. Today we have over 350,000 surveyors and now cover airlines, bars, dining, entertaining, fast food, golf, hotels, movies, music, resorts, shopping, spas, theater and tourist attractions in over 100 countries.

INTERACTIVE: Up-to-the-minute news about restaurant openings plus menus, photos and more are free on **ZAGAT.com** and the award-winning **ZAGAT.mobi** (for web-enabled mobile devices). They also enable reserving at thousands of places with just one click.

VOTE AND COMMENT: We invite you to join any of our surveys at **ZAGAT.com.** There you can rate and review establishments year-round. In exchange for doing so, you'll receive a free copy of the resulting guide when published.

AVAILABILITY: Zagat guides are available in all major bookstores as well as on **ZAGAT.com.** You can also access our content when on the go via **ZAGAT.mobi** and **ZAGAT TO GO** (for smartphones).

FEEDBACK: There is always room for improvement, thus we invite your comments about any aspect of our performance. Did we miss anything? Just contact us at **world@zagat.com.**

Nina and Tim

New York, NY
May 19, 2009

Nina and Tim Zagat

What's New

This second edition of **World's Top Restaurants** brings together the finest dining experiences across Asia, Europe and North America. Covering the best and most popular establishments in 58 major cities, it illustrates the wonderful quality and diversity available to diners today.

YOU GOTTA EAT: It goes without saying that there's a global recession, and its impact is already being felt in the restaurant industry. We've recently surveyed thousands of restaurant-goers: One-third tell us they're eating out less, 28% say they're visiting less expensive places, and roughly 20% are cutting back on alcohol, appetizers or dessert. But despite the economic doom and gloom, we believe the restaurant industry is going to come through the recession better than some others for one reason - people always have to eat. Given the demands of modern life, it often makes more sense to eat out, since restaurants can buy wholesale and produce meals far more efficiently than at-home cooks. And the economic downturn will no doubt pressure restaurants to offer even greater value. Expect to see more low-priced prix fixe meals at upscale places and "recession specials."

THAT'S ENTERTAINMENT: Although the economy may dampen the enthusiasm for food and drink that has developed in recent years, the financial downturn may actually have an upside for restaurants. When times are tough, people naturally look for diversion, and in today's culture, dining out is a leisure activity in itself. As for the high-end restaurants featured in this book, while some may not be practical as weekly destinations, they offer a standard of excellence that remains sought after for business and travel. After all, if you're going to pay well to dine out, it makes sense to focus on getting the best overall value.

GOING GLOBAL: The restaurants in this guide illustrate how globalization has reshaped the dining landscape in recent years. While Paris is still your go-to city for Haute French Cuisine and Tokyo is the town for everything Japanese, many other destinations are studies in culinary diversity. To wit, Budapest's No. 1 for Food is Asian-Mediterranean (**Baraka**), Osaka's is French (**Lumière**), and two of Beijing's top scorers are Brazilian (**Alameda**) and Italian (**Danieli's**). Two of Amsterdam and Montréal's top spots are Japanese (**Yamazato**) and Greek (**Milos**), respectively, while Shanghai counts among its best an Indian eatery (**Vedas**).

TOPS IN OUR BOOK: Finally, as much as we'd like to bestow the title World's Top Restaurant City, it's impossible to say that any one destination has the best food. While Hong Kong, London, New York, Paris and Tokyo are widely recognized for their outstanding dining, every one of the cities in this book is a winner in its own right in terms of quality, diversity and innovation.

New York, NY
May 19, 2009

Nina and Tim

Nina and Tim Zagat

Top Food by City

ASIA

BEIJING

27 Made in China
26 Taj Pavilion
Alameda
25 Beijing Da Dong
Danieli's

HONG KONG

28 Lung King Heen
Sushi Hiro
27 Gaddi's
Petrus
L'Atelier de Joël Robuchon

OSAKA

29 Lumière
25 Agura
Honkogetsu
Arata
La Baie

SHANGHAI

28 Hanagatami
26 Guyi Hunan
Vedas
Jean Georges
Din Tai Fung

TOKYO

28 Raku-tei
27 Uguisudani-en
Kasumicho Suetomi
Sushi Mizutani
Yuji

CANADA

MONTRÉAL

28 La Chronique
27 Milos
Toqué!
Le Club Chasse
Ferreira

TORONTO

29 Sushi Kaji
28 Scaramouche
Chiado/Antonio
27 North 44°
Hiro Sushi

VANCOUVER

29 West
28 Bishop's
Vij's
Pear Tree
27 ToJo's

EUROPE

AMSTERDAM

28 Ron Blaauw
27 Yamazato
Van Vlaanderen
La Rive
26 Bordewijk

ATHENS

29 Spondi
26 48
Varoulko
24 Tudor Hall
Sale e Pepe

BARCELONA

28 Passadis del Pep
Drolma
Àbac
27 Gaig
Alkimia

BERLIN

26 VAU
24 Lorenz Adlon
Maxwell
Gabriele
23 Alt Luxemburg
Die Quadriga*

* Indicates a tie with restaurant above

BRUSSELS

- 28 Comme Chez Soi
- Bruneau
- 27 La Truffe Noire
- Sea Grill
- 26 La Maison du Cygne

BUDAPEST

- 28 Baraka
- Vadrózsa
- 27 Páva
- 25 Lou-Lou
- Kacsa

COPENHAGEN

- 27 Era Ora
- Restaurationen
- 26 Søllerød Kro
- Kong Hans Kælder
- 25 Krogs Fiskerestaurant

DUBLIN

- 27 Thornton's Restaurant
- Patrick Guilbaud
- 26 Seasons
- 25 L'Ecrivain
- One Pico

FLORENCE

- 27 Enoteca Pinchiorri
- La Giostra
- 26 Alle Murate
- Fuor d'Acqua
- Cibrèo

FRANKFURT

- 25 Gargantua
- Osteria Enoteca
- 24 Restaurant Français
- 23 Aubergine
- Sushimoto

GENEVA

- 29 Dom./Châteauvieux
- 26 Auberge du Lion d'Or
- 25 Patara
- 24 La Vendée
- Chez Jacky

HAMBURG

- 25 Haerlin
- 24 Atlantic Restaurant
- 23 Jacobs
- Landhaus Scherrer
- Le Canard Nouveau

ISTANBUL

- 26 Borsa
- 25 Körfez
- Develi
- Seasons Restaurant
- Tugra

LISBON

- 27 Varanda
- Ristorante Hotel Cipriani
- 24 Gambrinus
- Casa da Comida
- Adega Tia Matilde

LONDON

- 29 G. Ramsay/68 Royal
- Chez Bruce
- 28 La Trompette
- River Café
- Ledbury

MADRID

- 28 Santceloni
- 27 Zalacaín
- Goizeko
- 26 Príncipe de Viana
- Combarro

MILAN

- 29 Il Luogo/Aimo e Nadia
- 28 Sadler
- 27 Ristorante Cracco
- 25 Da Giacomo
- Boeucc

MOSCOW

- 25 Mario
- 24 Jeroboam
- Palazzo Ducale
- 23 Café Pushkin
- Cantinetta Antinori

MUNICH

- 27 Tantris
- 25 Vue Maximilian
- Schuhbeck's Restaurant
- Boettner's
- 24 Königshof

PARIS

- 28 Taillevent
- Le Cinq
- Guy Savoy
- L'Astrance
- Pierre Gagnaire

PRAGUE

26 Allegro
25 Aquarius
David
V Zátiší
Essensia

ROME

26 Vivendo
La Pergola
Alberto Ciarla
La Rosetta*
Agata e Romeo

STOCKHOLM

28 Paul & Norbert
Wedholms Fisk
27 Restaurant Mathias Dahlgren
F12
26 Lux Stockholm

VENICE

27 Vini da Gigio
26 Da Ivo
Osteria Da Fiore
Corte Sconta
25 Fortuny

VIENNA

28 Steirereck
26 Imperial
25 Coburg
24 Demel
Walter Bauer

WARSAW

25 Restauracja Polska Tradycja
Dom Polski
23 Restauracja Rubikon
U Kucharzy
Parmizzano's

ZURICH

27 Petermann's
26 Restaurant Français
Lindenhofkeller
24 Ginger
Casa Aurelio

UNITED STATES

ATLANTA

29 Bacchanalia
28 Quinones Room
Rathbun's
Restaurant Eugene
27 Aria

BALTIMORE

28 Charleston
Sushi King
27 Samos
Sushi Sono
Tersiguel's

BOSTON

28 L'Espalier
Aujourd'hui
Oleana
o ya
La Campania

CHICAGO

29 Alinea
Tallgrass
28 Carlos'
Les Nomades
Topolobampo

DALLAS/FT. WORTH

28 French Room
Tei Tei Robata
Local
Teppo Yakitori
Abacus

DENVER/MTN. RESORTS

28 Mizuna
Frasca
Fruition
Sushi Den
27 Sushi Sasa

HONOLULU

28 Alan Wong's
Sushi Sasabune
27 La Mer
Le Bistro
26 Nobu Waikiki

HOUSTON

28 Mark's
Da Marco
27 Tony's
Kanomwan
China View

KANSAS CITY

- 27 Bluestem
- 26 Oklahoma Joe's
- Le Fou Frog
- Tatsu's
- Plaza III

LAS VEGAS

- 28 L'Atelier de Joël Robuchon
- Joël Robuchon
- Rosemary's
- Nobu
- Todd's Unique Dining

LOS ANGELES

- 28 Mélisse
- Asanebo
- 27 Lucques
- Nobu Malibu
- Shiro

MIAMI

- 28 Michy's
- 27 Palme d'Or
- Nobu Miami Beach
- Romeo's Cafe
- Prime One Twelve

NEW ORLEANS

- 28 Brigtsen's
- Stella!
- Bayona
- Dakota
- Gautreau's

NEW YORK CITY

- 28 Per Se
- Le Bernardin
- Daniel
- Jean Georges
- Sushi Yasuda

ORLANDO

- 28 Victoria & Albert's
- Le Coq au Vin
- 27 Primo
- Chatham's Place
- Enzo's Restaurant

PALM BEACH

- 27 Chez Jean-Pierre
- Marcello's La Sirena
- L'Escalier
- Four Seasons
- Little Moir's

PHILADELPHIA

- 29 Fountain Restaurant
- 28 Little Fish
- Birchrunville Store
- Amada
- Le Bar Lyonnais

PHOENIX/SCOTTSDALE

- 28 Kai
- Sea Saw
- Binkley's Restaurant
- 27 Pizzeria Bianco
- 26 Atlas Bistro

SAN DIEGO

- 28 Sushi Ota
- WineSellar & Brasserie
- 27 El Bizcocho
- Karen Krasne's
- Pamplemousse Grille

SAN FRANCISCO BAY AREA

- 29 French Laundry
- Cyrus
- 28 Gary Danko
- Erna's Elderberry
- Kaygetsu

SEATTLE

- 29 Herbfarm
- 28 Rover's
- Cafe Juanita
- Sitka & Spruce
- Armandino's

ST. LOUIS

- 28 Sidney Street Cafe
- Paul Manno's
- 27 Tony's
- Trattoria Marcella
- Niche

WASHINGTON, DC

- 29 Makoto
- Inn at Little Washington
- 28 Komi
- L'Auberge Provençale
- CityZen

Most Popular by City

ASIA

BEIJING

1. Alameda
2. Din Tai Fung
3. Made in China
4. Beijing Da Dong
5. Courtyard

HONG KONG

1. Felix
2. Yung Kee
3. Gaddi's
4. Nobu
5. Spoon by Alain Ducasse

OSAKA

1. La Baie
2. Hagakure
3. Indian Curry
4. Calendrier
5. Ginpei

SHANGHAI

1. M on the Bund
2. Jean Georges
3. T8
4. Din Tai Fung
5. Laris

TOKYO

1. Ukai-tei
2. Jumbo
3. L'osier
4. Shotai-en
5. Au Goût Du Jour

CANADA

MONTRÉAL

1. Toqué!
2. Ferreira
3. Gibbys
4. L'Express
5. Chez L'Épicier

TORONTO

1. Canoe
2. North 44°
3. Scaramouche
4. Jamie Kennedy Wine Bar
5. Bymark

VANCOUVER

1. C Restaurant
2. West
3. Bishop's
4. Vij's
5. Le Crocodile

EUROPE

AMSTERDAM

1. D'Vijff Vlieghen
2. Dylan
3. La Rive
4. Christophe'
5. De Kas

ATHENS

1. Spondi
2. Daphne's
3. GB Corner*
4. 48
5. Milos*

BARCELONA

1. 7 Portes
2. Botafumeiro
3. Barceloneta
4. La Dama
5. Ca l'Isidre
6. Los Caracoles*

BERLIN

1. VAU
2. Borchardt
3. Lorenz Adlon
4. Margaux
5. Bacco/Bocca

BRUSSELS

1. Comme Chez Soi
2. Aux Armes de Bruxelles
3. Belga Queen
4. La Maison du Cygne
5. L'Ecailler du Palais Royal
6. L'Ogenblik*
7. Sea Grill*

BUDAPEST

1. Gundel
2. Páva
3. Kacsa
4. Café Kör
5. Centrál Kávéház
6. Spoon Café*

COPENHAGEN

1. Krogs Fiskerestaurant
2. Café Ketchup
3. Era Ora
4. Le Sommelier
5. Café Victor
6. Restaurationen*

DUBLIN

1. Patrick Guilbaud
2. Shanahan's
3. Seasons
4. Tea Room
5. Eden

FLORENCE

1. Enoteca Pinchiorri
2. Cibrèo
3. Il Latini
4. Villa San Michele
5. Cantinetta Antinori

FRANKFURT

1. Apfelwein Wagner
2. Holbein's
3. Edelweiss
4. Gargantua*
5. Aubergine

GENEVA

1. Auberge du Lion d'Or
2. Le Relais/l'Entrecôte*
3. Brasserie Lipp
4. Dom./Châteauvieux
5. Les Armures

HAMBURG

1. Jacobs
2. Doc Cheng's
3. Haerlin
4. Rive
5. Cox

ISTANBUL

1. Seasons Restaurant
2. Tugra
3. Laledan
4. Körfez
5. Ulus 29

LISBON

1. Gambrinus
2. Bica do Sapato
3. Alcântara Café
4. Varanda
5. A Travessa

LONDON

1. Ivy
2. J. Sheekey
3. Nobu London
4. Wolseley
5. Gordon Ramsay/68 Royal

MADRID

1. Botín Restaurant
2. Zalacaín
3. Viridiana
4. Balzac
5. La Trainera*

MILAN

1. Bice
2. Ristorante Cracco
3. Armani/Nobu
4. Trattoria Bagutta
5. Il Teatro

MOSCOW

1. Café Pushkin
2. Galereya
3. Shinok
4. Scandinavia
5. Cantinetta Antinori

MUNICH

1. Tantris
2. Dallmayr
3. Königshof
4. Käfer-Schänke
5. Lenbach
6. Schuhbeck's Restaurant*

PARIS

1. Taillevent
2. L'Atelier de Joël Robuchon
3. Le Grand Véfour
4. Alain Ducasse
5. La Tour d'Argent

PRAGUE

1. Kampa Park
2. Allegro
3. Bellevue
4. Pravda
5. U Modré Kachnicky

ROME

1. La Pergola
2. Imàgo
3. Harry's Bar
4. La Terrazza
5. Dal Bolognese

STOCKHOLM

1. Operakällaren
2. F12
3. Wedholms Fisk
4. Berns Asian
5. Sturehof*

VENICE

1. Harry's Bar
2. Fortuny
3. Osteria Da Fiore
4. La Terrazza
5. Al Covo

VIENNA

1. Demel
2. Steirereck
3. Imperial
4. Korso bei der Oper
5. Drei Husaren

WARSAW

1. Restauracja Polska Tradycja
2. Belvedere
3. Dom Polski
4. Malinowa
5. Oriental*

ZURICH

1. Kronenhalle
2. Petermann's
3. Widder
4. Brasserie Lipp
5. Restaurant Français

UNITED STATES

ATLANTA

1. Bone's Restaurant
2. Bacchanalia
3. Rathbun's
4. Chops Lobster Bar
5. Aria

BALTIMORE

1. Charleston
2. Prime Rib
3. Helmand
4. Petit Louis Bistro
5. Ruth's Chris

BOSTON

1. Legal Sea Foods
2. Blue Ginger
3. Hamersley's Bistro
4. L'Espalier
5. No. 9 Park

CHICAGO

1. Wildfire
2. Frontera Grill
3. Tru
4. Charlie Trotter's
5. Gibsons

DALLAS/FT. WORTH

1. Abacus
2. Mi Cocina
3. French Room
4. Stephan Pyles*
5. Del Frisco's

DENVER/MTN. RESORTS

1. Frasca
2. Sweet Basil
3. Mizuna
4. rioja
5. Barolo Grill

HONOLULU

1. Alan Wong's
2. Roy's
3. La Mer
4. Sansei
5. Duke's Canoe Club

HOUSTON

1. Mark's
2. Carrabba's
3. Cafe Annie
4. Perry's Steak
5. Da Marco

KANSAS CITY

1. Fiorella's Jack Stack
2. Plaza III
3. Lidia's
4. McCormick & Schmick's
5. Bristol B&G

LAS VEGAS

1. Picasso
2. Bouchon
3. Delmonico Steak
4. Bellagio Buffet
5. Aureole

LOS ANGELES

1. Spago
2. Mélisse
3. Café Bizou
4. Pizzeria Mozza*
5. A.O.C.

MIAMI

1. Joe's Stone Crab
2. Prime One Twelve
3. Nobu Miami Beach
4. Blue Door
5. Barton G.

NEW ORLEANS

1. Commander's Palace
2. Galatoire's
3. Bayona
4. August
5. Acme Oyster

NEW YORK CITY

1. Union Square Cafe
2. Gramercy Tavern
3. Babbo
4. Le Bernardin
5. Gotham B&G

ORLANDO

1. California Grill
2. Seasons 52
3. Victoria & Albert's
4. Emeril's Orlando
5. Jiko

PALM BEACH

1. Kee Grill
2. Abe & Louie's
3. Café Boulud
4. Chez Jean-Pierre
5. New York Prime

PHILADELPHIA

1. Buddakan
2. Amada
3. Le Bec-Fin
4. Alma de Cuba
5. Capital Grille

PHOENIX/SCOTTSDALE

1. T. Cook's
2. Binkley's Restaurant
3. Lon's at the Hermosa
4. P.F. Chang's
5. Eddie V's

SAN DIEGO

1. George's Ocean Terrace
2. Pamplemousse Grille
3. Prado
4. Sammy's Woodfired Pizza
5. Roppongi

SAN FRANCISCO BAY AREA

1. Gary Danko
2. Boulevard
3. Slanted Door
4. French Laundry
5. Michael Mina

SEATTLE

1. Wild Ginger
2. Dahlia Lounge
3. Metropolitan Grill
4. Canlis
5. Restaurant Zoë

ST. LOUIS

1. Sidney Street Cafe
2. Annie Gunn's
3. 1111 Mississippi
4. Trattoria Marcella
5. Tony's

WASHINGTON, DC

1. Citronelle
2. Zaytinya
3. Jaleo
4. Kinkead's
5. Central Michel Richard

ASIA RESTAURANT DIRECTORY

	FOOD	DECOR	SERVICE	COST

Beijing

TOP FOOD RANKING

	Restaurant	Cuisine
27	Made in China	Chinese
26	Taj Pavilion	Indian
	Alameda	Brazilian
25	Beijing Da Dong	Chinese
	Danieli's	Italian
	Din Tai Fung	Chinese
	Hatsune	Japanese
	Comptoirs de France	French
	Feiteng Yuxiang	Chinese
24	Pure Lotus	Vegetarian
	Liqun Roast Duck	Chinese
	Sichuan Provincial	Chinese
23	Courtyard	Eclectic
	Olive	European/Mediterranean
	Morel's	Belgian/French
	Haiku by Hatsune	Japanese
	Cafe Sambal	Malaysian

Alameda *Brazilian* 26 | 20 | 22 | M

Chaoyang | Nali Mall | Sanlitun Beijie (bet. Sanlitun Xiliujie & Sanlitun Xiwujie) | (86-10) 6417-8084

Trendy twenty- and thirtysomethings generate the "buzz" at Beijing's Most Popular restaurant, a "bustling" Brazilian whose "delicious-looking" crowd syncs up with the "chic", glass-walled Chaoyang setting and "consistently excellent", "constantly changing" "contemporary cuisine"; overall, it's "hard to find better", especially when you factor in the "gracious" service and "steal" of a lunch at 60 yuan.

Beijing Da Dong *Chinese* 25 | 17 | 18 | M

Chaoyang | Bldg. 3, Tuanjiehu Beikou, Dongsanhuan Lu (southeast corner of Changhong Qiao) | (86-10) 6582-2892
Dongcheng | Nanxincang Int'l Tower | 22 Dongsishitiao (bet. Chaoyangmen Beidajie & Chaoyangmen Beixiaojie) | (86-10) 5169-0329

"Spectacular Peking duck" that fans call "the best, hands down" is what this popular duo is prized for (they accept reservations only for the 6:30 PM seating - otherwise, expect a wait); the other Chinese fare is "thoroughly satisfying" too, so it's no wonder backers say they're "worth the trip from wherever you are"; P.S. the Dongcheng location features a glassed-in kitchen, and the Chaoyang setting is just as "modern."

Cafe Sambal ◐ *Malaysian* 23 | 20 | 21 | M

Xicheng | 43 Doufuchi Hutong (Jiugulou Dajie) | (86-10) 6400-4875

Deemed the "perfect neighborhood hangout", this hip, rustic, "mellow" Malaysian in Xicheng dishes up "excellent", spicy fare paired with "warm" service; an added attraction is the nearby Rear Lakes, around which pre- or post-dinner strolls are not uncommon.

	FOOD	DECOR	SERVICE	COST
Comptoirs de France	25	22	24	I
Courtyard, The	23	26	24	VE
Danieli's	25	23	26	VE
Din Tai Fung	25	18	20	M
Feiteng Yuxiang	25	17	15	I

Comptoirs de France ⇏ *French* 25 | 22 | 24 | I

Chaoyang | East Lake Villas | 35 Dongzhimenwai Dajie (Xindong Lu) | (86-10) 6461-1525

Chaoyang | Central Park Place, Bldg. 15 | 89 Jianguo Lu (Zhenzhi Lu) | (86-10) 6530-5480

NEW **Shunyi** | Europlaza | 99 Yu Xiang Lu (bet. Huoshayu & Xinyuan Xi Lu) | (86-10) 8046-6309

www.comptoirsdefrance.com

"So hard to choose" say surveyors of all the "decadently tasty", "visually appealing" breads, croissants and sandwiches at these "oases of deliciousness" opened by the son of a French bread-baking family who charges prices that equal Beijing's No. 1 Bang for the Buck; the East Lake location offers more space than the *mignardise*-size Central Park outlet, and the Shunyi spot has a terrace.

Courtyard, The *Eclectic* 23 | 26 | 24 | VE

Dongcheng | 95 Donghuamen Dajie (bet. Beichizi Dajie & Nanchizi Dajie) | (86-10) 6526-8883 | www.courtyardbeijing.com

"As good as any top NYC restaurant", this "magical" "remodeled courtyard house" in Dongcheng boasts "spectacular" panoramas of "the Forbidden City and its surrounding moat" from a "cool" interior with high ceilings, mirrored walls and "modern Chinese art"; the Eclectic cuisine, laying "Asian riffs on mostly Western food", is "expensive" but "worth it"; P.S. "don't miss" the upstairs cigar bar for the "best views."

Danieli's *Italian* 25 | 23 | 26 | VE

Chaoyang | St. Regis Beijing | 21 Jianguomenwai Dajie (Ritan Lu) | (86-10) 5050-6789, ext. 6370 | www.stregis.com/beijing

"Superb" service (voted Beijing's No. 1), a "lavish" selection of "high-quality" (and "expensive") Italian cuisine and a "tremendous wine list" make this a "perfect special-occasion destination" in Chaoyang; the restaurant and its home, the St. Regis Beijing, reopened in July 2008 after a refurbishment not reflected in the Decor score.

Din Tai Fung *Chinese* 25 | 18 | 20 | M

Chaoyang | 24 Xinyuan Xili Zhong Jie (bet. Xindong Lu & Zuojiazhuang Xijie) | (86-10) 6462-4502

Chaoyang | Shin Kong Pl. | 87 Jianguo Lu, 6th fl. (bet. Dongsanhuan Zhonglu & Jintai Lu) | (86-10) 6533-1536

The "outstanding", "perfectly light" soup dumplings are "little pieces of heaven" say allies of this "bright, airy" Chaoyang Chinese pair hosting "huge" crowds; "quick", "attentive" service only increases the "good-value" factor; P.S. the upstairs kids' room (at Xinyuan Xili Zhong) is "a plus."

Feiteng Yuxiang *Chinese* 25 | 17 | 15 | I

Chaoyang | Yanhua Yuan | 24 Jianguomenwai Dajie (southwest of Jianguomen Bridge) | (86-10) 6515-9600 ⇏

Chaoyang | A3 Xinyuan Nanlu (northwest of Yansha Bridge) | (86-10) 8455-2333

Chaoyang | Chunxiu Lu (bet. Gongti Beilu & Xingfucun Zhonglu) | (86-10) 6415-3764 ⇏

It's the "famed" shui zhu yu ('water-cooked fish', a misnomer since the fish is actually cooked in a lot of oil) that brings accolades to this

Chaoyang site that, aside from its signature dish, cooks up other "consistently good", reasonably priced Sichuan-style fare for a hip, young clientele; snaring one of the sunken booths is a challenge – the place is "popular" and no reservations are taken.

Haiku by Hatsune *Japanese* 23 | 24 | 21 | E

Chaoyang | Block 8 | 8 Chaoyang Gongyuan Xilu (bet. Liangmaqiao Lu & Nongzhanguan Nanlu) | (86-10) 6508-8585 | www.block8.cn

Located in the nightlife district near Chaoyang Park's west gate, this Japanese venture from Alan Wong (of Hatsune) is home to "amazing" cocktails, "flawless" sushi and "wonderful" cooked fare; the sparse space, set off in white and oak tones, draws local and foreign patrons, just about all of them ultrafashionable.

Hatsune *Japanese* 25 | 22 | 21 | M

Chaoyang | Heqiao Bldg. C | Jia 8 Guanghua Lu, 2nd fl. (bet. Jintai Lu & Zhenzhi Lu) | (86-10) 6581-3939

Marrying a "slick" setting with "unique" fare, this second-floor address in Chaoyang is acclaimed for its "fresh", "addictive" "American-style" sushi ("throw authenticity to the wind, and you'll love it"); it's a "lunchtime favorite" too, thanks to the "great" deals.

Liqun Roast Duck *Chinese* 24 | 9 | 13 | M

Dongcheng | 11 Beixiangfeng Hutong (Qianmen Dongdajie) | (86-10) 6705-5578

As the pictures in the corridors attest, everyone from Anthony Bourdain to Al Gore has sampled the famously "fabulous" duck roasted at this taste of the "real China" located in "what's left of" a "historic hutong" in Dongcheng (it's also known for "silky", "translucent" pancakes and "unhelpful service"); the "grease on the walls", "makeshift tables" and general "dilapidation" may prove "too authentic" for some, but "for the adventuresome", it's "quite the experience."

Made in China *Chinese* 27 | 26 | 24 | E

Dongcheng | Grand Hyatt | 1 Dong Chang'an Jie (bet. Dongdan Beidajie & Wangfujing Dajie) | (86-10) 8518-1234, ext. 3608 | www.beijing.grand.hyatt.com

"Popular with tourists", but "far from a trap", this "elite" eatery in Dongcheng's Grand Hyatt serves the "best Peking duck in the whole wide world" – or so say surveyors who've voted all of the "outstanding" "fancified" Northern Chinese fare the No. 1 Food in Beijing; a dash of "fun" is added to the "stylish", "stunning setting" with multiple "glass-walled" kitchens to view (which you won't be able to enjoy unless you "reserve well ahead"); P.S. your local "friends will be shocked by the price tag."

Morel's Ⓜ *Belgian/French* 23 | 14 | 18 | M

Chaoyang | 27 Liangmaqiao Lu (Lucky St.) | (86-10) 6437-3939

Chaoyang | 5 Xinzhong Jie (Gongti Beilu, opposite Workers' Indoor Arena north gate) | (86-10) 6416-8802 ◐

www.morelsgroup.com

Cross the street from Workers' Indoor Arena in Chaoyang and, voilà, "you're in a small Brussels bistro" where "authentic Belgian" and French tastes abound in dishes like "succulent mussels", "juicy steak" and "awesome waffles", all "well worth the money" (and they're "not even that expensive!"); the decor strikes some as "corny" and space is "cramped", but the "fabulous beer selection" obliterates protests; N.B. the Liangmaqiao sibling has bigger tables better for large groups.

Olive, The ◐ *European/Mediterranean* 23 | 17 | 18 | M

Chaoyang | 17 Gongti Beilu (opposite Workers' Stadium north gate) | (86-10) 6417-9669

Offering "healthier than average dining options" in Beijing, this "quaint eatery" across from Workers' Stadium in Chaoyang presents "fresh", "refreshing and flavorful" European and Mediterranean fare "cooked just right"; the "friendly" venue comprises several small rooms festooned with contemporary art, an open kitchen and a "relaxing" patio (the "perfect spot for brunch").

Pure Lotus Vegetarian *Vegetarian* 24 | 23 | 22 | M

Chaoyang | 10 Nongzhanguan Nanlu (bet. Chaoyang Gongyuan Lu & Dongsanhuan Beilu) | (86-10) 6592-3627

Chaoyang | Holiday Inn Lido | 6 Jiangtai Lu (Fangyuan Xilu) | (86-10) 6437-6688, ext. 3812

"How can this not be meat?" ask "amazed" carnivores when they taste what these monk-run Chaoyang veggie venues "accomplish": "intriguing", "inventive" dishes served in "stimulating artistic preparations"; with stone statues, prayer wheels and incense, the "temple"-like Holiday Inn Lido locale is the more ornate, but both are completely "serene" and blessed with servers who "genuinely care."

Sichuan Provincial Government Restaurant ⊄ *Chinese* 24 | 11 | 12 | I

Dongcheng | 5 Gongyuan Toutiao (Jianguomennei Dajie) | (86-10) 6512-2277

"Have your last meal in Beijing" at this "real slice" of Sichuan life in Dongcheng, because "you won't get anything this authentic until your next trip" (the "fresh chile oil makes all the difference" in the "zingingly tasty" dishes); you'll have to "wait for ages" to get into the "chaotic", pink-plastic-tablecloth-bedecked "government building", but it's "worth" it for "some of the best", "cheapest" fare to be found.

Taj Pavilion, The *Indian* 26 | 21 | 25 | M

Chaoyang | China World Mall | 1 Jianguomenwai Dajie (Dongsanhuan Zhonglu) | (86-10) 6505-5866

Chaoyang | Holiday Inn Lido | 6 Jiangtai Lu, 3rd fl. (Fangyuan Xilu) | (86-10) 6436-7678

www.thetajpavilion.com

"Absolutely the best Indian food" in Beijing can be found at these "ideally located" Chaoyang destinations whose "gracious" owner not only ensures the "consistency" of the "high-quality" fare, but "adds warmth" to the already "fantastic" service; the China World Mall branch feels "authentic" with candlelight illuminating the intricate wood carvings on the wall, while the Holiday Inn Lido iteration is "nice and bright."

FOOD DECOR SERVICE COST

Hong Kong

TOP FOOD RANKING

	Restaurant	Cuisine
28	Lung King Heen	Chinese
	Sushi Hiro	Japanese
27	Gaddi's	French
	Petrus	French
	L'Atelier de Joël Robuchon	French
26	Fook Lam Moon	Chinese
	Morton's	Steak
	Nadaman	Japanese
	Da Domenico	Italian
	Yan Toh Heen	Chinese
	Man Wah	Chinese
	Spring Moon*	Chinese
25	Mandarin Grill & Bar	Eclectic
	Caprice	French
	One Harbour Road	Chinese
	Nobu	Japanese

Caprice *French* 25 | 27 | 26 | VE

Central | Four Seasons | 8 Finance St. (Connaught Rd.) | (852) 3196-8888 | www.fourseasons.com

"One of the most beautiful" restaurants in Hong Kong is the Four Seasons' French in Central, where you "enter through carved doors" onto a "glass walkway lit from below" and arrive in an "elegant" room with "glorious views" of Victoria Harbour; add "impeccable" service from an "attentive" staff", chef Vincent Thierry's (ex Le Cinq in Paris) "exquisite" Gallic cuisine and an "epic" wine list, and you have a "wonderful", albeit "expensive", place for "special occasions."

Da Domenico *Italian* 26 | 14 | 15 | VE

Causeway Bay | Sunning Plaza | 8 Hoi Ping Rd. (Hysan Ave.) | (852) 2882-8013

"Simple but top-notch" Italian cooking and a "cult"-like following heavy on "tycoons and celebrities" are the claim to fame of this Causeway Bay scenester; everything down to the salt is "freshly flown in" from Italy - a mark of "authenticity" that's reflected in its "astronomical" prices - and while the "small" quarters are decidedly "down-to-earth" and the service "limited", nothing seems to stifle its "snob appeal."

Felix ◐ *Continental* 21 | 27 | 23 | VE

Tsim Sha Tsui | The Peninsula | Salisbury Rd., 28th fl. (Nathan Rd.) | (852) 2315-3188 | www.hongkong.peninsula.com

Philippe Starck makes his way to Hong Kong via this "lavish" "hipster" (voted Hong Kong's Most Popular restaurant) atop Tsim Sha Tsui's Peninsula hotel, where "jaw-dropping" 360-degree vistas of the harbor and city skyline meet "sexy" modern design with "stunning"

* Indicates a tie with restaurant above

results - and prices to match; maybe it's mostly about the "over-the-top atmosphere" and "beautiful-people" crowd here, but those who can focus on the Continental cuisine say it's "delicious"; N.B. "don't forget to check out" the "spectacular" men's WC, as well as the "must-visit" upstairs bar.

Fook Lam Moon *Chinese* 26 | 16 | 21 | VE

Wan Chai | Newman House | 35-45 Johnston Rd. (Luard Rd.) | (852) 2866-0633 | www.fooklammoon-grp.com

"Some of the best Cantonese food you can find in Hong Kong" comes out of the kitchen of this "old-school" Wan Chai institution known for its "to-die-for dim sum" and luxury specialties ("shark's fin soup, abalone", etc.); "upscale" prices and a "tycoon and *tai tai*"-heavy clientele have earned it the nickname the "millionaire's canteen", where "you must go with a regular" or service "can be lacking", but still to most it "doesn't get much better than this."

Gaddi's *French* 27 | 26 | 29 | VE

Tsim Sha Tsui | The Peninsula | Salisbury Rd. (Nathan Rd.) | (852) 2315-3171 | www.hongkong.peninsula.com

"Time stands still" (in a good way) at this "old-world", chandelier-bedecked "jewel box" in Tsim Sha Tsui's Peninsula hotel, a "European palatial"-style "landmark" that's "as fancy and classically French as can be found in Hong Kong"; the "world-class" fare and decor are surpassed only by the near-"perfect" "formal" service (Hong Kong's No. 1), and while such "not-to-be-missed" experiences come at a "stiff price", the "rich-and-famous" types who dine here swear it's "worth every cent"; P.S. for "extraordinarily special occasions", book the chef's table in the kitchen.

NEW Island Tang *Chinese* - | - | - | VE

Central | The Galleria | 9 Queen's Rd. Central (Ice House St.) | (852) 2526-8798 | www.islandtang.com

A magnet for financial elite types, this new haute Cantonese in Central is brought to you by lifestyle maven Sir David Tang (China Club) and purveys delicacies like shark's fin and bird's nest along with a variety of dim sum; set in a high-end shopping mall, the clubby room channels 1930s Shanghai with deco chandeliers, ceiling fans and wooden lacquered furniture, though the pricing is decidedly up to date.

L'Atelier de Joël Robuchon *French* 27 | 27 | 26 | VE

Central | The Landmark | 11 Pedder St., 4th fl. (Queen's Rd. Central) | (852) 2166-9000 | www.joel-robuchon.com

"Spend your children's inheritance" for a "fabulous experience" at this Robuchon production in Central, where you "sit at the counter and watch the show" unfold in the open kitchen, which produces a tasting menu of "superbly executed", "modern" French cuisine in "small portions", paired with one of the "best wine lists in town"; "beautiful, yet subdued" decor graces the "impressive" space, and the service is "excellent."

Lung King Heen *Chinese* 28 | 24 | 24 | E

Central | Four Seasons | 8 Finance St. (Connaught Rd.) | (852) 3196-8888 | www.fourseasons.com

"Everything from the menu is well executed" at this Chinese housed in the Four Seasons hotel in Central (voted Hong Kong's No. 1 for Food), where "innovative", "top-notch" Cantonese cuisine and an "excellent selection" of "scrumptious" dim sum are paired with an eclectic, China-centric wine list, while "amazing views of the harbor" serve as a backdrop to the "pretty", contemporary room accented with silver and glass; it's "expensive", but the consensus is that the experience is "worth it."

Mandarin Grill & Bar *Eclectic* 25 | 24 | 27 | VE

Central | Mandarin Oriental | 5 Connaught Rd. (Ice House St.) | (852) 2522-0111 | www.mandarinoriental.com

A "sure winner every time", this "expense-account" Eclectic in Central's Mandarin Oriental is a "class act", where the "attentive" staff has "everything down pat" and the kitchen turns out "excellent" fare, including the "freshest sashimi and oysters"; the "addition of windows was a tremendous improvement" to the "classic", "elegant" dining room, although a few prefer the old "formal club" setting to the present "glass, chrome and marble" look.

Man Wah *Chinese* 26 | 24 | 26 | VE

Central | Mandarin Oriental | 5 Connaught Rd. (Ice House St.) | (852) 2522-0111 | www.mandarinoriental.com

"Still worth a visit" after more than 40 years ("if you have the money"), this "old standby" in the Mandarin Oriental in Central delivers "superb" "traditional" Cantonese cuisine and "excellent" service in an "elegant" room with a "spectacular view of the harbor"; while a few fault the chef for "unimaginative" cooking, it's the "favorite" "upmarket Chinese" of many others.

Morton's of Chicago *Steak* 26 | 22 | 25 | VE

Tsim Sha Tsui | Sheraton | 20 Nathan Rd. (Salisbury Rd.) | (852) 2732-2343 | www.mortons.com

For a "taste of America" in Tsim Sha Tsui, carnivores commend this outpost of the chophouse chain in the Sheraton that cronies contend is a "step above most locations in the U.S.", thanks to "excellent" steaks, a "well-balanced wine list" and "prompt", "professional" service; the "clubby, sophisticated" setting and a "first-class view of the skyline" are "icing on the cake", and though the tabs are "hefty", many feel it's "worth it."

Nadaman *Japanese* 26 | 20 | 25 | VE

Admiralty | Island Shangri-La | Pacific Pl., 7th fl. (Supreme Court Rd.) | (852) 2820-8570 | www.shangri-la.com/island

A crowd of mostly "old-money" and "business clientele" gravitates to this "fabulous", "pricey" outpost of a venerable Tokyo-based Japanese chain in Admiralty's Island Shangri-La hotel for "amazing", "masterful" kaiseki courses, including "excellent" Wagyu beef, and "impeccable" service; the space, a modern take on "traditional" decor from Japan, includes sushi and teppanyaki counters and a private tatami room.

Nobu ◐ *Japanese* 25 | 24 | 23 | VE

Tsim Sha Tsui | Intercontinental | 18 Salisbury Rd. (Ave. of Stars) | (852) 2721-1211 | www.hongkong-ic.intercontinental.com

A "solid" addition to Nobu Matsuhisa's global "empire", this Tsim Sha Tsui outpost offers "outstanding" "nontraditional" Japanese, including a chef's menu that "always has something special" and "fresh", "super" sushi; a "stellar" harbor view is the backdrop to the Rockwell Group-designed space, which features an undulating ceiling and bamboo-embedded terrazzo walls, while the service is "quick and efficient.."

One Harbour Road *Chinese* 25 | 24 | 26 | VE

Wan Chai | Grand Hyatt | 1 Harbour Rd. (Convention Ave.) | (852) 2588-1234 | www.hongkong.grand.hyatt.com

"Impeccable" service, "high-quality" Cantonese fare (including "excellent" dim sum) and a "wonderful" space with a "spectacular view of the harbor" win raves for this Chinese in the Grand Hyatt in Wan Chai; it's "expensive", but that's "the price you pay" for "one of the best fine-dining places on Hong Kong Island."

Pawn, The *British* - | - | - | E

NEW **Wan Chai** | 62 Johnston Rd. (Ship St.) | (852) 2866-3444 | www.thepawn.com.hk

A former 100-year-old pawn shop has been transformed into this new British gastropub in Wan Chai, where Scottish eggs, bangers 'n' mash, and fish 'n' chips are the things to order; a colonial-chic setting, veranda seating and a rooftop garden supply the atmosphere.

Petrus *French* 27 | 26 | 27 | VE

Admiralty | Island Shangri-La | Pacific Pl., 56th fl. (Supreme Court Rd.) | (852) 2820-8590 | www.shangri-la.com/island

"Expensive, but worth it" according to *amis,* this haute French in the Island Shangri-La in Admiralty showcases "top-notch" toque Frederic Chabbert's "excellent", "inventive" cuisine, paired with an "amazing" wine selection; the "helpful staff" provides "impeccable" service while "jaw-dropping views" of Victoria Harbour complement the chandelier-lit room that some find "romantic", others a bit "gaudy"; while the tabs might approach the "Chinese GDP", most agree it's the "right place" to "impress a date or client."

Pierre *French/Mediterranean* - | - | - | VE

Central | Mandarin Oriental | 5 Connaught Rd. (Centre St.) | (852) 2825-4001 | www.mandarinoriental.com

Overseen by star toque Pierre Gagnaire, this luxurious French-Med in Central's Mandarin Oriental hotel (the former Vong space) offers avant-garde haute cuisine that's among the finest in town; formal service and an elegant setting, with windows overlooking Victoria Harbour, add to the sumptuous - and ultrapricey - experience.

NEW **Roka** *Japanese* - | - | - | E

Admiralty | Pacific Place Mall | 88 Queensway (Justice Dr.) | (852) 3960-5988 | www.rokarestaurant.com

Offering contemporary robatayaki cuisine, this Admiralty Japanese specializes in charcoal-grilled items accompanied by an extensive selection of soju; parked in the basement level of the Pacific Place Mall, it exudes a casual air, right down to lighting so perfect that everyone looks glam here.

Spoon by Alain Ducasse *French* 23 | 25 | 25 | VE

Tsim Sha Tsui | Intercontinental | 18 Salisbury Rd. (Ave. of Stars) | (852) 2313-2256 | www.hongkong-ic.intercontinental.com

"Superb" food, "impeccable" service and a "breathtaking view of the harbor" make this "chic" French export in Tsim Sha Tsui's Intercontinental hotel "a must for the total experience"; although some call the "eclectic" menu a bit "odd" (with "small portions") and wish that star chef "Alain would visit more often", most appreciate the "attention to detail and quality", recommending it for "impressing clients" on your "expense account" or for a "very special date"; P.S. "take a seat before 8 PM to enjoy the light show on the harbor."

Spring Moon *Chinese* 26 | 25 | 27 | VE

Tsim Sha Tsui | The Peninsula | Salisbury Rd. (Nathan Rd.) | (852) 2315-3160 | www.hongkong.peninsula.com

"Sublime" is the word on this "traditional" Cantonese in Tsim Sha Tsui that diners say "sets the standard for Chinese cuisine" across the country, with favorites including "fabulous dim sum" and "heavenly" Peking duck; its "exceptional Peninsula service", "classic art deco design" and "fine tea menu" further elevate the experience, making it well worth the "expensive" tab; N.B. jacket suggested.

Sushi Hiro *Japanese* 28 | 18 | 21 | VE

Causeway Bay | Henry House | 40-42 Yun Ping Rd., 10th fl. (Pak Sha Rd.) | (852) 2882-8752

It's "definitely one of the best sushi restaurants in town" declare diners about this find inside a Causeway Bay office building, serving "ultrafresh fish" that keeps it "popular among a Japanese clientele"; the minimally decorated room is relaxed but formal enough for a business meal, and most agree the "expensive" tab is "reasonable" considering the "excellent" quality - plus "lunch is a great deal"; P.S. be sure to "book ahead."

Yan Toh Heen ◐ *Chinese* 26 | 26 | 28 | VE

Tsim Sha Tsui | Intercontinental | 18 Salisbury Rd. (Ave. of Stars) | (852) 2721-1211 | www.hongkong-ic.intercontinental.com

"Magnificent in every way", this Chinese in Tsim Sha Tsui's Intercontinental hotel is "true decadence", offering "top-notch" service, "splendid" Cantonese cuisine, including some of the "best dim sum in the world", and an "elegant, beautiful" space featuring "jade place settings" and "amazing" views of the harbor; not surprisingly, "you'll pay through the nose", but "oh, is it worth it."

Yung Kee *Chinese* 23 | 14 | 17 | M

Central | 32-40 Wellington St. (D'Aguilar St.) | (852) 2522-1624 | www.yungkee.com.hk

A "classic Hong Kong establishment", this "famous" Central landmark (circa 1942) is a "must-try for visitors", serving "generous" portions of "wonderful" "traditional" Cantonese cuisine, including "out-of-this-world" roast goose and "perfectly done" preserved eggs, that "packs in the crowds"; the scene gets "hectic" in the "large", "bright" space that can accommodate "families and large groups", but you "don't come here for the ambiance or service."

FOOD DECOR SERVICE COST

Osaka

TOP FOOD RANKING

	Restaurant	Cuisine
29	Lumière	French
25	Agura	Japanese
	Honkogetsu	Japanese
	Arata	Japanese
	La Baie	French
24	L'heure Bleue	French
	Kashiwa-ya	Japanese
	Iwansui	Chinese
	Kahara	Eclectic/French
	La Tortuga	French
	Essence et Goût	French
	La Becasse	French
	Kuramata	Chinese
	Ristorante Matsumura	Italian
	Calendrier	French

Agura ◐ M *Japanese* 25 | 15 | 13 | M

Honmachi | 4-8-7 Honmachi (Honmachi) | Chuo-ku | (81-6) 6253-1129 S

Sakaisuji Honmachi | Excel 6 Bldg., 1st fl. | 2-4-9 Tokiwa-machi (Sakaisuji-Honmachi) | Chuo-ku | (81-6) 6943-0029

The staffers at this pair of yakiniku specialists are "so confident" in the quality of their "first-rate", "delectable" meats that they recommend BBQ seasoned with nothing more than salt, and regulars agree, rating it a "cut above the competition" and a "terrific value for the money"; the "bright", "unpretentious" interiors and "pleasant" service round out the "satisfying" experience.

Arata ◐ S M ≠ *Japanese* 25 | 7 | 13 | M

Nishi-Nakajima | 4-2-8 Nishi-Nakajima (Nishinakajima-Minamigata) | Yodogawa-ku | (81-6) 6304-5250 | www.fsic.net/arata

The daily lineup of raw giblets is "awesome" and the hotpot "superb" at this Nishi-Nakajima Japanese organ-meat specialist, one of the "city's jewels", where there's often a line outside the no-frills digs because it doesn't take reservations; since the veteran proprietor is "not so young anymore", some concerned loyalists wish he would "limit his customers" and "take it easy."

Calendrier M *French* 24 | 21 | 23 | VE

Honmachi | Ohara 3 Bldg., 1st fl. | 3-2-15 Honmachi (Honmachi) | Chuo-ku | (81-6) 6252-5010

This traditional French establishment in Honmachi is the showcase for chef Ryozo Kadoguchi's "brilliantly crafted, yet unpretentious" cuisine that's deemed "always reliable"; the disciplined, but still "casual" service is "lovely" and the atmosphere is "relaxed" in the "chic", if somewhat "narrow" room, and many surveyors feel "fortunate" to have the experience.

	FOOD	DECOR	SERVICE	COST
Essence et Goût	24	16	18	M
Ginpei	21	13	13	M
Hagakure	21	7	11	I
Honkogetsu	25	21	17	VE
Indian Curry	18	8	9	I

Essence et Goût Ⓜ⊄ *French*

Takatsuki | Forest Court, 1st fl. | 1-3-19 Tenjinmachi (Takatsuki) | Takatsuki-shi | (81-72) 685-0313

Carnivores "go out of their way" for some of the "region's best meats" served at this French located in a residential section of Takatsuki, where you "get a lot for your money", which is why landing a reservation "can be tricky"; the "warm" husband-and-wife team delivers "unpretentious" yet "surprisingly formal" service in the "tiny, casual" surroundings.

Ginpei ☒Ⓜ *Japanese*

Doutonbori | RITZ Building, 1st fl. | 2-2-20 Doutonbori (Nanba) | Chuo-ku | (81-6) 6211-9825 ⊄

Shinsaibashi | 2 Bangai Building, 1st fl. | 2-1-10 Shinsaibashi (Shinsaibashi) | Chuo-ku | (81-6) 6214-0519

Dojima | Hatsune Building, 1st fl. | 1-5-4 Dojima (Umeda) | Kita-ku | (81-6) 6341-6000

www.ginpei.com

The "only spots in this part of town" you can get such "marvelous" seafood "at such prices", this Japanese chain based in the city of Wakayama serves fin fare as "fresh as you can get in a fishing port", including "wonderful" sashimi, "superb" boiled fish and the "masterpiece" *taimeshi* (sea bream and rice); prices are reduced after 8 PM, but if you come too late most items will be sold out; P.S. the Doutonbori branch's private rooms are "ideal for entertaining clients."

Hagakure ☒Ⓜ⊄ *Japanese*

Umeda | Osaka Ekimae 3 Bldg., fl. B2 | 1-1-1 Umeda (Kitashinchi) | Kita-ku | (81-6) 6341-1409 | www.hagakure.cc

Devotees of Sanuki-style udon flock to this Umeda "mecca" for its "awesome" signature dish of "shiny, lovely" noodles in a "pure" soy sauce broth, and the "seconds on the house" also ensure "long lines all the time", but fortunately the "tables turn quickly" in the "cramped" space that's "not conducive to lingering"; the staff is "famous" for giving "lessons on how to eat" the pasta properly, but while some deem it "entertaining", critics find it "bothersome."

Honkogetsu ☒ *Japanese*

Doutonbori | Hozenji-Yokocho | 1-7-11 Doutonbori (Nanba) | Chuo-ku | (81-6) 6211-0201

"Osaka's finest" is what many dub this Japanese in Doutonbori's Hozenji-Yokocho, where "first-rate ingredients" go into its "consistently" "splendid" dishes that are full of "surprises" yet "always spot-on", although a few critics lament the "course-only" menu; the "austere" space is "serene" and "uncluttered", and the chef-owner is "friendly."

Indian Curry Ⓜ⊄ *Indian/Japanese*

Kitahama | Kitahama Chuo Bldg., fl. B2 | 2-2-22 Kitahama (Kitahama) | Chuo-ku | (81-6) 6203-0370 ☒

Minami-Senba | Nagahori Underground, 2-8 | 2 Minami-Senba (Sakaisuji-Honmachi) | Chuo-ku | (81-6) 6282-2040

Namba | 1-5-20 Namba (Namba) | Chuo-ku | (81-6) 6211-7630

Dojima | Dojima Abansa Bldg., fl. B | 1-6-20 Dojima (Kitashinchi) | Kita-ku | (81-6) 6345-5616 ☒

Nakanoshima | Asahi Shinbun Bldg. | 3-2-4 Nakanoshima (Higobashi) | Kita-ku | (81-6) 6202-5213 ☒

(continued)

Indian Curry

Shibata | Hankyu 3 Bangai | 1-3 Shibata (Umeda) | Kita-ku | (81-6) 6372-8813
Sonezaki-Shinchi | Dojima Underground | 1 Sonezaki-Shinchi (Kitashinchi) | Kita-ku | (81-6) 6344-3941 [S]
www.indiancurry.jp

"Osaka soul food" is what fans call the Japanese-style curry at this 60-year-old Nanba-based Eclectic chain that has earned a loyal following with its "addictive" signature fare that's "spicy, with a hint of sweetness"; the staff is "insolent" and the "wretched" counter-only spaces "need improvement", but since the "food comes as soon as you sit down", it's "good for a quick bite", and "women can dine alone comfortably" here.

Iwansui [S] [M] ≠ *Chinese* — 24 | 12 | 8 | M

Sakaisuji Honmachi | Osaka Honmachi Bldg., 1st fl. | 1-4-5 Azuchi-machi (Sakaisuji-honmachi) | Chuo-ku | (81-6) 6263-5190

An "exceptionally tough table" is this Chinese in Sakaisuji-Honmachi, where the "creative", "flawless" cuisine comes with "lots of surprises"; though the tiny counter-only space can accommodate no more than a dozen diners, since the chef-owner runs a "one-man operation", service can be "slow" and "inadequate."

Kahara [S] [M] *Eclectic/French* — 24 | 18 | 18 | VE

Sonezaki-Shinchi | Kishimoto Bldg., 2nd fl. | 1-9-2 Sonezaki-Shinchi (Kitashinchi) | Kita-ku | (81-6) 6345-6778

One of the "best in the Shinchi area", this popular, unassuming eight-seat counter spot elicits "sighs" of appreciation for all aspects of its innovative French-accented Eclectic fare, from the "high-quality ingredients to the preparations to the intriguing presentations" in attractive tableware; the "edgy" proprietor "adds some flair" to the menu with his explanations.

Kashiwa-ya [S] *Japanese* — 24 | 23 | 20 | VE

Senriyama-Nishi | 2-5-18 Senriyama-Nishi (Senriyama) | Suita-shi | (81-6) 6386-2234

While it's "hard to find" in a residential area of Senriyama-Nishi, as soon as you enter this veteran Japanese you find it as "relaxing as a country inn"; adding to the comfort level is the "authentic", "impressive" kaiseki menu that appeals to the "eyes as well as the palate" thanks to the "meticulous", "flawless" presentations.

Kuramata [M] *Chinese* — 24 | 25 | 23 | VE

Daito | 6-4-17 Haizuka (Kounoike-Shinden) | (81-72) 874-4323

Housed in a "splendid" traditional Japanese building in a residential section of Daito city, this Chinese (a sibling of Tokyo's Opus One) is "pricey" but "well worth the expense" for its original, seafood-centric cuisine and "corresponding" service; regulars would just as soon "keep it a secret" from the rest of the world.

La Baie *French* — 25 | 26 | 25 | VE

Umeda | The Ritz-Carlton Osaka, 5th fl. | 2-5-25 Umeda (Umeda) | Kita-ku | (81-6) 6343-7020 | www.ritz-carlton.co.jp

"Everything's superb" at the "Kansai region's exemplary high-end French", housed in the Ritz-Carlton Osaka, where the "delicate, inventive" cuisine is "memorable" and the atmosphere is "exceptional" in the "chic", "gorgeous" space; "no complaints" about the "warm, thoroughly attentive" service or the "abundant" wine list, which makes it a popular site for people "celebrating anniversaries."

La Becasse [S] *French* — 24 | 23 | 20 | VE

Koraibashi | Ginsenyokobori Bldg. | 4-2-6 Koraibashi (Yodoyabashi) | Chuo-ku | (81-6) 4707-0070

The "genuine article", this Koraibashi French near Yodoyabashi Station showcases chef Yoshinori Shibuya's "artistic", "refined" creations that are "impressive" for their "innovation" and "impeccable executions"; the "splendid" space is "dignified" yet "relaxing", the "thoughtful" service "unforgettable" and "for such a high-end" establishment, it's surprisingly "unpretentious."

La Tortuga [S][M] *French* — 24 | 13 | 14 | E

Koraibashi | 1-5-22 Koraibashi (Kitahama) | Chuo-ku | (81-6) 4706-7524

At this popular Koraibashi French near Kitahama Station, chef Hirokazu Mantani's cooking is the "pride of all Kansai bistros" according to fans who are "astonished" by the "volume" of his menu offerings, at such "reasonable" prices, and "impressed" by his "rustic" cuisine (including game in season) that features "accents of Asia and Africa" in its presentations; less impressive, however, are the "cramped" quarters and "slow" service.

L'heure Bleue [S][M] *French* — 24 | 17 | 18 | E

Edobori | Line Bldg., 1st fl. | 1-19-2 Edobori (Higobashi) | Nishi-ku | (81-6) 6445-3233

"Everything's top-notch", from the "flavorful" vegetable dishes to the "magnificent" seafood, at this French spot near Edobori's Higobashi Station serving up "generous portions" of Gallic fare that make it an "excellent value"; the chef "prepares meals in front of" customers seated at the counter while "entertaining" them with his "banter", adding to the comfort level in the "compact", "cozy" space.

Lumière [S][M] *French* — 29 | 29 | 29 | E

Higashi-Shinsaibashi | Unagidani-Block, 3rd fl. | 1-19-15 Higashi-Shinsaibashi (Shinsaibashi) | Chuo-ku | (81-6) 6251-4006 | www.k-coeur.com

This "shining star" of the city's French dining scene is Osaka's No. 1 for Food, Decor and Service; the "surprises keep coming" in chef Yasushi Karato's "bold, yet delicate use of produce" and "flamboyant", "complex" flavors, while the "high-end, yet comfortable" interior and "considerate" service are "consistent" with the stellar cuisine.

Ristorante Matsumura [M] ≠ *Italian* — 24 | 13 | 15 | E

Fukushima | Royal Heights Tango, 1st fl. | 1-2-1 Fukushima (Umeda) | Fukushima-ku | (81-6) 6455-7977

"Spot-on" Northern Italian cuisine is showcased at this Fukushima *cucina,* including "can't-miss" meat dishes and "exceptional" pastas, all of which "reflect the chef's passion" for his craft; critics, though, are full of complaints about "haughty, overbearing" service and warn of cramped conditions in the tiny, eight-seat space.

	FOOD	DECOR	SERVICE	COST

Shanghai

TOP FOOD RANKING

	Restaurant	Cuisine
28	Hanagatami	Japanese
26	Guyi Hunan	Chinese
	Vedas	Indian
	Jean Georges	French
	Din Tai Fung	Chinese
25	Kitchen Salvatore Cuomo	Italian
	Palladio	Italian
	T8	Asian/Mediterranean
	Crystal Jade	Chinese
	Danieli's	Italian
	South Beauty 881	Chinese
	Yi Café	Eclectic
	Bukhara Grill	Indian
	Vegetarian Lifestyle*	Chinese/Vegetarian
24	Di Shui Dong	Chinese
	Jade on 36	Eclectic/French
	Laris	Eclectic
	Nan Xiang	Chinese
	South Beauty	Chinese
23	1221	Chinese

Bukhara Grill *Indian* 25 | 20 | 23 | M

Gubei/Hongqiao | 3729 Hongmei Lu (Yan'an Xi Lu) | (86-21) 6446-8800

Granted, it's "a bit far" from the center of town in the expat enclave of Gubei, but this "consistently excellent", "family"-friendly Indian is "worth the trip" for its "delicious, authentic" dishes and "professional, friendly" staff; a pleasant bar/lounge on the ground floor broadcasts sporting events on a giant flat-screen.

Crystal Jade ◐ *Chinese* 25 | 19 | 19 | M

Huaihai/Xintiandi | South Block Xintiandi | House 6-7, Ln. 123 Xingye Lu, 2nd fl. (Madang Lu) | (86-21) 6385-8752

"Popular" is the word for this "always packed" Singapore import in Xintiandi, where the Cantonese-Shanghainese offerings are "excellent" and "affordable", despite the "upscale" neighborhood; "don't be put off by the shopping-mall setting" – it's beside the point once they roll out their "delicious" dim sum and "sublime" dumplings.

Danieli's *Italian* 25 | 24 | 25 | E

Pudong | St. Regis | 889 Dongfang Lu, 39th fl. (Weifang Lu) | (86-21) 5050-6789, ext. 632 | www.stregis.com

Although "a little out of the way", this "elegant" Italian in the St. Regis hotel is worth seeking out for an "impressive business dinner" owing to its "sublime" cooking and "fabulous view" of Pudong from its 39th-floor perch; sure, "you'll definitely pay for it", but economizers tout the

* Indicates a tie with restaurant above

"reasonable" set-menu lunch and Sunday brunch, a "well-kept secret" featuring free-flowing champagne.

Din Tai Fung *Chinese* 26 | 17 | 21 | M

Gubei/Hongqiao | Peace Sq. | 18 Shuicheng Lu (Hongqiao Lu) | (86-21) 6208-4188

Huaihai/Xintiandi | South Block Xintiandi | Unit 11, House 6, Ln. 123 Xingye Lu (Huangpi Lu) | (86-21) 6385-8378 ◐

www.dintaifung.com.tw

"Some of the best dumplings in the Far East" turn up at this "all-time favorite" Taiwanese chain serving "street food in restaurant settings", notably that "addictive" *xiaolongbao* that will "keep your mouth watering"; add in "quality service" and "modern", if "simple" decor, and it's no surprise that many say dining here is "mandatory for Shanghai newcomers."

Di Shui Dong ◐⊄ *Chinese* 24 | 11 | 13 | I

Xuhui | 5 Dongping Lu (Hengshan Lu) | (86-21) 6415-9448

Xuhui | 56 Maoming Nan Lu (Changle Lu) | (86-21) 6253-2689

"Cheap and tasty", this "popular" Xuhui duo serves "excellent" Hunan cuisine (in "spicy and not-too-spicy" versions) to a crowd of "locals and expats"; for some, the "alarmingly casual" settings may be too "downscale" and the acoustics too "boisterous", but a "big menu" brimming with "delicious" options and a "smiling, if harried", staff help distract.

NEW El Willy [S] *Spanish* - | - | - | E

Xuhui | 20 Donghu Lu (Huaihai Zhong Lu) | (86-21) 5404-5757 | www.elwilly.com.cn

Authentic tapas and tasty paellas combine with an impressive wine list at this new Xuhui Spaniard where Barcelonan chef Willy Trullàs Moreno is making a name for himself; set in a French Concession garden villa, it's attracting local and expat thirtysomethings with its Euro-chic interior and warm hospitality.

Fu 1039 ◐ *Chinese* - | - | - | VE

Changning | 1039 Yuyuan Lu (Jiangsu Lu) | (86-21) 5237-1878

Fu 1088 ◐ *Chinese*

Changning | 10 Yuyuan Lu (Jiangsu Lu) | (86-21) 5239-7878

Sophisticated Shanghainese cuisine is offered at these Changning siblings, serving both old-fashioned homestyle dishes like kao fu and smoked fish, as well as cutting-edge gourmet updates; set in historic mansions decorated with step-back-in-time antiques, they're a favorite of nostalgic locals and a handful of in-the-know expats.

Guyi Hunan *Chinese* 26 | 12 | 15 | M

Jing An | 87 Fumin Lu (Julu Lu) | (86-21) 6249-5628

"If you like it spicy", check out this "fiery hot" Hunan in Jing An that's "popular with locals" who "keep a few bottles of beer handy" to "cool their throats"; it's a "bustling, noisy" scene with "prices that are a throwback to the '50s", so naturally "ridiculous lines" and "long waits" come with the territory.

Hanagatami *Japanese* 28 | 21 | 26 | VE

Jing An | Portman Ritz-Carlton | 1376 Nanjing Xi Lu (Xikang Lu) | (86-21) 6279-8888, ext. 5898 | www.ritzcarlton.com

What just might be the city's "best sushi bar" lies in this Japanese "marvel" in Jing An's Portman Ritz-Carlton that also offers kaiseki, teppanyaki and a variety of sakes in a "comfortable" yet sophisticated space done up with plenty of light wood and screen dividers; maybe you'll wind up paying "higher-than-Japan" prices, but this "excellent" place does take Top Food (and Top Service) honors in our Shanghai Survey.

Jade on 36 *Eclectic/French* 24 | 26 | 24 | VE

Pudong | Pudong Shangri-La | 33 Fucheng Lu, 36th fl. (Huayuanshiqiao Lu) | (86-21) 6882-3636 | www.jadeon36.com

The "food is as spectacular" as the "stunning", picture-postcard views of the Bund from this glamorous 36th-floor aerie in the Pudong Shangri-La hotel, where the "unique" French-Eclectic dishes are truly "out of the ordinary" (think foams, infusions, etc.) and ordered from pricey, prix fixe-only menus; "impeccable service" and "inspirational" decor via Adam Tihany enhance the "crème de la crème" mood, leading many to swoon "does it get any better than this?"

Jean Georges *French* 26 | 27 | 26 | VE

Huangpu | Three on the Bund | 3 Zhongshan Dong Yi Lu, 4th fl. (Guangdong Lu) | (86-21) 6321-7733 | www.jean-georges.com

"Impress the boss or the wife (or both)" at Jean-Georges Vongerichten's "wow"-inducing French "splurge", a "world-class dining experience" set in Huangpu's "sophisticated" Three on the Bund complex; look for "exceptional" New French cooking, "super-attentive service", a "must-see" Michael Graves setting that includes a "million-dollar view" of the river and the "new Shanghai" and, of course, "money-is-no-object" pricing.

Kitchen Salvatore Cuomo *Italian* 25 | 23 | 21 | E

Pudong | 2967 Lujiazui Xi Lu (Fenghe Lu) | (86-21) 5054-1265

The eponymous Naples-born chef brings his Japanese franchise to Shanghai via this "authentic Italian" set along the river in Pudong with an "absolutely spectacular view of the Bund"; the "modern" menu (including some of the "best pizza" in the city) lives up to the "exceptional" setting, as does the "attentive staff."

Laris *Eclectic* 24 | 25 | 24 | VE

Huangpu | Three on the Bund | 3 Zhongshan Dong Yi Lu (Guangdong Lu) | (86-21) 6321-9922 | www.threeonthebund.com

This "elegant" Eclectic with "stunning" river views is parked in the swell Three on the Bund complex; given the "incredibly imaginative" menu, "attentive" service and "ultramodern", "white-on-white" decor courtesy of Michael Graves, it's no surprise that all this "high class comes with high tabs", but that doesn't seem to faze its "international" following one bit.

M on the Bund *Continental/Eclectic* 21 | 25 | 23 | VE

Huangpu | 5 Zhongshan Dong Yi Lu, 7th fl. (Guangdong Lu) | (86-21) 6350-9988 | www.m-onthebund.com

Swells seeking the "chic side of Shanghai" tout this circa-1999 Bund "trailblazer" that's still a "place to be seen" thanks to a "delicious" Continental-Eclectic menu, "knock-your-socks-off" river views from its outdoor terrace and the newly revamped Glamour Bar downstairs that some call an even "better scene"; sure, a few critics carp "you're paying for the address" not the "unspectacular" food, but then again, this "institution" was voted Shanghai's Most Popular restaurant.

Nan Xiang *Chinese* 24 | 13 | 14 | I

Old Town | Yu Gdn. | 85 Yuyuan Lu (adjacent to the Bridge of Nine Turnings) | (86-21) 6355-4206

"Be prepared to push and shove" for a taste of the "heavenly" soup dumplings (*xiaolongbao*) at this "tourist"-heavy Shanghainese triplex opposite Yu Garden; while the crowds can be "unbearable" at the ground-floor take-out counter, the more comfortable upper floors offer sit-down dining with "better service" but "higher prices."

Palladio *Italian* 25 | 23 | 25 | VE

Jing An | Portman Ritz-Carlton | 1376 Nanjing Xi Lu (Xikang Lu) | (86-21) 6279-8888 | www.ritzcarlton.com

"Exactly what you would expect from a restaurant in the Ritz-Carlton", this Jing An "special-occasion" Italian offers "flawless food" (from a wood-burning-oven–equipped kitchen), "great service" and, "of course, high prices"; swanky decor incorporating Palladian arches and columns and an "exceptional wine list" make it a natural for everything from power lunches to romantic suppers.

South Beauty *Chinese* 24 | 23 | 18 | M

Gubei/Hongqiao | 100 Zunyi Lu (Tianshan Lu) | (86-21) 6237-2885
Luwan | Times Sq. | 99 Huaihai Zhong Lu, 5th fl. (Pu'an Lu) | (86-21) 6391-0100
Pudong | Super Brand Mall | 168 Lujiazui Xi Lu (Fucheng Lu) | (86-21) 5047-1817
Xuhui | 28-1 Taojiang Lu (Hengshan Lu) | (86-21) 6445-2581

This Beijing-based chain specializes in "fiery hot" "modern Sichuan" cooking ("leave your tongue at home") hailing from Southwest China; the staff "really tries", and thanks to the "rich flavors", "hip settings" and "classy" vibes, they're a natural for "showing off to foreign guests."

South Beauty 881 *Chinese* 25 | 27 | 17 | E

Jing An | 881 Yan'an Zhong Lu (Shaanxi Nan Lu) | (86-21) 3222-0118

This "splashy" Jing An branch of the fast-growing chain offers "terrific" Sichuan dishes in a "beautiful" setting incorporating two buildings: an "elegantly renovated" period mansion and an ultramodern glass-lined garden house; the menu's heavy on seafood – and very spicy and rather pricey – but it's the glamorous old Shanghai vibe that draws in the movers, the shakers and the deep-pocketed "out-of-towners."

NEW **Stiller's** *European* - | - | - | VE

Huangpu | Building 3, 505 Zhongshan Nan Lu, 7th fl. (Fuxing Dong Lu) | (86-21) 6152-6501 | www.stillers-restaurant.cn

Top toque Stefan Stiller is manning the stove at this Huangpu Modern European whose building houses a restaurant, a deli, a bar/lounge and a cooking school on its four floors; the fine-dining options, offered either à la carte or as a set degustation menu, hint at the chef's German roots, while the sleek setting provides floor-to-ceiling windows with incomparable views of the river and the Pudong skyline.

T8 ◐ *Asian/Mediterranean* 25 | 27 | 23 | VE

Huaihai/Xintiandi | North Block Xintiandi | House 8, Ln. 181 Taicang Lu (Huangpi Nan Lu) | (86-21) 6355-8999 | www.t8shanghai.com

"High style" is alive and well at this "magical" Xintiandi "class act", one of the "most decorated" places in town, where the "elegant" setting complete with a "fun" open-fronted glass kitchen is matched by a "fancy" fusion menu of Asian and Mediterranean dishes, an "interesting wine list" and service that runs as "smoothly as a Swiss clock"; ok, it's "definitely not cheap", but that doesn't seem to faze its many fans one bit.

1221 *Chinese* 23 17 21 M

Changning | 1221 Yan'an Xi Lu (Fanyu Lu) | (86-21) 6213-6585

"Targeted to foreigners", this chic Changning Shanghainese is a "popular expatriate hangout" where the homestyle offerings may be "slightly tailored to non-Chinese palates" but are still plenty "authentic"; hidden "at the end of an alley", it's "not so easy to find" but worth seeking out for its "friendly service" and overall "good value."

Vedas *Indian* 26 22 21 M

Xuhui | 550 Jianguo Xi Lu (Wulumuqi Lu) | (86-39) 6445-8100 | www.vedascuisine.com

The unbeatable recipe of "great food" and "good prices" keeps the trade brisk at this much admired French Concession Indian that seals the deal with a spacious, classy setting that avoids the usual curry house decor clichés; a moodily lit bar area is ideal for pre-dinner drinks, while those hoping for entertainment with their meal can peer through a glass partition into the kitchen to see the chefs in action.

Vegetarian Lifestyle *Chinese/Vegetarian* 25 16 17 I

Gubei/Hongqiao | 848 Huangjincheng Dao (Shuicheng Nan Lu) | (86-21) 6275-1798

Huaihai/Xintiandi | 77 Songshan Lu, 1st fl. (Huaihai Zhong Lu) | (86-21) 6384-8000

Jing An | 258 Fengxian Lu (Nanjing Xi Lu) | (86-21) 6215-7566

www.jujubetree.com

"Traditional" Chinese dishes mainly "prepared with vegetables" fill out the menu of this "pleasant" mini-chain where they do a good enough job to "fool the most discernable carnivore" while supplying real "value for your money"; P.S. in keeping with the overall "healthy" mindset, the "no-smoking rules are strictly enforced" here.

Yi Café ◐ *Eclectic* 25 22 21 E

Pudong | Pudong Shangri-La | 33 Fucheng Lu (Huayuanshiqiao Lu) | (86-21) 6882-8888, ext. 210 | www.shangri-la.com

"Eat yourself silly" at this bustling, "something-for-everyone" Eclectic buffet in the Pudong Shangri-La hotel, where the walk-through layout is designed to replicate a public market equipped with "multiple food stations" drawn from around the globe; there is also an "impressive array of desserts" as well as a candy counter geared toward small fry.

FOOD | DECOR | SERVICE | COST

Tokyo

TOP FOOD RANKING

	Restaurant	Cuisine
28	Raku-tei	Tempura
27	Uguisudani-en	Yakiniku
	Kasumicho Suetomi	Japanese
	Sushi Mizutani	Sushi
	Yuji	Yakiniku
	Umi	Sushi
	Araki	Sushi
	Stamina-en*	Yakiniku
	Aroma-Fresca	Italian
	Kozasa-zushi	Sushi
26	Piatto Suzuki	Italian
	L'osier	French
	Ryugin	Japanese
	Cucina Hirata	Italian
	Il Grappolo da Miura*	Italian
	Sumita*	Udon
	Koju	Japanese
	Tempura Fukamachi	Tempura

Araki Ⓜ *Sushi* — 27 | 21 | 20 | VE

Nakamachi | Kaminoge Little Town 102 | 4-27-1 Nakamachi (Yoga) | Setagaya-ku | (81-3) 3705-2256

"Outstanding" ingredients go into the "superior" sushi at this establishment near Yoga Station that serves only an omakase menu, but cognoscenti crow that "everything" offered is a "delicacy" "anytime you go"; the chef-owner is "relaxed" yet "attentive" to his customers, although a few complain that he's showing "more and more favoritism toward his regulars", while the counter-only space accommodates just nine and there are "limited seatings" per day.

Aroma-Fresca Ⓢ Ⓜ *Italian* — 27 | 24 | 25 | VE

Minami-Azabu | M Tower, 2nd fl. | 1-7-31 Minami-Azabu (Azabu-Juban) | Minato-ku | (81-3) 5439-4010

Shinji Harada's "refined ristorante" – aka "Tokyo's top Italian" – is back after a hiatus and relocation from Hiroo to Minami-Azabu, showcasing his "uniformly excellent" menu of "innovative, seasonal" fare; while some grouse that it's "impossible to get a reservation", others point out that the room is "never overbooked" as a result, which together with the "refined, yet unpretentious" service ensures a "wonderful" experience.

Au Goût Du Jour Ⓜ *French* — 24 | 17 | 23 | E

Yonbancho | Nomura Bldg. | 4-8 Yonbancho (Kojimachi) | Chiyoda-ku | (81-3) 5213-3005

Au Goût Du Jour Merveille *French*

Nihonbashi | Karen Nihonbashi Bldg. | 3-8-13 Nihonbashi (Nihonbashi) | Chuo-ku | (81-3) 6202-1991

* Indicates a tie with restaurant above

(continued)

Au Goût Du Jour Nouvelle Ère Ⓜ *French*

Marunouchi | Shin Maru Bldg., 5th fl. | 1-5-1 Marunouchi (Tokyo) | Chiyoda-ku | (81-3) 5224-8070
www.augoutdujour-group.com

At this French near Kojimachi Station, the "carefully crafted", "exquisite and inspiring" fare, "lively", "impeccable" service and "terrific bang for the buck" make it easy to "overlook any flaws" - specifically, "cramped seating" and "plain" digs, according to critics; its Merveille offspring in Nihonbashi gets a shout-out for "marvelous" service, while Nouvelle Ère offers a "sweeping view" of historic Tokyo Station.

Cucina Hirata *Italian* 26 | 18 | 23 | VE

Azabu-Juban | Endo Bldg., 3rd fl. | 2-13-10 Azabu-Juban (Azabu-Juban) | Minato-ku | (81-3) 3457-0094

Fans are "amazed" by "how delicious" the Italian cuisine is at this venerable vet in Azabu-Juban where simple dishes made with "the freshest ingredients" are all "top-notch" and "flawless"; "polite" service with a "soft touch" and a "pleasant", "refined" decor are what many "expect from such a luxe restaurant", but because the menu "doesn't list prices", critics warn you might "suffer sticker shock" when the bill arrives.

Il Grappolo da Miura Ⓢ *Italian* 26 | 20 | 23 | E

Shirokanedai | Valubizon 32, fl. B1 | 4-9-18 Shirokanedai (Shirokanedai) | Minato-ku | (81-3) 5793-5300 |
www.ilgrappolo-damiura.com

The "handmade pasta" dishes at this Shirokanedai Italian are among the "best in Tokyo", but groupies gush that "everything is high quality" and makes for "superb wine pairings"; "terrific" desserts are another plus, as well as the "polite, not snooty" service and interior graced by "stylish, lovely" paintings; no wonder fans "keep coming back."

Jumbo ◐ *Yakiniku* 26 | 13 | 18 | E

Shinozakimachi | 4-13-19 Shinozakimachi (Shinozaki) | Edogawa-ku | (81-3) 3679-8929

Shirokane | Dai-Ichi Azabu Bldg. | 3-1-1 Shirokane (Shirokane-Takanawa) | Minato-ku | (81-3) 5795-4129 Ⓜ
www.yakiniku-jambo.com

Even though you "need a car" to get to this "out-of-the-way" yakiniku spot in Shinozakimachi (with a Shirokane spin-off), fans report it's "tough to get a table" nonetheless, thanks to its "can't-miss" fare, including "one-of-a-kind" rib-eye and "rare, off-the-menu" items, all of it "fresh enough to be eaten raw"; still, the owner who "coaches you on how to flash-grill your meat" gets mixed reviews; the more centrally located branch is "more subdued" in atmosphere and decor.

Kasumicho Suetomi Ⓜ *Japanese* 27 | 16 | 20 | VE

Nishi-Azabu | Yawata Bldg., 3rd fl. | 4-2-13 Nishi-Azabu (Hiroo) | Minato-ku | (81-3) 5466-1270

Among the "tops in Tokyo" for Japanese cuisine, this Nishi-Azabu establishment serves nearly "perfect" fare, the product of "fantastic" ingredients and "marvelous technique" that will "give your palate a reality check"; from "first course to last", the service is "prompt and smooth", "without pretense or attitude", and though some find the decor a "bit staid", most agree the "attention to detail", right down to the "tableware", makes it a "wonderful, relaxing experience."

Koju ◐ 🅂 *Japanese* 26 | 18 | 25 | VE

Ginza | Dai-Ni Sanyu Bldg. | 8-5-25 Ginza (Shinbashi) | Chuo-ku | (81-3) 6215-9544 | www.kojyu.jp

This "well-known" Ginza Japanese makes some fans "proud of their country" with its "refined", "top-notch" *kappo*-style cuisine made with "high-quality ingredients", which is matched with a "surprisingly excellent" wine list; the decor is "simple" but the digs are "squeaky clean", and regulars recommend "sitting at the counter" to "fully appreciate the craftsmanship" of popular chef-owner Toru Okuda - that is, "if you can get a reservation."

Kozasa-zushi 🅂 *Sushi* 27 | 17 | 23 | VE

Ginza | Dai-Go Shuwa Bldg. | 8-6-18 Ginza (Shinbashi) | Chuo-ku | (81-3) 3289-2227

At the "end of an alley" and behind an "inconspicuous entrance" lies this Ginza sushi institution where you "can see the respect" the "artisan" chef "has for the cuisine" in the "excellent", "robust" fin fare (which includes some "baked, grilled or steamed" offerings) that "melts in your mouth"; his "soft-spoken" mien is "attractive" to many, and some quip the experience is "well worth the overtime [they] put in to pay for it."

L'osier 🅂 *French* 26 | 25 | 27 | VE

Ginza | 7-5-5 Ginza (Ginza) | Chuo-ku | (81-3) 3571-6050 | www.shiseido.co.jp/losier

The cuisine is nearly "perfect" at this "world-class" French in Ginza where aficionados report chef Bruno Menard is "coming into his own" and "putting his own stamp" on the menu; fans "tip their hats" to the "flawless" service from the "impeccably groomed" staff, while the space, which resembles an "authentic *grande maison*" with "radiant", "art nouveau"-style decor, seals the deal.

Piatto Suzuki ◐ 🅂 *Italian* 26 | 18 | 21 | VE

Azabu-Juban | Hasebeya Bldg., 4th fl. | 1-7-7 Azabu-Juban (Azabu-Juban) | Minato-ku | (81-3) 5414-2116

An "excellent choice" for "grown-ups who appreciate simplicity in both food and ambiance" and a "popular" "late-night" option, this Azabu-Juban Italian is the showcase of chef Yahei Suzuki, who "works magic with veggies" and other ingredients to create "memorable", "vibrant" dishes; the only complaint is that the space is so "tiny" the staff is "almost tripping over you."

Raku-tei 🄼 ⊭ *Tempura* 28 | 23 | 22 | VE

Akasaka | Akasaka Music Inn | 6-8-1 Akasaka (Akasaka) | Minato-ku | (81-3) 3585-3743

Voted Tokyo's No. 1 for Food, this venerable tempura temple in Akasaka is a place "you must experience at least once in your life" according to groupies who gush over the chefs' "flawless artistry", "bringing out the full flavor of each ingredient" in their remarkably "light" fried fare, including the "addictive", "succulent" shrimp; the counter-only room is a "peaceful refuge", as "quiet as a teahouse", and since "lunch and dinner are equally expensive", there's "never a big lunchtime rush."

FOOD | DECOR | SERVICE | COST

Ryugin ◐ 🅂 *Japanese* — 26 | 21 | 24 | VE

Roppongi | Side Roppongi Bldg. | 7-17-24 Roppongi (Roppongi) | Minato-ku | (81-3) 3423-8006 | www.nihonryori-ryugin.com

Its "obscure, out-of-the-way location" in Roppongi doesn't deter devotees from descending on this Japanese establishment for "original", "innovative" "French-influenced" fare that's "attractively presented" and served on "beautiful tableware" by a "gracious", "impeccable" staff; the atmosphere is "soothing" and "relaxing" in the chic, mostly white space, which underwent a facelift in 2008.

Shotai-en ◐ *Yakiniku* — 26 | 16 | 14 | E

Machiya | AN Machiya 102 | 1-20-9 Machiya (Machiya) | Arakawa-ku | (81-3) 5901-2929 Ⓜ

Machiya | 8-7-6 Machiya (Machiya) | Arakawa-ku | (81-3) 3895-2423

Ginza | Cheers Ginza, 9th fl. | 5-9-5 Ginza (Ginza) | Chuo-ku | (81-3) 6274-5003 Ⓜ

Shiba-Daimon | Park Side Shiba-Daimon | 1-7-4 Shiba-Daimon (Daimon) | Minato-ku | (81-3) 5733-5025 Ⓜ

"High-quality meats at surprisingly low prices" are the draw at this Machiya-based yakiniku chain, serving "melt-in-your-mouth" kalbi with wasabi, "delish" sides and rib-eye cuts that "you have to reserve in advance"; you have to eat quickly, too, according to critics who complain that the staff "rushes you out the door"; still, many recommend the "trendy" Ginza and Shiba-Daimon branches as "good choices for dates."

Stamina-en Ⓜ ⊭ *Yakiniku* — 27 | 4 | 10 | E

Shikahama | 3-13-4 Shikahama (Oji) | Adachi-ku | (81-3) 3897-0416 | www.mode-web.jp/sutamina

Fans are willing to put up with "two-hour waits" at this Shikahama yakiniku for the "unmatched freshness" and "indescribably delicious" BBQ fare, including variety meats "so good you won't go anywhere else"; besides the lines, insiders advise you'll have to put up with "cramped" seating, a room so "smoky" it's "best to dress down" and a staff that some say "favors regulars over the rest of us."

Sumita Ⓜ *Udon* — 26 | 7 | 13 | I

Naka-Jujo | 2-5-11 Naka-Jujo (Higashi-Jujo) | Kita-ku | (81-3) 3905-0099

One of the "best in town", this Naka-Jujo specialist spot was voted Tokyo's No. 1 for udon, thanks to "artistic, lustrous" noodles that "define al dente" and other menu offerings such as the "must-try" tempura and *oden* (hot pot); the staff is "attentive even to those waiting for a table" in the "limited" space, another reason this spot is deemed "worth a long train ride."

Sushi Mizutani 🅂 ⊭ *Sushi* — 27 | 19 | 19 | VE

Ginza | Ginza Seiwa Silver Bldg., fl. B1 | 8-2-10 Ginza (Shinbashi) | Chuo-ku | (81-3) 3573-5258

Voted Tokyo's No. 1 for sushi, this Ginza establishment serves "exquisitely prepared", "unbelievable" dishes featuring a "delicate balance between the fish and rice" that are "world-class" "works of art"; in a "tranquil" environment, chef-owner Hachiro Mizutani is "unexpectedly congenial", and the rest of the staff is "on the ball", all of which contributes to a relaxing atmosphere.

Tempura Fukamachi *Tempura* 26 | 13 | 13 | VE

Kyobashi | Sabujudogurin Kyobashi Shinohara Bldg. | 2-5-2 Kyobashi (Kyobashi) | Chuo-ku | (81-3) 5250-8777

The nearly "perfect" tempura with a "delightful", "crisp" coating that leaves "no unpleasant aftertaste" is "thoroughly impressive" at this Kyobashi deep fryer according to fans; there's "limited seating" in the counter-only space, so "big parties" aren't welcome, and most say the service is "nothing special"; still, the "quiet" setting is "perfect" for owner Masao Fukamachi's "meticulous work."

Uguisudani-en *Yakiniku* 27 | 8 | 12 | M

Negishi | 1-5-15 Negishi (Uguisudani) | Taito-ku | (81-3) 3874-8717

Despite its "sketchy location" near Uguisudani Station, this yakiniku house has a loyal following of carnivores who are "happy to make the schlep" for the "terrific value" of its "melt-in-your-mouth" meats, including "outstanding beef prime rib and rump" cuts and "marvelous", "nicely marbled" kalbi; the only drawbacks are the "discouraging" decor, reservations-only policy and "two-hour time limit on each table."

Ukai-tei *Japanese* 24 | 24 | 23 | VE

Ginza | Jijitsushin Bldg. | 5-15-8 Ginza (Higashi-Ginza) | Chuo-ku | (81-3) 3544-5252

Jingumae | Omotesando Gyre Bldg., 5th fl. | 5-10-1 Jingumae (Omotesando) | Shibuya-ku | (81-3) 5467-5252

www.ukai.co.jp

"Destinations" for "elegant" dining (voted Tokyo's Most Popular), these Ginza and Jingumae outposts of a suburban-based teppanyaki chain offer steak that'll "make you forget about all others'", "excellent" abalone and other dishes hot off the griddle; the "gorgeous" interior "reminds you of the days of the bubble economy", and "from the moment you enter, until the time you leave", the service "doesn't miss a beat."

Umi *Sushi* 27 | 19 | 23 | VE

Minami-Aoyama | Sannan Bldg. | 3-2-8 Minami-Aoyama (Gaienmae) | Minato-ku | (81-3) 3401-3368

Some of the "world's best sushi" can be found at this Minami-Aoyama spot serving "top seafood from all over Japan" in "generous" portions "big enough to satisfy a varsity jock", served with "impeccable timing" by a "lively, pleasant" staff; it's "tough to book a table" in the "smallish" space, and it's undeniably "pricey", but fans insist it's "worth every yen."

Yuji *Yakiniku* 27 | 4 | 6 | M

Udagawacho | Matsunuma Bldg. | 11-1 Udagawacho (Shibuya) | Shibuya-ku | (81-3) 3464-6448

The menu seems "bottomless" at this yakiniku spot and organ meat specialist in Udagawacho near Shibuya Station popular for its "outstanding" variety meats (*horumon*) that many say are the "best in the city"; "service? - forget it" warn critics who find the staff "cold", but defenders insist that this and the "tiny" "smoke-filled" digs are "part of its charm."

CANADA RESTAURANT DIRECTORY

FOOD DECOR SERVICE COST

Montréal

TOP FOOD RANKING

	Restaurant	Cuisine
28	La Chronique	Eclectic/Québécois
27	Milos	Greek
	Toqué!	Québécois
	Le Club Chasse	Eclectic/Québécois
	Ferreira	Portuguese
26	Joe Beef	French/Seafood
	Moishe's Steak	Steak
	La Colombe	French
	Laloux	French
25	Au Pied de Cochon	French/Québécois
	Ginger	Pan-Asian
	Le Jolifou	French/Mexican
	Chez L'Épicier	Eclectic
	Mikado	Japanese
	Nuances	French
	Les Chenêts	French
	Chao Phraya	Thai
24	Queue de Cheval	Seafood/Steak
	L'Express	French
	Leméac	French
	Il Mulino	Italian

Au Pied de Cochon *French/Québécois* 25 18 22 E

Plateau Mont-Royal | 536, ave. Duluth Est (rue St-Hubert) | 514-281-1114 | www.restaurantaupieddecochon.ca

A "cult following" promotes the "heavy but oh-so-delicious" dishes of *enfant terrible* chef-owner Martin Picard at his Plateau French brasserie-"meets-rural Québec" "temple to excess"; the menu stars foie gras in "more ways than you can imagine", along with "superb duck in a can" and "delicious risotto served in a wheel of Parmesan" (offered in the fall); "enthusiastic waiters" and an open kitchen fuel the "party atmosphere."

Chao Phraya *Thai* 25 19 20 M

Mile End | 50, ave. Laurier Ouest (rue St-Urbain) | 514-272-5339 | www.chao-phraya.com

The "flavors actually do explode in your mouth" agree acolytes who come to this "favorite" on a "pretty" Mile End street for the "best Thai food in Montréal"; after nearly 20 years it's "still a pacesetter", offering "upscale, quality" dishes, including a signature crispy spinach, "spiced as requested" and served by a "thoughtful, attentive staff"; all this, in a sleek, red-walled setting, makes it especially "nice to visit with a group."

Chez L'Épicier *Eclectic* 25 22 23 E

Old Montréal | 311, rue St-Paul Est (rue St-Claude) | 514-878-2232 | www.chezlepicier.com

You know a place is "haute" "when the chef-owner comes out of the kitchen to a standing ovation" – a not-uncommon occurrence at Laurent

Godbout's "quaint renovated storefront" in Old Montréal; locals love "to take out-of-towners" here for "fanciful, fresh-market, French-influenced" Eclectic fare (say, a chocolate club sandwich and pineapple fries) and frequently changing "quirky presentations"; it "has a store too, where you can buy wonderful", "obscure ingredients."

Ferreira Café Ⓢ *Portuguese* 27 | 24 | 23 | VE

Downtown | 1446, rue Peel (rue Ste-Catherine O.) | 514-848-0988 | www.ferreiracafe.com

"Flawless" "fresh fish grilled simply" and "a festive atmosphere" will "transport you to the Azores" at this "ritzy", high-priced "Portuguese wonder" Downtown; the "hopping" "power scene" can get "clamorous" when "the music is cranked up", but the "nice staff" and colorful "smart setting" also "exude warmth", so even "if you're alone, you won't feel out of place eating at the bar" or sampling some of the "interesting ports."

Gibbys *Seafood/Steak* 23 | 22 | 23 | E

Old Montréal | Youville Stables | 298, pl. d'Youville (rue du Port) | 514-282-1837 | www.gibbys.com

"Dependable" "super-sized" "steakhouse standards" and "fresh seafood" served with a smile in a "weathered stone edifice" ensure this 18th-century "converted stable" "never disappoints"; "it's a little senior citizen/tourist-y" and, like its former equine occupants, gotten "long in the tooth" foes fume, but worshipers whinny with pleasure at this "ode to Old Montréal."

Ginger *Pan-Asian* 25 | 21 | 21 | E

Plateau Mont-Royal | 16, ave. des Pins Est (boul. St-Laurent) | 514-844-2121

Some of "the best damn sushi in Montréal", plus Pan-Asian dishes with a "modern edge", is sliced up at this "small" specialist whose quarters "close to the St-Laurent action" means it's "always full of beautiful people but without the chichiness"; partyers proclaim the "staff is a riot", especially after a "great lychee martini" or two.

Il Mulino Ⓢ Ⓜ *Italian* 24 | 19 | 24 | VE

Little Italy/Petite-Patrie | 236, rue St-Zotique Est (rue Alma) | 514-273-5776 | www.ilmulino.ca

"Old school meets the new world" in this "classy" yet "adorable" Little Italy "favorite" where chef/co-owner Tony de Rose offers the "warmest of welcomes" in addition to creating his "superb" *cucina* featuring "fresh seafood and tasty sauces"; true, paying the check "will take plenty of pennies", but acolytes urge "go, if only for the antipasti - you won't be sorry."

Joe Beef Ⓢ Ⓜ *French/Seafood* 26 | 19 | 23 | VE

St-Henri | 2491, rue Notre-Dame Ouest (bet. rues Charlevoix & Vinet) | 514-935-6504

"With that name, you'd never expect seafood, but that's what they specialize in" at this St-Henri "hot spot" run by "chef-owner *célèbres*" Frederic Morin and David McMillan; admirers have "no beef" with the "wonderful creations" of "retro-chic French comfort food", the "convivial" oyster bar or the "famous duo" "dabbling as waiters", but even they call the "prices a little high" and warn "getting in might be a challenge, as it only has 25 seats" indoors.

	FOOD	DECOR	SERVICE	COST
La Chronique	28	23	25	VE
La Colombe	26	20	23	E
Laloux	26	22	24	M
Le Club Chasse et Pêche	27	22	25	VE
Le Jolifou	25	21	25	E

La Chronique *Eclectic/Québécois*

Mile End | 99, ave. Laurier Ouest (rue St-Urbain) | 514-271-3095 | www.lachronique.qc.ca

Fans "float" in a "foodie heaven" at chef-owner Marc de Canck's Mile End Eclectic-Québécois, aka "one of the most consistently satisfying tables in town"; "plan for a long, sensual meal" of "market-fresh", "creative and classic" fare, enriched by wine pairings that are "second-to-none" and "warm waiters who are all passionate" about their work; small wonder that, though it's "*très cher*", the "intimate" "setting with black-and-white photos on the walls" is "alive with the sound of people enjoying their food."

La Colombe ◐ Ⓢ Ⓜ *French*

Plateau Mont-Royal | 554, ave. Duluth Est (rue St-Hubert) | 514-849-8844

"Bring your best wine" to this "intimate", pale-hued Plateau place that's perpetually "packed for a good reason" – it's BYO, which makes it an "incredible deal", considering the "enticing, eclectic" Classic French fare and "friendly, on-point" staff; the two nightly seatings (on Tuesdays, Fridays and Saturdays) are always "booked well in advance", but you can reserve at any hour on other days.

Laloux *French*

Plateau Mont-Royal | 250, ave. des Pins Est (ave. Laval) | 514-287-9127 | www.laloux.com

Though the refined French cuisine has been revamped (under a new chef) into a more informal and moderately priced bistro menu featuring reworked classics, this "off-the-beaten-path" Plateau veteran has kept its "attentive staff", fine wine list and the "secret feel" of "your own little Left Bank" place; N.B. the adjoining wine bar, Pop!, draws a youthful after-dinner crowd for live jazz.

Le Club Chasse et Pêche Ⓢ Ⓜ *Eclectic/Québécois*

Old Montréal | 423, rue St-Claude (rue Notre-Dame) | 514-861-1112 | www.leclubchasseetpeche.com

This expensive Eclectic-Québécois is "among the best", thanks to chef Claude Pelletier's "fresh-market cuisine" featuring wild game and fish that "will creep into your dreams", the way it "combines the crazy and the classic" – e.g. suckling pig risotto – and is "supported by" "informative service"; some say the atmosphere reminiscent of "an old, country hunt club" "is not my style", but to romantics it's a "cozy" "place to bring one's mistress" – especially as it's "on a tiny Old Montréal street"; N.B. it has a new dining terrace across the street where it serves lunch only.

Le Jolifou *French/Mexican*

Little Italy/Petite-Patrie | 1840, rue Beaubien Est (rue Cartier) | 514-722-2175 | www.jolifou.com

"New French food with a Mexican touch" – so "unique" and "excellent" "you have to pinch" yourself to believe it – makes this "truly charming", highly "reasonable" Petite-Patrie site a "labor of love" where the "congenial", enthusiastic husband-and-wife chef-owners see to it that "things work right"; on the tables are "cute" replicas of antique toys "for you to fiddle around with while you wait"; just "leave room for dessert."

Leméac ◐ *French* 24 | 22 | 22 | E

Outremont | 1045, ave. Laurier Ouest (ave. Durocher) | 514-270-0999 | www.restaurantlemeac.com

Sure, "French bistros are a dime a dozen in Montréal, but this one outdoes them all" claim converts of this "chic Outremont" specimen; the "competently served" dishes "never disappoint" and if they're a bit rich, "face it - everything tastes better with butter", anyway; some regulars recommend you "go during the day to enjoy the light flooding through the spectacular windows", but late-nighters love the "amazing after-10 PM" prix fixe (two courses for $22).

Les Chenêts *French* 25 | 20 | 22 | VE

Downtown | 2075, rue Bishop (rue Sherbrooke O.) | 514-844-1842 | www.leschenets.com

It's "a little on the stuffy side", but "old-world charm still reigns" at this 30-plus-year-old Downtowner serving "superb Classic French cooking" in a room where "a fortune in copper pots hangs on the walls"; while modernists may mock the menu as "a reminder of why nouvelle cuisine was invented", most opine this "pricey" veteran's "an oldie but a goodie"; P.S. "ask to visit the wine cellar, one of the best in Montréal."

L'Express ◐ *French* 24 | 21 | 21 | E

Plateau Mont-Royal | 3927, rue St-Denis (rue Roy E.) | 514-845-5333

On one of the "poshest streets" in the Plateau, its "sign cheekily embedded in floor tiles in front of the door", sits this "very Left Bank" bistro that's "Parisian to the core", from the "*extraordinaire*" classics ("marrow bones to die for") to the "traditional zinc bar" to the "black-and-white-attired" staff, which is "attentive despite the hectic pace" of the "pulsating, jam-packed scene."

Mikado *Japanese* 25 | 19 | 19 | E

Notre-Dame-de-Grâce | 5515, ave. Monkland (ave. Girouard) | 514-369-3659

Outremont | 368, ave. Laurier Ouest (ave. du Parc) | 514-279-4809

Plateau Mont-Royal | 1731, rue St-Denis (bet. boul. de Maisonneuve E. & rue Ontario E.) | 514-844-5705

www.mikadomontreal.com

Those not "afraid to try" "innovative" sushi will "be hooked" by such goodies as the Relax Maki at this trio with "lablike, minimalist decor" that rates among the "best Japanese in town"; just "ask the servers to explain the specials" - both raw and cooked - then "finish your meal" with an "artist's palette of sorbets and ice creams."

Milos *Greek* 27 | 23 | 25 | VE

Mile End | 5357, ave. du Parc (bet. ave. Fairmont O. & rue St-Viateur O.) | 514-272-3522 | www.milos.ca

Be transported from Mile End to a "Greek island taverna" by the "absolutely undisputed best seafood" - "fresh, fresh, fresh" "as if caught hours ago" - that's "perfectly served" amid the "boisterous atmospherics" of this "rustic-chic" "landmark of the rich and famous"; those objecting to the "outrageous prices" (you "pay by the pound") will find "the fabulous $20 lunch special" "a steal."

	FOOD	DECOR	SERVICE	COST

Moishe's Steak House *Steak* 26 | 18 | 23 | VE

Plateau Mont-Royal | 3961, boul. St-Laurent (bet. ave. Duluth & rue Napoléon) | 514-845-3509 | www.moishes.ca

"Serious steak in a Jewish restaurant in French Canadian Québec? yes, it's true" - and "red meat freaks" can rejoice, as this "schmaltzy" Main "original" "deserves its reputation" for "perfectly done" beef in portions "large enough to feed the Canadian army", plus "classic appetizers" and sides like chopped liver, pickles and twice-baked potatoes; a "who's who" clientele dines amid a "frayed" "Catskills hotel-like" grandeur; now, if only the waiters who "have been there forever" wouldn't "clear the table before you're done" ("most expensive fast food ever!").

Nuances *French* 25 | 25 | 26 | VE

Île Notre-Dame | Casino de Montréal | 1, ave. du Casino, 5th fl. | 514-392-2708 | www.casino-de-montreal.com

The flagship Casino de Montréal restaurant with its amazing sunset views has been given a post-Survey redo (not reflected in the ratings) and now boasts a more elegant, contemporary look and a revamped classic and New French menu featuring simplified dishes and luxury ingredients; the signature "classy" service (No. 1 in Montréal) and "superb" wine list remain, as does the high-roller tab.

Queue de Cheval Steak House & Bar *Seafood/Steak* 24 | 24 | 23 | VE

Downtown | 1221, boul. René-Lévesque Ouest (rue Drummond) | 514-390-0090 | www.queuedecheval.com

Totally "OTT (over the top)", this "solid contender" among surf 'n' turfers "spares no effort" to "pamper" celebs and expense-accounters with "gargantuesque" portions "you could cut with a butter knife" and served "with the seriousness of a science presentation"; some scoff it's "overpriced" - "had I known the cost of the lobster, I'd have kept it as a pet" - but most say go on and "spoil yourself" in a "hyper-macho" space fittingly located opposite Bell Centre.

Toqué! S M *Québécois* 27 | 24 | 25 | VE

Old Montréal | 900 Place Jean-Paul-Riopelle (bet. rues de Bleury & St-Antoine) | 514-499-2084 | www.restaurant-toque.com

"The inventor of Québec fusion cuisine", chef-owner Normand Laprise, has "influenced a generation", using regional ingredients - his treatment of "foie gras alone is worth the significant damage to the wallet" - in "minimal" "masterpieces" that trigger "a taste bud orgasm" (don't worry, the "professional" staff is "discreet"); many "miss the old digs" on St-Denis - the Old Montréal venue, while "elegant", can be "cold" - but this is a minority gripe for a mainstay that's "often called the city's finest", not to mention Montréal's Most Popular.

Toronto

TOP FOOD RANKING

	Restaurant	Cuisine
29	Sushi Kaji	Japanese
28	Scaramouche	Continental
	Chiado/Antonio	Portuguese/Seafood
27	North 44°	Continental
	Hiro Sushi	Japanese
	Lai Wah Heen	Chinese
	Lee	Asian Fusion/Mediterranean
	Splendido	Mediterranean
	Oro	Mediterranean
	Perigee	French/Mediterranean
	Célestin	French
	Scaramouche Pasta	Italian
26	George	Canadian
	Truffles	French
	Canoe	Canadian
	Starfish Oyster	Seafood
	Boba	American
	Opus	Continental
	Il Mulino	Italian
25	Harbour Sixty	Steak

Boba *American* 26 | 21 | 24 | VE

Bloor Yorkville | 90 Avenue Rd. (bet. Bloor St. & Davenport Rd.) | 416-961-2622 | www.boba.ca

This "high-end" Bloor Yorkville vet remains "a favorite year after year" due to its "exquisite", "savory" New American cuisine and the "gems" on the "well-selected wine list"; the husband-and-wife chef-owners are "consummate hosts" to boot, so most don't mind the "small" confines – just "hope your neighbors are interesting conversationalists"; the Decor score does not reflect a post-Survey modern-minimalist remodel.

Bymark *Continental* 25 | 25 | 23 | VE

Financial District | 66 Wellington St. W. (bet. Bay & York Sts.) | 416-777-1144 | www.bymark.ca

This "subterranean Valhalla" in the Financial District is frequented by "brokers and bankers" bullish on Mark McEwan's "innovative" Continental cookery; whether in the minimalist, "soothing" (if "dark") dining room, the "intimate" lounge or out on the warm-weather patio, an "efficient" crew provides "personalized service"; and if "outrageous" tabs have some figuring this spot's "reputation exceeds its price/value quotient", plenty more deem it "worth every cent."

Canoe *Canadian* 26 | 26 | 25 | VE

Financial District | Toronto Dominion Bank Tower | 66 Wellington St. W., 54th fl. (Bay St.) | 416-364-0054 | www.canoerestaurant.com

Voted the city's No. 1 for both Decor and Popularity, this literally "top-tier" "destination" on the 54th floor of the Toronto Dominion Bank

Tower lives up to its "stunning location" with "exquisitely flavored" Canadian cuisine that's "presented with class" by a "first-rate" staff; prices that are "as lofty as the setting" don't deter devotees who say the view alone justifies "the cost of your meal" ("wait or bribe" to snag the large table "in the southwest corner" for the best panorama); N.B. closed Saturdays.

Célestin M *French* 27 | 22 | 22 | VE

Midtown | 623 Mt. Pleasant Rd. (Manor Rd. E.) | 416-544-9035

Best "savored one plate at a time", chef-owner Pascal Ribreau's "refined", "creative" New French cuisine makes this Midtown "haute bistro" one of "the top spots in town"; "everything is above par here", including "knowledgeable" personnel and a renovated 1920s bank building interior that's "upscale", "clean" and "calm"; P.S. fans of the "to-die-for handmade bread" can stop by the "exquisite bakery next door" and get some to go.

Chiado/Senhor Antonio *Portuguese/Seafood* 28 | 21 | 25 | VE

Little Italy | 864 College St. (Concord Ave.) | 416-538-1910 | www.chiadorestaurant.com

"Melt-in-your-mouth" seafood lures pescavores to this "top-notch" Little Italy Portuguese where "simple preparations emphasize" "superb" ingredients and the cellar contains what may be the "best Portuguese wine list in Canada"; staffers work so smoothly as to be "almost invisible" within the "intimate" old-world dining room and the minimalist tapas bar next door; yes, tabs are "steep" - but then "you've got to be terrific to charge these prices in this part of town."

George S *Canadian* 26 | 24 | 24 | VE

Downtown Core | Queen Richmond Ctr. | 111C Queen St. E. (bet. Church & Jarvis Sts.) | 416-863-6006 | www.georgeonqueen.com

By George, it's "amazing" assert admirers of this onetime chocolate factory in the Downtown Core's Queen Richmond Centre; "master chef" Lorenzo Loseto's "flavorful", seasonal Canadian cuisine comes on "small plates [that] allow for maximum sampling" and can be paired with three- or six-oz. pours; the antique "industrial" open-plan setting manages to be both "stylish" and "soothing", helped along by "smooth, accommodating service."

Harbour Sixty Steakhouse *Steak* 25 | 23 | 22 | VE

Harbourfront | Toronto Harbour Commission Bldg. | 60 Harbour St. (Bay St.) | 416-777-2111 | www.harboursixty.com

To "celebrate special occasions" - e.g. "a Leafs victory" at the nearby Air Canada Centre - well-heeled carnivores come to this Harbourfront spot for "slabs of meat" that are "cooked to perfection" and "generous sides" ordered à la carte; the "engaging" "old gentlemen's club setting" in a historic "port office building" and "excellent" if "snooty" service - not to mention "large price tags" on food and wine - make it an "expense-account favorite."

Hiro Sushi S M *Japanese* 27 | 15 | 21 | VE

St. Lawrence | 171 King St. E. (Jarvis St.) | 416-304-0550

Hiro worshipers say "sitting at the sushi bar is the only way to experience" this small, traditional St. Lawrence Japanese; they adore the "genius" chef-owner's "amazing" omakase (a culinary "walk on the wild side") but caution that since "you'll eat at the master's pace" you may spend "a few hours" here.

Il Mulino *Italian* 26 20 24 VE

Forest Hill | 1060 Eglinton Ave. W. (Bathurst St.) | 416-780-1173 | www.ilmulinorestaurant.com

Bolstered by a "magnificent wine list" to "suit every taste and budget", the "innovative" *cucina* at this "outstanding" Forest Hill Italian evokes "trips to Tuscany"; *amici* also adore "friendly" staffers and owners who "greet you like family", so although the simple 65-seat room with vaulted ceiling can get "noisy", locals' "only complaint is that more people are getting to know about it."

Jamie Kennedy Wine Bar *Canadian/French* 25 21 21 VE

St. Lawrence | 9 Church St. (south of Front St.) | 416-362-1957 | www.jamiekennedy.ca

"Superstar" chef Jamie Kennedy's "legions of fans" laud his "fabulous" spot in St. Lawrence, where an open kitchen "churns out" "explosively flavorful" Canadian-French small plates for pairing with "outstanding" vintages "often unavailable elsewhere"; not surprisingly, this "finger food [comes] at full torso prices", just as the "knowledgeable" crew exhibits a touch of "attitude."

kaiseki-SAKURA *Japanese* - - - VE

Downtown Core | 556 Church St. (Wellesley St.) | 416-923-1010 | www.kaisekisakura.com

Those who love Japanese cuisine appreciate this Downtown Core temple to kaiseki-style small plates, where chef Daisuke Izutsu offers monthly changing tasting menus that range from five to eight courses ($80–$100); a relative secret, this dinner-only destination also serves intricate, artfully presented à la carte choices in a quiet setting that's ideal for relaxed conversation; N.B. closed Tuesdays.

Kultura Social Dining *Eclectic* - - - E

Downtown Core | 169 King St. E. (bet. George & Jarvis Sts.) | 416-363-9000 | www.kulturarestaurant.com

Delivering small plates that are big on taste and creativity, this ultra-romantic Downtown Core restaurant offers an Eclectic menu rooted in Caribbean and Japanese cuisine; it attracts a business and celebrity clientele that appreciates the deft wine list with 50 selections by the glass.

Lai Wah Heen *Chinese* 27 22 25 VE

Downtown Core | Metropolitan Hotel | 108 Chestnut St. (bet. Bay St. & University Ave.) | 416-977-9899 | www.metropolitan.com/lwh

Renowned for "divine" dim sum "made with tremendous care" and served similarly by a "top-notch" staff, this "superior" Sino in the Downtown Core's Metropolitan Hotel is likely to "make visitors from Hong Kong feel right at home"; dining in this "serene" "white-tablecloth" setting may be "expensive by Chinese standards", but it's "a bargain" for such "a wonderful experience."

Lee ☒ *Asian Fusion/Mediterranean* 27 23 22 VE

King West | 603 King St. W. (Portland St.) | 416-504-7867 | www.susur.com

The comparatively "affordable little sister" to the late and lamented Susur, this King West "favorite" allows fans of "the master" to "get a taste" of Susur Lee's "sensational", "surprising" Asian-Med "fusion food" ("tapas meets dim sum") "without breaking the bank"; the "stylish" loftlike space with pink Lucite tables is a "hip", "hopping" (if "chaotic") scene that's "good for groups", as is the outdoor patio.

North 44° ☒ *Continental* 27 | 25 | 25 | VE

North Toronto | 2537 Yonge St. (Eglinton Ave.) | 416-487-4897 | www.north44restaurant.com

"Sophisticated" and "serene", Mark McEwan's North Toronto "showpiece" guarantees a "memorable" "special occasion" rave respondents, reporting that the chef-owner's "magnificent" Continental cuisine evinces "superb quality and craftsmanship" while service is simply "state-of-the-art"; it's undoubtedly "pricey" and may be a "hassle to get to", but foodies urge their fellows to "walk, crawl, hitchhike . . . do whatever is necessary."

Opus Restaurant ◐ *Continental* 26 | 24 | 24 | VE

Annex | 37 Prince Arthur Ave. (Bedford Rd.) | 416-921-3105 | www.opusrestaurant.com

"Discriminating" diners are "delighted" by this "top-notch" Annex veteran known for its "sublime" Continental cuisine and a "comprehensive" "wine book" (2,500 labels); "warm, sincere" staffers let you "take your time" in the brownstone's "formal" yet "soothing" monochromatic dining room or on the "lovely" atriumlike patio, making this a "great spot for a special occasion" (e.g. "impressing the in-laws").

Oro ☒ *Mediterranean* 27 | 22 | 26 | VE

Downtown Core | 45 Elm St. (bet. Bay & Yonge Sts.) | 416-597-0155 | www.ororestaurant.com

"Somehow seeming out of the way while right in the middle of town", this "quiet" Downtown Core Med delivers with "exceptional", "innovative" cuisine ("melt-in-your-mouth calamari", "delectable desserts") as "attentive" owners circulate and "make everyone feel like family"; the interior is a "pleasantly odd mix" of "upscale" and retro, with three fireplaces adding both atmosphere and warmth ("first-class for a first date").

Perigee ☒ Ⓜ *French/Mediterranean* 27 | 23 | 25 | VE

Distillery District | Cannery Bldg. | 55 Mill St. (Trinity St.) | 416-364-1397 | www.perigeerestaurant.com

For "pure theater", "adventurous" gastronomes gather at this "fantastic" French-Med in the historic Distillery District and settle into "arenaside seats" by the open kitchen to be served a "blissful" blind tasting menu; "social", "creative and charming" chef Pat Riley "explains each course to you" amid converted industrial environs with thick wooden beams and exposed brick; N.B. early-birds and night owls can try pretheater and dessert menus, respectively.

Scaramouche ☒ *Continental* 28 | 26 | 27 | VE

Forest Hill | 1 Benvenuto Pl. (bet. Avenue Rd. & Edmund St.) | 416-961-8011 | www.scaramoucherestaurant.com

Devotees of this "consistently" "top-notch" Forest Hill Continental declare its staff is "second to none" – indeed, surveyors voted this veteran Toronto's No. 1 for Service, citing "expert", "exquisite" ministrations that make you "feel like a millionaire" while chef/co-owner Keith Froggett feeds you his "delectable", "trustworthy, superb" cuisine; the "quiet, elegant" room is also renowned for "magnificent views of Downtown" ("without the Downtown traffic"), so "movers and shakers" recommend "lingering over a wonderful meal" to "savor" the "magic."

Scaramouche Pasta Bar & Grill ☒ *Italian* 27 | 25 | 27 | VE

Forest Hill | 1 Benvenuto Pl. (bet. Avenue Rd. & Edmund St.) | 416-961-8011 | www.scaramoucherestaurant.com

Sharing its Forest Hill building and "gorgeous views of Downtown", this "sophisticated sibling to Scaramouche" "continues to excel" as well, offering "lighter meals" of "marvelous" Italian fare ("not just pasta") and "exceptional" service for a comparatively "reasonable price"; overall, it's a "more casual yet no less worthy" experience.

Splendido *Mediterranean* 27 | 24 | 25 | VE

South Annex | 88 Harbord St. (Spadina Ave.) | 416-929-7788 | www.splendido.ca

"Splendido indeed" rhapsodize respondents about this South Annex Med where chef David Lee's "sublime", "celestial" cuisine ("one of the city's best tasting menus") is complemented by an "impressive wine cellar" and served in a "classy", "modern", "clean"-lined dining room by a staff that offers a "perfect combination of professional and friendly" ministrations; "for a special occasion, you can't go wrong" here.

Starfish Oyster Bed & Grill *Seafood* 26 | 19 | 22 | VE

St. Lawrence | 100 Adelaide St. E. (bet. Church & Jarvis Sts.) | 416-366-7827 | www.starfishoysterbed.com

Everyone knows "great things come in small packages", and that goes for the "exceptional" bivalves at this St. Lawrence seafooder (owned by World Oyster Opening Champion Patrick McMurray) as well as the "memorable" pleasures to be found within its "cozy", "understated" confines; for a "lesson" in freshness, "sit at the bar" and chat with "knowledgeable" shuckers over a mug of microbrewed stout.

Sushi Kaji Ⓜ *Japanese* 29 | 19 | 25 | VE

Mimico | 860 The Queensway (Islington Ave.) | 416-252-2166 | www.sushikaji.com

"Don't let your first impressions cloud your judgment" - this "unassuming" 30-seat Mimico Japanese, voted Toronto's No. 1 for Food, is a "hidden treasure"; with "talent and a wry sense of humor", "artist" Mitsuhiro Kaji creates "sumptuous sashimi and sublime sushi" from sea creatures who "move from packing crate to dinner plate in seconds" ("fish so fresh it really does flop around"), while his "intriguing and expertly presented" omakase incorporates "exquisite hot dishes" as well; N.B. prix fixe only.

Truffles ☒ Ⓜ *French* 26 | 26 | 26 | VE

Bloor Yorkville | Four Seasons Hotel | 21 Avenue Rd. (Bloor St. W.) | 416-928-7331 | www.fourseasons.com/toronto

"They don't trifle" at this "exceptional" New French destination, a "gourmand's delight" in Bloor Yorkville's Four Seasons, where the "delectable", almost "flawless" dishes are "adeptly paired with appropriate wines" from a "superb" list; what with the staff's "courtesy" and "attention to detail", diners love to "linger for hours" in the "intimate" room.

Vancouver

TOP FOOD RANKING

	Restaurant	Cuisine
29	West	Pacific NW
28	Bishop's	Pacific NW
	Vij's	Indian
	Pear Tree	Continental
27	ToJo's	Japanese
	Le Crocodile	French
	La Régalade	French
26	Cioppino's	Mediterranean
	Il Giardino/Umberto	Italian
	Villa del Lupo	Italian/Pacific NW
	Vij's Rangoli	Indian
	Diva at the Met	Pacific NW
	Cru	Pacific NW
	Gotham Steak	Steak
	C Restaurant	Seafood
25	Raincity Grill	Pacific NW
	Parkside	European
	Bin 941/942	Eclectic
	Five Sails	French/Pacific NW
	Kitanoya	Japanese
	Kirin Mandarin	Chinese
	Blue Water	Seafood
	Morton's*	Steak
	Blue Water	Seafood

Bin 941 Tapas Parlour ◐ *Eclectic* 25 | 19 | 19 | M

West End | 941 Davie St. (bet. Burrard & Howe Sts.) | 604-683-1246

Bin 942 Tapas Parlour ◐ *Eclectic*

West Side | 1521 W. Broadway (bet. Fir & Granville Sts.) | 604-734-9421

www.bin941.com

"Be ready to cuddle up to strangers" – you'll almost "be sitting on their laps" – at Gord Martin's "boisterous" West End and West Side "shoeboxes"; "ingenious" Eclectic small plates like Digby scallops wrapped in prawns put these "funky" joints "at the top of the tapas bin", though some yearn for "a side of earplugs."

Bishop's *Pacific NW* 28 | 23 | 27 | VE

West Side | 2183 W. 4th Ave. (bet. Arbutus & Yew Sts.) | 604-738-2025 | www.bishopsonline.com

Thanks to the "sincerity and warmth" of "unsurpassed host" John Bishop and his "amazing" team of professionals, this "intimate" West Side "classic" ranks No. 1 for Service in Vancouver; the kitchen, too, is "brilliant", using mostly "organic ingredients" to prepare "top-of-the-

* Indicates a tie with restaurant above

line" fare that reflects the "Pacific Northwest at its best"; "save your pennies for a splurge" at this "perennial favorite."

Blue Water Cafe & Raw Bar *Seafood* — 25 | 24 | 22 | E

Yaletown | 1095 Hamilton St. (Helmcken St.) | 604-688-8078 | www.bluewatercafe.net

"The fish are still flopping just before they reach your table" at this "bustling" seafood "hot spot" in a "trendy Yaletown" warehouse where the "top-notch raw bar", "amazing tower" of crustaceans and "innovative" sushi are a "religious experience"; the "service is accommodating" - if you "dress to impress" - and "celeb-sighting" abounds, but some protest prices that "leave them blue."

NEW **Boneta** *French* — - | - | - | E

Gastown | 1 Cordova St. W. (Carrall St.) | 604-684-1844 | www.boneta.ca

Thanks to a talented trio with serious pedigrees (ex Lumière, Chambar) this lively, high-ceilinged, heritage room (renovated by the three owners) is setting the pace in a rejuvenated Gastown; chef Jeremie Bastien's detail-driven French plates roam from scallops with celeriac ravioli over braised oxtail to duck breast perched on barley with maple-glazed beets, and are paired with often esoteric wines by sommelier Neil Ingram.

Cioppino's Mediterranean Grill *Mediterranean* — 26 | 23 | 25 | VE

Yaletown | 1133 Hamilton St. (bet. Davie & Helmcken Sts.) | 604-688-7466 | www.cioppinosyaletown.com

"Brilliant" chef-owner Pino Posteraro "turns out amazing" Med dishes from the "open kitchen" of his "outstanding" Yaletowner, run by a "helpful staff"; it's a "fine destination for wine weenies" - the "serious list" includes 1,200 labels - and while it's "not inexpensive", *amici* aver that this "epitome of sublime cuisine and service" is "one of the town's best."

C Restaurant *Seafood* — 26 | 24 | 26 | VE

Downtown | 2-1600 Howe St. (Beach Ave.) | 604-681-1164 | www.crestaurant.com

"The passion shows" affirm fin-atics of "wildly innovative" chef Robert Clark's "superlative seafood", "superbly presented" and "expertly served" in a "stylish", "stunning" "waterfront setting" Downtown overlooking False Creek; environmentalists applaud the spot's "eco-friendly" support for "sustainable fishing practices", and everyone agrees that, while you'll "C your wallet shrink" ("the prices are unbelievably high"), it's a "must-visit."

Cru *Pacific NW* — 26 | 21 | 24 | E

West Side | 1459 W. Broadway (bet. Granville & Hemlock Sts.) | 604-677-4111 | www.cru.ca

Oenophiles appreciate the "unique, color-coded" list of "scrumptious wines" that match with "fantastic" Pacific Northwest "plates to share" or one of the "best prix fixes in the city" at this "intimate" West Side bistro; though the storefront is "small" and "minimalist", a grape-savvy staff that encourages you to "try something new" "without a bit of snobbery" at "relatively affordable prices" "allows you to be a regular."

	FOOD	DECOR	SERVICE	COST
Diva at the Met *Pacific NW*	26	23	25	VE

Downtown | Metropolitan Hotel | 645 Howe St. (bet. Dunsmuir & W. Georgia Sts.) | 604-602-7788 | www.metropolitan.com

At lunch when "deals are made", "prior to the opera" or "for a splurge night", this Downtown "delectable diva" draws ovations for "beautifully plated" Pacific Northwest dishes and "orgasmic desserts"; "prepare to be impressed" by the "witty staff" in this "airy" space, particularly if you sit near "the open kitchen that shows the chefs working their magic."

	FOOD	DECOR	SERVICE	COST
Five Sails *French/Pacific NW*	25	26	26	VE

Downtown | Pan Pacific Hotel | 300-999 Canada Pl. (Howe St.) | 604-891-2892 | www.fivesails.ca

"Breathtaking vistas over the harbor" and "white-glove service" lend a "romantic aura" to this "formal" Downtowner; the "creative" French-influenced Pacific NW fare is "beautifully prepared and presented", and the "amazing wine list" reads "like a novel", so "go on your anniversary or birthday" - just "be prepared to flex your credit card limit."

	FOOD	DECOR	SERVICE	COST
Gotham Steakhouse *Steak*	26	25	24	VE

Downtown | 615 Seymour St. (bet. Dunsmuir & W. Georgia Sts.) | 604-605-8282 | www.gothamsteakhouse.com

"Wear a power suit" and "impress your carnivore friends" with "the best steak in the city" at this "top-notch" Downtown chophouse boasting the "gorgeous vaulted ceilings" and "dark-leather" interior "you'd expect" from "old-school" "fine dining"; the "knowledgeable" servers treat you like you "belong to a private club", but with the à la carte pricing ("which means 'no potato' in French"), you might hope that "someone else is picking up the tab."

	FOOD	DECOR	SERVICE	COST
Il Giardino di Umberto ☒ *Italian*	26	24	25	E

Downtown | 1382 Hornby St. (Pacific St.) | 604-669-2422 | www.umberto.com

Some of "the best Italian fare" is served in this "rustic yet regal" Tuscan-style "period house" Downtown that's "romantic" enough "for any intimate celebration"; owner Umberto Menghi ("Vancouver's Wolfgang Puck") presides over a "power patio" that makes for "good beautiful-people viewing" at a "little gem" that's all about "consistent" "fine dining" and "warm hospitality."

	FOOD	DECOR	SERVICE	COST
Kirin Mandarin *Chinese*	25	17	21	M

Downtown | 1166 Alberni St. (bet. Bute & Thurlow Sts.) | 604-682-8833 | www.kirinrestaurant.com

"Authentic" Northern Chinese fare, including "Peking duck that can't be beat" and "fresh seafood" fished live from the tanks, attracts Sinophiles to this "elegant Asian" Downtown for "big, banquet-style dinners" or business lunches; "dim sum is always a treat", brought by a "knowledgeable, helpful staff."

	FOOD	DECOR	SERVICE	COST
Kitanoya Guu ◐ *Japanese*	25	19	20	M

Downtown | 105-375 Water St. (W. Cordova St.) | 604-685-8682
Downtown | 1698 Robson St. (Bidwell St.) | 604-685-8678
Downtown | 838 Thurlow St. (bet. Robson & Smithe Sts.) | 604-685-8817
www.guu-izakaya.com

"Unbelievably good", "shockingly cheap" "small dishes with big tastes" are the hallmark of this "chaotic" Japanese *izakaya* trio Downtown, where the "lively staff hollers your order across the packed restaurant"; "you might wait, but it's worth it" for a "unique" experience that's popular with the "young and hip" - despite "the hearing loss you may suffer."

La Régalade S M *French* 27 | 19 | 25 | E

West Vancouver | 102-2232 Marine Dr. (bet. 22nd & 23rd Sts.) | 604-921-2228 | www.laregalade.com

"*C'est magnifique*" rave regulars who "adore *la cuisine française*" at this "mighty authentic" West Vancouver bistro that's "well worth the trip over a bridge - any bridge" - to tuck into "ample portions" of "heartwarming" "French country" fare "meticulously prepared" by chef-owner Alain Rayé; the "quarters are close", but it's "like finding yourself in France."

Le Crocodile S *French* 27 | 23 | 26 | VE

Downtown | 100-909 Burrard St. (Smithe St.) | 604-669-4298 | www.lecrocodilerestaurant.com

"Are we in France?" clientele query chef-owner Michel Jacob, an "Alsatian prince" whose "sublime" cuisine bears the "Gallic consistency of a master"; there are "no crocodile tears" shed in this "stylish" Downtown "oasis" where the "discreet" staff "spoils" you (and the diners, *bien sûr,* are "expected to behave"), so whether "for a civilized lunch or a romantic evening", it is "worth every penny."

Morton's The Steakhouse *Steak* 25 | 22 | 25 | VE

Downtown | 750 W. Cordova St. (bet. Granville & Howe Sts.) | 604-915-5105 | www.mortons.com

"Order your meat rare and your drinks stiff" advise patrons of this "upscale American chain outpost" Downtown noted for its "flavorful" steaks of "monolithic proportions" served in an "old-boys'-club atmosphere"; just "pack your wallet" - this "classy" act doesn't come cheap.

Parkside M *European* 25 | 23 | 25 | E

West End | 1906 Haro St. (Gilford St.) | 604-683-6912 | www.parksiderestaurant.ca

"Mouth orgasms" - that's what smitten surveyors call chef-owner Andrey Durbach's "seasonally changing" Modern European inventions, made with "the freshest ingredients" and served on a prix fixe for "one of the best deals in town"; the staff is "attentive but not hovering" at this "intimate" West End "hideaway" where, from "succulent cocktails" to "delicious desserts", a "brilliant" meal leaves you "feeling happy-happy."

Pear Tree, The S M *Continental* 28 | 22 | 27 | E

Burnaby | 4120 E. Hastings St. (bet. Carleton & Gilmore Aves.) | 604-299-2772 | www.peartreerestaurant.net

At this "sophisticated", "welcome find in the culinary desert of Burnaby", "one of the country's top talents", chef-owner Scott Jaeger, puts out "fabulous", "imaginative" Continental plates; Stephanie Jaeger heads up a "stellar front-of-house" team, and "recent renovations have added a high-end touch" to the "small" but "charming" room.

Raincity Grill *Pacific NW* 25 | 19 | 24 | E

West End | 1193 Denman St. (Morton Ave.) | 604-685-7337 | www.raincitygrill.com

"For a true taste of Vancouver", regionalists rave about this "Pacific Northwest winner" with its "commitment to local suppliers", "seasonal" "menu variations that keep it interesting" and an "incredible" BC wine list; add "terrific" service and a "fabulous" West End setting "with an English Bay view", and this spot "defines West Coast" dining.

ToJo's 🅂 *Japanese* | 27 | - | 23 | VE

West Side | 1133 W. Broadway (bet. Heather & Willow Sts.) | 604-872-8050 | www.tojos.com

For some of "the best sushi in North America", "put yourself in the hands" of chef-owner Tojo Hidekazu and order the "mind-blowing omakase", then "taste pure decadence" in an array of "inventive" "nouvelle" creations; always an "undisputed winner" gastronomically, it offers a complete experience of "Japanese food heaven - in credit-card-limit hell"; N.B. a post-Survey move outdated the Decor score.

Vij's *Indian* | 28 | 22 | 25 | E

West Side | 1480 W. 11th Ave. (bet. Granville & Hemlock Sts.) | 604-736-6664 | www.vijs.ca

"Every meal is a sensual experience" at "consummate host" Vikram Vij's West Sider, known equally for the "genial" chef-owner's "personal touches" and for the "world-class", "inventive interpretations" of Indian cuisine; while "the single detractor is a no-reservations policy" that can lead to "hour-plus line-ups", the "back lounge is the best cocktail party in town", with "complimentary tasty treats" to "soothe the wait."

Vij's Rangoli *Indian* | 26 | 19 | 20 | M

West Side | 1488 W. 11th Ave. (bet. Granville & Hemlock Sts.) | 604-736-5711 | www.vijs.ca

"If you don't want to face the wait next door", or if you're looking for the "best bet for lunch" on the West Side, this "poor-man's Vij's" is "a cheaper, quicker alternative", offering a "limited selection" of "succulent" Indian fusion dishes; with the option to bring these "big flavors" home in the frozen "take-out boil-in bags", the "time-stressed" wonder "who cooks anymore."

Villa del Lupo *Italian/Pacific NW* | 26 | 23 | 26 | E

Downtown | 869 Hamilton St. (bet. Robson & Smithe Sts.) | 604-688-7436 | www.villadellupo.com

"Take a date" (or "your trophy wife") "for a romantic rendezvous" at this "intimate", "elegant" Downtown heritage house where the "superb service" "makes you feel like royalty" and the "high-end" Italian-Pacific Northwest fare is "outstanding"; the "artfully presented plates" are matched with an "excellent wine list" for a meal that is "*delizioso* in any language."

West *Pacific NW* | 29 | 26 | 27 | VE

West Side | 2881 Granville St. (W. 13th Ave.) | 604-738-8938 | www.westrestaurant.com

Ranked No. 1 for Food in Vancouver, this "jewel in the city's culinary crown" is "exquisite in every way"; chef Warren Geraghty creates "extraordinary" Pacific Northwest "dishes with divine flavors" that are paired with "superb" wines "graciously served" by an "exemplary" staff in a "stunning" West Side room; "it'll cost you a pretty penny", but for a "superlative" experience that will have "you floating home in a state of perfect serenity", "go West as quickly as possible."

EUROPE RESTAURANT DIRECTORY

FOOD | DECOR | SERVICE | COST

Amsterdam

TOP FOOD RANKING

	Restaurant	Cuisine
28	Ron Blaauw	French/International
27	Yamazato	Japanese
	Van Vlaanderen	French/Mediterranean
	La Rive	French/Mediterranean
26	Bordewijk	French/Mediterranean
	Christophe'	French
	Blauw aan de Wal	French/Mediterranean
	Visaandeschelde	International/Seafood
25	Excelsior	French/Mediterranean
24	Chez Georges	French
	Vermeer	French/International
	De Silveren Spiegel	Dutch
	Dylan	French
	Beddington's	French/Asian
23	Tempo Doeloe	Indonesian
	De Kas	Dutch/Mediterranean
	Blue Pepper	Indonesian
	Sichuan Food	Chinese
22	Tomo Sushi	Japanese
	Ciel Bleu	French
	Gala	Catalan
	Sophia	French/International

Beddington's S M *French/Asian* — 24 | 18 | 18 | E

Frederiksplein | Utrechtsedwarsstraat 141 | (31-20) 620-7393 | www.beddington.nl

"Long live Jean!" exclaim fans of this "nice place" in the Frederiksplein area that's "run by female chef" Jean Beddington, who is always cooking up a "hot menu" of "excellent", "inventive" French-Asian fare; still, some find the "small", "sober" space with "only a few tables" somewhat "cold" and suggest the "informal (but correct) service" "could use some work", saying the "restaurant just misses being really superior."

Blauw aan de Wal S M *French/Mediterranean* — 26 | 22 | 23 | E

Centrum | Oudezijds Achterburgwal 99 | (31-20) 330-2257

"Hidden away" at the end of an alley in the Centrum, this "serene spot" with its own "private dining terrace" offers a "respite from the Red Light District" "around the corner"; its "cozy setting" is home to "sweet", "enthusiastic" staffers who "are happy to explain" their "terrific" French-Med "fare made from the best ingredients" and accompanied by a "solid wine list"; no wonder so many consider it a "special place."

Blue Pepper *Indonesian* — 23 | 20 | 22 | M

Oud-Zuid | Nassaukade 366 | (31-20) 489-7039 | www.restaurantbluepepper.com

If you "want something other than" "the standard rijsttafel", "go straight to this top-notch" Oud-Zuid "treat" where a "creative" "nouveau Indonesian" kitchen delivers "delicious dishes" that are "full of flavor" and "out of the ordinary"; the "friendly staff" provides equally "sizzling service" and will happily "inform you about the details of the menu", but insiders insist that "the tasting menu is a must."

Bordewijk 🅼 *French/Mediterranean* 26 | 18 | 23 | E

Jordaan | Noordermarkt 7 | (31-20) 624-3899 | www.bordewijk.nl

The "chef visits" "your table" and "takes your order" at this "terrific place" "in a charming Jordaan location", a "favorite" of many for its "incredible" French-Med "haute cuisine", "comprehensive wine list" and "fantastic" service; still, some sigh it's "too bad" the "noisy room" "doesn't do justice to the rest of the experience", adding that "the restaurant is less inviting" to tourists since the staff is not as welcoming "if you are not a native."

Chez Georges 🅂 *French* 24 | 21 | 23 | E

Jordaan | Herenstraat 3 | (31-20) 626-3332

"It's always full" at this tiny Jordaan French in the nicest part of Amsterdam, because the "beautifully classic" cuisine is "superb", particularly the "fine" five-course tasting menu, which is a "great value"; a "staff that takes such pride in what it serves" and a "charming", "cozy" and "civilized" interior are other pluses.

Christophe' 🅂🅼 *French* 26 | 22 | 24 | VE

Jordaan | Leliegracht 46 | (31-20) 625-0807 | www.restaurantchristophe.nl

"Brilliantly inventive" and "beautifully presented" "dishes that combine upscale French cuisine" with "Mediterranean ingredients" and "African influences" "delight the eye and palate" at this "perfectly located" "canal-side" Jordaan "jewel" manned by an "eager-to-please staff"; those who think the "atmosphere is rather dull" quip that the "lovely" interior is "as quiet and peaceful as the floral arrangements, and about as lively", but most report "a special night out."

Ciel Bleu *French* 22 | 21 | 21 | E

Pijp | Hotel Okura | Ferdinand Bolstraat 333, 23rd fl. | (31-20) 678-7450 | www.cielbleu.nl

"Go on a clear night" to this "peaceful" establishment on the 23rd floor of the Hotel Okura in the Pijp to enjoy "marvelous views" (perhaps the "best in the city") along with "exquisite", "original and delicate" New French dishes that are delivered by a "helpful staff"; all agree that the "food is up to the level of the location"; N.B. the restaurant was refurbed in summer 2007.

De Kas 🅂 *Dutch/Mediterranean* 23 | 26 | 21 | E

Oost | Frankendael Park | Kamerlingh Onneslaan 3 | (31-20) 462-4562 | www.restaurantdekas.nl

Set in an "impressively large" and "beautiful greenhouse" "situated in the Park" Frankendael in Oost, "this sparkling glass temple to food" takes its "sensitivity and passion for local", mostly "organic ingredients" "to a whole new level", creating "a daily prix fixe menu" of "stellar" Dutch-Mediterranean fare "based upon the day's harvest"; whether seated in "the stunning dining room" or on the "lovely terrace", expect an "absolutely enchanting" experience as you "inhale the heady fragrances" of "fresh vegetables and herbs" growing all around you.

De Silveren Spiegel *Dutch* — 24 | 22 | 22 | VE

Centrum | Kattengat 4-6 | (31-20) 624-6589 | www.desilverenspiegel.com

This "beautiful little historic" Centrum treat "tucked away" "near Centraal Station" may be so "old" (circa 1614) that it "looks as though it's falling over", but its kitchen actually "impresses" with an "interesting" array of "well-executed dishes" that are some "of the best" examples of "nouvelle Dutch" cuisine; the "quaint" setting with "lead-glass windows and candles" is an "old-world delight" whose "warm", "intimate atmosphere" is abetted by "gracious service" from a "staff with exceptional knowledge of" the "great wine list."

D'Vijff Vlieghen *Dutch* — 21 | 23 | 20 | E

Centrum | Spuistraat 294-302 | (31-20) 530-4060 | www.thefiveflies.com

"Small rooms connected by narrow winding corridors" spanning "five charming old houses" in the Centrum form a "marvelous" backdrop for this "Amsterdam institution" that's "still going strong", serving up a "great variety" of "flavorful" Dutch dishes that are more "contemporary" than you'd expect; still, some say it's "living on its reputation" and complain that it's "chronically overfilled" with "tons of tourists" and "complacent", "slow" servers – so "be prepared" for a "long (though memorable) evening"; P.S. "the name means 'The Five Flies.'"

Dylan, The *French* — 24 | 26 | 23 | VE

Jordaan | Dylan Hotel | Keizersgracht 384 | (31-20) 530-2010 | www.dylanamsterdam.com

This "don't-miss place" "within the hip, tasteful" Dylan Hotel in the Jordaan is "trendy", in part because its "sleek, cool interior" continues to "wow" the city's "handsome people", but also because the kitchen creates "beautifully presented" modern French cuisine; in fact, it's so "tremendous across the board" most overlook that the "stuck-up staffers" still "take themselves too seriously."

Excelsior *French/Mediterranean* — 25 | 24 | 25 | VE

Centrum | Hotel de L'Europe | Nieuwe Doelenstraat 2-8 | (31-20) 531-1705 | www.restaurantexcelsior.nl

"Fine dining in Amsterdam" is found at this "luxurious" venue "within the Hotel de L'Europe", a "beautiful" Centrum establishment "with old European charm", where chef Jean-Jacques Menanteau creates "delicious" "traditional French-Med dishes" that are "worth the splurge"; fans feel the "excellent service" and "elegant" interior "recall the graciousness of times past", but even "bored" sorts who say the "stuffy decor" "could use an upgrade" are "simply delighted" by the "lovely" terrace with its "romantic view" of the Amstel River.

Gala *Catalan* — 22 | 20 | 20 | E

Leidseplein | Reguliersdwarsstraat 38 | (31-20) 623-6303

This "hip" and "trendy" "place to be seen" in the Leidseplein area offers a narrow, sexy and stylish setting with a moodily lit bar that makes for a "romantic evening"; influenced by contemporary Catalan cooking, the kitchen turns out "excellent Spanish tapas" that are indeed a gala "celebration of good eating."

	FOOD	DECOR	SERVICE	COST
La Rive	27	26	26	VE
Ron Blaauw	28	21	24	VE
Sichuan Food	23	16	18	M
Sophia	22	21	20	E
Tempo Doeloe	23	15	19	M

La Rive Ⓢ Ⓜ *French/Mediterranean* — 27 | 26 | 26 | VE

Oost | InterContinental Amstel | Professor Tulpplein 1 | (31-20) 520-3264 | www.restaurantlarive.nl

"You know you've a-Rived when you" visit "this breathtaking waterfront restaurant" "right on the river" "in the city's premier hotel", the "elegant" InterContinental Amstel in Oost, where the "fabulous views" are actually trumped by the "phenomenal" French-Mediterranean culinary creations; furthermore, "you'd be hard-pressed to find a grander dining room" or more "wonderful" staff to "wait on you hand and foot", so it's no surprise "sated" surveyors swear the experience produces "ecstasy"; P.S. "in summer, dine waterside" on the "beautiful terrace."

Ron Blaauw Ⓢ Ⓜ *French/International* — 28 | 21 | 24 | VE

Ouderkerk aan de Amstel | Kerkstraat 56 | (31-20) 496-1943 | www.ronblaauw.nl

Expect "a real feast" at this "wonderful" winner, rated No. 1 for Food in Amsterdam, that "can be counted on" for "consistently high-quality" French-International cuisine offered in "surprising" multicourse meals of "gorgeous, creative tapaslike dishes"; servers who ensure "you're really pampered" and "great" decor also make it "worth" "the journey" to an "out-of-the-way" location in Ouderkerk aan de Amstel; P.S. "on a hot summer evening, head for a seat on the terrace."

Sichuan Food *Chinese* — 23 | 16 | 18 | M

Centrum | Reguliersdwarsstraat 35 | (31-20) 626-9327

"Extraordinary Peking duck" and "great oysters from the wok" are the stars of the show at this "classic" Chinese in the Centrum that fans call a "wonderful place" for its "high-quality" cuisine, including "some dishes that are actually authentic"; still, heat-seekers say there's "not much spice" in the Westernized fare, while others insist that "service can be slow when it's busy" and the "outdated decor" is "slightly gaudy."

Sophia *French/International* — 22 | 21 | 20 | E

Oud-Zuid | Sophialaan 55 | (31-20) 305-2760 | www.restaurantsophia.nl

Scenesters say "if you only have one night in Amsterdam", this "hip", new French in Oud-Zuid with its "chic" decor and "plenty of eye candy" to ogle is a "good choice"; most maintain the "trendy" tasting "dishes are delicious" but "small", so "you may be surprised when you see the size of your bill."

Tempo Doeloe *Indonesian* — 23 | 15 | 19 | M

Rembrandtplein | Utrechtsestraat 75 | (31-20) 625-6718 | www.tempodoeloerestaurant.nl

"Fantastic fare" "keeps patrons coming back" to this "classic Indonesian rijsttafel restaurant", a "moderately priced" and "always crowded" "Amsterdam favorite" "on a beautiful block" in the Rembrandtplein area, where the "attentive owner" and his "friendly", "patient servers will explain the entire menu" ("let them guide you"); some "critics claim the decor", "stuffy atmosphere" and "tight quarters" "take away from the experience", "but real foodies would travel far for cooking this authentic."

Tomo Sushi *Japanese*

22 | 16 | 20 | M

Centrum | Reguliersdwarsstraat 131 | (31-20) 528-5208

"Don't tell too many people" plead patrons panicked that this "small" Japanese place "hidden away" "near the Rembrandtplein" "will become overcrowded" with customers clamoring for its "excellent sushi" "cut well and served imaginatively" ("awesome" yakitori too); other pluses include "good", "friendly service", "hip decor" with a "clean", "modern design" and relatively "low prices" that make it "a good value."

Van Vlaanderen *French/Mediterranean*

27 | 20 | 24 | E

Leidseplein | Weteringschans 175 | (31-20) 622-8292

"An antidote to overly trendy places" is this "lovely, low-key" spot in the Leidseplein area featuring "fantastic" French-Mediterranean fare that "always pleasantly surprises"; perhaps the "informal", "quite-small" interior "with not much space between the tables" doesn't fully do justice to "the caliber of cuisine", but it's nevertheless "a quiet" refuge from "the heart of the action", plus the "capable waiters do their utmost to make your dinner a success."

Vermeer *French/International*

24 | 23 | 24 | VE

Centrum | NH Barbizon Palace Hotel | Prins Hendrikkade 59-72 | (31-20) 556-4885 | www.restaurantvermeer.nl

"Outstanding cuisine" is a hallmark of this "top-class" "favorite" in the Centrum's NH Barbizon Palace Hotel, where the French-International "food is amazing" and the "wine list elaborate"; some find "the majorly elegant dining room" "pretty", others "a bit stiff", but all agree the "friendly yet professional staff" provides "impeccable service", leading most to insist that you "couldn't have a more enjoyable evening."

Visaandeschelde *International/Seafood*

26 | 20 | 21 | E

Rivierenbuurt | Scheldeplein 4 | (31-20) 675-1583 | www.visaandeschelde.nl

"Visitors to Holland" in search of "wonderful" International cuisine "with a focus on seafood" should follow the hordes of locals who crowd this "very hip place" that's "a little out of the way" in the Rivierenbuurt; after all, "you come here for really great fish" dishes, which incorporate Japanese, French and Mediterranean influences and are "nicely served" at "well-situated tables" by a "stellar" staff; P.S. "don't forget the excellent wines."

Yamazato *Japanese*

27 | 19 | 25 | VE

Pijp | Hotel Okura | Ferdinand Bolstraat 333 | (31-20) 678-8351 | www.yamazato.nl

"For real Japanese food, this is the place to be in the Netherlands" say fans of this "absolute treat" in the Pijp's Hotel Okura that serves "fresh", "fabulous presentations" of "some of the best sushi in Europe" along with other "outstanding" offerings, all backed up by an "extensive sake list"; "alas", some say, it's a "shame the decor doesn't quite reach the same level", but "excellent service" from the "trilingual staff" more than compensates - "be prepared" for the bill, though, as it's definitely "costly."

Athens

		FOOD	DECOR	SERVICE	COST

TOP FOOD RANKING

	Restaurant	Cuisine
29	Spondi	French/Mediterranean
26	48	Greek
	Varoulko	Mediterranean/Seafood
24	Tudor Hall	French/Mediterranean
	Sale e Pepe	Italian
	Pil Poul et Jérôme Serres	French/Mediterranean
	Thalassinos	Seafood
23	Parea	Greek
	Kiku	Japanese
	Ta Kioupia	Greek/Mediterranean
	Vassilenas	Greek
	Daphne's	Greek/Mediterranean
22	Papadakis	Greek
	Milos	Greek/Seafood
	7 Thalasses	Greek/Seafood
	St'Astra	Mediterranean
21	GB Corner	Mediterranean
	Lalu	International
20	Kafeneio	Greek
	Balthazar	Mediterranean

Balthazar ◐ *Mediterranean* 20 | 24 | 18 | E

Ampelokipi | Tsoha 27 & Bournazou | (30-210) 641-2300 | www.balthazar.gr

This "dangerously trendy" Mediterranean in "hip" Ampelokipi is "great in summer" when diners forgo an "amazing" modern interior in favor of the "superb" garden; the fare is "up to par" as well, and there are "beautiful" people at the bar.

Daphne's *Greek/Mediterranean* 23 | 23 | 21 | E

Plaka | Lysikratous 4 | (30-210) 322-7971 | www.daphnesrestaurant.gr

Set in a restored 19th-century townhouse, this "wonderful" Greek-Med in the Plaka is "a find", starting with its "beautiful", enclosed courtyard and continuing on to its "superb" old-world decor replete with "lovely" Pompeii-esque frescoes painted by the owner; the interior's "warmth and charm" extends to an "attentive staff" and a menu of "traditional" favorites – "by all means, don't miss the rabbit *stifado* (stew)."

48, The Restaurant ◐ⓢ *Greek* 26 | 26 | 25 | VE

Ampelokipi | Armatolon & Klefton 48 | (30-210) 641-1082 | www.48therestaurant.com

"Easily the coolest place I've ever been to" assert admirers of this "beautiful", "modern" Ampelokipi Greek featuring dramatic lighting and a "magical" courtyard where patrons literally "dine over the water" via a see-through platform; chef Christoforos Peskias caters to a "hip", "pretty" clientele with pricey, "innovative takes" on traditional fare, while "friendly service" and an extensive international wine list round out the "wonderful experience."

FOOD | DECOR | SERVICE | COST

GB Corner ◐ *Mediterranean* — 21 | 22 | 22 | VE

Syntagma | Hotel Grande Bretagne | Syntagma Sq. | (30-210) 333-0000 | www.grandebretagne.gr

Situated in the lobby of the stately Hotel Grande Bretagne, this "bit of old Europe" in a "beautiful space" attracts power-lunchers with its "good", "very expensive" Mediterranean cuisine, an "attentive but not intrusive" staff and an "excellent wine list, including Greek vintages"; P.S. for a more "serene" experience, romantics recommend the GB Roof Garden upstairs, with its "incredible, magical views of the Acropolis to your left and Parliament to your right."

Kafeneio ▣ *Greek* — 20 | 14 | 19 | M

Kolonaki | Loukianou 26 | (30-210) 723-7757

"For a true Kolonaki dining experience", try this trendy but "traditional" "treat" serving "quite original" takes on "affordable" Greek favorites; the simple, nondescript interior boasts "little atmosphere", so a mostly local clientele advises "eat outside" at one of the sidewalk tables that are "great for people-watching" in this "hot" section of Athens.

Kiku ◐▣ *Japanese* — 23 | 16 | 21 | VE

Kolonaki | Dimokritou 12 | (30-210) 364-7033

Considered "the best sushi restaurant in town", this Japanese located on a busy side street in Kolonaki is an "excellent" choice "for a business meal" of "good" raw fish, albeit at "expensive" prices; the minimalist setting – think blond wood and hanging scrolls – strikes some as "boring", but its "authentic" cooked dishes make it a "favorite of Japanese tourists" as well as those "living in Athens."

Lalu ◐ *International* — 21 | 19 | 19 | E

Kolonaki | 4 Anagnostopoulou St. | (30-210) 623-3933

This new Athens "hot spot" in a 19th-century mansion overlooking trendy Kolonaki square has become "the talk of the town"; the International menu is "very good", but the quietly opulent "atmosphere", "great nightly DJ" and music that "swings from jazz to soul to more" mean "the crowds" also come for a "cheerful night out."

Milos ◐ *Greek/Seafood* — 22 | 22 | 23 | VE

Kolonaki | Hilton Athens | Vassilissis Sofias 46 | (30-210) 724-4400 | www.hilton.com

With long-standing restaurants in New York City and Montréal, chef-owner Costas Spiliades came home to open this "starkly modern" Greek seafooder with a "convenient" location in the landmark Hilton Athens; an "elegant" dining room (complete with open kitchen and marble display cases) and outdoor terrace set the stage for "superb" seasonal specialties and grilled fish "so fresh, you'll have to wash the salt spray off of your face" – much as you'll do with your smile once the über-"expensive" check arrives.

Papadakis ◐▣ *Greek* — 22 | 19 | 21 | E

Kolonaki | Voukourestiou 47 & Fokilidou | (30-210) 360-8621

On a citrus-tree-lined street in Kolonaki lies this "popular" Greek import "straight from Paros Island" that specializes in "excellent", "imaginative" fish dishes, along with "ample alternatives for carnivores and vegetarians", all at "fairly reasonable" prices; a "welcoming staff" presides over a small but "beautiful" setting that evokes "a seaside taverna."

Parea ◐☒ *Greek* 23 | 22 | 22 | E

Kerameikos | Eridanus Hotel | Pireos 78 | (30-210) 520-0630 | www.eridanus.gr

Top toque Lefteris Lazarou of the highly rated Varoulko is producing "excellent food" at this Hellenic in the basement of the Eridanus Hotel; come summer it moves up to the roof terrace to take advantage of views of the Acropolis, Keramikos cemetery and Philoppapou Hill; whatever season, it all adds up to "a wonderful evening and great memories" - "everything anyone could ask for the full Greek experience."

Pil Poul et Jérôme Serres ◐☒ *French/Mediterranean* 24 | 25 | 22 | E

Thisio | Apostolou Pavlou 51 & Poulopoulou | (30-210) 342-3665 | www.pilpoul.gr

Star chef Jérôme Serres (ex his own namesake spot and Spondi) has joined forces with this establishment in a beautiful restored mansion in Thisio and the result is "great" "creative" French-Mediterranean cuisine served by an "excellent" staff; the "incredible" setting includes "a dream-like" terrace with "one of the most magnificent views of the Acropolis."

Sale e Pepe ◐☒ *Italian* 24 | 18 | 22 | E

Kolonaki | Aristippou 34 | (30-210) 723-4102

A "lovely dining experience", this "high-class Italian" "aims to please" with simple, "well-executed" dishes and a "pleasant", antiques-filled setting; "great service" and a chef who "adds a personal touch" draw a chic crowd from surrounding Kolonaki, although most visit this "gem" for "one of the best wine lists in Athens" (over 5,000 bottles).

7 Thalasses ◐☒ *Greek/Seafood* 22 | 20 | 22 | E

Kolonaki | Omirou 11 & Vissarionos | (30-210) 362-4825

The name of this Kolonaki Greek means 'seven seas', so the fact that it specializes in "excellent" fish should come as no surprise; the nautically decorated setting "could use an update", but "good value for the money" keeps luring locals back.

Spondi ◐ *French/Mediterranean* 29 | 24 | 26 | VE

Pangrati | Varnavas Sq. | Pyrronos 5 | (30-210) 756-4021 | www.spondi.gr

At this elegant Pangrati restaurant rated No. 1 for Food in Athens, travelers and the city's well-to-do are "totally blown away" by chef Arnaud Bignon's "excellent", "creative" French-Mediterranean fare that's praised for its "outstanding taste and presentation"; set on three "beautiful" floors with a "spectacular" courtyard and terrace, this pricey 'offering to the gods' (the meaning of its name) rounds out the experience with "wonderfully attentive" service and a "superb wine list", including a "nice selection of Greek" labels.

St'Astra ◐☒ *Mediterranean* 22 | 20 | 22 | E

Pedion tou Areos Park | Park Hotel | Alexandras Ave. 10 | (30-210) 889-4500 | www.park-hotel.gr

"What more are you looking for?" ask aesthetes about this "enjoyable" rooftop bar and Med restaurant in the Park Hotel where "dining under the stars" includes "a breathtaking view" of Athens from the

Acropolis and Lycabettus Hill to the coast; throw in "delicious food", a cool interior with colorful contemporary Murano glass chandeliers and "attentive service" and it all adds up to an "unforgettable evening."

Ta Kioupia ◐ *Greek/Mediterranean* 23 | 19 | 21 | E

Kolonaki | Dinokratous & An. Polemou 22 | (30-210) 740-0150 | www.takioupia.gr

For 35 years, this family-run Greek-Mediterranean in Kolonaki has been serving "authentic", "utterly delicious" traditional dishes complemented by an extensive local wine list; the setting is a classic and comfortable high-ceilinged two-story space, and in summer the small dining terrace overlooking Lycabettus Hill beckons.

Thalassinos ◐M *Seafood* 24 | 17 | 23 | M

Tzitzifies | Irakleous & Lysikratous 32 | (30-210) 940-4518

Seafood lovers from around the city descend on this "Athens treasure", a "quality" Tzitzifies taverna that's a good choice for "exquisite fish" and a "great variety" of other "delicious" dishes; some deem the rustic, tchotchke-filled interior "dull", but moderate prices help this local favorite "stay busy."

Tudor Hall ◐ *French/Mediterranean* 24 | 23 | 23 | VE

Syntagma | King George Palace | Vas. Georgiou A' St. 3 | (30-210) 322-2210 | www.classicalhotels.gr

"What an awesome view of Athens" enthuse admirers of this French-Med "perfectly located" on the seventh floor of the King George Palace hotel, with its "unbeatable classic" panorama of the Acropolis and proximity to the Greek Parliament houses on Constitution Square; the "food is wonderful" and the "service excellent", making for an "all-around impressive", albeit very "expensive, experience."

Varoulko ◐S *Mediterranean/Seafood* 26 | 20 | 23 | VE

Kerameikos | Pireos 80 | (30-210) 522-8400 | www.varoulko.gr

This "can't-miss" Med seafooder in historic Kerameikos from acclaimed chef-owner Lefteris Lazarou "continues to surprise" a host of regulars who appreciate a "uniquely executed", ever-changing menu that exhibits the wealth of "Poseidon's bounty"; a simple, elegant interior dotted with modern sculpture lets the "fresh" fish shine, although wallet-watchers warn the fin fare also "really bites - once you get the check."

Vassilenas ◐M *Greek* 23 | 20 | 23 | M

Piraeus | Aitolikou 72 | (30-210) 461-2457 | www.vassilenas.gr

"One of the best" tavernas in Athens, this stalwart "has modernized its cuisine while maintaining some original" Greek dishes, with an emphasis on fish; moderate prices lead locals to the simple street level space near Piraeus, but in summer the action moves to the flower-bedecked rooftop.

FOOD | DECOR | SERVICE | COST

Barcelona

TOP FOOD RANKING

	Restaurant	Cuisine
28	Passadis del Pep	Mediterranean/Seafood
	Drolma	Catalan
	Àbac	Catalan
27	Gaig	Catalan
	Alkimia	Catalan
26	Cinc Sentits	Catalan/Mediterranean
	Hofmann	Mediterranean
	Cal Pep	Mediterranean/Seafood
25	Comerç 24	Spanish/International
	Ca l'Isidre	Catalan/Mediterranean
	Lasarte	Catalan/Basque
	La Dama	Catalan/Mediterranean
	Botafumeiro	Seafood/Galician
24	Els Pescadors	International/Seafood
	Neichel	Mediterranean
	Gorría	Basque/Navarraise
	Arola	Catalan

Àbac S M *Catalan* 28 | - | 26 | VE

Sarrià-Sant Gervasi | Avenida Tibidado 1 | (34-93) 319-6600 | www.restaurantabac.com

Foodies and the fashionable flock to this "exciting" modern Catalan for top toque Xavier Pellicer's "original" "cutting-edge" cuisine with an "amazing combination of flavors" and textures, "especially the tasting menu"; the staff works the room with "choreographed gracefulness", leading gastronomic groupies to conclude it's "top-notch in every way"; N.B. post-Survey the restaurant moved from the Born district to this new locale in Sant Gervasi.

Alkimia S *Catalan* 27 | 21 | 22 | E

Eixample | Indústria 79 | (34-93) 207-6115

It's "currently one of the best restaurants in Barcelona" state supporters of star chef Jordi Vilà's new-wave Catalan in the Eixample, with its "excellent" and "unusual amalgam of explosive flavors"; the "white minimalist" setting evokes a "sense of purity that is carried over into the food", while alchemy symbols on the wall stylishly suggest the restaurant's name.

Arola M *Catalan* 24 | 25 | 24 | VE

Port Olímpic | Hotel Arts | Marina 19-21 | (34-93) 483-8090 | www.arola-arts.com

Chef Sergi Arola, a Ferran Adrià disciple who also runs Madrid's groundbreaking La Broche, heads up this "trendy" modern Catalan located in the "fantastic" Hotel Arts; a "beautiful"-looking staff serves the "creative", "attractive small plates" in a "perfect location" complete with "wonderful views" of the Olímpic Harbor and the sea; N.B. also closed Tuesdays.

Barceloneta ◐ *Mediterranean/Seafood* 21 | 18 | 18 | M

Barceloneta | Moll dels Pescadors | L'Escar 22 | (34-93) 221-2111 | www.rte-barceloneta.com

This big, "boisterous", "fairly priced" Med with "top-quality fish" and a "cordial" staff has an "excellent location on the water" in Barceloneta; the "dining room doesn't need a lot of decoration because the view is enough", and in summer "a table on the terrace" is even more ideal.

Botafumeiro ◐ *Seafood/Galician* 25 | 18 | 23 | VE

Gràcia | Gran de Gràcia 81 | (34-93) 218-4230 | www.botafumeiro.es

For the "freshest seafood", particularly the "pristine cold shellfish platter", many head to this 32-year-old "emblematic" Galician in Gràcia with a "good" regional wine list, "warm" setting and popular bar; the sprawling, "hustle-bustle" space can be "noisy", and it's "expensive", but that doesn't keep loyal crowds from coming back.

Ca l'Isidre ☒ *Catalan/Mediterranean* 25 | 18 | 23 | VE

El Raval | Les Flors 12 | (34-93) 441-1139 | www.calisidre.com

"Creative but not froufrou" describes the "culinary delights" found at this family-run Catalan-Med in El Raval, where chef Núria Gironés, the daughter of the owner and former noted chef, especially excels at "superb" desserts like the "best chocolate soufflé"; a "most accommodating and helpful staff" presides over a quietly "elegant" room with original art - Picasso, Miró - on the walls; "it's expensive, but you leave with the sense that you invested your money very well."

Cal Pep ☒ *Mediterranean/Seafood* 26 | 17 | 21 | E

Born-Ribera | Plaça de les Olles 8 | (34-93) 310-7961 | www.calpep.com

"You have no business being a foodie if you are in Barcelona and miss this place" declare disciples of this Born-Ribera Med, which specializes in "super-fresh" seafood and tapas "simply prepared, the way they should be"; owner Pep Manubens oversees a "diminutive" "high-energy" space with about 30 stools at the "packed" bar and a back room with a handful of tables; "line up early" and "don't expect a menu" - "just go with the flow" for "an exceptional" experience.

Cinc Sentits ☒ *Catalan/Mediterranean* 26 | 22 | 24 | E

Eixample | Aribau 58 | (34-93) 323-9490 | www.cincsentits.com

"Barcelona is the new capital of world dining" and this family-run Catalan-Med in the Eixample showcasing Jordi Artal's "creative but intelligible cuisine" is "one of its heads of state"; surveyors single out the tasting menus paired with "surprising but always exquisite wines" as providing not only "a great meal but a great foodie deal"; "service is a rare blend of refinement and genuine hospitality", and the setting is sleek contemporary chic.

Comerç 24 ☒ M *Spanish/International* 25 | 23 | 22 | E

Born-Ribera | Comerç 24 | (34-93) 319-2102 | www.comerc24.com

"Exciting, unpredictable" and "adventurous" sums up this avant-garde Spanish-International in the Born-Ribera district run by "dynamic" chef-owner Carles Abellán, a disciple of legendary Ferran Adrià of El Bulli; "inventive", "unforgettable" tapas are "taken to a sexy new level" and served by a "charming staff" in a cooler than cool, colorful minimalist setting, making this a "must-eat-at in Barcelona."

	FOOD	DECOR	SERVICE	COST
Drolma *Catalan*	28	25	27	VE

Eixample | Hotel Majestic | Passeig de Gràcia 68 | (34-93) 496-7710 | www.hotelmajestic.es

Chef Fermí Puig's "outstanding" modern Catalan in the Hotel Majestic features "out-of-this-world", cutting-edge cuisine (glazed baby goat is his signature) and a small but "stylish" setting with views of the Passeig de Gràcia; it's "exceptionally expensive", but that hasn't kept it from becoming a "bastion for Barcelona's rich and powerful."

	FOOD	DECOR	SERVICE	COST
el Bulli *Eclectic/Spanish*	-	-	-	VE

Roses | Cala Montjoi, Ap. 30 | (34-97) 215-0457 | www.elbulli.com

On the Costa Brava coastline near Roses, this deceptively rustic-looking lair of molecular gastronomy originator Ferran Adrià draws epicureans from around the world for extravagant 33-course modern Spanish tasting menus featuring the surrealist likes of freeze-fried eggs and caviar made from olive oil (the dishes change annually); a polished staff, quaint bulldog-themed dining room and terrace overlooking an Arcadian inlet complete the picture; N.B. if you score a reservation – it's open April-September only and books up a year in advance – bring your sense of humor and a fat wallet.

	FOOD	DECOR	SERVICE	COST
Els Pescadors *International/Seafood*	24	19	21	E

Poblenou | Plaça Prim 1 | (34-93) 225-2018 | www.elspescadors.com

This large International stalwart with "great seafood" ("amazing salt-baked fish") and a strong Spanish wine list is "worth the trip to Poblenou" (about a mile down the waterfront north of the Olympic Port); there's a trio of dining rooms to choose from, and in summer terrace tables are a cool alternative.

	FOOD	DECOR	SERVICE	COST
Gaig *Catalan*	27	21	24	VE

Eixample | Cram Hotel | Aragó 214 | (34-93) 429-1017 | www.restaurantgaig.com

Though this family-owned establishment in the Eixample dates back to 1869, its current chef, Carles Gaig, produces "creative" modern Catalan cuisine that's "among the best in Barcelona", with the "emphasis on elegant dishes made with the best ingredients"; an "intimate", "quiet" setting and "superb service" add to the "fine-all-around", "very expensive" experience.

	FOOD	DECOR	SERVICE	COST
Gorría *Basque/Navarraise*	24	16	20	E

Eixample | Diputació 421 | (34-93) 245-1164 | www.restaurantegorria.com

Long-standing, family-run Basque-Navarraise in the Eixample featuring "classic" dishes like suckling pig and "meat as good as Peter Luger's in Brooklyn"; a timeless "rustic" setting with wood, brick walls and stained glass, an "excellent wine list" and "doable" prices add to the laid-back vibe.

	FOOD	DECOR	SERVICE	COST
Hofmann *Mediterranean*	26	19	21	E

Born-Ribera | La Granada del Penedès 14-16 | (34-93) 218-7165 | www.hofmann-bcn.com

"They aim high in the kitchen and succeed most of the time" at this restaurant/culinary school in the Born-Ribera district run by chef/owner/teacher Mey Hofmann; "fantastic" Mediterranean dishes and "work-of-art" desserts are served in a series of "charming" dining rooms housed in a 19th-century building; N.B. closed Saturdays and Sundays.

La Dama *Catalan/Mediterranean* 25 | 26 | 25 | VE

Eixample | Avinguda Diagonal 423 | (34-93) 202-0686 | www.ladama-restaurant.com

"Absolutely elegant", this "grand, old" dame excels with a "gorgeous", "romantic" art nouveau setting in a 1918 Eixample building; "very good" creative Catalan-Mediterranean food, an exceptional wine list and "immaculate", "not stuffy", service also lead devotees to declare "it's a gem that could hold its own anywhere."

Lasarte S *Catalan/Basque* 25 | 23 | 23 | E

Eixample | Hotel Condes de Barcelona | Mallorca 259 | (34-93) 445-3242 | www.restaurantlasarte.com

This modern Catalan-Basque "masterpiece" owned by star chef Martín Berasategui and located in the Hotel Condes de Barcelona was one of the city's most anticipated openings; "outstanding food and attention to detail" and a "beautiful" split-level contemporary space make it a "must-stop" hot spot for foodies and fashionistas alike.

Los Caracoles ◐ *Spanish/Catalan* 20 | 18 | 17 | M

Barri Gòtic | Escudellers 14 | (34-93) 302-3185 | www.loscaracoles.es

The name of this "cavernous", "rustic" 1835 "landmark" Spanish-Catalan in Barri Gòtic translates as 'snails', and that's the specialty here along with "wonderful, spit-roasted chicken" and "paella served in skillets the size of flying saucers"; sure, it's "touristy", "campy" and "service is slap-dash", but most maintain it's a "must for first-time" visitors and "reasonable prices."

Neichel S M *Mediterranean* 24 | 21 | 22 | VE

Pedralbes | Beltrán i Rózpide 1-5 | (34-93) 203-8408 | www.neichel.es

"Everything is great" enthuse admirers of this 27-year-old Med where chef-owner Jean-Louis Neichel's "fantastic food" and a "superb wine list" are served by an "impeccable" staff in a room overlooking a garden in residential Pedralbes; but the less-impressed assess the experience as "old-fashioned" and "very expensive."

Passadis del Pep S *Mediterranean/Seafood* 28 | 21 | 25 | E

Ciutat Vella | Plaça de Palau 2 | (34-93) 310-1021 | www.passadis.com

"Don't expect a written menu or a choice" at this "difficult-to-find gem", a Mediterranean seafooder in Ciutat Vella that's voted No. 1 for Food in the city; the second you sit down, you'll be served sparkling *cava* and an "extravaganza" of "plate-after-plate" of appetizers that "just keep coming" ("don't forget to say stop"), followed by a main course ("if you can still fit it in") that's "the best fish in the world"; it all adds up to a down-to-earth "awesome experience."

7 Portes ◐ *Catalan* 21 | 21 | 20 | E

Ciutat Vella | Passeig Isabel II 14 | (34-93) 319-3033 | www.7portes.com

"An old standard that's still going strong", this sprawling 1836 Catalan "institution" and "paella palace" in Port Vell is "one of the oldest continuously operating restaurants in the world"; although "touristy" and "hectic", most maintain that "good value for the money" and a "festive" atmosphere that "reeks of old-world charm" "make up for it."

FOOD | DECOR | SERVICE | COST

Berlin

TOP FOOD RANKING

	Restaurant	Cuisine
26	VAU	International
24	Lorenz Adlon	French
	Maxwell	French/International
	Gabriele	Italian/Mediterranean
23	Alt Luxemburg	French/Mediterranean
	Die Quadriga*	French/Mediterranean
	44	French/International
	Vox	Asian/French
	Ana e Bruno	Italian/Mediterranean
22	Hartmanns	German/Mediterranean
	Margaux	French
21	Aigner	Viennese
	Guy	French/Mediterranean
	Balthazar	Mediterranean
	San Nicci	Italian
	Grill Royal	Seafood/Steak
	Borchardt	French/German
	Bacco/Bocca di Bacco	Tuscan

Aigner *Viennese* — 21 | 19 | 19 | E

Mitte | Französische Str. 25 | (49-30) 203-751-850 | www.aigner-gendarmenmarkt.de

"Fashionable people" flock to this "popular" "place in Mitte", "on the Gendarmenmarkt", where you'll "want to order seconds" of the "excellent Viennese cooking" that's "well-rounded" with German influences – the signature roast "duck is spectacular" – and served by a "friendly" staff; though located within a typical GDR-style 'Plattenbau' (concrete building), its "wonderful" 19th-century bistro setting is transplanted from the former Café Aigner in Vienna.

Alt Luxemburg ⊠ *French/Mediterranean* — 23 | 21 | 25 | E

Charlottenburg | Windscheidstr. 31 | (49-30) 323-8730 | www.altluxemburg.de

"One expects the old Kaiser to walk in" to this "wonderful place", a "Berlin standard" not far from the Charlottenburg Castle, where the "fast service" provided by Ingrid Wannemacher's "nice" staff always "satisfies", as does her husband Karl's "comprehensive menu" of "delicious" New French-Med cuisine ("no schnitzel") offered amid "quiet" surroundings; no wonder so many regulars are "happy" to call it a "favorite."

Ana e Bruno ⊠ M *Italian/Mediterranean* — 23 | 17 | 22 | E

Charlottenburg | Sophie-Charlotten-Str. 101 | (49-30) 325-7110 | www.ana-e-bruno.de

"Made for a lovely, quiet evening", this "cozy" Charlottenburg spot is home to "accommodating chef" Bruno Pellegrini, whose "ambitious"

* Indicates a tie with restaurant above

menu offers a taste of "*bella Italia*" via "excellent, inventive" Italian-Mediterranean cuisine at prices that may be "high" but are "appropriate for the quality of the food"; some call the decor "less than striking", but at least "you know you're in good hands" with the "polite staff"; P.S. "be sure to make reservations, as tables are limited."

Bacco *Tuscan* 21 | 19 | 19 | E

Charlottenburg | Marburger Str. 5 | (49-30) 211-8687 | www.bacco.de

Bocca di Bacco ◐ *Tuscan*

Mitte | Friedrichstr. 167/168 | (49-30) 2067-2828 | www.boccadibacco.de

The Mannozzi family oversees this Tuscan pair, the original an old-fashioned trattoria "with history" that's been serving "good, traditional cuisine with no surprises" in Charlottenburg since the late-'60s, and its 'mouth of Bacchus' offshoot in Mitte a more "sophisticated", "upmarket" eatery offering "nouvelle" fare and a "good selection of wines" in a "modern, stylish" setting; both are often "star-studded" and feature "fresh ingredients" and "charming" staffers, making either one "worth a try."

Balthazar *Mediterranean* 21 | 20 | 20 | E

Wilmersdorf | Kurfürstendamm 160 | (49-30) 8940-8477 | www.restaurant-balthazar.de

Tucked into a classical Berlin townhouse in Wilmersdorf, at the "less-fashionable end of Kurfürstendamm", is this urbane-looking Mediterranean with Asian accents that offers "enjoyable", "high-class cuisine", a "great wine list" and a "warm staff"; moreover, the practical point out there's a bargain 10 euro business lunch and at dinner "you can walk away without emptying your wallet."

Borchardt ◐ *French/German* 21 | 20 | 19 | E

Mitte | Französische Str. 47 | (49-30) 8188-6262

"Popular" with "politicians, movie stars" and other "celebrity patrons", this "classic" in Mitte is known for a "wonderful menu" of French-German fare - including "delicious fish" dishes and some of "the best Wiener schnitzel in Berlin" - "hospitably" presented in a "large", "beautiful" "brasserie" setting with "pre-war flair"; still, those with "unfulfilled expectations" posit that "one pays for the stargazing" and "glam" scene, adding that certain "snooty" staffers are "less accommodating when serving Mr. and Ms. Average."

Die Quadriga ⊠ *French/Mediterranean* 23 | 25 | 23 | E

Charlottenburg | Brandenburger Hof | Eislebener Str. 14 | (49-30) 2140-5650 | www.brandenburger-hof.com

"A memorable meal" awaits at this "nice hotel dining" venue whose two rooms flank a "beautiful [Japanese] garden" in Charlottenburg's Brandenburger Hof; chef Bobby Bräuer creates a "varied menu" of "exquisite" New French-Mediterranean cuisine, which is accompanied by an extensive all-German wine list and "incredible service" from a "helpful, charming" staff; sure, it's "somewhat expensive", but it's definitely a "first-class" experience; N.B. there's live jazz on Tuesdays.

44 ⊠ *French/International* 23 | 18 | 21 | VE

Charlottenburg | Swissôtel | Augsburger Str. 44 | (49-30) 220-100 | www.restaurant44.de

"Excellent", "inventive" New French-International cooking that "never fails to excite" makes "multiple" visits to this "quiet, romantic" venue on the third floor of Charlottenburg's modern Swissôtel "a joy"; critics, though, claim the menu "tries very hard to be interesting" but "overwhelms the taste buds with competing flavors"; N.B. ask for a table on the small terrace overlooking the famous Kurfürstendamm.

Gabriele S M *Italian/Mediterranean* — 24 | 23 | 24 | E

Mitte | Hotel Adlon Kempinski | Behrenstr. 72 | (49-30) 2062-8610 | www.gabriele-restaurant.de

This "wonderful" Italian-Med newcomer is in the restored "iconic" Hotel Adlon Kempinski, near the Brandenburg Gate and U.S. Embassy; a "charming" staff presides over an eclectic setting with cushy leather chairs and banquettes, brass chandeliers and contemporary art.

Grill Royal ● M *Seafood/Steak* — 21 | 20 | 20 | E

Mitte | Friedrichstr. 105B | (49-30) 2887-9288 | www.grillroyal.com

"Great" steakhouse and seafooder in trendy Mitte (the "best location in Berlin") that offers "delicious" food and is "often packed" with a chic crowd that doesn't complain about the "expensive" tabs; the spacious wood and marble setting boasts a vintage motor boat, a "spectacular" terrace and a view of the Spree River.

Guy S *French/Mediterranean* — 21 | 19 | 19 | E

Mitte | Jägerstr. 59–60 | (49-30) 2094-2600 | www.guy-restaurant.de

Ensconced "in a courtyard" in Mitte between the Gendarmenmarkt and the Friedrichstrasse shopping area, this French-Med is a "favorite regular stop in town", "satisfying" surveyors with "delicious" fare that's "hard to beat", not to mention "tasteful decor" and "excellent service" from a "well-trained staff"; "it isn't cheap, but the bill isn't irritating" – especially if you "go on someone else's tab"; P.S. though the "dining area is beautiful", "the terrace is an oasis."

Hartmanns ● S *German/Mediterranean* — 22 | 20 | 19 | E

Kreuzberg | Fichtestr. 31 | (49-30) 6120-1003 | www.hartmanns-restaurant.de

Chef-owner Stefan Hartmann's intimate and "enjoyable" spot combines German and Mediterranean influences and the result is a "delicious" and "very creative" combination; set in the basement of a classical turn-of-the-century Kreuzberg townhouse, the serene minimalist space gets a kick of color from modern art and strikingly spare floral arrangements.

Lorenz Adlon S M *French* — 24 | 24 | 22 | VE

Mitte | Hotel Adlon Kempinski | Unter den Linden 77 | (49-30) 22610 | www.hotel-adlon.de

"Indulge yourself" at this "romantic" "gourmet restaurant" in Mitte's Hotel Adlon Kempinski, "just steps from the Brandenburg Gate"; it features classic French cuisine, a "comprehensive list" of "exquisite wines", a "stylish" setting and a "refined staff" that gives one a "feeling of being pampered"; yes, it's "very expensive", but most are prepared "to pay a little more" for such a "luxe" experience – after all, "you have to spoil yourself sometime."

Margaux S *French* — 22 | 23 | 20 | VE

Mitte | Unter den Linden 78 | (49-30) 2265-2611 | www.margaux-berlin.de

With its "impressive decor", this "fine-dining" venue in Mitte is a "chic", "cosmopolitan" showcase for the "world-class" creations of chef-owner Michael Hoffmann, whose "high-end" "classic French fare" is "prepared with amazing care" (and some avant-garde touches) and complemented by "an extraordinary wine list"; many are also "wowed" by the "excellent staff", though a few feel they "could do better"; P.S. the desserts are "unbelievable."

Maxwell *French/International* 24 | 21 | 16 | E

Mitte | Bergstr. 22 | (49-30) 280-7121 | www.restaurant-maxwell.de

For "some of the coolest dining" around, hipsters head to this "trendy" spot set in a "former brewery" "tucked away in a courtyard" in Mitte, where "inventive" French-International dishes (incorporating Asian, Italian and German influences) are offered in a "beautiful high-ceilinged" space with "modern but not chilly furnishings"; sure, "the service could be more efficient", but at least "the staff is friendly."

San Nicci ◐ *Italian* 21 | 19 | 21 | E

Mitte | Friedrichstr. 101 | (49-30) 3064-54980 | www.san-nicci.de

"Who knew Italian in Germany translates well?" but that's what supporters say about this Mitte sibling of Berlin's very popular Borchardt that's being touted as the "place to go" for breakfast, lunch and dinner; it boasts a "great location" a stone's throw from the Admiralspalast theater, and the "cosmopolitan" brasserie setting includes dramatic columns and an expansive courtyard.

VAU ☒ *International* 26 | 23 | 25 | VE

Mitte | Jägerstr. 54-55 | (49-30) 202-9730 | www.vau-berlin.de

"You can't miss" this Mitte "must", an "exquisite-in-every-way" "oasis" "next to the famous Gendarmenmarkt" that's rated No. 1 in Berlin for Food; chef and TV personality Kolja Kleeberg's "heavenly menu" of "excellent", "extremely creative" International cuisine, a "quality wine list", "wonderful service" from a "thoughtful, unintrusive" staff and "cool", "crisp, modern" decor add up to a "superb dining experience" that most insist is "worth the splurge", even if your "wallet still hurts" long after (at least the "lunch prices are more reasonable").

Vox ◐ *Asian/French* 23 | 23 | 24 | E

Tiergarten | Grand Hyatt | Marlene-Dietrich-Platz 2 | (49-30) 2553-1234 | www.berlin.grand.hyatt.com

"Everything is top-notch" at this hotel restaurant overlooking the Potsdamer Platz shopping area in Tiergarten's Grand Hyatt, where the service from the "well-trained staff" is "discreet and attentive", the "unconventional decor" is "posh and stylish" and the "great open kitchen's" "fantastic" food - ranging from "excellent sushi" to "interesting" New French-Asian dishes - "is a pleasure for the palate"; no wonder some say they "would fly to Berlin just to have dinner here again."

FOOD | DECOR | SERVICE | COST

Brussels

TOP FOOD RANKING

	Restaurant	Cuisine
28	Comme Chez Soi	French
	Bruneau	French
27	La Truffe Noire	French/Italian
	Sea Grill	International/Seafood
26	La Maison du Cygne	French
25	Chez Marie	French
24	L'Ecailler du Palais	Seafood
	Villa Lorraine*	Belgian/French
	L'Ogenblik	French
	Le Pain et le Vin	French
	Café des Spores	European
	Bon-Bon	Belgian/French
23	Blue Elephant	Thai
	Le Fourneau	French/Tapas
	La Maison du Boeuf	French
	Le Bistrot du Mail	French
	Scheltema	French
	L'Idiot du Village	Belgian/French
	La Manufacture	French

Aux Armes de Bruxelles 🄼 *Belgian* 21 | 19 | 19 | E

Ilôt Sacré | Rue des Bouchers 13 | (32-2) 511-5550 | www.armesdebruxelles.be

It's "a jewel in the otherwise" tourist-trap-laden Rue des Bouchers say supporters of this Belgian "favorite"; "few things are better than mussels in Brussels", so those are a "must" here, along with "wonderful *waterzooi*"; it's a "popular", "prototypical brasserie" for "eating like the locals."

Belga Queen ◐ *Belgian* 18 | 27 | 17 | E

Lower Town | Rue du Fossé aux Loups 32 | (32-2) 217-2187 | www.belgaqueen.be

"Sexy" describes the "fab" setting - an "ornate" "domed", stained-glass ceiling, moody lighting and cool loos - of this Belgian brasserie housed in what was a former belle epoque bank in the Lower Town; gourmands gripe that the "food is nothing to write home about" and say "stick to the seafood platter" and raw bar, but scenesters simply shrug and check out the "beautiful people."

Blue Elephant *Thai* 23 | 22 | 21 | E

Uccle | Chaussée de Waterloo 1120 | (32-2) 374-4962 | www.blueelephant.com

For 28 years, this Thai in Uccle (with other outposts from London to Dubai) has been leading loyalists on a "wonderful culinary journey" with "fine", "wonderfully spiced" fare; a "beautiful" setting "complete

* Indicates a tie with restaurant above

with coconuts and flowers" leads to thoughts of "lush" lands and away from the realities of "Belgian weather."

Bon-Bon Ⓢ Ⓜ *Belgian/French* 24 | 19 | 19 | E

Uccle | Rue des Carmélites 93 | (32-2) 346-6615 | www.bon-bon.be

Chef Christophe Hardiquest's market-driven "modern and refined" Belgian-French cuisine is improvisational and "excellent" and earns him "rising star" status; located in a quiet residential street in Uccle, his intimate bistro relies on claret-colored walls and gray banquettes for its attractive, unpretentious appeal.

Bruneau *French* 28 | 25 | 28 | VE

Ganshoren | Avenue Broustin 73-75 | (32-2) 421-7070 | www.bruneau.be

"Exquisite" exclaim admirers of this 33-year-old Classic French in an elegant double townhouse in residential Ganshoren, about a 15-minute taxi ride from the City Center; chef-owner Jean-Pierre Bruneau's "outstanding" cuisine is complemented by equally "excellent service", a "tremendous" wine list, handsome dining rooms and a summer garden terrace; in all, it's a very "costly" but "outstanding" experience; N.B. closed Tuesdays and Wednesdays.

Café des Spores *European* 24 | 20 | 23 | E

Saint-Gilles | Chaussée D'Alsemberg 103-108 | (32-2) 534-1303 | www.cafedesspores.be

Fungi fans sprout up at this small, simple European cafe in Saint-Gilles for the namesake spores - namely, "delicious" and "varied fresh mushroom dishes" that are market-driven; oenophiles can also be accommodated, since there is "a fine array of wines" to complement the earthy ingredients.

Chez Marie Ⓢ Ⓜ *French* 25 | 21 | 22 | E

Ixelles | Rue Alphonse de Witte 40 | (32-2) 644-3031

A firm favorite with EU professionals, this Classic French in Ixelles features chef Lilian Devaux's "delicious" cuisine, including a great "value" prix fixe lunch at 18 euros; "tiny", "warm" and "cozy" with "low lights", mirrors and candles, it's also "romantic."

Comme Chez Soi Ⓢ Ⓜ *French* 28 | 24 | 27 | VE

Lower Town | Place Rouppe 23 | (32-2) 512-2921 | www.commechezsoi.be

Pierre Wynants and his son-in-law Lionel Rigolet's "sublime" French in the Lower Town is Voted No. 1 for Food in Brussels; a "very attentive but unobtrusive" staff presides over a "fantastic" art nouveau setting with stained-glass flower motifs, although the chef's table in the kitchen is also a coveted spot; it's "extremely expensive", but it's a "gem that's a joy to visit" and "one of the world's great restaurants."

La Maison du Boeuf Ⓢ *French* 23 | 18 | 22 | E

Upper Town | Hilton Brussels | Boulevard de Waterloo 38 | (32-2) 504-1334 | www.hilton.com

"When you miss USA prime ribs, this is the place to go" urge enthusiasts of this beef-focused Classic French in the Upper Town that's "fantastic for a Hilton"; a "tremendous wine list", "attentive" service and a warm setting with views of palatial gardens make for an "enjoyable experience even if dining alone."

La Maison du Cygne [S] *French* 26 | 27 | 24 | VE

Grand' Place | Rue Charles Buls 2 | (32-2) 511-8244 | www.lamaisonducygne.be

"Beautifully decorated" and in a "stunning location" "overlooking the historic Grand' Place" is this long-standing Classic French in a former 17th-century guildhall; velvet banquettes and paintings by Belgian masters are the "magnificent" backdrop for "excellent" cuisine, "exceptional service" and an "extensive wine list"; given the stratospheric prices, it's ironic that Karl Marx once worked on his Communist Manifesto here.

La Manufacture [S] *French* 23 | 24 | 20 | E

Ste-Catherine | Rue Notre Dame du Sommeil 12-20 | (32-2) 502-2525 | www.manufacture.be

Housed in a "famous old" former handbag factory - hence the name - this "innovative", "delicious" and fashionable French in the up-and-coming Ste-Catherine district is "not expensive if you compare the price with the quality of the meals"; the "great atmosphere" comes from an expansive, dramatic industrial space with leather banquettes, stone tables and a "sexy staff."

La Truffe Noire [S] [M] *French/Italian* 27 | 22 | 25 | VE

Ixelles | Boulevard de la Cambre 12 | (32-2) 640-4422 | www.truffenoire.com

A "must for truffle lovers", this "excellent" French-Italian in Ixelles features the unearthed fungus from start (with carpaccio) to finish (substituting its sweet chocolate namesake at dessert); "perfect service" and a "sophisticated" room with modern paintings round out the extravagant experience; of course, you'll be digging deep too when it comes time to pay the big bill.

Le Bistrot du Mail [S] [M] *French* 23 | 18 | 20 | E

Ixelles | Rue du Mail 81 | (32-2) 539-0697 | www.bistrotdumail.be

This "memorable" "upmarket bistro" in Ixelles offers "fine" French fare that includes "great game in season" served in a straightforward minimalist setting with a "Paris-without-the-attitude" vibe; surveyors say it represents "good value", particularly the 20 euro prix fixe lunch.

L'Ecailler du Palais Royal [S] *Seafood* 24 | 21 | 22 | VE

Grand Sablon | Rue Bodenbroek 18 | (32-2) 512-8751 | www.lecaillerdupalaisroyal.be

Since 1967, not a morsel of meat has passed through the portals of this "top-quality" seafooder in the Grand Sablon featuring "fish, just fish, but the best" of the catch; "excellent service" and a "wonderful" two-story setting (one room with soothing traditional plaid decor, the other a scarlet salon) make it "great for business lunches", but the exuberant bar with "turquoise fish-scale tiles" is "good for single diners too."

Le Fourneau [S] [M] *French/Tapas* 23 | 20 | 21 | E

Ste-Catherine | Place Sainte-Catherine 8 | (32-2) 513-1002

A "must-visit" is what supporters say about this "excellent" French small-plates specialist whose "sophisticated" "handling of ingredients on a continuously changing menu" "makes it a place to return to whenever the season changes"; you'll "love the location" on medieval Sainte Catherine square, and inside, a handful of tables, a long bar and an open kitchen are set against a spare but stylish black-and-white room punctuated with snappy red lights.

Le Pain et le Vin *French* 24 20 22 E

Uccle | Chaussée D'Alsemberg 812A | (32-2) 332-2774 | www.painvin.be

It's "definitely worth a try" declare devotees of chef-owner Olivier Morland's "excellent" "subtly flavored" French cuisine that elevates "fresh" market fare, particularly fish, in Uccle; both dining rooms - a warm burgundy space and a sunny white one - are "comfortable", but "if the weather allows try the wonderful terrace" overlooking a lovely leafy garden.

L'Idiot du Village *Belgian/French* 23 21 21 E

Marolles | Rue Notre-Seigneur 19 | (32-2) 502-5582

You'd be the idiot if you didn't book way ahead at this popular tiny boîte tucked away in a 17th-century house in Marolles; "inventive" Belgian-French cuisine that "soars with flavor" and a "quirky" "bohemian-chic" atmosphere with "whimsical" flea-market decor attract "Eurocrats wanting to get in touch with their inner hippie."

L'Ogenblik *French* 24 18 20 E

Ilôt Sacré | Galerie des Princes 1 | (32-2) 511-6151 | www.ogenblik.be

"What a bistro should be" declare devotees of this French that's in part of the "beautiful" glassed-in Galeries Saint-Hubert, the "oldest shopping arcade in Europe"; there's "delicious food", an "excellent wine list", "attentive service" and a homey setting, so although it's been a "favorite Brussels haunt" since 1969, it still attracts a cosmopolitan crowd.

Scheltema *French* 23 19 19 E

Ilôt Sacré | Rue des Dominicains 7 | (32-2) 512-2084 | www.scheltema.be

Named after a Dutch poet, this "bustling", bi-level Classic French brasserie in the Ilôt Sacré features "excellent seafood and desserts" and a burnished wood setting; "friendly waiters" and an "Old Europe without the stiff upper lip atmosphere" add to the "wonderful experience."

Sea Grill *International/Seafood* 27 23 27 VE

Lower Town | Radisson SAS Royal Hotel | Rue du Fossé aux Loups 47 | (32-2) 217-9225 | www.seagrill.be

"Embedded in the Radisson SAS Royal Hotel" in the Lower Town is this "top-class" International seafooder with "superb" cuisine, "an excellent wine list" and "incomparable service"; still, some carp about the corporate atmosphere and sky-high prices - it's so "expensive" that even "expense accounts will get strained here."

Villa Lorraine *Belgian/French* 24 25 25 VE

Uccle | Chaussée de la Hulpe 28 | (32-2) 374-3163 | www.villalorraine.be

Nestled on the fringes of the "beautiful" Bois de la Cambre in Uccle, about a 20-minute taxi ride from the City Center, is this "landmark" "temple of Belgian-French haute cuisine" in a 19th-century villa; a "posh" setting, "fine food", sterling service and a "stellar wine cellar" lead to long, lovely lunches or "romantic evenings", particularly out on the summer garden terrace; N.B. jacket required.

Budapest

TOP FOOD RANKING

	Restaurant	Cuisine
28	Baraka	Asian/Mediterranean
	Vadrózsa	Hungarian/International
27	Páva	Italian
25	Lou-Lou	French
	Kacsa	Hungarian/International
24	Gundel	Hungarian/International
	Fausto's	Tuscan
23	Café Kör	Hungarian/International
	Rézkakas	Hungarian
	Segal*	International
	Bistro Jardin	Hungarian/International
	Kisbuda Gyöngye	Hungarian/International
22	Csalogány 26	International
	Donatella's Kitchen	Tuscan
21	Cyrano	Hungarian/French
	Kárpátia*	Hungarian

Baraka *Asian/Mediterranean* 28 | - | 27 | E

Andrássy út | MaMaison Andrássy Hotel | Andrássy út 111 | (36-1) 462-2189 | www.andrassyhotel.com

"Truly one of Budapest's great finds", this "outstanding" Asian-Med ranking No. 1 for Food in the city moved Uptown from Belváros to a glam silver-and-black art deco-style space in the MaMaison Andrássy Hotel; "running the show" is the "husband-and-wife team" of David and Leora Seboek, who oversee a "regularly changing menu" of "inventive" "world cuisine" that's "complemented by" an "expensive wine list" and "excellent service"; P.S. you'll also stand "a good chance of seeing local celebrities."

Bistro Jardin *Hungarian/International* 23 | 22 | 21 | E

Belváros | Kempinski Hotel Corvinus | Erzsébet tér 7-8 | (36-1) 429-3777 | www.kempinski-budapest.com

You "can bring the most fastidious of guests" to this "favorite" in the Kempinski Hotel Corvinus in Belváros since you "can always rely on" "high standards", as evidenced by "delicious" Hungarian-International fare; the "pleasant atmosphere", "elegant" setting (including a "nice outside" terrace) and "first-class service" further "justify" the "expense"; meals here are accompanied by live jazz on Sundays, which adds to "the grand experience."

Café Kör *Hungarian/International* 23 | 18 | 23 | M

Lipótváros | Sas utca 17 | (36-1) 311-0053 | www.cafekor.com

Anyone "looking for delicious food at reasonable prices" - from "intellectuals" to "tourists" to "expats" - should check out this "charming", "classic" "hot spot near St. Stephen's" Basilica in Lipótváros, where a

* Indicates a tie with restaurant above

"wide choice" of "excellent" "traditional Hungarian fare" "and International dishes" are offered in "generous portions" by "friendly, upbeat" staffers who make you "feel as if you were surrounded by friends"; P.S. "don't skip dessert", as "you won't believe the variety of cakes and pastries!"

Centrál Kávéház *Hungarian/International* 17 | 19 | 16 | M

Belváros | Károlyi Mihály utca 9 | (36-1) 266-2110 | www.centralkavehaz.hu
There's "always an interesting crowd" at this coffeehouse, "an island of peace and quiet" in bustling Belváros with an "authentic" 19th-century "period feeling" and a "welcoming atmosphere"; true, "there are better choices" for Hungarian-International food, and "service can be a bit perfunctory", but the staffers are "friendly" (save for "one or two grumpy ones") and "they don't rush you", which makes it a "great place to hang out, have strong coffee and chat with friends."

Csalogány 26 *International* 22 | 18 | 22 | E

Viziváros | Csalogány utca 26 | (36-1) 201-7892 | www.csalogany26.hu
Locals in-the-know head for this small, unassuming International in Viziváros, where the emphasis is on a frequently changing menu of "delicious" dishes that include organic vegetables from the retaurant's own garden; the simple bistro setting is enlivened by enormous arched windows and a closed-circuit flat-screen monitor that allows curious customers sneak-peeks into the chefs' doings in the kitchen.

Cyrano *Hungarian/French* 21 | 22 | 19 | E

Terézváros | Kristóf tér 6 | (36-1) 266-3096
"Trendy and posh", this Hungarian-French boasts an "elegant" yet "relaxing ambiance" (and an unusual chandelier shaped like an inverted Christmas tree); the "consistently creative" kitchen is "always experimenting" with the "very good" menu, and the "attentive, polite" staff is "well trained and helpful"; in short, it's "one of the better places for a stylish lunch or dinner off of Váci utca" - especially on the "outside terrace."

Donatella's Kitchen *Tuscan* 22 | 19 | 21 | E

Terézváros | Király utca 30-32 | (36-1) 878-0515
"You won't go Hungary" at this new Tuscan in Terézváros, from the original founders of the so-hip Tom-George; "a varied menu with well-prepared entrees" is served in a sprawling, "boisterous" setting with an open kitchen and quirky decor that includes antler chandeliers and copper fittings, which draws a "trendy" young crowd.

Fausto's *Tuscan* 24 | 18 | 24 | E

Erzsébetvaros | Székely Mihály utca 2 | (36-1) 877-6210 | www.fausto.hu
"A great evening" of "chic eating" awaits at this "excellent Italian" "in the old Jewish quarter" in Erzsébetvaros, where "top-notch service" from an "attentive" but "not constantly hovering" staff is matched by chef Fausto Di Vora's "outstanding" Tuscan fare; perhaps the food's "expensive", but fans insist there's "value" for the money, saying you'll "pay more for less in many other restaurants - on either side of the river."

Gundel *Hungarian/International* 24 | 26 | 25 | VE

Városliget | Állatkerti út 2 | (36-1) 468-4040 | www.gundel.hu
"Memories are made" at this "venerable" Hungarian "legend" "near Hero's Square", a "palatial", "elaborately decorated", ultra-expensive

"salon" with "turn-of-the-century grandeur" and "beautiful views" of Városliget; within its "elegant setting", a "cultured" staff "indulges" "lucky" patrons with "the epitome" of "quality service" and a "delicious menu" of "national and International cuisine"; factor in "marvelous strolling musicians" playing "wonderful" "live gypsy music" and you can expect a "magical evening in a magical city"; N.B. jacket required.

Kacsa ◐ *Hungarian/International* 25 | 19 | 23 | E

Viziváros | Fö utca 75 | (36-1) 201-9992 | www.kacsavendeglo.hu

Its "name means 'duck'", and "as you'd expect" you'll find "excellent" examples of that fowl's flesh on the "wide-ranging and delicious menu" of "magnificent" Hungarian-International fare at this "stellar" spot in Viziváros, where the "amazing meals" are heightened by "wonderful service" from a "lovely staff"; it's "pricey but not outrageous", and while the "not particularly captivating" "decor could be improved", at least the "atmosphere is romantic", making it "a must when you're in Budapest."

Kárpátia *Hungarian* 21 | 23 | 19 | E

Belváros | Ferenciek tere 7-8 | (36-1) 317-3596 | www.karpatia.hu

"The historic past makes its mark" on the present at this "fairly pricey" venue set in a circa-1877 Belváros building in which there's "not an unadorned inch" in the "over-the-top" yet mostly "tasteful" interior; the "varied" menu of "excellent" cuisine - including a "great Sunday smorgasbord" in winter - is "authentically Hungarian", the service is a "pleasure" (even if a few fault certain "indifferent" staffers) and a "nice gypsy violin ensemble" helps cement its status as a true "taste of Budapest."

Kisbuda Gyöngye ☒ *Hungarian/International* 23 | 19 | 23 | E

Óbuda | Kenyeres utca 34 | (36-1) 368-9246 | www.remiz.hu

A 'pearl' in Óbuda, this "favorite" is peopled by "observant" staffers with "high standards" who serve "exceptionally well-prepared" Hungarian-International fare featuring "all the good flavors of home cooking"; a few find the flea-market ambiance of its "intimate" setting "a little contrived", but most are won over by its old-world atmosphere and live piano, "wondering what else do you need?"

Lou-Lou ☒ *French* 25 | 18 | 20 | E

Belváros | Vigyázó Ferenc utca 4 | (36-1) 312-4505 | www.loulourestaurant.com

"Always a treat", this French bistro in Belváros brings a "modern" approach to its "delicious" fare, while its "excellent" staff provides "quick, attentive service", making for an "overall good dining experience"; as for the setting, perhaps the "tables are too close together for intimate conversation", but "the food is so scrumptious you don't mind the slightly cramped dining room."

Páva ☒ *Italian* 27 | 26 | 25 | VE

Belváros | Four Seasons Gresham Palace | Roosevelt tér 5-6 | (36-1) 268-6000 | www.fourseasons.com/budapest

"First-rate Italian food on the banks of the Danube" is found at this "winner" (whose name means 'Peacock') within the "gorgeous" "art nouveau" Four Seasons Gresham Palace hotel "across from the Chain Bridge"; its "cutting-edge" cuisine is complemented by "a perfect

Hungarian wine list", "classically elegant decor (radiant but not ostentatious)", "lovely views" and "excellent service" from a "considerate" staff; in short, it's "one of the city's best" "for the real connoisseur."

Rézkakas ◐ *Hungarian* 23 | 22 | 25 | E

Belváros | Veres Pálné utca 3 | (36-1) 318-0038 | www.rezkakasrestaurant.com

An "excellent attitude toward customers" distinguishes the "professional" staff's "unusually" "top-notch service" at this "truly captivating" Belváros venue, a "lovely", "romantic" wood-paneled dining room where "terrific traditional Hungarian cuisine is complemented by a wonderful live musical ensemble"; for such a "magical" (albeit "somewhat touristy") experience, most say "never mind the cost - what's important is that you enjoy yourself."

Segal ◐ *International* 23 | - | 22 | E

Terézváros | Ó utca 43-49 | (36-1) 354-7888 | www.segal.hu

"Superstar" chef Viktor Segal (ex top-rated Baraka) opened his own namesake establishment and the result is "innovative" and "excellent" International cuisine that "advances the Budapest palate to the next level" and is complemented by "attentive service"; N.B. a post-Survey move from Belváros to these new larger digs in Terézváros also comes with a garden.

Spoon Café & Lounge *Hungarian/International* 17 | 22 | 18 | E

Belváros | Vigadó tér 3 Kikötö | (36-1) 411-0934 | www.spooncafe.hu

Set "on a boat" "docked on the Danube" by the Chain Bridge in Belváros, this "stylish" tri-level "floating restaurant" and "fashionable lounge" attracts a "cooler-than-thou crowd" of "trendy and chic" "hipsters" with its "novel concept"; some find "the wide-ranging menu" of Hungarian-International fare to be "not particularly enticing", but most are content to "sit back and enjoy" "the spectacular view of Castle Hill across the river"; P.S. "visiting the restrooms is a must" experience!

Vadrózsa ◐ *Hungarian/International* 28 | 24 | 24 | E

Rózsadomb | Pentelei Molnár utca 15 | (36-1) 326-5817 | www.vadrozsa.hu

"Come hungry" to this "outstanding" "off-the-beaten-path" Rózsadomb 'Wild Rose' whose "fresh" Hungarian-International fare is "lovingly prepared" "with the finest ingredients" and full of "interesting flavors"; its "classic, elegant" setting (complete with a "charming private garden terrace") is "lovely, romantic and a little magical" thanks in part to "polite" staffers who provide "wonderful old-world service" "and a pianist who plays requests" - so "if you can't live in a mansion", at least "you can dine in one."

Copenhagen

TOP FOOD RANKING

	Restaurant	Cuisine
27	Era Ora	Italian
	Restaurationen	Danish/French
26	Søllerød Kro	French
	Kong Hans Kælder	French/Danish
25	Krogs Fiskerestaurant	French/Seafood
	Alberto K at The Royal	Italian/Scandinavian
24	Pierre André	French
	Paul	French/International
	Koriander	Indian
23	Slotskælderen hos Gitte Kik	Danish
	Kanalen	French/Danish
	Le Sommelier	French
22	Royal Cafe	Danish
	D'Angleterre	French/Danish
	Den Sorte Ravn*	French/Danish
	Leonore Christine	Danish/French
	Fifty Fifty	Japanese

Alberto K at The Royal ⊠ *Italian/Scandinavian* — 25 | 24 | 23 | E

Vesterbro | Radisson SAS Royal | Hammerichsgade 1, 20th fl. | (45-33) 42-61-61 | www.alberto-k.dk

The "superb" Italian-Scandinavian cuisine "melts in your mouth" at this "fantastic location" with "to-die-for views" on the 20th floor of the Radisson SAS Royal in Vesterbro; its "so-cool interior" is overseen by a staff that will "treat you like dignitaries", and if the cost is as "high" as the altitude, most maintain it's "worth the krona."

Café Ketchup *International* — 17 | 18 | 15 | E

Indre By | Pilestræde 23 | (45-33) 32-30-30 ⊠

Tivoli | Tivoli Gardens | Vesterbrogade 3 | (45-33) 75-07-55

"Night after night, young beauties pack" this "large" "place to be seen" "in Tivoli" to "enjoy the view of the gardens" (and each other) "while dining on good food from" a "modern" International menu; foes, though, find factors "going against it", including "pricey" fare that's "nicely presented" "but nothing extraordinary", "dull decor" "lacking intimacy", "lagging service" and too many "tourists"; P.S. insiders assert that "its more sophisticated sibling across town" in Indre By "is better" – plus it's open year-round.

Café Victor *French/Danish* — 17 | 17 | 14 | E

Kongens Nytorv | Ny Østergade 8 | (45-33) 13-36-13 | www.cafevictor.dk

"Sharpen your elbows to get past" the "pretty people" "packed into" this "classic but hip" Kongens Nytorv "fixture" that's "still hot" with "the well-heeled crowd" that "loves" "to be seen" "on either side" of its divided space – "trying the cafe", with its "limited menu", then "returning

* Indicates a tie with restaurant above

another night" to the restaurant for its "good French" cuisine (at lunch the dishes are Danish); some suggest it's too "snobbish", with "slack service" from a "pretentious staff", but few fault the "fun atmosphere."

D'Angleterre *French/Danish* 22 | 25 | 22 | VE

Kongens Nytorv | Hotel D'Angleterre | Kongens Nytorv 34 | (45-33) 37-06-45 | www.dangleterre.dk

"Passersby must envy diners" at this "don't-miss" destination (formerly known as Wiinblad) in the "charming old-world" Hotel D'Angleterre that's graced with a "spectacular setting overlooking Kongens Nytorv" and a burnished brown-and-gold formal dining room; the kitchen produces "wonderful" New French-Danish creations that are served by a staff that is "attentive without being overbearing."

Den Sorte Ravn *French/Danish* 22 | 20 | 21 | E

Nyhavn | Nyhavn 14 | (45-33) 13-12-33 | www.sorteravn.dk

Occupying a "great location on the canal", "on the main street of the Nyhavn neighborhood", this "small cellar" spot (whose name means 'The Black Raven') is one of the area's more "high-class" venues, where "delicious" French-Danish fare is "pleasantly" served by a "friendly, attentive" staff; some dub the decor "a bit worn", quipping that "the shiny black feathers are molting a bit", but most find the "simple" interior "inviting" - and if it's "expensive", at least the "quality matches the price."

Era Ora [S] *Italian* 27 | 21 | 24 | VE

Christianshavn | Overgaden Neden Vandet 33B | (45-32) 54-06-93 | www.era-ora.dk

For "a meal you'll remember", "you just have to go" to this "always-crowded" Northern Italian along the canal in Christianshavn, whose "authentic" Tuscan and Umbrian fare "bursting with natural flavors" (and "accompanied by delicious wines") earns it the ranking of No. 1 for Food in Copenhagen; "excellent in every way", it's manned by a "warm, extremely efficient" staff providing "impeccable service" "from start to finish" and features a "gorgeous atmosphere to match the gorgeous food"; "bring a really fat wallet", though, as it's "wildly expensive."

Fifty Fifty [S] [M] *Japanese* 22 | 20 | 21 | E

Vesterbro | Vesterbrogade 42 | (45-33) 22-47-57 | www.fiftyfiftyfood.dk

There's far more than a 50/50 chance both carnivores and finatics will "love" this "cool" Japanese in Vesterbro since it offers grilled meats and raw fish; "good value and high standards" also have made it a "fast favorite of the hungry 'beautiful people.'"

Kanalen [S] *French/Danish* 23 | 20 | 22 | E

Christianshavn | Wilders Plads 2 | (45-32) 95-13-30 | www.restaurant-kanalen.dk

"Good-size portions" of "delicious" French-Danish fare "will make you smile" at this "charming", "upmarket" spot in a "superb location" in "beautiful" Christianshavn, providing it with a "lovely canal view"; the "simple" space is "a bit tight", but most find its "intimate atmosphere" "delightfully" "cozy" "and romantic", and the "excellent wine list" is another reason it's considered "a true pleasure."

	FOOD	DECOR	SERVICE	COST

Kong Hans Kælder ☒ *French/Danish* 26 | 25 | 24 | VE

Kongens Nytorv | Vingaardsstræde 6 | (45-33) 11-68-68 | www.konghans.dk
"One of the best culinary experiences" in Copenhagen can be found at "this historic, vaulted-ceiling wine cellar" "situated in King Hans'" 16th-century royal mint (the city's "oldest" building) in the Kongens Nytorv area; "out-of-this-world" French-Danish cuisine - with an emphasis on "top-notch" fish dishes - is offered in a "lovely" setting with "nicely spaced tables" by a "personable" staff that "looks after you really well"; yes, you'll "pay through the nose", but "you should visit at least once in your lifetime."

Koriander ☒ *Indian* 24 | 23 | 21 | E

Kongens Nytorv | Store Kongensgade 34 | (45-33) 15-03-15 | www.restaurantkoriander.dk
This trendy, "excellent" Indian that's set in a glittering ultramodern space in Kongens Nytorv takes its name from coriander, a key ingredient in that cuisine, and is complemented by an expansive wine list that leans toward German whites; on the downside, it's "expensive" and service can be "slow."

Krogs Fiskerestaurant ☒ *French/Seafood* 25 | 20 | 22 | VE

Indre By | Gammel Strand 38 | (45-33) 15-89-15 | www.krogs.dk
The "fabulous" "fresh fish" is "fit for a king" at this "old-fashioned", "high-class" French seafooder in Indre By; though the "sublime food" (with "wonderful wine pairings") is certainly "the center of attention", "everything about the place is elegant" - from the "superb service" to the "lovely setting" - which may explain why faithful fans forgive that the fare is "ferociously expensive", the room can be "stuffy" and some staffers are "a bit pretentious."

Leonore Christine *Danish/French* 22 | 19 | 22 | E

Nyhavn | Nyhavn 9 | (45-33) 13-50-40 | www.leonore-christine.dk
"Pleasant without being intrusive", the "very competent staff" of this "crowded and popular" Nyhavn spot, "in the sailor part of town", performs a "table ballet" nightly while delivering "gorgeous" plates of "super" Danish-French fare, accompanied by a "good wine selection"; perhaps the interior of its circa-1681 building with low ceilings and crooked floors "feels a bit faded", but a redo may have remedied that, and there's "lovely alfresco dining" as an alternative.

Le Sommelier *French* 23 | 18 | 23 | E

Kongens Nytorv | Bredgade 63-65 | (45-33) 11-45-15 | www.lesommelier.dk
"As the name indicates", the "fantastic wine list" at "this friendly restaurant" in the Kongens Nytorv area "is in a class of its own", but rest assured that the "excellent French cuisine" is also "outstanding" ("well prepared" and "quite flavorful") - as is the "warm welcome" from the "professional" staff; a few feel the decor of its "large, open" and "very white" interior "could be better", but more are put "at ease" by the "peaceful", "relaxed" and "well laid-out" space.

Paul, The ☒ *French/International* 24 | 21 | 21 | VE

Tivoli | Tivoli Gardens | Vesterbrogade 3 | (45-33) 75-07-75 | www.thepaul.dk
"Small dishes with gigantic flavors" are featured on chef-owner Paul Cunningham's "very expensive" French-International menu at this

"impeccable" venue whose "modern" setting is an "enjoyable refuge from the masses in Tivoli Gardens"; "yes, you do pay the usual premium" for the area, but affluent "gourmets" insist it's "worth the money", while clever folks of lesser means advise "this is your pick when somebody else is paying"; N.B. open mid-April through late-September and most of November and December.

Pierre André 🅂 🄼 *French* 24 | 18 | 23 | E

Indre By | Ny Østergade 21 | (45-33) 16-17-19 | www.pierreandre.dk

Named for the proprietors' two sons, this "classic French" in Indre By features chef-owner Philippe Houdet's "exciting, well-prepared", "elegant" dishes, which are offered by an "observant" staff overseen by his wife, Sussie; some see a "romantic edge" to the "traditional" decor, while others sigh that it's "not the most exciting in the city", but all agree the "choice of prix fixe menus to fit both mid and high budgets" adds up to "great value for the money."

Restaurationen 🅂 🄼 *Danish/French* 27 | 21 | 27 | VE

Indre By | Møntergade 19 | (45-33) 14-94-95 | www.restaurationen.com

"Run by people who truly love good food", this "amazing" Danish-French in Indre By offers a "well-rounded" five-course prix fixe menu nightly - "no à la carte!" - of "innovative, gorgeous dishes" made from "the best ingredients", accompanied by an "excellent wine" list and "presented by owner Bo Jacobsen" and his wife, Lisbeth, or by their "attentive" staff; a few find "nothing to cheer about" in the "nice-but-nothing-special" decor, but most maintain the overall "experience is absolutely superb."

Royal Cafe, The *Danish* 22 | 21 | 20 | E

Indre By | Strøget | Amagertorv 6 | (45-38) 14-95-27 | www.theroyalcafe.dk

"Delicious" Danish 'smushies' - sushi-inspired riffs on *smørrebrød,* which are traditional open-faced sandwiches - and "superb pastries" are the order of the day at this newcomer "conveniently located" in the middle of the Strøget designer shopping district and main pedestrian street; it's geared for those "on the run", but loyalists like to linger in the funky baroque interior with its glittering chandeliers, George Jensen cutlery, fine china and royal portraits.

Slotskælderen hos Gitte Kik 🅂 🄼 *Danish* 23 | 21 | 21 | E

Indre By | Fortunstræde 4 | (45-33) 11-15-37

"One of the outstanding purveyors" of "good, old-fashioned Danish open sandwiches" is this lunch-only Indre By "classic" *smørrebrød* specialist dating back to 1910; choose from the likes of herring or tiny shrimp, beer or schnapps and join the crowd of MP's from the nearby parliament building that frequents this popular place.

Søllerød Kro 🄼 *French* 26 | 24 | 25 | VE

Holte | Søllerødvej 35 | (45-45) 80-25-05 | www.soelleroed-kro.dk

For French "food at its best", a "to-die-for wine list" and "an evening to remember" "this is it" say supporters of this 1677 "charmer" in Holte, about a 20-minute cab ride from the city center; housed in an "authentic Danish cottage" surrounded by a garden and pond, it comes with an "impossibly romantic atmosphere" and a very "expensive" price tag.

		FOOD	DECOR	SERVICE	COST

Dublin

TOP FOOD RANKING

	Restaurant	Cuisine
27	Thornton's Restaurant	Irish/French
	Patrick Guilbaud	French
26	Seasons	Irish/European
25	L'Ecrivain	Irish/French
	One Pico	French/Irish
	Shanahan's on the Green	Steak/Seafood
24	Mint Restaurant	French
	Tea Room	Irish/International
23	Balzac	French/Irish
	Chapter One Restaurant	International
	O'Connells	Irish
	Poulot's	French/Irish
22	Lobster Pot	Seafood
	Fallon & Byrne	French
	Jaipur	Indian
	Dax	French
	Eden	Irish
	Jacob's Ladder	Irish/International
21	Mermaid Café	French/American

Balzac *French/Irish* 23 | 23 | 21 | E

St. Stephen's Green | La Stampa Hotel & Spa | 35 Dawson St. | (353-1) 677-4444 | www.balzac.ie

"One of the loveliest rooms in Dublin" and "an 'it' spot" is this French-Irish brasserie "on trendy Dawson Street" that serves "grown-up food" "worthy of its surroundings"; "vaulted ceilings" and a Victorian cocktail bar are an "elegant" backdrop for "excellent" albeit "expensive" cuisine.

Chapter One Restaurant S M *International* 23 | 23 | 24 | E

Parnell Square | Dublin Writers Museum | 18-19 Parnell Sq. | (353-1) 873-2266 | www.chapteronerestaurant.com

"You can almost hear Joyce and Yeats reading their work while you're dining on delicious food" at this International in the Dublin Writers Museum; considered one of the city's "finest" spots, with a "good value pre-theater menu" from Tuesday–Saturday, it's a "must" for literate libation-lovers who like to salute the "inspirational" setting with the establishment's infamous Irish Coffee.

Dax S M *French* 22 | 20 | 21 | E

City Center | 23 Upper Pembroke St. | (353-1) 676-1494 | www.dax.ie

"It's not overpriced for great ingredients" and the "limited menu changes often so there is usually something new" at this chef-owned French brasserie in the City Center; the basement setting in a Georgina town-house is "subdued" but "suave" and comfortable, making it a pleasant place to "while away an evening."

	FOOD	DECOR	SERVICE	COST
Eden *Irish*	22	21	22	E

Temple Bar | Meeting House Sq. | (353-1) 670-5372 | www.edenrestaurant.ie

"Located in throbbing Temple Bar", this "buzzy" Irish "staple" boasts "sophisticated food", a "modern" setting and "friendly" service; "lots of locals" descend to dine on the legendary 'smokies' (smoked haddock with crème fraîche and cheddar cheese), and in summer the gaslamp-lit terrace is a "great scene" and place to watch films and shows.

	FOOD	DECOR	SERVICE	COST
Fallon & Byrne *French*	22	21	20	E

City Center | 11-17 Exchequer St. | (353-1) 472-1010 | www.fallonandbyrne.com

"Keep it up" order admirers of this French brasserie that's "conveniently located" in the City Center and "consistently good", with a particularly "excellent-value lunch menu"; a "polished staff" presides over a New-York-as Dublin-gets loftlike high-ceilinged setting; there's also a "very good" wine bar in the cellar for sips, "fine cheese and cold plates" and a "lovely grocer on the ground floor."

	FOOD	DECOR	SERVICE	COST
Jacob's Ladder S M *Irish/International*	22	20	22	E

City Center | 4-5 Nassau St. | (353-1) 670-3865

"A real winner" "bang in the center of town" is what supporters say about this chef-owned, bi-level Irish-International with "innovative", "enjoyable" cuisine and "solid service"; spectacular Georgian windows dominate the "pleasing" minimalist space and provide a "great view over Trinity College's playing fields."

	FOOD	DECOR	SERVICE	COST
Jaipur *Indian*	22	15	17	M

City Center | 41 S. Great George's St. | (353-1) 677-0999 | www.jaipur.ie

It's "probably the best Indian in Dublin" declare devotees of this "authentic" Asian in a trendy part of the bustling City Center, where low-key decor - light wood, chrome and floor-to-ceiling windows - makes for a "nice environment"; prices are moderate to begin with, but there's a "great early-bird special" too crow wallet-watchers.

	FOOD	DECOR	SERVICE	COST
L'Ecrivain S *Irish/French*	25	23	24	VE

City Center | 109A Lower Baggot St. | (353-1) 661-1919 | www.lecrivain.com

"High-end" Irish-New French that's one of the city's "top picks" for "loquacious" chef-owner Derry Clarke's "excellent, imaginative" fare; "staffers that make you feel like a guest in their home" preside over a quietly luxurious split-level setting that's "full of suits" during the week, while a pianist on Thursdays-Saturdays attracts the "special-occasion" crowd.

	FOOD	DECOR	SERVICE	COST
Lobster Pot, The S *Seafood*	22	17	21	E

Ballsbridge | 9 Ballsbridge Terrace | (353-1) 668-0025 | www.thelobsterpot.ie

A local favorite is this long-standing, family-run, "old-school" seafooder (Mornay sauce, anyone?) with "frolicking fresh fish" in Ballsbridge, the embassy district, just south of the City Center; a "veteran staff" presides over a warm, "walking-back-through-a-time-machine" setting (i.e. an open fireplace, maritime memorabilia and a dessert cart), which is scheduled for a major rehab.

	FOOD	DECOR	SERVICE	COST
Mermaid Café, The *French/American*	21	18	22	E

Temple Bar | 69-70 Dame St. | (353-1) 670-8236 | www.mermaid.ie
This "lively" stalwart, on the edge of Temple Bar, is still going strong with "exceptionally well-prepared" French-American fare served by a "professional staff"; the high-ceilinged, open-kitchen setting is simple but that doesn't keep it from being "one of the city's best loved eateries"; N.B. the daily changing lunch menu is one of Dublin's biggest bargains.

	FOOD	DECOR	SERVICE	COST
Mint Restaurant S M *French*	24	20	21	E

Ranelagh | 47 Ranelagh Village | (353-1) 497-8655 | www.mintrestaurant.ie
"Beautifully presented" and "inspired" New French cuisine makes for a "lovely dining experience" in Ranelagh; the small, stylish spot attracts tony types who tout that it's in mint condition for prime people-watching, particularly at lunchtime; N.B. a post-Survey renovation may outdate the above Decor score.

	FOOD	DECOR	SERVICE	COST
O'Connells *Irish*	23	19	19	M

Ballsbridge | Bewley's Hotel | Merrion Rd. | (353-1) 647-3304 | www.oconnellsballsbridge.com
This "excellent" traditional and modern Irish owned by foodie Tom O'Connell relies on organic "locally sourced ingredients"; some find the sprawling setting in Ballsbridge's Bewley's Hotel a bit like an "airport lounge", though an establishment that responds to dietary needs (most menu items are gluten-free), has reasonable prices, including an "incredible value early-bird", and features an appealingly "quirky", affordable wine list wins way more yeas than nays.

	FOOD	DECOR	SERVICE	COST
One Pico S *French/Irish*	25	23	23	VE

City Center | 5-6 Molesworth Pl., Schoolhouse Ln. | (353-1) 676-0300 | www.onepico.com
Set in an 18th-century coach house that's "tucked away" in a lane off St. Stephen's Green is chef-owner Eamonn O'Reilly's French-Irish "gem"; a "subtly elegant setting" is the backdrop for "wonderful", "top-quality" food, "very accommodating service" and "amazing wines"; of course, dining at "one of Dublin's better restaurants" comes at a price.

	FOOD	DECOR	SERVICE	COST
Patrick Guilbaud S M *French*	27	25	26	VE

City Center | Merrion Hotel | 21 Upper Merrion St. | (353-1) 676-4192 | www.restaurantpatrickguilbaud.ie
"Every city has its famous restaurant and this is Dublin's"; at Patrick Guilbaud's "excellent all-round" French in City Center, there's Guillaume Lebrun's "revelatory" cuisine, 500 "world-class wines", "outstanding service" and "amazing", "luxe surroundings" with 20th-century Irish art (and "it doesn't hurt that Bono may be at the next table"); "if you really want to treat someone, this is the place", "so go on, blow the budget" big, big, big time.

	FOOD	DECOR	SERVICE	COST
Poulot's S M *French/Irish*	23	18	19	E

Donnybrook | Mulberry Garden | (353-1) 269-3300 | www.poulots.ie
On the site of the former Ernie's in Donnybrook is this French-Irish from chef-owner Jean-Michel Poulot, whose "delicious" cuisine relies on exceptional local produce, much of it organic, and is backed up by what some say is "the best wine list for value in Dublin"; the setting in-

cludes a bright modern interior decorated with contemporary paintings and an exterior with a "lovely" courtyard garden and fountain.

Seasons *Irish/European* 26 | 25 | 27 | VE

Ballsbridge | Four Seasons Hotel | Simmonscourt Rd. | (353-1) 665-4000 | www.fourseasons.com/dublin

"Exactly what you'd expect from the Four Seasons" is what fans of this Irish-European in Ballsbridge say; "outstanding service", "excellent cuisine" and a "posh" setting with conservatory windows, a fireplace and an abundance of flowers add up to a "top-tier", "high-priced" experience; P.S. some swear the "Sunday brunch here is the best in the world."

Shanahan's on the Green *Steak/Seafood* 25 | 24 | 26 | VE

St. Stephen's Green | 119 St. Stephen's Green | (353-1) 407-0939 | www.shanahans.ie

"Great steaks but gosh do you pay for them" at this opulent chophouse "conveniently located" on St. Stephen's Green; "portions are mammoth" ("I hope they have a defibrillator on the premises"), and the glamorous Georgian setting is far from the typical "testosterone"-oriented atmosphere found in most meat meccas; throw in a seafood selection, an "amazing wine list", a celeb clientele and service that exudes "Irish charm" and no wonder it's "loved by the locals"; P.S. be sure to "check out JFK's rocker in the Oval Office bar."

Tea Room *Irish/International* 24 | 23 | 20 | E

Temple Bar | The Clarence | 6-8 Wellington Quay | (353-1) 407-0813 | www.theclarence.ie

"A cathedral to fine food" in the "über-hip", U2-owned Clarence hotel is this "chic" and "spacious" Irish-International with a 20-ft. "soaring ceiling", "beautiful tall windows", "acres of blond wood" and "heavenly" cuisine; "it's perfect for romance, business" or "people-watching", so if you're big on "buzz" and "you're only in town for a short time", this is the place.

Thornton's Restaurant [S] [M] *Irish/French* 27 | 19 | 25 | VE

St. Stephen's Green | Fitzwilliam Hotel | 128 St. Stephen's Green | (353-1) 478-7008 | www.thorntonsrestaurant.com

Voted No. 1 for Food in the city, chef Kevin Thornton's "highly personal and poetic" Irish-French cuisine, which relies on the "highest quality fresh local ingredients", is "unsurpassed" and served by a "perfect yet friendly" staff; sure, it's "very expensive", but most maintain it's a "great way to start or finish a trip to Dublin"; P.S. a refurbishment may outdate the above Decor score and make some who found the Fitzwilliam Hotel setting "stark" change their minds.

	FOOD	DECOR	SERVICE	COST

Florence

TOP FOOD RANKING

	Restaurant	Cuisine
27	Enoteca Pinchiorri	Italian
	La Giostra	Tuscan
26	Alle Murate	Italian
	Fuor d'Acqua	Seafood
	Cibrèo	Italian
	Taverna del Bronzino	Italian
25	Omero	Tuscan
	Baccarossa Bistrot	Mediterranean/Seafood
	Zibibbo	Italian/Mediterranean
	Villa San Michele	Italian
	Cavolo Nero	Tuscan/International
24	Cantinetta Antinori	Italian
	Sabatini	Tuscan
	Ora d'Aria	Tuscan/Mediterranean
	InCanto	Italian
	PORTOfino	Italian/Seafood
	Il Latini	Tuscan
23	Il Santo Bevitore	Italian/Mediterranean
	Olio & Convivium	Italian
	Buca Lapi	Tuscan

Alle Murate M *Italian* — 26 | - | 24 | VE

Duomo | 16R Via del Proconsolo | (39-055) 240-618 | www.allemurate.it

This "lovely, modern" Italian near the Duomo features an exceptional wine list and a "friendly" staff that oversees an "intimate" room with unearthed 14th-century frescoes; the "overall package puts them in a higher class", so expect to pay accordingly; N.B. a post-Survey move outdated the Decor score.

Baccarossa Bistrot *Mediterranean/Seafood* — 25 | 22 | 23 | E

Santa Croce | Via Ghibellina 46R | (39-055) 240-620 | www.baccarossa.it

"Paradisical preparations" of wild-caught fresh fish that rely on "innovative combinations of flavors" as well as "excellent homemade pastas" and desserts are complemented by an ample wine list (60 selections by the glass) at this "off-the-beaten-track" Santa Croce Mediterranean; the service is "smooth", and the setting is "intimate" with "warm woods and antiques."

Buca Lapi S *Tuscan* — 23 | 19 | 21 | E

City Center | 1R Via del Trebbio | (39-055) 213-768 | www.bucalapi.com

At this "hospitable", "old" 1880 Tuscan in the basement of an 11th-century palazzo off tony Tornabuoni, the "famous *bistecca alla fiorentina* is the star" and the atmospheric setting with "postered walls still charms"; a few sniff it's "touristy" and say "unless you are a saber-toothed tiger the beef is too rare and big", but they're outvoted.

FOOD | DECOR | SERVICE | COST

Cantinetta Antinori [S] *Italian* 24 | 23 | 23 | E

Duomo | 3 Piazza Antinori | (39-055) 292-234 | www.antinori.it
"Owned by the famous wine family", this "wonderful" Italian in a Renaissance building in a "beautiful location" near the Piazza Duomo showcases 60 of their vintages (both by the bottle and the glass); "equally impressive" food is served by a "friendly" staff in a polished, wood-paneled setting filled with the fashionable who like to lunch here; N.B. closed Saturdays and Sundays.

Cavolo Nero *Tuscan/International* 25 | 20 | 23 | E

San Frediano | Via dell' Ardiglione 22 | (39-055) 294-744 | www.cavolonero.it
"For a real Florentine experience", head to this "delightful" chef-owned contemporary Tuscan-International in the San Frediano district, "tucked away" behind the Carmine church, with its not-to-be-missed Masaccio frescoes; surveyors say the "innovative" food is "wonderful", "service is gracious" and there's a "great quality-to-price ratio"; the space is "small" but "upscale" and atmospheric, and in summer dining in the garden is "particularly enjoyable."

Cibrèo [S] [M] *Italian* 26 | 21 | 23 | VE

St. Ambrogio | 8R Via Andrea del Verrocchio | (39-055) 234-1100 | www.cibreo.com
Chef-owner Fabio Picchi's "captivating" St. Ambrogio Italian is "one of the best in Florence" - the food is "original" (just note it's as likely to be "cock's combs and animal organs" as it is a signature ricotta, pesto and potato soufflé) and there's "no pasta" in sight; the tabs are high, but most maintain "even the memory feels satisfying"; N.B. on the same corner there is Picchi's less expensive Trattoria Cibrèo, which shares the same kitchen, as well as a cafe and the Teatro del Sale, with a buffet and entertainment.

Enoteca Pinchiorri [S] [M] *Italian* 27 | 27 | 26 | VE

Santa Croce | 87 Via Ghibellina | (39-055) 242-757 | www.enotecapinchiorri.com
"If there is a dining room in heaven it's taking lessons" from this Santa Croce Italian, where Annie Féolde's "fantastic mix of flavors" and "masterful cuisine" is voted No. 1 for Food in Florence, partner Giorgio Pinchiorri's "incredible wine cellar" is praised as the "finest in Europe" and an "impeccable" staff presides over a "gorgeous", gardenlike setting with swagged drapes, massive flowers and the best crystal and china; while foes feel it's "more bloated than an old Englishman", most find the "incredible experience" is worth the "obscenely expensive" tab.

Fuor d'Acqua [S] *Seafood* 26 | 19 | 21 | E

San Frediano | 37R Via Pisana | (39-055) 222-299
The darling of the fashion and entertainment set is this San Frediano seafooder where the "best fresh fish in town with a presentation to match" tempts the trendy; a vaulted-brick-ceiling setting with minimalist decor doesn't distract from "star- and people-watching."

Il Latini [M] *Tuscan* 24 | 18 | 21 | M

City Center | 6R Via dei Palchetti | (39-055) 210-916 | www.illatini.com
"Be prepared to queue big-time" at this "eternally popular" "true Tuscan" in City Center where "hungry tourists" and locals are "packed in" at

communal tables ("it's like eating with one giant Florentine family you never knew you had") to "revel in" gutsy food; "forget about the menu, let the waiter take care of you", sit back and enjoy the "congenial" atmosphere and "inexpensive" prices.

Il Santo Bevitore *Italian/Mediterranean* 23 | 20 | 20 | E

Oltrarno | Via di Santo Spirito 64-66R | (39-055) 211-264 | www.ilsantobevitore.com

Admirers insist "you can't go wrong" at this Italian-Med *osteria*, an informal and "delicious find" in Santo Spirito, "a charming part of Florence"; "good ingredients simply prepared", "an extensive wine list" with less-well-known Tuscan labels and "good value" for the quality pricing make for "a winning combination."

InCanto *Italian* 24 | 22 | 22 | VE

Ponte Vecchio | Grand Hotel | 1 Piazza Ognissanti | (39-055) 2716-3767 | www.starwoodhotels.com

"Grand views" of the Arno and the Ponte Vecchio can be had from this very "expensive" Italian "refuge" in the Grand Hotel; "fine food" and an "excellent wine list" are proferred in an intimate, "inviting" room with leather armchairs and an open kitchen.

La Giostra ◐ *Tuscan* 27 | 22 | 24 | E

Duomo | 12R Via Borgo Pinti | (39-055) 241-341 | www.ristorantelagiostra.com

The "handsome" twin sons of the late owner-chef still run this "wonderful" Tuscan near the Duomo, where "delicious" food based on ancient recipes is served in a small, "romantic" setting where celebrity photos line the walls and "little white lights twinkle from the ceiling"; a few mutter it "oozes as much cheese as charm", but they're outvoted.

Olio & Convivium ⊠ *Italian* 23 | 21 | 23 | E

Oltrarno | 4 Via Santo Spirito | (39-055) 265-8198 | www.conviviumfirenze.it

This classically decorated "tiny gem" with "inventive" Italian food in the Renaissance Palazzo Capponi is good for lunch if you're in the Oltrarno area; it's also a gourmet take-out shop where you can get picnic fixings, wines and a selection of about 40 olive oils.

Omero *Tuscan* 25 | 21 | 22 | E

Arcetri | 49 Via Piandei Giullari | (39-055) 220-053 | www.ristoranteomero.it

"Take a taxi" and "go when it's light so you can enjoy" the "beautiful views of Florence" from the second dining room or terrace of this "unassuming", 107-year-old Tuscan trattoria in the cool hills of Arcetri, about five kilometers from the City Center; order the "best" fried chicken, rabbit and *bistecca alla fiorentina* and you'll join those who say: "eat here once and you'll want to return forever"; N.B. closed Tuesdays.

Ora d'Aria ⊠ *Tuscan/Mediterranean* 24 | 21 | 22 | E

Santa Croce | 3 CR Via Ghibellina | (39-055) 200-1699 | www.oradariaristorante.com

"Wow" - "amazing food" (from "both their traditional and creative menus"), a "charming locale" in trendy Santa Croce, "elegant" modern decor with "ever-changing art on display" and "lovely service" make this Tuscan-Mediterranean "popular" with the "beautiful and stylish people", so "forget about the exchange rate" and focus on the "enchanting evening that awaits."

PORTOfino Ⓜ *Italian/Seafood* 24 | 21 | 22 | E

Campo di Marte | Viale Mazzini 25/27R | (39-055) 244-140 | www.ristoranteportofino.it

Outside the City Center, near Florence's secondary train station, the Campo di Marte, is this "excellent" Italian newcomer specializing in "unique" seafood dishes like shrimp gratin with Gorgonzola, as well as "fantastic pastas"; serene spans of white-on-white walls, fabric and furniture are enlivened by a colorful painting of the charming namesake port, and there's a terrace tucked behind hedges for alfresco eating.

Sabatini Ⓜ *Tuscan* 24 | 21 | 22 | VE

Duomo | 9A Via Panzani | (39-055) 282-802 | www.ristorantesabatini.it

Since 1929 this "traditional", high-profile Tuscan with "excellent" but "expensive" food and "refined service" has been "one of the better Florentine restaurants", and it's conveniently located near the Duomo; fans of the surprisingly "spacious", "formal", wood-paneled room with paintings praise its lovely garden, but others disdain the "dated setting."

Taverna del Bronzino Ⓢ *Italian* 26 | 21 | 26 | E

Piazza Indipendenza | 25 Via delle Ruote | (39-055) 495-220

"No hype or hipness", just "wonderful food" is found at this Italian set in a 16th-century former artist's studio that's "a bit off the beaten path", near San Marco, where a "wonderful, attentive staff always tries to please the demanding international clientele that frequents" the place.

Villa San Michele *Italian* 25 | 28 | 25 | VE

Fiesole | Hotel Villa San Michele | 4 Via Doccia | (39-055) 567-8200 | www.villasanmichele.com

"This is living" say sybarites about this Italian in Fiesole's Villa San Michele, a former 15th-century monastery with a facade attributed to Michelangelo; sure, the food is "very good", the "wine list outstanding", service "exceptional" and the dining areas "beautiful", but what surveyors "really remember is seeing night falling on Florence from a terrace table", "champagne glass in hand"; the less romantic also recall the "astronomical prices."

Zibibbo Ⓢ *Italian/Mediterranean* 25 | 20 | 25 | E

Careggi | 3R Via di Terzollina | (39-055) 433-383 | www.trattoriazibibbo.it

Chef-owner Benedetta Vitali (ex co-founder Cibrèo) is a "magician" when it comes to cooking "great" Italian-Mediterranean cuisine at this "out-of-the-way temple of food" in the Careggi hills, about eight kilometers from the City Center; devotees declare it's "worth the trek" to dine on "outstanding" culinary combinations in her modern room with a skylight and Medici tower view.

FOOD | DECOR | SERVICE | COST

Frankfurt

TOP FOOD RANKING

	Restaurant	Cuisine
25	Gargantua	French/Mediterranean
	Osteria Enoteca	Italian
24	Restaurant Français	French
23	Aubergine	Italian/French
	Sushimoto	Japanese
	Gerbermühle	German/International
22	M Steakhouse	Steak/Seafood
21	Gusto	Italian/Mediterranean
	Zarges Restaurant	French
20	Medici	Mediterranean
	Erno's Bistro	French
	Edelweiss	Austrian

Apfelwein Wagner ◐ *German* — 16 | 14 | 14 | M

Sachsenhausen | Schweizer Str. 71 | (49-69) 612-565 | www.apfelwein-wagner.com

For a taste of "typical Frankfurt", try this "typical apple-wine pub" in Sachsenhausen; the "down-to-earth" digs may be "bleak", the "simple" German fare "unexceptional" ("pork, pork and more pork") and the "rough", "gruff" staffers "uncouth", but "fast service", "moderate prices" and the city's "signature beverage" make it "popular among locals and tourists alike."

Aubergine ☒ *Italian/French* — 23 | 22 | 23 | E

City Center | Alte Gasse 14 | (49-69) 920-0780 | www.aubergine-frankfurt.de

There's a small red awning marking this "superb" City Center spot where one can expect "extravagant, freshly prepared" Italian-French fare as well as "attentive service" from a "nice, young, friendly" staff; owner and native Sardinian Paolo Vargiu's "incredible attention to detail" extends from the "excellent" wine list and "tasteful decor" "right down to the Versace plates" that grace the few tables.

Edelweiss ◐ *Austrian* — 20 | 15 | 21 | M

Sachsenhausen | Schweizer Str. 96 | (49-69) 619-696 | www.edelweiss-ffm.de

"Friendly service" combined with a "relaxed atmosphere" lends a "holiday" feel to this "comfortable" Sachsenhausen pseudo-ski lodge where the "really good flavors" of "authentic Austrian food", including "wonderful dishes like Wiener schnitzel", are accompanied by a selection of "super brews to wash everything down"; N.B. don't miss the large heated terrace.

Erno's Bistro ☒ *French* — 20 | 15 | 21 | VE

Westend | Liebigstr. 15 | (49-69) 721-997 | www.ernosbistro.de

"Attentive" service from a "caring" staff overseen by longtime owner Eric Huber sets the tone at this "ultrareliable, top-flight French" in Westend, "a surprising oasis in a city full of heavy food" thanks to chef

Valéry Mathis' "small but exquisite menu" of "excellent" fare; not only is it "a welcome break from German cuisine", but the "comfy atmosphere" of its "lively, friendly" digs makes it just the kind of place to which many "would go every day if they could."

Gargantua 🅂 *French/Mediterranean* 25 | 19 | 20 | VE

Westend | Liebigstr. 47 | (49-69) 720-718 | www.gargantua.de

It's the "creative, well-executed menu" of "incredible" New French-Mediterranean fare from chef-owner and cookbook author Klaus Trebes that makes this "exceptional small bistro" in Westend justifiably "famous" and earns it the ranking of No. 1 for Food in Frankfurt; "very good service", a winning wine list and a shady terrace are other reasons it's "well worth" a visit; yes, it's quite expensive, but such an "excellent" experience offers "good value for the money."

Gerbermühle *German/International* 23 | 21 | 22 | E

Sachsenhausen | Hotel Gerbermühle | Gerbermühlstr. 105 | (49-69) 689 7779 | www.gerbermuehle.de

The city's movers and shakers are hitting this new Sachsenhausen German-International in a boutique hotel "idyllically located on the banks of the River Main", which is also the site where Goethe met his great first love, Marianne; these days, trendies are served "great classics" and updated dishes in a handsome series of dining rooms, but in summer it's the big beer garden with its view of the water and Frankfurt skyline in the distance that's the draw.

Gusto *Italian/Mediterranean* 21 | 24 | 22 | E

Sachsenhausen | Forte Villa Kennedy | Kennedyallee 70 | (49-69) 717-12-1200 | www.villakennedy.com

This "good" Italian-Mediterranean in the "gorgeous" Rocco Forte-owned Forte Villa Kennedy hotel in Sachsenhausen is a "lovely addition" to the city; a "simpatico" staff presides over a "beautiful" expansive setting overlooking a lush courtyard garden, which becomes a dining terrace in summertime.

Holbein's 🄼 *German/International* 19 | 21 | 16 | E

Sachsenhausen | Städel Kunstmuseum | Holbeinstr. 1 | (49-69) 6605-6666 | www.holbeins.de

"Beautiful, stylish decor" is the point at this "posh joint" that's "nicely located in the Städel museum" in Sachsenhausen, "a wonderful setting for a great meal" of "tasty" German-International fare made from "particularly fresh ingredients"; still, some complain about "long waits" and suggest that the generally "well-trained staff" is "not accommodating" when "stressed"; P.S. "in summer, sit on the terrace" overlooking the gardens.

Medici 🅂 *Mediterranean* 20 | 19 | 19 | E

City Center | Weißadlergasse 2 | (49-69) 2199-0794 | www.restaurant-medici.de

Most maintain that this centrally located City Center Mediterranean housed in an insurance company building is a "popular" and "secure bet for a business lunch or dinner"; for those who find the modern minimalist interior with its massive painting of bare-breasted females a bit of a "turnoff", there's the alternative of alfresco eating out on the terrace.

M Steakhouse [S] *Steak/Seafood*

FOOD	DECOR	SERVICE	COST
22	15	18	E

Westend | Feuerbachstr. 11A | (49-69) 7103-4050 | www.the-steakhouse.de

"A piece of America in Frankfurt", this Westend steakhouse packs in "lots of English-speaking customers" who come to sample its "delicious" fare - including "really tender" beef, "satisfying jumbo prawns" and "fantastic salads" - served by "good-humored" staffers in a "sparse" setting with "cowboy photos on the walls"; yes, it's "expensive", but most feel the "cost is appropriate given the quality" and "generous portions."

Osteria Enoteca [S] *Italian*

FOOD	DECOR	SERVICE	COST
25	18	23	E

Rödelheim | Arnoldshainer Str. 2 | (49-69) 789-2216 | www.osteria-enoteca.de

Chef Carmelo Greco's "fresh", "delicious Italian food" (including "great antipasti") draws urbanites to this bi-level venue in the somewhat "remote suburb" of Rödelheim, where guests must ring a bell to gain access to the romantically lit, off-white dining room; add in a "good wine list" and an "accommodating, attentive" staff and you'll see why many lauders label it "a special-occasion place" that's "a bit out of the way but worth the trip."

Restaurant Français [S] *French*

FOOD	DECOR	SERVICE	COST
24	22	24	VE

City Center | Steigenberger Frankfurter Hof | Am Kaiserplatz | (49-69) 215-118 | www.frankfurter-hof.steigenberger.de

Set "in Frankfurt's dowager hotel", City Center's Steigenberger Frankfurter Hof, this "formal special-occasion restaurant" has been "nicely upgraded" in recent years and now attracts a "less-stuffy clientele" with its "gourmet New French selections", "excellent service" and "extremely civilized" decor with cream-colored walls and opulent oil paintings; "make sure you have plenty of room on your credit card", though, because "you may feel like royalty but you'll need access to the state treasury to settle the bill."

Sushimoto [M] *Japanese*

FOOD	DECOR	SERVICE	COST
23	16	18	E

City Center | The Westin Grand Hotel | Konrad Adenauer Str. 7 | (49-69) 131-0057 | www.sushimoto.eu

Guests "wonder if you can eat as well in" Tokyo after a visit to this "unexpected" Japanese in City Center's Westin Grand; despite decor that "isn't world-shaking" and a staff that could use "a better knowledge of German" and English, it's "a must for fans" seeking "fantastic and fresh meals" featuring "excellent sushi" and teppanyaki selections; P.S. those who find the tabs "too high" should check out the more "moderately priced set menu" at lunch.

Zarges Restaurant & Bistro [S] [M] *French*

FOOD	DECOR	SERVICE	COST
21	17	20	E

City Center | Kalbächer Gasse 10 | (49-69) 299-030 | www.zarges.zweckgemaess.de

Highly regarded chef Alfred Friedrich produces "fine classic French cuisine" along with some modernized and lightened regional German dishes at this newcomer in City Center; plush red velvet furnishings, "flickering candles" and mirrors add to the intimate atmosphere, and in summer the tiny terrace attracts the alfresco oriented.

FOOD | DECOR | SERVICE | COST

Geneva

TOP FOOD RANKING

	Restaurant	Cuisine
29	Domaine de Châteauvieux	French
26	Auberge du Lion d'Or	French
25	Patara	Thai
24	La Vendée	French
	Chez Jacky	French
	Restaurant du Parc	French
	La Favola	Italian
	Miyako	Japanese
	L'Auberge d'Hermance	French
	Spice's	Asian Fusion
23	L'Entrecôte Couronnée	French
	Vertig'O*	French/Mediterranean
	Il Lago	Italian
	Le Grill	International
	Le Relais de l'Entrecôte	Steak
	Le Chat-Botté	French
22	Roberto	Lombardian

Auberge du Lion d'Or ☒ *French* — 26 | 24 | 25 | VE

Cologny | 5 Place Pierre Gautier | (41-22) 736-4432 | www.liondor.ch

"Worth" the trip "outside of town", this "excellent, old-school" inn in Cologny boasts a "contemporary" "gastronomic restaurant" and a "pretty", more casual bistro, "both of which serve fabulous French food"; the setting "overlooking the lake" is "magnificent" and the staff is "impeccable", ensuring "an experience that should not be missed."

Brasserie Lipp ● *French* — 18 | 17 | 15 | E

Left Bank | Confédération Centre | 8 Rue de la Confédération | (41-22) 318-8030 | www.brasserie-lipp.com

"Modeled on its Paris namesake", this "buzzy" Left Bank boîte is "everything you'd expect" in a "typical French brasserie" - "noisy" "art nouveau" digs "packed" with patrons at "too-small tables" enjoying "consistently good" "traditional" fare ("shellfish is a specialty") served by sometimes abrupt staffers; it also offers "salvation for those who don't eat on a Swiss timetable", as it's "seemingly always open"; P.S. you "must dine" on the "terrace overlooking the ramparts of the Old Town."

Chez Jacky ☒ *French* — 24 | 15 | 21 | E

Right Bank | 9-11 Rue Necker | (41-22) 732-8680 | www.chezjacky.ch

For a "distinguished dining experience", visit this "great little restaurant" whose "setting slightly off the beaten track" on the Right Bank "adds to its cachet as 'a find'"; eponymous "chef Gruber's truly imaginative" French food offers "value" (regulars recommend you "stick to the excellent, affordable set menu"), and a "friendly staff" further enhances the "pleasant" atmosphere; P.S. "dining on the patio is just wonderful."

* Indicates a tie with restaurant above

Domaine de Châteauvieux ⓢⓜ *French* 29 25 27 VE

Satigny | Domaine de Châteauvieux | Chemin de Châteauvieux 16, Peney-Dessus | (41-22) 753-1511

"Wow!" is how fans sum up this "deluxe" venue in a "marvelous setting" overlooking the Rhône in Satigny that offers "the best table" around town, ranking No. 1 for Food in Geneva; "creative" chef "Philippe Chevrier's alchemy" produces "superb" New French fare, which is paired with a "fantastic wine list" and "impeccably served" by an "attentive, efficient" staff in "a lovely room" with "panoramic countryside views"; true, you'll need "a well-filled billfold", but everyone should experience such a "true gastronomic delight", "even if it's just once."

Il Lago *Italian* 23 26 23 VE

Right Bank | Four Seasons Hôtel des Bergues | 33 Quai des Bergues | (41-22) 908-7110 | www.fourseasons.com/geneva

"If you like dining in hotels, this restaurant is as good as they come" say supporters of this Northern Italian in the Four Seasons Hôtel des Bergues on the Right Bank; "excellent" cuisine and a "great wine list" that includes bottles from France, Switzerland and The Boot are proffered in a "beautiful" "formal setting" with extravagant floral displays, paintings and Rhône views; of course, "prices that are off the charts" also make for an "elite" experience.

La Favola ⓢ *Italian* 24 22 19 E

Old Town | 15 Rue Jean Calvin | (41-22) 311-7437 | www.lafavola.com

It's no fairy tale: "a most memorable meal" can in fact be found at this "tiny gem", "a wonderful retreat" "in the heart of Old Town", where "fabulous Italian" "dishes and wines from Ticino" are served with "personalized attention" in a "cute" little "jewel-box" space; though both floors are "sweet", regulars recommend that "those who can navigate the tight staircase" should "make sure to get a table upstairs"; P.S. don't miss "the best tiramisu ever."

L'Auberge d'Hermance *French* 24 23 24 E

Hermance | L'Auberge d'Hermance | 12 Rue du Midi | (41-22) 751-1368 | www.hotel-hermance.ch

Peripatetic patrons who are willing "to drive 15 minutes outside of the city" will be rewarded with an undeniably "great meal" at this "idyllic" French inn ensconced "in the medieval village" of Hermance, where a "friendly, professional" staff will seat you within the "intimate" "antique" dining room, in the "delightful" glass-walled winter garden or on the "beautiful terrace"; wherever you sit, though, expect "attractively presented dishes" from a "superb kitchen."

La Vendée *French* 24 17 20 VE

Petit-Lancy | Hostellerie de la Vendée | 28 Chemin de la Vendée | (41-22) 792-0411 | www.vendee.ch

"Inventive" French fare - including especially "well-prepared fresh fish" dishes - served by a staff with "plenty of savoir faire" makes this "high-quality" destination in a Petit-Lancy hotel "worth the trip", despite its "steep" prices; some suggest the "rather somber" surroundings "don't suit the standing" of such an otherwise "first-class" venue, but all agree "the veranda is very nice."

Le Chat-Botté *French* 23 | 22 | 23 | VE

Right Bank | Hôtel Beau-Rivage | 13 Quai du Mont-Blanc | (41-22) 716-6666 | www.beau-rivage.ch

"A favorite for years", this "elegant" French venue in the Right Bank's Hôtel Beau-Rivage features "enchanting" cuisine and a "very nice wine list", all "effortlessly served" by an "impeccable" staff "in a refined setting" with decor resembling a "grand palace"; yes, "it will cost you", but most feel "the quality equals the price", though a few wonder "what's with the hype?", saying the fare would do well by "a touch of originality."

Le Grill ☒ⓜ *International* 23 | 22 | 23 | VE

Right Bank | Grand Hotel Kempinski | 19 Quai du Mont-Blanc | (41-22) 908-9220 | www.kempinski-geneva.com

At this expensive but "enjoyable" new International in the Grand Hotel Kempinski you can start by selecting your own status steak (Swiss Simmental or French Charolais?) or seafood (Scottish salmon or Brittany blue lobster?) from two glassed-in refrigerators, then watch them being prepared in the open kitchen; you can also just sit back and relax by the floor-to-ceiling windows offering "beautiful" views of Lake Geneva, its iconic Jet d' Eau and snow-capped Mont Blanc.

L'Entrecôte Couronnée ☒ *French* 23 | 18 | 19 | E

Right Bank | 5 Rue du Pâquis | (41-22) 732-8445

Of course, this "lively" little French place on the popular Right Bank features an "excellent" namesake entrecôte with "endless frites", but other "quality" dishes (many based on local ingredients) "will have you coming back for more"; wooden furnishings, mirrors and ceiling fans help produce an appealing archetypal bistro ambiance.

Le Relais de l'Entrecôte ☒ *Steak* 23 | 18 | 17 | M

Left Bank | 49 Rue du Rhône | (41-22) 310-6004

"Choice is not the strong" suit at this "single-dish" steakhouse "institution" on the Left Bank, but fans "know why they go" - for the "same quality" entrecôte "with a twist (an addictive sauce that's guaranteed to have you licking the plate)" and "classic frites" that are served at its Paris siblings; "the only disadvantage" is that it's "difficult to get a table" in the "noisy", "cramped" space, but most "don't mind standing in line" since "the meat is divine and the prices fair."

Les Armures *French/Swiss* 19 | 19 | 17 | E

Old Town | Hôtel Les Armures | 1 Rue du Puits-Saint-Pierre | (41-22) 310-3442 | www.hotel-les-armures.ch

Just "steps from all the points of interest in Old Town", this "charming" "longtime favorite" "in the lovely" Hôtel Les Armures is "crowded" with "conventioneers and tourists" seeking "stereotypical" "Swiss-style" dining from a "traditional menu" with "wonderful specialties" such as "great fondue and raclette", along with classic French dishes; be warned, though, that the "overpowering smell" "of melted cheese" may stay with you "for a long" time.

Miyako ☒ *Japanese* 24 | 18 | 22 | VE

Right Bank | 11 Rue de Chantepoulet | (41-22) 738-0120 | www.miyako.ch

"One of the best Japanese restaurants in Geneva", this Right Bank spot serves up "fresh", "delicious sushi and sashimi", plus "wonderful teppanyaki", to an "international and business clientele" amid "traditional" (some say "a bit stuffy") decor that makes "you think you're in" the East; though the "excellent" staffers are "all very willing to help" ensure that guests "enjoy a nice evening", some still wonder whether the experience "justifies the excessive prices."

Patara *Thai* 25 | 19 | 19 | E

Right Bank | Hôtel Beau-Rivage | 13 Quai du Mont-Blanc | (41-22) 731-5566 | www.patara-geneve.com

"Part of a high-class chain" with locations in Singapore, Taipei and London, this "deluxe" Thai in a "great location" on the Right Bank offers "excellent" (albeit "high-priced") Siamese cuisine delivered by "attentive" staffers in a "pretty setting" with ceiling fans, wooden blinds and fresh flowers; still, some purists pout that the fare's "not authentic enough", while others say service suffers when it's "overcrowded."

Restaurant du Parc des Eaux-Vives [S] [M] *French* 24 | 25 | 20 | VE

Left Bank | Hôtel du Parc des Eaux-Vives | 82 Quai Gustave-Ador | (41-22) 849-7575 | www.parcdeseauxvives.ch

"What a view!" report fans of this "elegant" venue in the Left Bank's Hôtel du Parc des Eaux-Vives; a "wonderful menu" of "superb" New French fare made from "quality ingredients" is presented in a "smart", "classical" interior with "the lake in the background"; true, "you pay for" the "enchanted setting", but note that the downstairs "brasserie offers excellent food for decent prices"; P.S. "go when the roses are in bloom."

Roberto [S] *Lombardian* 22 | 18 | 21 | VE

Left Bank | 10 Rue Pierre-Fatio | (41-22) 311-8033

"Viva Roberto!" proclaim proponents of owner Mr. Carugati, who have "nothing but positive things to say" about this "high-priced" eponymous "Italian institution in the center of Geneva's" Left Bank, where a "creative menu" of "delicious" Lombardian dishes is served by a "superb staff"; a "power-lunch" "favorite" of "the old-money" "business crowd", its "flashy red" room is "always busy" at midday, so regulars recommend you "go for dinner and relax."

Spice's *Asian Fusion* 24 | 21 | 22 | VE

Right Bank | Hôtel Président Wilson | 47 Quai Wilson | (41-22) 906-6666 | www.hotelpwilson.com

"If you like great food but want something other than typical French cuisine", this "pleasant surprise" in the Right Bank's Hôtel Président Wilson "is for you"; its "creative", "excellent" Asian fusion cooking is served by an "impeccable" staff in a "hip", "modern" setting with "nice views"; no wonder most insist it's "worth" the "astronomical prices."

Vertig'O [S] *French/Mediterranean* 23 | 22 | 24 | VE

Right Bank | Hôtel de la Paix | 11 Quai du Mont-Blanc | (41-22) 909-6066 | www.hoteldelapaix.com

Alright, you may well get vertigo from the "exorbitant" prices at this French-Med that replaced the former Café de la Paix in the venerable and recently renovated hotel of the same name; still, most maintain "very pleasing cuisine", "excellent service", "stunning" slate-blue and copper contemporary decor and a "beautiful location on the lake shore" make for a "winning" experience; N.B. closed Saturdays and Sundays.

	FOOD	DECOR	SERVICE	COST

Hamburg

TOP FOOD RANKING

	Restaurant	Cuisine
25	Haerlin	French/Mediterranean
24	Atlantic Restaurant	International
23	Jacobs	French/Mediterranean
	Landhaus Scherrer	German
	Le Canard Nouveau	Mediterranean/Turkish
	Doc Cheng's	Eurasian
	Fischereihafen	Seafood
	Saliba	Syrian
22	Stock's Fischrestaurant	German/Seafood
	Cox	French/Mediterranean
20	Tafelhaus	German/International
	Allegria	Austrian
19	Nil	German

Allegria Ⓜ *Austrian* 20 | 17 | 22 | M

Winterhude | Hudtwalcker Str. 13 | (49-40) 4607-2828 | www.allegria-restaurant.de

"You'll be happy you went" to this "charming place" adjacent to the Winterhuder Komödie theater, as the staff is "attentive but not pushy" and will "answer all questions" about the "interesting" Med-influenced Austrian cuisine of "ingenious chef" Alexander Tschebull; the "modern" glass-and-steel setting is "chic [yet] cozy", and there's also summer dining in the garden outside, with a view of the river Alster.

Atlantic Restaurant Ⓢ *International* 24 | 22 | 25 | VE

St. Georg | Hotel Atlantic Kempinski Hamburg | An der Alster 72-79 | (49-40) 288860 | www.kempinski.atlantic.de

Supporters say "although you can't go wrong with anything" on the menu, the "seafood is amazing" at this "*echt*" International in the "beautiful old-world" Hotel Atlantic Kempinski; "everything is top-drawer" here - from the "perfect service" to the "classic" setting with its view of Lake Alster; just remember that "excellence comes at a price"; N.B. jacket required.

Cox *French/Mediterranean* 22 | 15 | 18 | E

St. Georg | Lange Reihe 68 | (49-40) 249-422 | www.restaurant-cox.de

Some "satisfied" surveyors are "surprised" by the "creativity" of the "excellent" New French-Med cuisine at this "place to meet people" in St. Georg given its "restrained" decor, which elicits "contradictory opinions" - some term it "tasteful", while others call it "boring"; at least almost all agree that the staff offers "good advice" on what to order from the "innovative", if "short, menu."

Doc Cheng's Ⓢ *Eurasian* 23 | 22 | 23 | E

Neustadt | Fairmont Hotel Vier Jahreszeiten | Neuer Jungfernstieg 9-14 | (49-40) 349-4333 | www.hvj.de

An "all-round" winner, this "high-class establishment" in the Fairmont Hotel Vier Jahreszeiten in Neustadt boasts "a nice team - both in" its "show kitchen", where chefs who've "mastered the contrasting flavors" of their "great Eurasian fusion fare" "prepare it in front of you", and on the floor, where "accommodating and polite" staffers "make every effort" to ensure visitors "feel well cared for"; rounding out the "top-notch dining" experience is the "posh, stylish Shanghai Express decor", which also helps the "elevated prices" seem "quite appropriate."

Fischereihafen *Seafood* 23 14 19 E

Altona | Große Elbstr. 143 | (49-40) 381-816 | www.fischereihafenrestaurant.de

"Excellent quality and outstanding selection" are hallmarks of this "traditional" ("not trendy") fish house that "does honor to its name" with "skillfully prepared", "classic seafood" that's "as fresh as it comes", served by a "friendly and competent" staff that really "knows the menu"; some say its "dignified" decor is "a bit dowdy" and "could use an update", but all appreciate its "great" dockside location in Altona, complete with a "wonderful view" - ask for a "table next to the window."

Haerlin *French/Mediterranean* 25 21 25 VE

Neustadt | Fairmont Hotel Vier Jahreszeiten | Neuer Jungfernstieg 9-14 | (49-40) 3494-3310 | www.hvj.de

Rated No. 1 for Food in Hamburg, this "top spot" in the Fairmont Hotel Vier Jahreszeiten is "distinguished" by chef Christoph Rüffer's "superb" French-Med cuisine, "gracious service" from staffers who are "so attentive they know what you want before you do" and an "excellent location" affording "lovely views of the Alstersee through picture windows"; in short, this "dream" of a place makes "you feel special", even if you're not one of its "famous guests from radio, television or politics."

Jacobs *French/Mediterranean* 23 19 22 VE

Nienstedten | Hotel Louis C. Jacob | Elbchaussee 401-403 | (49-40) 8225-5407 | www.hotel-jacob.de

"Exquisite" French-Med fare, an "excellent wine list", a "charming", "confident" staff and "classic decor" combine at this "elegant" establishment in Nienstedten's Hotel Louis C. Jacob; whether you enjoy "top chef Thomas Martin's" "surprisingly" "imaginative dishes" in an interior with a "wonderful collection of oil paintings" or out on the "magnificent terrace overlooking the Elbe river", the experience will "remain in your memory a very long time" - but be sure to bring a "fat wallet."

Landhaus Scherrer *German* 23 16 20 VE

Ottensen | Elbchaussee 130 | (49-40) 880-1325 | www.landhausscherrer.de

"Old-world charm, grace and quality abound" at this German in a former country house close to the river Elbe, where an "obliging" staff provides guests with "super recommendations from" the "creative menu's" "wide selection" of "first-class" modern dishes; some suggest its "decor could be better", but more insist that its "homelike atmosphere" makes it "ideal for a cozy get-together"; P.S. those who cry "oh, my poor wallet!" may find relief in its "less-expensive" bistro space.

Le Canard Nouveau *Mediterranean/Turkish* 23 20 20 VE

Ottensen | Elbchaussee 139 | (49-40) 8812-9531 | www.lecanard-hamburg.de

"One of the best restaurants in town" also comes with perhaps "the most stunning view of the Elbe River" report respondents about this "excellent" Med with Turkish accents in Ottensen; it's "very expensive" but "always worth it", particularly if you get a seat on the terrace.

Nil German 19 16 13 M

St. Pauli | Neuer Pferdemarkt 5 | (49-40) 439-7823 | www.restaurant-nil.de
"All the beautiful people" still crowd this "relaxed yet classy" St. Pauli spot, "for years a trendsetter" with its "fresh", "delicious food" - lately "high-quality", "medium-priced" Med-influenced "new German cuisine"; insiders advise that you "enjoy the stylish", "colorful" gallery above and avoid "the poorly lit basement", while first-timers report that "folks have to be regulars to get a smile" from the merely "civil" staffers whose idea of service seems to be Nil; N.B. closed Tuesdays.

Rive *Mediterranean/Seafood* 17 19 17 E

Altona | Van-der-Smissen-Str. 1 | (49-40) 380-5919 | www.rive.de
"For those romantic moments, a table by the window" or "on the wonderful, sunny [heated] terrace" of this "posh" Med seafooder in Altona "is a must" according to fans of its "fantastic location" and "exceptional view of the Elbe"; there's "something for everyone on its menu" of "fresh", "imaginative creations", though some are "disappointed" with the "simple", "nothing-special decor", "long waits", "ok service" and "high cost", declaring it "better for a light snack and drinks than an evening out."

Saliba *Syrian* 23 20 19 E

Altona | Leverkusenstr. 54 | (49-40) 858-071 | www.saliba.de
"An adventure for the senses" awaits at this "wonderful" Altona venue, set in a former power station, that offers a break from the "monotonous" with its "delicious" Syrian fare (a "whole new taste experience"); neophytes needn't worry, as the "friendly, patient" staff "provides the necessary information" to those who "don't know" "this exceptional cuisine", and aesthetes add that its "imaginative, appealing decor" helps take you to "another world."

Stock's Fischrestaurant M *German/Seafood* 22 15 21 M

Poppenbüttel | An Der Alsterschleife 3 | (49-40) 602-0043 | www.stocks.de
"Congratulations to Mr. Stock" say fans of this German seafooder set in a replica of a thatched, half-timbered 18th-century house "pleasantly located near Treudelberg" Park in residential Poppenbüttel; "you get the feeling" that the "excellent local fish" "jumped directly out of the water onto your plate with a brief stopover in the frying pan", and you "can't complain" about the moderate cost, so it's no wonder most don't mind that the "simple decor" is a bit "meager."

Tafelhaus S M *German/International* 20 22 18 E

Övelgönne | Neumühlen 17 | (49-40) 892-760 | www.tafelhaus-hamburg.de
This "wonderful place" blessed with "a great view of the harbor" in Övelgönne "exceeds expectations" with "sober but stylish decor" and "simply delicious" "German specialties" as well as some International dishes; still, surveyors are split over service, with some reporting "no complaints" about "caring" attendants who are "always at hand" and others offering "no special praise" for certain "slow" staffers.

Istanbul

TOP FOOD RANKING

	Restaurant	Cuisine
26	Borsa	Turkish
25	Körfez	Seafood/Turkish
	Develi	Turkish
	Seasons Restaurant	Turkish/Mediterranean
	Tugra	Turkish/Ottoman
	Poseidon	Seafood
	Tike	Turkish
	Balikçi Sabahattin	Seafood
24	Lokanta	Turkish/Finnish
	Ulus 29	Turkish/International
	Zuma	Japanese
	Laledan	Seafood
23	Feriye Lokantasi	Turkish/Ottoman
	Pandeli*	Turkish/Ottoman
	Del Mare	Seafood
	Kösebasi	Turkish
	Sunset Grill & Bar	International
22	Paper Moon	Italian
	Mezzaluna	Italian
	Changa/Müzedechanga	Asian Fusion/International
21	Spice Market	Asian
	Asitane	Turkish/Ottoman

Asitane *Turkish/Ottoman* 21 | 16 | 19 | M

Edirnekapí | Kariye Hotel | Kariye Camii Sokak 16 | (90-212) 534-8414 | www.kariyeotel.com

Dine like a sultan - as in Suleiman the Magnificent - for less than a king's ransom at this "gem" in the Kariye Hotel that features "authentic" Turkish specialties from royal recipes dating back to 1539; while a few find the onetime Ottoman mansion "stuffy", the "garden is lovely."

Balikçi Sabahattin/The Fisherman ◐ *Seafood* 25 | 17 | 20 | M

Sultanahmet | Seyit Hasan Koyu Sokak 1 | (90-212) 458-1824 | www.armadahotel.com.tr

"Wonderful", "authentic" and "freshly made mezes", "excellent fish and moderate prices" lure loyalists to this Sultanahmet seafooder in a restored mansion "near the Blue Mosque"; menus are nonexistent - all meals are fixed-price and include drinks and dessert - so just "sit at an outside table", relax and enjoy the "classic Turkish experience."

Borsa ◐ *Turkish* 26 | 16 | 25 | E

Harbiye | Istanbul Lütfi Kirdar Convention & Exhibition Ctr. | (90-212) 232-4201 | www.borsarestaurants.com

Voted Istanbul's No. 1 for Food, this Harbiye institution is renowned for "excellent traditional" Turkish cuisine ("best doner kebab in town")

* Indicates a tie with restaurant above

ably presented by a courteous staff; the bonus of a "handy address" in the Lütfi Kirdar convention center ("five minutes from major hotels") draws a "businesslike" "older crowd" that also appreciates the "lovely" glassed-in terrace "overlooking the sea and the city."

Changa ☒ *Asian Fusion* 22 | 25 | 21 | E

Taksim | Siraselviler Caddesi 47 | (90-212) 249-1205

Müzedechanga Ⓜ *Turkish/International*

Emirgan | Sakip Sabanci Museum | Sakip Sabanci Cad. 22 | (90-212) 323-0901

www.changa-istanbul.com

"The F word" - fusion - "still rules" at what some call "Istanbul's best" (and possibly only) multiculti eatery, where "good" Asian dishes are enhanced by local ingredients; located near the sights and sounds of Taksim, the setting is equally eclectic, with a "historical" art nouveau exterior that belies its extremely stylish "modern" interior - small wonder it's popular with "the city's young movers and shakers"; N.B. the newer Müzedechanga offshoot features Turkish-International fare and is in the Sakip Sabanci Museum overlooking the Bosphorous.

Del Mare *Seafood* 23 | 18 | 20 | E

Cengelköy | Kuleli Caddesi 53/4 | (90-216) 422-5762 | www.del-mare.com

The menu is extensive, the seafood is "delicious", the "service is kind" and the setting in a historic building is atmospheric at this Cengelköy spot; but it's "dining alfresco in the moonlight" on the expansive terrace with its "fantastic view of the Bosphorus" and bridge that's its "biggest asset" and what leaves most "breathless."

Develi *Turkish* 25 | 13 | 21 | M

Etiler | Tepecik Yolu 22 | (90-212) 263-2571

Kalamis | Kalamis Marina | Münir Nurettin Selçuk Caddesi | (90-216) 418-9400

Samatya | Gümüsyüzük Sokak 7 | (90-212) 529-0833

www.develikebap.com

"Fun, frantic and fabulous", this trio of "outstanding kebab houses" specializing in spicy Southeastern Turkish-style fare is "where the locals go" to fill up for mere "pennies", but it's also "friendly to business travelers" who "can't go wrong" with any of the "multitude of meat selections" ("try the pistachio kebab"); ok, "the decor isn't great", but the Samatya original's "pleasant open-air rooftop" provides a panoramic "view of the harbor."

Feriye Lokantasi *Turkish/Ottoman* 23 | 24 | 22 | E

Ortaköy | Çiragan Caddesi 124 | (90-212) 227-2216 | www.feriye.com

"Summer is the best time" to dine at this "beautiful" converted police station in Ortaköy because you'll want to sit on its "lovely terrace" to take in "one of Istanbul's most spectacular views" of the Bogazici Bridge ("unforgettable at sunset"); the location is so "breathtaking" it's "almost difficult to focus" on the "succulent" Turkish-Ottoman fare, comparatively extensive wine list and service that's "as good as it gets."

Körfez *Seafood/Turkish* 25 | 22 | 24 | VE

Kanlica | Körfez Caddesi 78 | (90-216) 413-4314 | www.korfez.com

"Exquisite seafood" (e.g. "fantastic" salt-crusted sea bass) and "gorgeous" views of the Mehmet II Bridge and Rumeli Hisar make dinner at this pricey, nautical-themed Turkish "a great experience"; getting to the waterside villa can be half the "fun", since guests can choose to cross the Bosphorus on the restaurant's "private" ferry.

Kösebasi *Turkish* 23 | 16 | 20 | M

Beylikdüzü | Kaya Ramada Plaza Yani E5 | (90-212) 886-6699
Fenerbahce | Fuatpasa Caddesi, Kurukahveciler Sokak | (90-216) 363-5856
Levent | Çamlik Sokak 153 | (90-212) 270-2433
Macka | Bronz Sokak 5 | (90-212) 230-3868
www.kosebasi.com.tr

"You can't miss" at this modern and "upscale" Turkish chain, a "local favorite" with a "wide array" of "tantalizing", "sizzling" kebabs, "plentiful" meze and a large, affordable wine list; execs from the nearby business districts readily entertain foreign clients here, although a few folks fear the owners have now "opened too many branches" to sustain the high quality.

Laledan *Seafood* 24 | 27 | 26 | VE

Besiktas | Çiragan Palace Kempinski | Çiragan Caddesi 32 | (90-212) 326-4646

This "stunning" seafooder in the Çiragan Palace Kempinski has respondents rhapsodizing over its patio's "spectacular" Bosphorus views, gardens and elegant interiors ("like dining in a museum"); staffers deliver practically "perfect service" along with "world-class food and wine" to a well-heeled clientele, leaving a dazed few to sigh that with surroundings "so pretty" they "can't remember how the meal was."

Lokanta ◐ *Turkish/Finnish* 24 | 18 | 19 | E

Beyoglu | Mesrutiyet Caddesi 149/1 | (90-212) 245-6070 | www.lokantadaneve.com

What lures the thirtysomething crowds to this hip Beyoglu eatery is "talented" chef-owner Mehmet Gürs' "cool take" on Turkish treats, incorporating elements of Finnish cuisine; the modern interior is "understated", but for a truly "magical" experience, savor your fusion fare at a rooftop table overlooking the Golden Horn.

Mezzaluna *Italian* 22 | 15 | 18 | M

Nisantasi | Abdi Ipekçi Caddesi 38/1 | (90-212) 231-3142 | www.mezzaluna.com.tr

With a wood oven producing "wonderful pizzas" and an extensive menu full of "high-quality", affordable *cucina,* this big, colorful Italian mainstay in fashionable Nisantasi remains a "good choice" for an informal meal; the staff can be overwhelmed during the dinner rush, but overall this place is "always satisfactory" - which is why it's "always full."

Pandeli *Turkish/Ottoman* 23 | 20 | 20 | M

Eminönü | Misir Çarsisi 1 | (90-212) 522-5534

"Yes, it's a bit touristy", but this "bustling" "traditional" Turkish-Ottoman is nevertheless a "magical place" thanks to its "historic setting", a 17th-century edifice above the entrance to the Egyptian Spice Bazaar in Eminönü; colorfully tiled, domed rooms provide "Old Istanbul atmosphere" plus "excellent views" of the bustling market, and it's conveniently located for shoppers to stop in for a moderately priced midday meal (only lunch is served, from noon-4 PM).

Paper Moon ◐ *Italian* 22 | 22 | 21 | VE

Etiler | Akmerkez Residence | Nispetiye Caddesi | (90-212) 282-1616

"Playboys, models" and other "beautiful" specimens populate the "scene" at this upscale Italian in Etiler's Akmerkez Residence hotel, so "go for the people-watching" but "stay for the food" too suggest surveyors; "good" pastas, risottos and wood-fired pizzas are served in the modern Milano-"chic" dining room or the garden, but because the experience can be "über-expensive", it's best for those "with expense accounts."

Poseidon ◐ *Seafood* 25 | 20 | 22 | E

Bebek | Cevdetpasa Caddesi.58A | (90-212) 263-3823 | www.poseidonbistro.com

It's not surprising that an establishment named after the Greek god of the sea specializes in piscatory plates, but this popular one in posh Bebek may be the "best" fish house in town, offering a "wonderful variety of extremely well-prepared dishes" served by an "attentive staff"; the aquatic emphasis expands to their "unforgettable dining terrace" and its "fantastic view of the Bosphorus."

Seasons Restaurant *Turkish/Mediterranean* 25 | 26 | 27 | VE

Sultanahmet | Four Seasons Hotel | Tevkifhane Sokak 1 | (90-212) 638-8200 | www.fourseasons.com/istanbul

At the center of what was a "former prison" in Sultanahmet, this "intimate", "peaceful" glass-walled restaurant is now the place to "mingle with Istanbul's upper crust" over "marvelous" and costly Turkish-Mediterranean meals ("order with abandon - it's all good") enhanced by "excellent local wines"; best of all, report respondents, is the "extraordinary" service from an "attentive" and "friendly" staff, but then again all agree that's "typical Four Seasons quality."

NEW **Spice Market** *Asian* 21 | 22 | 20 | E

Besiktas | W Hotel Akaretler | Suleyman Seba Caddesi 22 | (90-212) 381-2121 | www.culinaryconcepts.com

Jean-Georges Vongerichten's sexy Manhattan Meatpacking district Asian sprouts a new offshoot in Beşiktas' "wonderful" W Hotel Akaretler in the Financial District; the "good" "fresh food" is "flavorful", but the real "wow factor" comes from the Bosphorus view, atmospheric Oriental-meets-Ottoman interior and "see-and-be-seen vibe."

Sunset Grill & Bar *International* 23 | 26 | 25 | VE

Ulus Park | Adnan Saygun Caddesi Yol Sokak 2 | (90-212) 287-0357 | www.sunsetgrillbar.com

"Out of the City Center" but nevertheless a "must-go", this Ulus Park destination with "terrace tables overlooking the whole city and the Bosphorus" is "one of Istanbul's best options for summer dining", plus the "magnificent" vistas are visible from the spare, open interior as well; "great" International eats (e.g. "unbeatable" but "expensive" sushi and steaks) come courtesy of a "wonderful" staff, so in all ways "it's worth the trip."

Tike *Turkish* 25 | 18 | 20 | E

Günesli | Koçman Caddesi Ziyal Plaza 38 | (90-212) 630-5930 ☒

Kadiköy | Kazim Özalp Caddesi 58 | (90-216) 467-5914

Kemerburgaz | Göktürk Mahallesi Sadik Sok. 3A | (90-212) 322-3255

Levent | Haci Adil Caddesi 4, Aralik 1 | (90-212) 281-8871

(continued)

Tike

Nisantasi | Sair Nigar Sokak 4/A | (90-212) 233-3540
www.tike.com.tr

"Everyone knows" this chain of "upscale kebab houses" assert aficionados who say you've "got to love" its "delicious", "perfectly seasoned" grilled meat skewers, "great vegetarian dishes" and "tasty" meze and salads; all branches' "modern", "trendy" settings and ample alfresco seating appeal to "crowds" of affluent thirtysomethings, as do the indoor and outdoor bars featured at the original Levent location.

Tugra *Turkish/Ottoman* 25 | 28 | 27 | VE

Besiktas | Çiragan Palace Kempinski | Çiragan Caddesi 32 | (90-212) 326-4646

"Mind-blowingly beautiful, ornate and colorful", this "fabulous" jewel box "overlooking the glittering Bosphorus" makes it clear you're "dining in the palace" of a sultan (now the Çiragan Palace Kempinski in Besiktas); similarly exalted are the "wonderful", "perfectly" presented Turkish and Ottoman specialties, a wine list that's among the city's best, "excellent" live piano music performed nightly and tabs that may necessitate dipping into the royal treasury.

Ulus 29 *Turkish/International* 24 | 26 | 22 | VE

Ulus Park | Ahmet Adnan Saygun Caddesi Yol Sokak 1 | (90-212) 358-2929 | www.club29.com

Perched on a hilltop in residential Ulus, this "always 'in'" eatery offers "drop-dead" vistas - not only a "famous" panoramic Bosphorus view of both bridges, but also glimpses of the "beautiful people" who frequent this "elegant" mod-minimalist boîte to dine on "top-level", premium-priced Turkish-International cuisine; afterward, the young, fashionable crowd happily heads to the "fun" adjacent club for late-night dancing.

NEW Zuma ◐ *Japanese* 24 | 22 | 20 | VE

Ortaköy | Radisson SAS Bosphorus | Salhane Sok 7 | (90-212) 236-2296 | www.zumarestaurant.com

"Even if you are already stuffed you can't resist" the "fantastic fare" at this new Japanese in the Radisson SAS that's a spin-off of its buzzy brothers in London and Hong Kong; ultra-expensive sushi and robata are served in a "truly memorable" modernist glass-and-bamboo setting centering around a "lovely dining terrace" with "great views of the Bosphorus" and the celeb/jet-set clientele.

FOOD DECOR SERVICE COST

Lisbon

TOP FOOD RANKING

Score	Restaurant	Cuisine
27	Varanda	French
	Ristorante Hotel Cipriani	Italian
24	Gambrinus	Portuguese/International
	Casa da Comida	Portuguese
	Adega Tia Matilde	Portuguese
	O Mercado do Peixe	Seafood
	Olivier	Mediterranean
23	A Travessa	International
	Solar dos Presuntos	Portuguese
22	Gemelli	Italian
	Solar dos Nunes	Portuguese
	Valle Flôr	French/Mediterranean
	Pap'Açorda	Portuguese
	A Casa do Bacalhau	Portuguese/Seafood
21	Panorama	International
	Ad Lib	French/Portuguese
	Conventual	Portuguese
	Tavares Rico	Portuguese/International
20	Alcântara Café	International
	BBC - Belém Bar Café*	French/Portuguese
	XL	Portuguese/International
19	Bica do Sapato	Portuguese/Japanese

A Casa do Bacalhau ⊠ *Portuguese/Seafood* 22 | 21 | 17 | M

Beato | Rua do Grilo 54 | (351-21) 862-0000 | www.acasadobacalhau.restaunet.pt

You are at the 'House of the Codfish' at this Beato Portuguese specialist serving over 20 "good" versions of the revered local staple; prices are moderate, so if you're bananas for *bacalhau,* this one is a good catch.

Adega Tia Matilde *Portuguese* 24 | 16 | 21 | M

Praça de Espanha | Rua da Beneficencia 77 | (351-21) 797-2172

Since 1937, locals have been flocking to this "delicious and authentic" Portuguese in Praça de Espanha for classic dishes; the spacious, tiled setting is traditionally decorated, and the price is right.

Ad Lib *French/Portuguese* 21 | 20 | 21 | E

Liberdade | Hotel Sofitel | Avenida da Liberdade 127 | (351-21) 322-8350 | www.sofitel.com

Supporters spontaneously say this "good, innovative" French-Portuguese in the Hotel Sofitel "adds a bit of global chic to Avenida da Liberdade", the city's main thoroughfare, making it appropriate either for a business lunch or romantic dinner; it's a "beautiful find", but "bring your wallet" because "it's expensive" by local "standards."

* Indicates a tie with restaurant above

FOOD	DECOR	SERVICE	COST

Alcântara Café ◐ *International* — 20 | 22 | 18 | E

Alcântara | Rua Maria Luísa Holstein 15 | (351-21) 363-7176 | www.alcantaracafe.com

Even after 19 years it's "still one of the most beautiful rooms in Lisbon" is what supporters say about this "stunning" Alcântara International in "an old industrial setting" with steel beams, ornate mirrors, classic statues, candlelight and a sexy bar; even though it's "more like a nightclub than a restaurant", the food is "surprisingly good", and the crowd is a nice "mix of tourists and locals."

A Travessa Ⓢ *International* — 23 | 23 | 22 | E

Madragoa | Travessa do Convento das Bernardas 12 | (351-21) 390-2034 | www.atravessa.com

This long-standing International in the 17th-century Convento das Bernardas in Madragoa has "all the charm of a historic location"; a "nice" selection of "excellent Belgian dishes and local Portuguese favorites" is served in an "inviting" setting by a "very polite staff"; regulars recommend "have dinner alfresco on a warm night" on the terrace.

BBC - Belém Bar Café ◐ Ⓢ Ⓜ *French/Portuguese* — 20 | 23 | 20 | E

Belém | Avenida Brasília, Pavilhão Poente | (351-21) 362-4232 | www.belembarcafe.com

In a "very beautiful location" in a "happening neighborhood" is this well-frequented French-Portuguese restaurant/bar/club in Belém, a "little far from the City Center" but in a popular redeveloped area with a "good view" of the Tejo river and bridge; a "hip" crowd comes for a "lively" time and an exceptionally "atmospheric" glassed-in setting.

Bica do Sapato Ⓢ *Portuguese/Japanese* — 19 | 22 | 16 | E

Santa Apolónia | Avenida Infante D. Henrique, Armazém B, Cais da Pedra | (351-21) 881-0320 | www.bicadosapato.com

"As cool as you can get in Lisbon" is this "trendy", "inventive" Santa Apolónia Portuguese with a separate upstairs sushi bar in a "huge waterfront warehouse" that's co-owned by actor John Malkovich; "portions are small" ("the ideal quantity for models") and service could be "friendlier and more attentive", but it's the "grooviest" "place to see local celebs", and there are "beautiful views" of the Tagus River too.

Casa da Comida Ⓢ *Portuguese* — 24 | 23 | 22 | E

Jardim das Amoreiras | Travessa das Amoreiras 1 | (351-21) 388-5376 | www.casadacomida.pt

Among the "tops in town" is this refined, "romantic" Portuguese in a pretty, 18th-century townhouse in Jardim das Amoreiras; start by sipping a crisp white port while perusing the menu in the wood-paneled lounge before moving into the "wonderful" interior garden room and enjoying an "excellent" meal served by a "cordial staff."

Conventual Ⓢ *Portuguese* — 21 | 19 | 21 | E

Bairro das Mercês | Praça das Flores 45 | (351-21) 390-9196

Many of this long-standing restaurant's dishes are inspired by old recipes from Portuguese convents or monasteries, and the result is "deliciously flavored" "traditional" food; an "attentive" staff presides over the "sedate", white-walled space in the Bairro das Mercês that is, appropriately enough, decorated with "interesting religious art."

Gambrinus ◐ *Portuguese/International* — 24 | 20 | 24 | VE

Baixa | Rua das Portas de Santo Antão 23-25 | (351-21) 342-1466 | www.gambrinuslisboa.com

"Excellent seafood and game" are the focus at this Portuguese-International, "one of the oldest and most traditional restaurants" in the Baixa, where "waiters and customers seem to be longtime friends"; its decor - "dark-paneled rooms", stained glass and leather chairs - appeals to "mostly male" patrons, but everyone exclaims 'holy mackerel' when it comes to the "very expensive" prices.

Gemelli ◐Ⓢ *Italian* — 22 | - | 16 | E

Bairro das Mercês | Rua Nova da Piedade 99 | (351-21) 395-2552 | www.augustogemelli.com

Insiders insist "let chef-owner Augusto Gemelli make the choice" as to what you'll order at this newly relocated Bairro das Mercês "excellent Italian" where many recipes rely on Portuguese products; the bistro-style room is small but "warm" and welcoming.

Olivier ◐Ⓢ *Mediterranean* — 24 | 15 | 20 | E

Bairro Alto | Rua do Teixeira 35 | (351-21) 343-1405 | www.restaurante-olivier.com

The menu at chef-owner Olivier da Costa's Bairro Alto dinner-only Mediterranean may be limited, but the cuisine is "unique", "sophisticated" and "delicious"; no wonder the charming, "tiny" wood-paneled room with paintings is always "full."

O Mercado do Peixe *Seafood* — 24 | 13 | 16 | E

Monsanto | Estrada Pedro Teixeira, Vila Simâo, Caramão da Ajuda | (351-21) 361-6070 | www.mercadodopeixe.web.pt

There's a "large diversity" of the "freshest" fish and shellfish on ice to choose from, and then you watch your selection "grilled to perfection" in front of you at this favorite in Monsanto; aesthetes say the plain decor is not the lure, but even they insist it's all "simple, direct and wonderful."

Panorama *International* — 21 | 22 | 22 | E

São Sebastião da Pedreira | Sheraton Lisboa Hotel & Spa | Rua Latino Coelho 1, 30th fl. | (351-21) 312-0000 | www.starwoodhotels.com

Indeed, this "enjoyable" International on the 30th floor of the Sheraton Lisboa Hotel & Spa does provide a "gorgeous" panoramic view of the city; admirers urge: "go there for an early dinner", "get a table by the window" and "enjoy the glorious sunset as a bonus."

Pap'Açorda ⓈⓂ *Portuguese* — 22 | 17 | 19 | E

Bairro Alto | Rua da Atalaia 57-59 | (351-21) 346-4811

Still "very popular" and "eternally trendy" "after more than 25 years" is this "Portuguese with a twist" up in the hopping Bairro Alto; dishes like the traditional namesake açorda (a bread stew cooked with shellfish, garlic and coriander) and an "excellent chocolate mousse" have their fans, but it's the "people-watching" that's the real order of the day.

Ristorante Hotel Cipriani *Italian* — 27 | 25 | 27 | VE

Lapa | Lapa Palace Hotel | Rua do Pau de Bandeira 4 | (351-21) 394-9494 | www.lapapalace.com

Housed in the lush and "lovely" Lapa Palace Hotel in the "ritzy" embassy area is this "great" Italian with equally highly rated service; the softly lit room is patrician and pretty, plus in summer there's a "nice dining terrace overlooking the garden"; in sum, it's "very elegant" and "very expensive."

Solar dos Nunes Ⓢ *Portuguese* 22 | 14 | 18 | M

Alcântara | Rua dos Lusíadas 70 | (351-21) 364-7359

At this "Lisbon fixture" in the Alcântara, there's a "large choice" of "delightful" Alentejo specialties; a "friendly" staff, country-casual decor and moderate prices add to its appeal.

Solar dos Presuntos *Portuguese* 23 | 17 | 22 | M

Baixa | Rua das Portas de Santo Antão | (351-21) 342-4253 | www.solardospresuntos.com

"Lots of locals and tourists" hit this "very good" Restaurant Row pioneer in the Baixa for a plethora of "classic" and "simple" Portuguese staples that range from meats to seafood dishes like "perfect paella", all complemented by a substantial wine cellar; "service is excellent", the decor is "traditional" and prices are "acceptable"; P.S. "try to get a table upstairs."

Tavares Rico ⓈⓂ *Portuguese/International* 21 | 22 | 19 | E

Chiado | Rua da Misericórdia 35-37 | (351-21) 342-1112

"Still good after all these years" assert admirers of this 1784 Chiado Portuguese-International - maybe that's because its drop-dead opulent interior with gilt, mirrors and chandeliers was recently restored; the finest appointments - Riedel crystal and Christofle silver - ensure this "institution" remains elegant.

Valle Flôr *French/Mediterranean* 22 | 28 | 23 | VE

Alcântara | Pestana Palace Hotel | Rua Jau 54 | (351-21) 361-5600 | www.pestana.com

"Probably the most beautiful and historic dining room in Lisbon" is this French-Mediterranean with frescoes, boiserie and garden views in the Pestana Palace Hotel, which is also a national monument; chef Aimé Barroyer does a "wonderful job modernizing classic dishes", and the result is an "expensive" but "great experience."

Varanda *French* 27 | 24 | 27 | VE

São Sebastião da Pedreira | Four Seasons Hotel Ritz | Rua Rodrigo da Fonseca 88 | (351-21) 381-1400 | www.fourseasons.com/lisbon

Voted No. 1 for Food in the city is this "very expensive" French venue that "like most other Four Seasons' restaurants could easily stand on its own without the hotel"; an "impeccable" staff serves "exquisite" food in a luminous room with a view of Eduardo VII park; P.S. the "sumptuous and well-presented lunchtime buffet" is "where all of Lisbon meets."

XL ◐Ⓢ *Portuguese/International* 20 | 18 | 20 | E

Lapa | Calçada da Estrela 57-63 | (351-21) 395-6118

At this chef-owned Portuguese-International in the aristocratic Lapa district, "delicious steaks" and "good soufflés" are the stars; a "friendly, helpful" staff and "cool", "informal" vibe make it "a hit with a younger clientele."

FOOD | DECOR | SERVICE | COST

London

TOP FOOD RANKING

	Restaurant	Cuisine
29	Gordon Ramsay/68 Royal	French
	Chez Bruce	British
28	La Trompette	European/French
	River Café	Italian
	Ledbury	French
	Marcus Wareing	French
	New Tayyabs	Pakistani
27	Jin Kichi	Japanese
	Square	French
	Le Gavroche	French
	St. John	British
	L'Atelier Robuchon/La Cuisine	French
	Pied à Terre	French
	Rasoi Vineet Bhatia	Indian
	Nobu London	Japanese
	Hunan	Chinese
	Zuma	Japanese

NEW BORD'EAUX *French* — | - | - | - | VE |

Mayfair | Grosvenor House | Park Ln., W1 (Marble Arch) | (44-20) 7399-8460 | www.bord-eaux.com

The Grosvenor House's new high-ceilinged, huge-windowed restaurant overlooking Park Lane is kitted out like a classic Gallic brasserie, circa 1930s; jolly chef Ollie Couillaud (ex Tom's Kitchen and The Dorchester's Grill) brings the gutsy tastes of his native Aquitaine to a "solid" Southwestern French menu that's "highly expensive, but at least the surroundings and services back up the top prices."

Chez Bruce *British* — | 29 | 21 | 26 | VE |

Wandsworth | 2 Bellevue Rd., SW17 (Balham/Wandsworth Common Rail) | (44-20) 8672-0114 | www.chezbruce.co.uk

Despite relinquishing London's No. 1 Food ranking to Mr. Ramsay this year, this "gastronomic outpost" remains "first-class" cry the many boosters of its "brilliantly conceived" Modern British cuisine that "never falters" – and is a "phenomenal value" to boot; augmented by "fantastic advice from the sommelier", the "high-caliber" service is "outstandingly orchestrated", navigating the "reassuringly informal", if slightly "cramped", setting; all told, it's "really worth it in Wandsworth."

Gordon Ramsay at 68 Royal Hospital Rd. ⊠ *French* — | 29 | 25 | 28 | VE |

Chelsea | 68 Royal Hospital Rd., SW3 (Sloane Sq.) | (44-20) 7352-4441 | www.gordonramsay.com

"He may not be there every day" (other restaurants to open, TV shows to star in, etc.), but Gordon Ramsay's "original emporium" in Chelsea "remains true to his cooking credo and intensity" and has regained London's No. 1 for Food title to prove it; the "amazing", "ambrosial"

New French fare is served within a white-on-white "jewel box" setting by a staff that ranks as the No. 1 for Service, neither "shunning the first-time visitor nor fawning over the regular" (thanks to "charming" manager Jean-Claude Breton); just remember to "bring a large sack of gold bullion" to settle up.

Hunan *Chinese* | 27 | 13 | 20 | E |

Belgravia | 51 Pimlico Rd., SW1 (Sloane Sq.) | (44-20) 7730-5712 | www.hunanlondon.com

"The only way to dine" at this "quiet, intimate" Pimlico Chinese is to "put yourself in the hands" of chef-owner Michael Peng, who brings "a roller coaster of flavors" from a "sophisticated", "authentic" menu "until you can eat no more"; that, and an "incredibly fairly priced wine list", makes up for "long waits between dishes" and "decor that could use some updating."

Ivy, The *British/European* | 22 | 21 | 23 | VE |

Covent Garden | 1-5 West St., WC2 (Leicester Sq.) | (44-20) 7836-4751 | www.the-ivy.co.uk

"Once you successfully navigate the Byzantine reservation system" and snag a seat in the "dark-wood-paneled inside", this "timeless" Theatreland "thespian stalwart" will "pamper you in an understated way"; while "surprisingly good", the "homely" Modern British-Euro cuisine is perhaps "not worthy of what they charge", "but then you don't come here to eat - you come to experience the star-studded energy."

Jin Kichi *Japanese* | 27 | 12 | 18 | M |

Hampstead | 73 Heath St., NW3 (Hampstead) | (44-20) 7794-6158 | www.jinkichi.com

This "little hole-in-the-wall" in Hampstead "transports you directly to Downtown Tokyo", partly because it's "packed and noisy", but more importantly because of its "out-of-this-world", "proper Japanese" victuals (the "sashimi's always fresh", but "the yakitori excels"); just "make sure to order everything at once, or you may find that extra piece of sushi takes a one-hour wait."

J. Sheekey *Seafood* | 26 | 21 | 24 | VE |

Covent Garden | 28-32 St. Martin's Ct., WC2 (Leicester Sq.) | (44-20) 7240-2565 | www.j-sheekey.co.uk

Located down a "Dickensian" alleyway, the "ultimate clubby" Covent Gardener "is uninspiring from the outside, but inside it has a cozy atmosphere, with wood paneling, signed photos" and "tables that are a bit close together (but they're all [occupied by] celebrities, so who cares?)"; the fare's "nothing fancy, nothing adventurous - just superb seafood", admittedly "expensive" but "artfully prepared" and served by a "witty staff" who'll "get you to the theater on time - if you can bear to leave."

L'Atelier de Joël Robuchon *French* | 27 | 24 | 24 | VE |

Covent Garden | 13-15 West St., WC2 (Leicester Sq.) | (44-20) 7010-8600

La Cuisine *French*

Covent Garden | L'Atelier de Joël Robuchon | 13-15 West St., 1st fl., WC2 (Leicester Sq.) | (44-20) 7010-8600
www.joel-robuchon.com

Enjoy "a serious workout for the eyes and the taste buds" at "true genius" chef-restaurateur Joël Robuchon's "slick, chic and expensive"

New French; bringing "cutting-edge to Covent Garden", his "mini-portions of perfection" are "served by people who obviously care", either in the "elegant" kitchen-themed, dinner-only La Cuisine or the "dark" ground-floor L'Atelier ("less formal", but "much better" some say); "high prices are the only dampener" - "not everyone wants to sit on stools to spend this kind of money" - otherwise, it's a "memorable" "delight."

La Trompette *European/French* 28 | 22 | 25 | VE

Chiswick | 5-7 Devonshire Rd., W4 (Turnham Green) | (44-20) 8747-1836 | www.latrompette.co.uk

"Sound *la trompette*" for this "professionally run" yet "unpretentious" bit of "Paris in Chiswick", whose "sophisticated" Modern European-New French cuisine represents "*une triomphe*" of "culinary genius and class"; it's supported by an "excellent wine list" "across all price ranges and regions", "lovely" hardwood decor and a "quick, well-informed staff", and since all of this "would be twice the price in the West End", it's definitely "worth the journey" out.

Ledbury, The *French* 28 | 23 | 25 | VE

Notting Hill | 127 Ledbury Rd., W11 (Notting Hill Gate/Westbourne Park) | (44-20) 7792-9090 | www.theledbury.com

"A perfect place for a first, or a 5,001st, date" declare devotees of this "classy, almost-world-class" venue that "adds glamour to a less-than-glamorous end of" Notting Hill; as a rising Food rating reveals, chef Brett Graham's "worth-every-penny", "sophisticated" New French menu just keeps getting better - even "better than sibling The Square's" some say - and it's "served up with no attitude, just a discreet, helpful staff"; the "swish, modern decor" may be "a bit *ordinaire*", but it affords "sufficient room between tables, so a quiet dinner for two stays that way."

Le Gavroche ☒ *French* 27 | 24 | 26 | VE

Mayfair | 43 Upper Brook St., W1 (Marble Arch) | (44-20) 7408-0881 | www.le-gavroche.co.uk

"If you like eating in the lap of luxury", this "timeless" Mayfair "institution" gives any meal "a real sense of occasion", with "crème de la crème" cooking that "sets the standard of Classic French cuisine" in the capital, capped by "legendary service" that, "without being cloying", "makes every customer feel like a king"; sophisticates sigh it's "*so* old hat", especially the subterranean setting, and it's certainly "not for the faint of wallet", but legions of fans profess it "faultless in every way"; P.S. "the set lunch is a steal."

Marcus Wareing at The Berkeley ☒ *French* 28 | 25 | 27 | VE
(fka Pétrus)

Belgravia | The Berkeley | Wilton Pl., SW1 (Hyde Park Corner) | (44-20) 7235-1200

As the new name suggests, longtime chef Marcus Wareing assumed overall control of The Berkeley's dining room in September 2008 - but little else has changed: "managing to be both posh and unpretentious", the room provides a vividly colored canvas for the "silky smooth execution of supreme" "modern" French dishes that are "always of the highest order", "the wine list reads like a superb novel" and "nothing is a problem" for the "outstanding" staff; even if it will put "a big dent in your wallet", "you get what you pay for" - so "save up and go"; N.B. former manager Gordon Ramsay plans to open another Pétrus at a different site.

New Tayyabs ◐ *Pakistani* 28 | 14 | 16 | I

Whitechapel | 83-89 Fieldgate St., E1 (Aldgate/Whitechapel) | (44-20) 7247-6400 | www.tayyabs.co.uk

"Why bother with Brick Lane" when there's this "wonderful" Whitechapel warhorse whose "authentic Pakistani food" is "absolutely tops"; there's "always a queue", it's always "cramped" and you "always feel like you're getting rushed out", but the cuisine "quality makes you look past any shortcomings."

Nobu London *Japanese* 27 | 20 | 22 | VE

Mayfair | Metropolitan Hotel | 19 Old Park Ln., W1 (Hyde Park Corner) | (44-20) 7447-4747 | www.noburestaurants.com

"Despite it's being a big-name celebrity hangout, the cuisine remains top-notch" at Nobu Matsuhisa's "fine-dining mainstay" in Mayfair; the "simple" yet "inspired" Japanese-Peruvian creations and "inventive" sushi are presented by "polite but not obsequious" servers amid "sophisticated", if slightly "dated", decor; given the number of Nobus nowadays, it's "getting to feel like an international chain" cynics say, but the quality's just "so damn consistent", few really care - even if they have to "pay exorbitant sums"; P.S. some "prefer to eat at the sushi bar where they've always found space without reservations."

Pied à Terre ☒ *French* 27 | 21 | 25 | VE

Fitzrovia | 34 Charlotte St., W1 (Goodge St.) | (44-20) 7636-1178 | www.pied-a-terre.co.uk

"The *pied* may be *à terre,* but the food is heavenly" at this "Fitzrovia townhouse" where chef Shane Osborne "deserves all the accolades he gets" - and "the fortune one spends" - for his "interpretation of modern French fare" "with playful touches", backed by a "serious wine list"; all's served by an "unobtrusive" but "helpful" staff in a "sophisticated", if "slightly claustrophobic", setting; "intimate rather than lively", it's "perfect for a quiet celebration."

Rasoi Vineet Bhatia ☒ *Indian* 27 | 22 | 24 | VE

Chelsea | 10 Lincoln St., SW3 (Sloane Sq.) | (44-20) 7225-1881 | www.rasoirestaurant.co.uk

"One reaches nirvana without trying" at this "transporting" townhouse in Chelsea, where owner-chef Vineet Bhatia uses a "spectacular variety of spices and flavors" to produce "adventurous", "refined" subcontinental fare - especially on the tasting menu, aka "seven courses to heaven"; add in the recently redone environs, "decorated like a peaceful candlelit temple", and "wonderful service", and "if there's a better Indian restaurant around, do let me know."

River Café *Italian* 28 | 22 | 25 | VE

Hammersmith | Thames Wharf | Rainville Rd., W6 (Hammersmith) | (44-20) 7386-4200 | www.rivercafe.co.uk

"An Italian masterpiece beside the Thames" in Hammersmith, this "bright", "bustling" legend is "larger than life", serving "gargantuan portions" of "the finest ingredients", with "perfect service to match"; so "who cares if it's a little pricey" - the "result is pure magic", and "heaven if you can sit outside on a beautiful day"; N.B. the Decor score doesn't reflect a midsummer revamp after a fire.

Square, The *French* 27 | 23 | 25 | VE

Mayfair | 6-10 Bruton St., W1 (Bond St./Green Park) | (44-20) 7495-7100 | www.squarerestaurant.com

Get "the feel of being in the centre of London's power elite" at this "clean, modern space" in Mayfair, where chef-owner Philip Howard's "impeccable" New French cooking - "creative and classical at the same time" - is matched by a "spot-on, professional" staff and an "amazing wine list" with "many half-bottles"; sure, it's "not cheap" and "others may have a slight edge on decor and service", but this "wonderfully sophisticated" venue "delivers every time."

St. John *British* 27 | 18 | 23 | E

Farringdon | 26 St. John St., EC1 (Farringdon) | (44-20) 7251-0848 | www.stjohnrestaurant.com

"If you want the whole hog, literally", this "convivial" Smithfield Modern Brit caters to "adventurous eaters" with an "innovative, nose-to-tail" menu - "a vegetarian's nightmare, but a carnivore's dream" - "and then there's baked goods" too, all served by a "no-nonsense" staff; the "canteen-style", "clinical surroundings" are "not as comfortable as I'd like", given the "steep prices" - but otherwise, "this place is offaly good"; N.B. a midsummer 2008 revamp may outdate the Decor score.

Wolseley, The ◐ *European* 22 | 26 | 21 | E

Piccadilly | 160 Piccadilly, W1 (Green Park) | (44-20) 7499-6996 | www.thewolseley.com

With its "buzzing atmosphere", "unique, grand setting" ("Viennese-style" cafe "meets former bank" in Piccadilly) and "always some celebrity-spotting", this "well-oiled machine" remains "hot, hot, hot"; while some growl it's "more glamour than good food" here, the Modern European "comfort" menu "covers the gamut" from "brilliant breakfasts" to "delicious dinners", so "you can eat cheap and cheerful or top-end", and the "service is surprisingly friendly"; it's "impossible to book", of course, but "their policy of keeping tables for walk-ins is a wonderful touch."

Zuma *Japanese* 27 | 24 | 20 | VE

Knightsbridge | 5 Raphael St., SW7 (Knightsbridge) | (44-20) 7584-1010 | www.zumarestaurant.com

Seven years old and "still packed to the rafters" with a mix of "beautiful people, the famous" and "corporate types", this "luscious"-looking Knightsbridge "icon" of the "achingly hip" has an "extensive menu" of Japanese fare, including a "dynamite" "first come, first served robata grill" and "sushi that'll make you moan with delight", plus a "hopping bar" with 25 types of sake; so even though prices keep zuma-ing up and their "numerous-sittings policy makes you feel rushed all the time", "deal with it" - the place is "divine."

FOOD | DECOR | SERVICE | COST

Madrid

TOP FOOD RANKING

	Restaurant	Cuisine
28	Santceloni	Mediterranean
27	Zalacaín	International
	Goizeko Kabi/Wellington	Basque
26	Príncipe de Viana	Basque/Navarraise
	Combarro	Galician/Seafood
	Viridiana	International
	La Terraza del Casino	Spanish
	El Chaflán	Mediterranean
25	Sergi Arola Gastro	Mediterranean
	Horcher	International
	Jockey	International
	El Amparo	Basque/Mediterranean
	Goya	International/Spanish
	Kabuki	Japanese/Mediterranean
24	Asia Gallery	Chinese
	Astrid y Gastón	Peruvian
	Arce	Basque
	Diverxo	International
	El Pescador	Seafood
	La Broche	Mediterranean
	La Trainera	Seafood
23	El Bodegón	Basque/International
	El Olivo	Mediterranean
	Lavinia Espacio	Mediterranean

Arce ◐ [S] *Basque* — 24 | 16 | 21 | E

Centro | Augusto Figueroa 32 | (34-91) 522-0440

Admirers advise on planning for an interactive evening at this "fine" modern Basque in El Centro, where "attentive" chef-owner Iñaki Camba may "come out of the kitchen and help you design your meal", which can be complemented with wine from an impressive 900-bottle list; the cozy, "comfortable" setting reminds some of "eating at home."

Asia Gallery ◐ *Chinese* — 24 | 24 | 24 | E

Centro | Hotel Westin Palace | Plaza las Cortes 7 | (34-91) 360-0049 | www.westinpalacemadrid.com

"It's hard to find Asian food this good in Spain" say supporters of this Chinese in the Hotel Westin Palace; an "amazing", "luxurious" setting with silks and antiques and "great service" add to the experience, making it "ideal for a romantic evening."

Astrid y Gastón [S] *Peruvian* — 24 | 21 | 22 | E

Chamberí | Paseo de la Castellana 13 | (34-91) 702-6262 | www.astridygaston.com

One of the city's biggest culinary buzzes is about this "awesome" new Peruvian, an upscale offshoot from Gastón Acurios' highly regarded

South American restaurant empire; the focus on "sophisticated seafood", both cooked and raw (as in ceviche and carpaccios), a "great location" on the central Paseo de la Castellana and an appealing interior in earth tones have also helped it become a "place to see and be seen"; P.S. the "pisco sour cocktail here is splendid."

Balzac ◐ ☒ *Mediterranean* 22 | 19 | 21 | E

Retiro | Moreto 7 | (34-91) 420-0177 | www.restaurantebalzac.net

"An epicurean delight" is how devotees describe the cuisine at this "inventive", "modern" Med in the Retiro, near the Prado Museum; "pleasing" service and a series of softly lit, minimally decorated rooms with modern art provide an "enjoyable atmosphere."

Botín Restaurante ◐ *Castilian* 22 | 22 | 21 | E

Centro | Cuchilleros 17 | (34-91) 366-4217 | www.casabotin.com

"Although touristy, it's no trap" assert admirers of this 1725 Castilian "institution" and former Hemingway haunt off Plaza Mayor that bills itself as "the oldest restaurant in the world"; the food is "great" ("particularly roast suckling pig, baby lamb" and "mouthwatering Iberian ham"), the "warren of rickety rooms" is "atmospheric" and service is "gracious", making it "a must-see" and "must-do" in Madrid.

Combarro *Galician/Seafood* 26 | 18 | 21 | E

Tetuán | Reina Mercedes 12 | (34-91) 554-7784 | www.combarro.com

Many surveyors say this Tetuán establishment is the "best place in town" for simply prepared seafood with a Galician accent; it imports its fin fare from its own fish farm in that region, along with local wines like the crisp Albariños, and if the "bill can add up", "you'll leave satisfied."

Diverxo ☒ *International* 24 | 15 | 19 | E

Tetuán | Calle Francisco Medrano 5 | (34-91) 570-0766

The name translates as "different", which accurately reflects young chef-owner and rising "star" David Muñoz's approach to cooking at his tiny, "trendy" new International in Tetuán; he fuses a variety of unexpected ethnic influences, and the result is "innovative", "impressive" cuisine; some surveyors sigh it's too bad that the "drab" informal setting and "service are not on the same level", but prices here are more reasonable than at others of its ilk.

El Amparo ☒ *Basque/Mediterranean* 25 | 22 | 22 | VE

Salamanca | Callejón de Puigcerdá 8 | (34-91) 431-6456

"It really doesn't get much better than this" "outstanding" Basque-Mediterranean in the "ritzy" Salamanca district, where "perfectly prepared" modern cuisine and a substantial wine list are proffered by a solidly rated staff in a "relaxing", "romantic" triplex setting; of course, such excellence comes at a very high price.

El Bodegón ☒ *Basque/International* 23 | 21 | 21 | E

Salamanca | Pinar 15 | (34-91) 562-8844 | www.grupovips.com

Housed in a stone cottage in Salamanca is this Basque-International bastion serving "quality" "classic" cooking; "top-notch service" and a comfortable and "tasteful dining room" with wood beams and "beautiful art" make it "excellent for entertaining clients."

	FOOD	DECOR	SERVICE	COST

El Chaflán *Mediterranean*

	FOOD	DECOR	SERVICE	COST
El Chaflán	26	22	24	VE

Chamartín | Hotel Aristos | Avenida de Pío XII 34 | (34-91) 350-6193 | www.elchaflan.com

One of the most talked about restaurants in town is cutting-edge chef Juan Pablo Felipe's "inventive" modern Mediterranean, which makes the most of white Alba truffles in autumn; housed in the Hotel Aristos, the "minimalist" pale-green-and-white space is enlivened by a skylight and gleaming open kitchen.

El Olivo ◐⊠ *Mediterranean*

	FOOD	DECOR	SERVICE	COST
El Olivo	23	18	22	E

Chamartín | General Gallegos 1 | (34-91) 359-1535 | www.elolivorestaurante.es

As its name implies, this "first-class" Mediterranean in Chamartín is devoted to olives as well as their oils (there's a trolley of them for sampling and for sale), and the ingredient turns up in "subtle and delicate" dishes, even including a signature ice cream; a "kind" staff, "comfortable" setting and swell selection of 120 sherries are added attractions.

El Pescador ◐⊠ *Seafood*

	FOOD	DECOR	SERVICE	COST
El Pescador	24	15	20	E

Salamanca | José Ortega y Gasset 75 | (34-91) 402-1290

"Fabulous fresh seafood" like "big-as-a-whale sole" is the lure at this long-standing "no-attitude" spot in Salamanca; the "casual nautical decor" could use "refurbishing", but that doesn't keep the likes of the Royal Family from frequenting the place.

Goizeko Kabi ◐⊠ *Basque*

	FOOD	DECOR	SERVICE	COST
Goizeko Kabi	27	19	20	VE

Tetuán | Comandante Zorita 37 | (34-91) 533-0214

Goizeko Wellington ◐⊠ *Basque*

Salamanca | Wellington Hotel | Villanueva 34 | (34-91) 577-0138

www.goizekogaztelupe.com

"A bastion of the fur-wearing Tetuán ladies and their banking husbands" is this very expensive Basque that boosters boast is "one of the best choices in town", with "fine food" and a "great wine list"; P.S. those who find the ambiance here "stuffy" prefer the newer, more modern and relaxed branch in the Wellington Hotel.

Goya *International/Spanish*

	FOOD	DECOR	SERVICE	COST
Goya	25	26	26	VE

Retiro | Hotel Ritz | Plaza de la Lealtad 5 | (34-91) 701-6767 | www.ritzmadrid.com

This "grand" Spanish-International on the ground floor of the Ritz comes with "pampering" service that's a "tribute to the art of fine dining"; the interior, with its chandeliers and palms, evokes "old-world elegance to the nth degree", and in summer, eating in the "garden is magical"; like one of its namesake's paintings, its cost is "excessive", but the "well-heeled" clientele doesn't dwell on such mundane matters.

Horcher ⊠ *International*

	FOOD	DECOR	SERVICE	COST
Horcher	25	24	26	VE

Retiro | Alfonso XII 6 | (34-91) 522-0731 | www.restaurantehorcher.com

Family-owned International dowager with a German accent near Retiro Park that's been turning out "classic" cuisine like stroganoff and game dishes for decades; an "excellent" solicitous staff ("in his heyday Franco would not have been treated better") oversees an "old-world" room with floral fabrics and porcelain figurines; of course, you pay for a "formal evening out" like this "big time"; N.B. jacket and tie required.

FOOD | DECOR | SERVICE | COST

Jockey ☒ *International* — 25 | 23 | 25 | VE

Chamberí | Amador de los Ríos 6 | (34-91) 310-0411 | www.restaurantejockey.net

This "old-school", über-expensive International in Chamberí has been putting itself through its paces since 1945 and still draws a formally dressed crowd of the "who's who of the Madrid business and aristocratic worlds"; they come for "classic" cuisine, a "great wine list", "attentive service" and a "clubby" setting; N.B. jacket and tie required.

Kabuki ◐☒ *Japanese/Mediterranean* — 25 | 16 | 19 | E

Chamartín | Presidente Carmona 2 | (34-91) 417-6415

For the "best toro in town" and other "top-quality sushi", loyalists head to this chef-owned Japanese-Mediterranean in Chamartín, where a "charming" and "friendly" staff presides over a small, minimalist black-and-yellow space that spills over onto an appealing terrace in summer.

La Broche ☒ *Mediterranean* — 24 | 24 | 23 | VE

Chamberí | Miguel Ángel Hotel | Miguel Ángel 29-31 | (34-91) 399-3437 | www.labroche.com

Top toque and Ferran Adrià disciple Sergi Arola's modern Med in the Miguel Ángel Hotel is "controversial": aficionados admire his "unbelievable imagination" and "exquisite and daring" deconstructed dishes, while detractors declare them "weird" and the puzzled plead "who wants to eat rooster combs?"; note that the "stark white setting" "couldn't be more minimalist", and the tab is about the "price of a Picasso"; N.B. closed Saturday and Sunday.

La Terraza del Casino ☒ *Spanish* — 26 | 24 | 25 | VE

Puerta del Sol | Casino de Madrid | Alcalá 15 | (34-91) 532-1275 | www.casinodemadrid.es

"You'll feel like a king" (or at least "Cary Grant") dining in a "breathtaking" rooftop room in one of the city's oldest "exclusive" clubs just off the Puerta del Sol; El Bulli's touted Ferran Adrià is the consulting chef, and his "high-quality", "high-tech" deconstructed Spanish dishes with foams are complemented by "great wines" and served by an "incredibly attentive" staff in a see-and-be-seen-in space; it's "quite expensive", but the experience is "incomparable."

La Trainera ☒ *Seafood* — 24 | 15 | 19 | E

Salamanca | Lagasca 60 | (34-91) 576-0575 | www.latrainera.es

For "simple, satisfying and consistently excellent" "classical" dishes like clams and the signature turbot, fanatics flock to this sprawling seafooder in Salamanca; just be warned that its "unassuming" decor - "wood paneling" and a "nautical theme" with ships' lanterns and wheels - "belies how expensive it is."

Lavinia Espacio Gastronómico ☒ *Mediterranean* — 23 | 19 | 22 | E

Salamanca | Calle José Ortega y Gasset 16 | (34-91) 426-0599 | www.lavinia.es

This lunch-only Mediterranean is on the mezzanine of a prestigious, well-established Salamanca wine shop (with branches in Paris and Kiev) that bills itself as the largest in Europe; it offers "well-prepared, imaginative" dishes served by a "lovely, friendly staff", but since the international "wines are very impressive", with a two-story display of some 4,500 bottlings, oenophiles often opt for teaming up a tipple or two - priced at less than the usual restaurant markup - with tapas at the bar.

Príncipe de Viana ◐ 🅂 *Basque/Navarraise* 26 | 18 | 25 | VE

Chamartín | Manuel de Falla 5 | (34-91) 457-1549

"They don't take risks" at this "classic" Basque-Navarraise in Chamartín, but "top ingredients" and "extremely fresh, tasty and delicate food" make it "one of Madrid's perennial greats"; an older crowd appreciates the comfortable split-level space and serious service and can cope with the "pricey" tabs.

Santceloni 🅂 *Mediterranean* 28 | 25 | 28 | VE

Chamberí | Hotel Hesperia | Paseo de la Castellana 57 | (34-91) 210-8840 | www.restaurantesantceloni.com

Voted No. 1 for Food in Madrid is star chef Santi Santamaría's (of the acclaimed Can Fabes outside Barcelona) "fantastic", "cutting-edge" Med that's "never over the top" in the Hotel Hesperia; the staff is the "best", plus there's a "great wine list, good sommelier advice" and a "chic" white skylit setting that provides well-spaced tables and "lots of privacy"; not surprisingly, such an "extraordinary experience" is "very, very expensive."

Sergi Arola Gastro 🅂 *Mediterranean* 25 | 22 | 23 | VE

Chamberí | Calle Zurbano 31 | (34-91) 310-2169 | www.sergiarola.es

Sergi "Arola is synonymous with innovation and excellence" declare devotees of this chef and showman who owns this new Chamberí Mediterranean where Manuel Berganza is manning the stoves and producing "*fantastico*", "foamy" cuisine that's served in a minimalist setting with modern art; portions can be "small (but Arola has said it takes a lot of food to make a small dish)", and prices will make you "gasp", but gastronomic groupies are buzzing.

Viridiana ◐ 🅂 *International* 26 | 18 | 21 | VE

Retiro | Juan de Mena 14 | (34-91) 523-4478 | www.restauranteviridiana.com

Fans of chef-owner Abraham García and his "innovative-in-all-senses" International near Retiro Park say he's been doing "superb" "fusion cuisine in his own inimitable style for nigh on 20 years", making it almost "impossible not to be surprised here"; an "attentive professional" staff presides over a black-and-white setting dominated by stills from the Buñuel film for which it is named; considered "one of Madrid's best", it's "worth taking out a mortgage for."

Zalacaín 🅂 *International* 27 | 24 | 27 | VE

Salamanca | Álvarez de Baena 4 | (34-91) 561-4840 | www.restaurantezalacain.com

"It's seldom that a restaurant can keep its standards up for more than 30 years", but this "winner" in Salamanca has; "innovative" International cuisine using the best seasonal ingredients is served by an "excellent professional" staff in a "handsome" setting with salmon-colored walls and dark wood; you'll need "mucho dollars, but you'll see it's a good investment", as it's a gastronomic landmark that "lives up to its large reputation"; P.S. "jackets and ties are mandatory for gents."

FOOD	DECOR	SERVICE	COST

Milan

TOP FOOD RANKING

	Restaurant	Cuisine
29	Il Luogo di Aimo e Nadia	Italian
28	Sadler	Italian
27	Ristorante Cracco	Italian
25	Da Giacomo	Seafood/Tuscan
	Boeucc	International/Italian
	Il Teatro	Italian/Mediterranean
24	Joia	Vegetarian
	Armani/Nobu	Japanese
	Dongio'	Calabrian
	Bebel's	Italian/Mediterranean
23	Acanto	International/Italian
	Giannino	Italian
	La Veranda	International/Italian
	Park	Italian/Mediterranean
	Ristorante Teatro*	Italian
	Dal Bolognese	Emilian
22	Trattoria Milanese	Milanese
	Innocenti Evasioni	Italian

Acanto *International/Italian* 23 25 21 VE

Repubblica | Hotel Principe di Savoia | Piazza della Repubblica 17 | (39-02) 6230-2026 | www.hotelprincipedisavoia.com

"Not your typical hotel restaurant" assert aesthetes about this "charming and full of grace" "old-world" room in the Principe di Savoia, featuring "fantastic" creative Italian cuisine from rising chef Paola Budel, a protégé of celebrated Gualtiero Marchesi; N.B. a post-Survey renovation, expansion and addition of a garden dining terrace may outdate the above Decor score.

Armani/Nobu *Japanese* 24 22 21 VE

Montenapoleone | Via Pisoni 1 | (39-02) 6231-2645 | www.armaninobu.it

"What could possibly be more chic" than this "internationally acclaimed" Japanese with a Peruvian accent housed in a stylish Armani shop in the heart of the fashion district in Montenapoleone?; "excellent", "inventive" and "artistic" cuisine, "hip" Eastern decor with screens and natural wood and a "stylish crowd" lead customers to conclude "beautiful food, people and ambiance" but "terrible prices."

Bebel's *Italian/Mediterranean* 24 19 20 E

Brera | Via San Marco 38 | (39-02) 657-1658

This long-standing, popular Italian-Med on the edge of the Brera district serves "fantastic authentic" grilled meat, fish and pizzas to locals like Miuccia Prada; the narrow room has art nouveau accents and stained-glass windows, plus there are "wonderful market displays" of the day's "fresh vegetables, seafood and cheeses"; N.B. closed Wednesdays.

* Indicates a tie with restaurant above

FOOD | DECOR | SERVICE | COST

Bice ☒ *Tuscan* 22 | 19 | 21 | VE

Montenapoleone | Via Borgospesso 12 | (39-02) 7600-2572 | www.bicemilano.it

"Good things never change" at this 1926 Montenapoleone Tuscan, the original "flagship" of a third-generation, family-run franchise; "loyal patrons" like its "reliable", "classic" cuisine and "chic" clientele and setting, but cynics shrug at the "rich, tourist-trap" prices and conclude "better for ogling - I kept tripping over all the tall models' feet - than eating."

Boeucc *International/Italian* 25 | 22 | 24 | VE

Duomo | Piazza Belgioioso 2 | (39-02) 7602-0224 | www.boeucc.com

With over "300 years of experience", this "distinguished" 1696 Italian-International near the Duomo excels with "excellent" "classic" dishes, a "wine list that's a bible of Italian vintages", "impeccable service" and an "exquisite setting" with vaulted ceilings; a few say it's "stuffy", but "power brokers and beautiful people" pronounce it "the only choice for business dinners and special occasions"; N.B. closed Saturdays.

Da Giacomo *Seafood/Tuscan* 25 | 20 | 23 | E

Porta Vittoria | Via Pasquale Sotto Corno 6 | (39-02) 7602-3313

The "seafood-laced spaghetti is a triumph" at this long-standing Tuscan fish house near Porta Vittoria, but you can also order *bistecca alla fiorentina* complemented by a "serious" wine list that's strong on that region's reds; an "in" crowd of fashionistas and arty types frequents the gracious space with arches and mosaic-tiled floors.

Dal Bolognese ☒ *Emilian* 23 | 19 | 20 | E

Repubblica | Piazza della Repubblica 13 | (39-02) 6269-4843

This hot Emilian next door to the stylish Hotel Principe di Savoia is a "posh" "place to see and be seen", just like its legendary flagship in Rome; foodies may fume about "unexciting" cuisine, but that doesn't stop fashionistas from praising the "delightful" dishes, then hitting its smoky bar, surveying the scene and declaring it a "must when in Milan."

Dongio' ☒ *Calabrian* 24 | 19 | 20 | E

Porta Romana | Via B. Corio 3 | (39-02) 551-1372

Located in Porta Romana, where fashionistas from nearby Prada offices and techies from Yahoo mingle, is this welcoming Calabrian trattoria that's also a favorite of foodies who praise the "fine" homemade pastas; it's "simple" and "noisy", but that's "part of its charm."

Giannino ◐ *Italian* 23 | 20 | 21 | E

Repubblica | Via Vittor Pisani 6 | (39-02) 6698-6998 | www.giannino.it

A Milan landmark since 1899, this Italian has changed hands (and even addresses), but its current Repubblica incarnation still offers "excellent" traditional fare and "first-class service"; its "cool New York-style interior" and expansive terrace are also a "hangout" for "beautiful women and soccer players."

Il Luogo di Aimo e Nadia ☒ *Italian* 29 | 20 | 28 | VE

Bande Nere | Via Montecuccoli 6 | (39-02) 416-886 | www.aimoenadia.com

Voted No. 1 for Food in Milan is Aimo and Nadia Moroni's "superb from start to finish", "innovative" and expensive Italian with top-notch ingredients, "sparkling, fresh" flavors, the "best wine list" and "incredible service"; it's a "bit out of the way" in Bande Nere and some don't care for "the room decorated with modern art", but proponents proclaim don't let that keep you from "one of the most rewarding eating experiences of your life."

Il Teatro ☒ *Italian/Mediterranean* 25 | 26 | 26 | VE

Montenapoleone | Four Seasons Hotel | Via Gesù 8 | (39-02) 7708-1435 | www.fourseasons.com/milan

"Everything is exceptional" at this Italian-Med in the Four Seasons Hotel - from chef Sergio Mei's "superb creative cuisine" and "excellent wines" to the "reliably efficient" service and "warm, comfortable" and "serene setting"; of course, it's so "blindingly expensive", "it will cost you your shirt", but you're in Milan, so "just visit Zegna for another."

Innocenti Evasioni ☒ *Italian* 22 | 20 | 20 | E

Certosa | Via Privata della Bindellina | (39-02) 3300-1882 | www.innocentievasioni.com

At this intimate Italian in Certosa there's "excellent", "innovative cuisine", an "extensive wine list" and "friendly but discreet service"; the "warm and welcoming", rustically "romantic" room with well-spaced tables overlooks "a wonderful garden" with Asian accents and adds to the opinion that dining here is "a treat for all the senses."

Joia ☒ *Vegetarian* 24 | 18 | 24 | VE

Porta Venezia | Via Panfilo Castaldi 18 | (39-02) 2952-2124 | www.joia.it

Wags wager the "best place to go with a model on a diet" is probably chef-owner Pietro Leemann's "very pricey" vegetarian in Porta Venezia, where "beautifully presented" "creative" cuisine "with a lively twist" is served in a wood-and-stone setting that reflects his attraction to an Asian aesthetic.

La Veranda *International/Italian* 23 | 26 | 25 | VE

Montenapoleone | Four Seasons Hotel | Via Gesù 8 | (39-02) 7708-1478 | www.fourseasons.com/milan

The less-formal sister of the Four Seasons' Il Teatro is this Italian-International in Montenapoleone, the center of Milan's fashion scene; "good across-the-board" is the verdict on "excellent food" (with light choices for the style-conscious clientele), a "gracious" staff and an "airy setting" with frescoes and a "great view" of a cloistered courtyard.

Park, The ☒ *Italian/Mediterranean* 23 | 25 | 23 | VE

Duomo | Park Hyatt Milan | Via Tommaso Grossi 1 | (39-02) 8821-1234 | www.milan.park.hyatt.com

On the ground floor of the luxurious Park Hyatt Milan, this Italian-Mediterranean makes a strong "modern" design statement with expanses of cool, cream travertine marble and black leather banquettes; "creative and delicious" dishes and "the nicest staff in town" add up to a "high-end" and "enjoyable" experience.

Ristorante Cracco ☒ *Italian* 27 | 22 | 24 | VE
(fka Cracco-Peck)

Duomo | Via Victor Hugo 4 | (39-02) 876-774

Chef Carlo Cracco is no longer affiliated with the nearby prestigious gourmet shop Peck, but his experimental recipes and innovative techniques continue to make this "top-class" Italian a "temple of modern cuisine"; a "wonderful wine list" and an "amazingly knowledgeable staff" are added pluses; a few fault the cellar setting, but most maintain the elevated eating experience offsets it and the "expensive" prices.

NEW Ristorante Teatro alla Scala - Il Marchesino *Italian* 23 | 23 | 22 | E
(fka Ristorante alla Scala)
Piazza della Scala | Teatro alla Scala | Via Filodrammatici 2 | (39-02) 7209-4338 | www.ilmarchesino.it
What could possibly be more "convenient for a night at the opera" than this "memorable" new Italian right in La Scala that's owned by top toque and music lover Gualtiero Marchesi?; its "elegant", talk-of-the-town design includes a dramatic open kitchen, towering granite columns and splashes of scarlet.

Sadler *Italian* 28 | - | 24 | VE
Navigli | Via Ascanio Sforza 77 | (39-02) 5810-4451 | www.sadler.it
"One of the best restaurants in town" is what supporters say about this "wonderful" Italian "institution" that after 21 years in a tiny Navigli space has moved to new digs in that same neighborhood; celebrity chef-owner Claudio Sadler's "excellent", "creative" cuisine with "well-balanced flavors" is complemented by an extensive wine list and a "friendly and efficient staff."

Trattoria Bagutta *Lombardian/Tuscan* 22 | 19 | 19 | E
San Babila | Via Bagutta 14 | (39-02) 7600-2767 | www.bagutta.it
Since 1924, this big, "vibrant" San Babila trattoria has been feeding cultural icons and business leaders from a Lombardian-Tuscan menu, and the result has been "consistently good over the years", particularly the "wonderful pastas and antipasti"; the frescoed setting is "charming", but the alfresco-oriented advise "sit in the garden if the weather permits."

Trattoria Milanese *Milanese* 22 | 19 | 21 | E
Duomo | Via Santa Marta 11 | (39-02) 8645-1991
If you want to "eat where the locals eat", head for this family-run Milanese trattoria near the Duomo that dates back to 1933 and is known for its "great classic dishes" like osso buco with risotto or *cassoeula* (pork, sausage and cabbage stew); the brick-arched, stone-columned setting is as "typical" and "authentic" as the cooking.

	FOOD	DECOR	SERVICE	COST

Moscow

TOP FOOD RANKING

	Restaurant	Cuisine
25	Mario	Italian
24	Jeroboam	French
	Palazzo Ducale	Italian
23	Café Pushkin	French/Russian
	Cantinetta Antinori	Tuscan
22	Vogue Café	International
21	Bistrot	Italian
	Cheese	Italian
	Uzbekistan	Uzbeki/Chinese/Arabic
20	Galereya	International
	Shinok	Ukrainian
	Vanil	French/Japanese
19	White Sun of the Desert	Uzbeki/Chinese/Arabic
	Scandinavia	Scandinavian

Bistrot ◐ *Italian* 21 21 17 VE

Savvinskaya naberezhnaya | Bolshoi Savvinskiy pereulok 12/2 | (7-495) 248-4045 | www.restsindikat.com

The setting and menu of the award-winning Bistrot in Italy's Forte dei Marmi inspired this collaboration in the up-and-coming neighborhood of Savvinskaya naberezhnaya between the owner of the aforementioned Tuscan and some Russian restaurateurs; the result is a "great looking" re-created two-storied villa with a courtyard and fountain, serene white-and-cream decor, working fireplaces and candlelight that's a backdrop for "very good food" from The Boot; but wallet-watchers note "as always, Moscow restaurants are overpriced."

Café Pushkin ◐ *French/Russian* 23 27 23 E

Tverskaya | Tverskoy bulvar 26a | (7-495) 739-0033 | www.cafe-pushkin.ru

This "delicious", "classic" Russian-French "must" is set in a "richly decorated mansion" in Tverskaya that's overseen by an "attentive", graceful staff that's been trained by a ballet-master; the "magical" multilevel space consists of a first floor decorated like a "beautiful" 19th-century chemist's shop that's open 24/7 so "you can indulge in caviar and champagne at 6 AM", and a "more expensive" and formal "upstairs Imperial library" where jackets are required; either way, it's "high-priced and touristy", but most say don't miss the chance to hang with an "illustrious" clientele of "movers, shakers and mafia."

Cantinetta Antinori ◐ *Tuscan* 23 23 20 VE

Arbat | Denezhny pereulok 20 | (7-495) 241-3771 | www.antinori.it

"The latest hangout for oligarchs" is this "fashionable" Tuscan in the Arbat, an affiliate of the Florence-based namesake original; Antinori family wines (100 by the bottle and 30 by the glass) are complemented by "superb" "authentic" cuisine and a rustic-chic setting with a fireplace; for some "it's hard to justify the price", but sybarites cite the "buzz" and say "when you're sick of sour cream and borscht, this is the place."

Cheese ◐ *Italian* 21 | 20 | 17 | VE

Tsvetnoy Boulevard | Sadovaya-Samotechnaya ulitsa 16/2 | (7-495) 650-7770 | www.cheese-restaurant.ru

So you've always wanted to know what it's like to sit inside a huge, hollow chunk of cheese? well, here's your chance because that's what the first-floor decor of this Italian near Tsvetnoy Boulevard looks like; an open kitchen turns out expensive, "high-quality" dishes like octopus carpaccio and "great pasta"; for a less-cheesy experience, head for the more conventionally decorated burgundy-colored dining room upstairs.

Galereya ◐ *International* 20 | 21 | 18 | E

Boulevard Ring | Petrovka ulitsa 27 | (7-495) 937-4544 | www.cafegallery.ru

"If you like beautiful women who are taller than you are" and "would give Claudia and Giselle inferiority complexes", then head to the Boulevard Ring and one of the "trendiest" spots in town owned by Russian restaurant czar Arkady Novikov; the "beautifully presented" International food is "fine" and the gallery-like space with changing artwork is dramatic, but the "crowd is even better" and it's open 24/7; "it costs an arm and a leg", but scenesters sniff "who cares?"

Jeroboam ☒ *French* 24 | 25 | 23 | VE

Tverskaya | Ritz-Carlton | Tverskaya 3 | (7-495) 225-8888 | www.ritzcarltonmoscow.ru

You definitely have to have champagne tastes to afford this "spectacularly expensive" French in the new "puttin' on the Ritz" Ritz-Carlton next to the Kremlin; German top toque Heinz Winkler's "excellent" lightened menu is complemented by a world-class wine list that includes a collection of rare Pétrus vintages and is served in a "voluptuously elegant" soaring setting done in glass, steel and marble.

Mario ◐ *Italian* 25 | 15 | 19 | VE

Presnya | Klimashkina ulitsa 17 | (7-495) 253-6505

Voted No. 1 for Food in the city and judged by many to be the "best Italian" in town, this split-level spot in Presnya offers "excellent" pasta and fish dishes; outside there's an expansive summer garden and Ferraris and Lamborghinis in the parking lot, inside there's glam owner Tatiana Kurbatskaya and a clubby, salon vibe that attracts rich young Russians who all seem to know each other; "prices are outrageous" and the "service is like the weather, but the kitchen is Gibraltar."

Palazzo Ducale ◐ *Italian* 24 | 22 | 21 | VE

Tverskaya | Tverskoy bulvar 3/1 | (7-495) 789-6404

"Great pasta for the price of caviar" can be had at this über-expensive, "authentic" Italian in Tverskaya run by the owner of Mario; while a few fume about it being a "poseur paradise", most maintain a "wine list strong on Tuscan reds", "top-notch service" and "rich decor" evocative of a Venetian palace with paintings, mirrors, chandeliers and a gilded, gondola-shaped bar make it "a good place for romantic dinners."

Scandinavia *Scandinavian* 19 | 16 | 18 | E

Tverskaya | Malye Palashevsky pereulok 7 | (7-495) 937-5630 | www.scandinavia.ru

A "popular expat place" in Tverskaya that's "consistently good" is this Scandinavian with a "varied menu" that ranges from herring to halibut;

a "friendly" staff presides over a "sleek, chic" but cozy Swedish country house setting, and in summer its "famous garden" with a less-expensive menu is "one of the best outdoor hangouts in Moscow."

Shinok ◐ *Ukrainian* 20 | 23 | 18 | E

Presnya | 1905 Goda ulitsa 2 | (7-495) 255-0888 | www.shinok.ru

To say this 24-hour Ukrainian in Presnya has the most "unique decor of any restaurant in the world" may be an understatement since it consists of a glassed-in "faux farmhouse in the center" filled with "live domestic animals" like cows, hens and horses tended to by a lady who sits and knits when not otherwise occupied with her charges; the rustic food is "filling" and "satisfying", but clearly it plays second fiddle to the setting.

Uzbekistan ◐ *Uzbeki/Chinese/Arabic* 21 | 25 | 20 | E

Tsvetnoy Boulevard | Neglinnaya ulitsa 29/14 | (7-495) 623-0585 | www.uzbek-rest.ru

This Uzbeki/Chinese/Arabic near Tsvetnoy Boulevard shares space and the same menu with its sister restaurant, The White Sun of the Desert; a "cavernous" palatial space filled with sofas, pillows and carpets makes guests "feel like sultans" and encourages lingering over "tasty" dishes; a summer garden and belly dancing add to the indolent atmosphere.

Vanil *French/Japanese* 20 | 19 | 18 | VE

Kropotkinskaya | Ostozhenka ulitsa 1/9 | (7-495) 202-3341 | www.novikovgroup.ru

Admirers enamored of this "trendy" French-Japanese fusion in posh Kropotkinskaya assert "if you bring your better half here for a date, all your sins will be forgotten", thanks to pricey but "very good" food and a comfortable, candlelit modern setting with brick walls, banquettes and views of the reconstructed 19th-century Christ the Savior Cathedral.

Vogue Café ◐ *International* 22 | 19 | 19 | E

Bolshoy Theatre | Kuznetsky most ulitsa 7/9 | (7-495) 623-1701 | www.novikovgroup.ru

Not surprisingly, given its moniker and affiliation with the Russian magazine of the same name, the "fashionable" flock to this "trendy" International, another venue from Moscow restaurant magnate Arkady Novikov, located near the Bolshoi Theatre; a few sniff it's more for "meeting than eating", but proponents praise the "stylish" setting and "very good food" that's fairly priced for "such quality."

White Sun of the Desert, The ◐ *Uzbeki/Chinese/Arabic* 19 | 23 | 18 | E

Tsvetnoy Boulevard | Neglinnaya ulitsa 29/14 | (7-495) 209-6015 | www.bsp-rest.ru

Named after and inspired by a cult Soviet film, this Uzbeki/Chinese/Arabic theme restaurant near Tsvetnoy Boulevard shares space and the same menu with its sibling, Uzbekistan; a kitschy setting - a tree trunk, life-size papier-mâché soldiers and wizened hookah smokers - is the bizarre backdrop for "fresh and authentic" dishes that feature some "startling options" like an "entire roast lamb on a spit" that you can pre-order.

FOOD | DECOR | SERVICE | COST

Munich

TOP FOOD RANKING

	Restaurant	Cuisine
27	Tantris	French/International
25	Vue Maximilian	Bavarian/International
	Schuhbeck's Restaurant	Bavarian/Mediterranean
	Boettner's	International
24	Königshof	French/International
	Mark's	Mediterranean/International
	Dallmayr	Mediterranean/Seafood
23	Sushibar	Japanese
	Retter's	German/International
	Acquarello	Italian
22	Paulaner am Nockherberg	German
	Käfer-Schänke	Italian/International
	Hippocampus	Italian
	Austernkeller	French/Seafood
	Restaurant Einstein	International
21	Mangostin Asia	Pan-Asian
20	Brenner	Mediterranean

Acquarello *Italian* 23 | 15 | 21 | VE

Bogenhausen | Mühlbaurstr. 36 | (49-89) 470-4848 | www.acquarello.com

Touted by some as "the best Italian in town", this small spot in residential Bogenhausen draws diners with "excellent" fare that "reflects the creativity of the chef", an expansive wine list and a "knowledgeable" staff; despite its "good reputation", though, detractors cite "too-expensive" eats and "kitschy decor."

Austernkeller *French/Seafood* 22 | 19 | 21 | E

Innenstadt | Stollbergstr. 11 | (49-89) 298-787 | www.austernkeller.de

This "favorite" in the Altstadt section of Innenstadt has been serving up "quality" French cuisine for more than 30 years; the "cellar" setting is "romantic", and the service is reliably "friendly", but the "highlight" that keeps regulars returning is "fantastic seafood", such as "excellent lobster Thermidor" and (as the name indicates) some of "the best" oysters in town – including a platter of 24 featuring four varieties in season.

Boettner's S *International* 25 | 22 | 26 | VE

Innenstadt | Pfisterstr. 9 | (49-89) 221-210 | www.boettners.de

For a "terrific slice of old Munich", locals head to this elegant Innenstadt International (in a "great location" in the historic Altstadt section) that's been run by the same family for more than a century; its "innovative chef brings the world to" German palates with his "grand selection of specialties", and the "attentive, competent" staff also helps ensure that its "beautiful" interior is the "perfect place for a really good meal."

	FOOD	DECOR	SERVICE	COST

Brenner *Mediterranean* — 20 | 23 | 20 | E

Innenstadt | Maximilianstr. 15 | (49-89) 452-2880 | www.brennergrill.de
Set behind the opera house, in Innenstadt, this former royal stable has been restored and modernized, creating a bright, expansive space with "big" pillars and vaulted ceilings; the "unparalleled" interior is divided into "various dining areas", with chefs at a "large open grill" cooking up Med specialties for a chic clientele that "enjoys" the "satisfying" fare.

Dallmayr *Mediterranean/Seafood* — 24 | 20 | 21 | E

Innenstadt | Dienerstr. 14-15 | (49-89) 213-50 | www.dallmayr.de
An Innenstadt "institution", this "upmarket" venue features a "gourmet emporium" downstairs that's "akin to a food museum" thanks to a "tremendous selection of delicacies", some of "the finest coffee" in town and a champagne-and-oyster bar for "hedonists" seeking "paradise"; "upstairs", there's a "top-notch restaurant" serving "delicious" Mediterranean and seafood dishes, which are complemented by a "posh" setting and "smart" service - but "don't expect to get a table without a reservation, even for lunch."

Hippocampus *Italian* — 22 | 21 | 21 | E

Bogenhausen | Mühlbaurstr. 5 | (49-89) 475-855 | www.hippocampus-restaurant.de
"Anyone with a hippocampus" will remember that it's expensive joke jesters about this Italian in Bogenhausen, but "always fresh" and "absolutely delicious" cuisine keeps the place "quite popular"; the "exquisite" setting consists of dark-walnut paneling, marble floors and bronze art nouveau lamps, as well as a torch-lit terrace in summer.

Käfer-Schänke *Italian/International* — 22 | 20 | 19 | E

Bogenhausen | Prinzregentenstr. 73 | (49-89) 416-8247 | www.feinkost-kaefer.de
"Excellent Italian food" and "out-of-the-ordinary" International dishes are served in an "old-world", country house-style dining area or in one of 12 "beautiful" private rooms at this "classic" in suburban Bogenhausen; the service is generally "friendly", even if it "sometimes takes too long" when things get "hectic", but "great people-watching" helps pass the time; P.S. "don't miss their gourmet store downstairs", "the ultimate German delicatessen."

Königshof *French/International* — 24 | 21 | 24 | E

Innenstadt | Hotel Königshof | Karlsplatz 25 | (49-89) 551-360 | www.geisel-hotels.de
With "superior" New French-International creations courtesy of chef Martin Fauster and "accommodating" service from a "discreet" staff, this "fine-dining" venue in the Hotel Königshof offers an "elegant experience" befitting a "king's court"; the "exclusive ambiance" is enhanced by "plush" design details, a dramatic view of Innenstadt's Karlsplatz and live piano music on Friday and Saturday evenings; P.S. the prix fixe "gourmet dinner, including wines with each course, is spectacular."

Lenbach *International* — 18 | 20 | 18 | E

Innenstadt | Ottostr. 6 | (49-89) 549-1300 | www.lenbach.de
"Hip comes to Munich" in the form of this 19th-century Innenstadt palace-turned-"modern"-urban ode to the Seven Deadly Sins, thanks

to the "über-trendy" design of Sir Terence Conran; a "fast", "friendly", "pretty" staff serves International dishes (including "great sushi") that are "varied" and "fanciful" - though some quip "you may need to view them with a magnifying glass"; the "catwalk atmosphere" and late-night hours also help keep it "in vogue."

Mangostin Asia *Pan-Asian* 21 | 19 | 16 | E

Thalkirchen | Maria-Einsiedel-Str. 2 | (49-89) 723-2031 | www.mangostin.de

"Unusual atmosphere and unusually delicious" Pan-Asian fare make it "easy to think you're in a different country" at this Thalkirchen "jewel" near the zoo, where "authentic", "attractive" dishes are delivered to a trio of Japanese-, Thai- and Colonial-style dining rooms (or outside in the beer garden); some cynics say "it's past its prime" and find the service "lacking", but most maintain it's "a real joy", especially for its "great" dinner and Sunday brunch buffets.

Mark's *Mediterranean/International* 24 | 21 | 24 | VE

Innenstadt | Mandarin Oriental | Neuturmstr. 1 | (49-89) 2909-8862 | www.mandarinoriental.com

"Inspired" Med-International cuisine is "perfectly executed and flawlessly" delivered by a "well-trained, friendly" staff at this "awesome place" in the Mandarin Oriental hotel in Innenstadt; a few find the "quiet, elegant" dining room a "little boring" and say the "surreal prices" make for "excessive" tabs, but the monthly changing, six-course menu (including wine) and the special late-night, three-course dinner offered during the Opera Festival in summer are especially "worth a try."

Paulaner am Nockherberg *German* 22 | 20 | 18 | M

Giesing | Hochstr. 77 | (49-89) 459-9130 | www.nockherberg.com

The Paulaner brewery folks are behind the "authentic Bavarian feel" of this "typical beer garden" in Giesing, and they continue to have one of the largest Oktoberfest tents each year (it's "enormous", as are all those "liter brews everyone's drinking"); suds aside, though, the moderately priced, "good German" fare - such as "well-made" and well-priced Weißwurst and roast pork - is itself "worth stopping" for.

NEW **Restaurant Einstein** *International* 22 | 20 | 22 | E

(fka Fleming's Koscher Restaurant)

Innenstadt | St.-Jakobs-Platz 18 | (49-89) 202-400-333 | www.einstein-jakobsplatz.de

Though the owner and name have changed, the menu and chef remain the same at this International in the Innenstadt Jewish community center that bills itself as the only glatt kosher restaurant in Bavaria; wags wager that since the "tasty traditional" "food is excellent", "it looks like the chef cooks with a high IQ"; N.B. closed for Friday dinner and all day Saturday.

Retter's S M *German/International* 23 | 18 | 22 | E

Innenstadt | Frauenstr. 9 | (49-89) 2323-7923 | www.retters.de

Oenophile Nicole Retter has opened this German-International restaurant/wineshop in Innenstadt, and while the cuisine is "creative" and "inspired" (often by the ingredients in the adjacent Viktualienmarkt, or food market), it's the potential "great pairings" with any of 300 "excellent" selections by the bottle and 25 by the glass that's generating the buzz; the setting is a handsome, wood-paneled townhouse with ample garden seating in summer.

Schuhbeck's Restaurant in den Südtiroler Stuben ☒ *Bavarian/Mediterranean* 25 | 20 | 25 | VE

Innenstadt | Platzl 6 + 8 | (49-89) 216-6900 | www.schuhbeck.de

"Traditional Bavarian cuisine" is given a "contemporary Mediterranean cutting edge" (read: "not so heavy") at this gourmet spot, owned by "famous" TV-chef Alfons Schuhbeck, just next door to the Hofbräuhaus in Innenstadt; "clever" food combinations, "exceedingly attentive" service and a "superb" wine selection may come at a price that's even "beyond expense-account" status, but it adds up to one of "the best restaurants in Munich" for a truly "adult dining" experience.

Sushibar *Japanese* 23 | 19 | 21 | E

Innenstadt | Maximilianstr. 34 | (49-89) 2554-0645 ☒
Schwabing | Marschallstr. 2 | (49-89) 3889-9606
www.sushibar-muc.de

Like the name says, sushi is showcased here at this small specialist that some say serves the "freshest raw fish in town", including sashimi; the setting is light, modern and urbane, and the location is in one of the quieter quarters of tourist hot spot Schwabing; N.B. the Maximilian Strasse offshoot opened post-Survey.

Tantris ☒☒ *French/International* 27 | 23 | 26 | VE

Schwabing | Johann-Fichte-Str. 7 | (49-89) 361-9590 | www.tantris.de

Austrian chef Hans Haas incorporates regional influences and culinary trends at his "outstanding" French-International out in Schwabing, earning it the ranking of No. 1 for Food in Munich; his "superb" daily changing prix fixe menus are paired with sommelier Paula Bosch's "inspired wines" and complemented by "remarkable service" ("you'll feel like a king!"), so though a few fault the "truly weird" "over-the-top" decor and "outrageous" prices, most insist "you get what you pay for" at this "classic."

Vue Maximilian *Bavarian/International* 25 | 23 | 25 | VE

Innenstadt | Hotel Vier Jahreszeiten Kempinski | Maximilianstr. 17 | (49-89) 2125-2125 | www.kempinski-vierjahreszeiten.com

This venue in the historic Hotel Vier Jahreszeiten Kempinski takes its name from the wonderful view of Maximilian Strasse, the city's most beautiful and exclusive boulevard; the redone interior, a lighter, less "stuffy" room than what went before, is a "lovely" but "very expensive" backdrop for "top-notch" Bavarian-International cuisine, which relies on local and seasonal ingredients.

FOOD | DECOR | SERVICE | COST

Paris

TOP FOOD RANKING

	Restaurant	Cuisine
28	Taillevent	Haute Cuisine
	Le Cinq	Haute Cuisine
	Guy Savoy	Haute Cuisine
	L'Astrance	New French
	Pierre Gagnaire	Haute Cuisine
	L'Ambroisie	Haute Cuisine
	Alain Ducasse	Haute Cuisine
	L'Atelier de Joël Robuchon	Haute Cuisine
	Le Grand Véfour	Haute Cuisine
	Les Ambassadeurs	Haute Cuisine/New French
27	Lasserre	Haute Cuisine
	Michel Rostang	Classic French
	La Braisière	Gascony
	Le Bristol	Haute Cuisine
	Dominique Bouchet	Haute Cuisine
	Le Meurice*	Haute Cuisine
	Le Pré Catelan	Haute Cuisine
	Relais d'Auteuil	Haute Cuisine
26	Apicius	Haute Cuisine

Alain Ducasse au Plaza Athénée ☒ *Haute Cuisine* — 28 | 27 | 27 | VE

8e | Plaza-Athénée | 25, av Montaigne (Alma Marceau/Franklin D. Roosevelt) | (33-1) 53-67-65-00 | www.alain-ducasse.com

The legendary Alain Ducasse serves up "a meal of a lifetime" at his Paris flagship, an "*ancien régime* meets high-tech" setting in the Plaza-Athénée; "from the amuse-bouches to the delightful candy cart" and tea made from "live herbs snipped by white-gloved waiters", the Haute Cuisine is "probably similar to what the angels are eating", while "exceptional" service "without the starch" makes each diner feel like "the most important client in the world"; it's all "divine", and if the bill seems "hellish", consider it "tuition toward [learning] the art of eating."

Apicius ☒ *Haute Cuisine* — 26 | 26 | 26 | VE

8e | 20, rue d'Artois (George V/St-Philippe-du-Roule) | (33-1) 43-80-19-66 | www.restaurant-apicius.com

It's easy to "fall in love" with "movie-star-handsome" chef-owner Jean-Pierre Vigato and his Haute Cuisine establishment, a "stunning" mansion in the centrally located 8th with "spectacular decor" and a "hidden garden", plus "welcoming service" that's "close to perfection"; "but the food trumps all", "combining the very best of the French classics with creative modern influences"; in short, supporters swear this place "outshines" the rest, though "alas, it's impossible to get a reservation."

* Indicates a tie with restaurant above

	FOOD	DECOR	SERVICE	COST
Dominique Bouchet *Haute Cuisine*	27	21	24	VE

8e | 11, rue Treilhard (Miromesnil) | (33-1) 45-61-09-46 | www.dominique-bouchet.com

Although it's "hidden" in the upper 8th, those who find this Haute Cuisine haven declare it "delivers 100% on the promise of greatness reflected in Bouchet's résumé", which includes Les Ambassadeurs; a "joy of a man", the chef-owner makes "creative preparations" of French classics while steering clear of trendy "foams and froths"; converts also compliment the "modern but warm interior" and "polite, attentive service from English-speaking waiters"; so, travelers, take note: "this is the food that you went to Paris for."

	FOOD	DECOR	SERVICE	COST
Guy Savoy, Restaurant *Haute Cuisine*	28	25	27	VE

17e | 18, rue Troyon (Charles de Gaulle-Etoile) | (33-1) 43-80-40-61 | www.guysavoy.com

Clearly, his "ventures in Las Vegas haven't distracted" chef-owner Guy Savoy - his "modern", "elegantly understated" Rue Troyon flagship remains "consistently superior in every way"; the "innovative" cooking "brings Haute Cuisine as close to art as it can come", the "formal but friendly" service hits a "high watermark" ("the staff all but spoon-fed us") "and - unusual for a big-name chef - M. Savoy often is actually at the restaurant"; yes, they charge "ridiculous prices", but since "you can't take it with you, leave some of it here."

	FOOD	DECOR	SERVICE	COST
La Braisière *Gascony*	27	19	23	E

17e | 54, rue Cardinet (Malesherbes) | (33-1) 47-63-40-37

The "quiet contented murmurings" attest to the "masterful" cuisine found in this "hidden gem" for "imaginative" Gascon gastronomy in the 17th, with connoisseurs claiming it offers "more value for the money than the better-knowns"; the "neutral" decor was recently redone, but the ambiance is still "cozy" and "down-to-earth", while the "relaxed service encourages you to linger over your meal and savor every bite."

	FOOD	DECOR	SERVICE	COST
L'Ambroisie *Haute Cuisine*	28	27	26	VE

4e | 9, pl des Vosges (Bastille/St-Paul) | (33-1) 42-78-51-45 | www.ambroisie-placedesvosges.com

It's like "dining in a nobleman's home" at this "smoothly run", "aptly named" Haute Cuisine haven "serving food of the gods" along with a "top flight wine list" that helps to "rationalize" the "damage the bill inflicts"; "the most intimate of Paris' grand restaurants" (only 40 seats), it's also possibly the "toughest table in town" - and beware of "being exiled to the back room" - but "who wouldn't want to be king of the Place des Vosges, even just for a few hours?"

	FOOD	DECOR	SERVICE	COST
Lasserre *Haute Cuisine*	27	28	28	VE

8e | 17, av Franklin D. Roosevelt (Franklin D. Roosevelt) | (33-1) 43-59-02-13 | www.restaurant-lasserre.com

Experience "elegance personified" at this "old-world" "orchid-filled" establishment in an 8th-arrondissement mansion; combining "great classics with innovations", chef Jean-Louis Nomicos' "brilliant" Haute Cuisine bags bushels of compliments, as does the "flawless" staff, but the real raves are for the "fabulously '60s" technical touches, "from the James Bond entrance by the mini-lift" to the "unique open roof" (it's the "best topless place in town!"); "it all adds up to one magical evening for which you'll pay - but without the sense of being robbed."

L'Astrance S M *New French* 28 | 22 | 27 | VE

16e | 4, rue Beethoven (Passy) | (33-1) 40-50-84-40

"Young, passionate" chef/co-owner Pascal Barbot "manages to wow the most blasé palates" with "inventive" New French cuisine that's "otherworldly", "intellectual" and always "surprising" (especially at dinner, when the "no-choice" tasting menu is the only option) at this "hard-to-get-into" table in the 16th, where a near-"flawless" staff with a "personal touch" services the small, "sophisticated" room; aesthetes argue "they could rethink the decor, but with bookings two months in advance, why - and when?"

L'Atelier de Joël Robuchon ◐ *Haute Cuisine* 28 | 24 | 24 | VE

7e | Hôtel Pont Royal | 5, rue de Montalembert (Rue du Bac) | (33-1) 42-22-56-56 | www.joel-robuchon.com

In the tony 7th, the idolized chef's "Asian-sleek" "canteen for the rich" has them queuing at the door, then sitting "on a stool at a counter" ("singles welcomed") and watching the kitchen turn out "sublime", "cutting-edge" Haute Cuisine; tapas-size portions offer "a great way to sample the offerings" from the Robuchon repertoire, though the "hearty of appetite" must be "prepared to pay a fortune"; cynics snap the staff, while "attentive", displays "typical French insouciance", but the only really "irksome" item is the no-reservations policy (except for very early and very late).

La Tour d'Argent M *Haute Cuisine* 25 | 28 | 26 | VE

5e | 15-17, quai de la Tournelle (Cardinal Lemoine/Pont-Marie) | (33-1) 43-54-23-31 | www.latourdargent.com

Defiant (and dominant) devotees "don't care if it's considered uncool" - this Haute Cuisine table "is still one of the most magical of Parisian places", with its "spectacular views of Notre Dame"; "make sure you ask for a window table when you book, and for heaven's sake order the pressed duck" "with its numbered certificate" - though new chef Stéphane Haissant has "finally updated" the menu with some "excellent" options, served by an initially "haughty", but truly "outstanding staff"; so let the grouches grimace she's "a grande dame in decline" - this tower remains "a reason to sell off your worldly goods for one meal here before you die."

Le Bristol *Haute Cuisine* 27 | 28 | 27 | VE

8e | Hôtel Le Bristol | 112, rue du Faubourg St-Honoré (Miromesnil) | (33-1) 53-43-43-40 | www.lebristolparis.com

When an "extravagant experience" is in order, this "special-night-out kind of place" in the 8th is "close to perfect", with "two separate dining rooms, depending upon the season": an oak-paneled, "sumptuous circular room" in winter and an "exquisite" garden in summertime; chef Eric Frechon's "phenomenal", "cutting-edge" Haute Cuisine is worth the "ooh-la-la" prices, "particularly for those who like strong tastes in original combinations", while the "exceptional" service extends to "a silver tray of cleaning items" in case a customer should splash gravy on his recommended jacket.

Le Cinq *Haute Cuisine* 28 | 29 | 28 | VE

8e | Four Seasons George V | 31, av George V (Alma Marceau/George V) | (33-1) 49-52-71-54 | www.fourseasons.com/paris

"Come here for the meal of your life" swoon sated surveyors who promise this Haute Cuisine table in the George V, voted Tops in Decor and Service, is "perfect in every way", from the "delectable", oft-"adventurous" menu to the "exquisite" classic decor with "vases of flowers everywhere" to the "surprisingly friendly service", "as personal as it is professional" (even offering "a box of reading glasses" to farsighted diners); yes, this "splendid splurge" "will just about rob you of every last euro", but "the experience is so wonderful, somehow one doesn't mind"; N.B. the Food score doesn't reflect the recent replacement of chef Philippe Legendre by Eric Briffard (Elysées).

Le Grand Véfour ☒ *Haute Cuisine* 28 | 29 | 28 | VE

1er | Palais Royal | 17, rue de Beaujolais (Palais Royal-Musée du Louvre) | (33-1) 42-96-56-27 | www.grand-vefour.com

Chef Guy Martin's "exquisite" Haute Cuisine offers "a glorious feast for the senses in the midst of old-world luxury" at this "mythic address" in the 1st; "dripping with atmosphere", the "exceptional setting", a gilded box of a room with a painted ceiling and brass plaques engraved with the names of its celebrated clientele (Colette, Maria Callas), is animated by a staff that's "professional, courteous and welcoming"; true, this "royal treatment needs a royal treasury" when the bill comes - but "it meets each and every expectation."

Le Meurice ☒ *Haute Cuisine* 27 | 28 | 27 | VE

1er | Hôtel Meurice | 228, rue de Rivoli (Concorde/Tuileries) | (33-1) 44-58-10-55 | www.meuricehotel.com

"One of the great French chefs in one of Paris' prettiest dining rooms" sums up "the Haute Cuisine experience" at the Hôtel Meurice; loaded with luxe items like truffles and caviar, "culinary wizard" Yannick Alléno's "food is just exquisite", and "the cuisine's matched" by the "balletlike service" "gliding" within the "grand, gorgeous" and "gilded" space recently redone with Philippe Starck's silver chairs and abstract glass sculpture; "yes, it's expensive" - but "the experience is magnificent."

Le Pré Catelan ☒M *Haute Cuisine* 27 | 28 | 26 | VE

16e | Bois de Boulogne, Route de Suresnes (Pont-de-Neuilly/Porte Maillot) | (33-1) 44-14-41-14 | www.precatelanparis.com

"Haute Cuisine of the highest order", "impeccable service" and, of course, that "beautiful location" in the Bois de Boulogne - small wonder that a "phenomenal dining experience" awaits at this "elegant, enduring" classic; though recently redone in contemporary tones of beige, bronze and gray, the decor retains its "magical" imperial aura; even advocates allow the "prices are budget-busting", but "cost be damned" - "lunch in the garden on a summer afternoon is pure bliss."

Les Ambassadeurs M *Haute Cuisine/New French* 28 | 29 | 28 | VE

8e | Hôtel de Crillon | 10, pl de la Concorde (Concorde) | (33-1) 44-71-16-16 | www.crillon.com

The "sumptuous" "gold and marble" surroundings of the Crillon hotel are "like being inside a jewel box", a "perfect showplace" for the "incredibly inventive" New French Haute Cuisine of chef Jean-François

Piège (who has "enchanted" "serious foodies" ever since he was at Alain Ducasse); the 1,100-label wine list is "*extraordinaire*", the service is "choreographed to perfection" while remaining "refreshingly friendly" and though the experience may "relieve you of many euros", "you get a lot for the price"; P.S. "the lunch menu at 88€ is a delight" – and a relative deal.

Michel Rostang ☒ *Classic French* 27 | 24 | 27 | VE

17e | 20, rue Rennequin (Péreire/Ternes) | (33-1) 47-63-40-77 | www.michelrostang.com

"Where charm and sophistication intersect", you find chef-owner Michel Rostang's "chic" table in the 17th, whose "every detail is perfect", from the "superb" cuisine ("rich, rich" "but delicious none the same") to the "charming maitre d'" and "flawless staff" to the "wood-paneled beauty" of the decor; yes, it's "a bit too pricey" – but after 30 years, this is "still among the best of the Classic French" establishments; P.S. "in season, ask to be truffled for the entire meal."

Pierre Gagnaire ☒ *Haute Cuisine* 28 | 25 | 27 | VE

8e | Hôtel Balzac | 6, rue Balzac (Charles de Gaulle-Etoile/George V) | (33-1) 58-36-12-50 | www.pierre-gagnaire.com

"Let your senses explore uncharted territory" during a "breathtaking meal" at this "brilliant", completely "unforgettable" Haute Cuisine haven in the 8th, serving what many describe as "the most innovative food" in Paris ("Pierre Gagnaire is to gastronomy what Picasso was to contemporary art"); yes, the master's "science experiment"-like creations, while "out of this world", are "too out there" for some; but the "exceptional service" in the discreet dove-gray and blonde-wood dining room makes you "feel like royalty", and to the vast majority, it's "worth every euro (damn dollar!)."

Relais d'Auteuil "Patrick Pignol" ☒ Ⓜ *Haute Cuisine* 27 | 20 | 26 | VE

16e | 31, bd Murat (Michel-Ange-Molitor/Porte d'Auteuil) | (33-1) 46-51-09-54

"If you're adventuresome", join the "well-to-do neighborhood clientele" that congregates at this Haute Cuisine table out toward the Porte d'Auteuil; while "outrageously expensive", it's "one of the best in Paris" for the eponymous chef-owner's traditional French food and "outstanding wine", plus the "warm welcome of Madame Pignol", within the wood-paneled, slightly "dim" setting; a "lovely" experience, all 'round.

Taillevent ☒ *Haute Cuisine* 28 | 28 | 28 | VE

8e | 15, rue Lamennais (Charles de Gaulle-Etoile/George V) | (33-1) 44-95-15-01 | www.taillevent.com

"You're at home the minute you enter" this "elegant", "spectacular modern art"-adorned townhouse in the 8th, which – though mourning the loss of legendary owner Jean-Claude Vrinat – shines on as Paris' No. 1 for Food and Popularity; guests would "gladly borrow from the kids' college fund" to sample "service that's not just an art form, but a religion" as it delivers chef Alain Solivérès' "classic", sometimes "inventive", but always "decadent and luscious" Haute Cuisine, backed by "a prodigious wine list"; in short, "why wait for heaven, when you can go to Taillevent?"

FOOD | DECOR | SERVICE | COST

Prague

TOP FOOD RANKING

	Restaurant	Cuisine
26	Allegro	Italian/Mediterranean
25	Aquarius	Czech/Mediterranean
	David	Czech/International
	V Zátiší	Czech/International
	Essensia	Eurasian
24	Flambée	International
	U Zlaté Hrušky	Czech/International
	Rybí trh	International/Seafood
	U Modré Ruze	Czech/International
23	U Modré Kachnicky	Czech
	Maze	French
	Kampa Park	International/Seafood
	Mlýnec	International
	Café Imperial	Czech
	Fish*	Czech/Seafood
	Oliva	Mediterranean
	La Perle de Prague	French

Allegro *Italian/Mediterranean* 26 | 24 | 27 | VE

Old Town | Four Seasons Hotel | Veleslavínova 2A | (420) 221-426-880 | www.fourseasons.com/prague

"Not your typical hotel dining" room, this "truly first-rate" Old Town venue "wows" with an "ultimate experience" that's just as "wonderful" "as you'd expect" from the Four Seasons; indeed, it's ranked No. 1 for Food in Prague for "fantastic" Italian-Med cuisine, "beautifully presented" in "a lavish environment" by "charming" staffers; P.S. "come early to get a window seat" for a "particularly" "spectacular view" of "the Vltava River's Charles Bridge" and the "fairy-tale" castle.

Aquarius *Czech/Mediterranean* 25 | 23 | 19 | E

Little Quarter | Alchymist Grand Hotel & Spa | Tržište 19 | (420) 257-286-019 | www.alchymisthotel.com

This Czech-Med is located in the Little Quarter's Alchymist Grand Hotel & Spa, four richly and romantically refurbished 16th-century buildings; "great" cuisine and a "fantastic" setting - a vaulted, mirrored space that opens to a courtyard on one side - make for "an enchanting experience", plus the practial pronounce "the price is very good value"; N.B. there's live music Thursday-Saturday.

Bellevue *Czech/International* 23 | 23 | 24 | VE

Old Town | Smetanovo nábrezí 18 | (420) 222-221-443 | www.zatisigroup.cz

"An incredible dining experience" is in store for guests of this "grand" Old Town venue who enjoy a "magnificent view of the river, Charles Bridge and Prague Castle" as "impeccable" staffers deliver

* Indicates a tie with restaurant above

"delicious", "up-to-date" Czech-International cuisine; some suggest the same can't be said about the somewhat "faded" decor, but more maintain the "elegant setting" is "stylish and romantic", so they'd "happily return again."

Café & Restaurant Imperial *Czech* 23 | 25 | 25 | E

Prague 1 | Prague Imperial Hotel | Na Poříčí 15 | (420) 246-011-600 | www.hotel-imperial.cz

Located in the recently renovated art deco Prague Imperial Hotel, on the edge of Old Town, is this "beautiful" new Czech offering breakfast, lunch and dinner; the "glorious setting" - Moorish-inspired tiles, elaborate towering columns, marble tables, expansive windows and a high ceiling - is an over-the-top backdrop for "food that is very good for this part of the world."

David *Czech/International* 25 | 22 | 24 | E

Little Quarter | Trzište 21 | (420) 257-533-109 | www.restaurant-david.cz

For "a fantastic trip to another era", step inside the "country-style dining rooms" of "this relaxing haven" "tucked into a hillside" "in a quiet corner of" the Little Quarter, where "carefully prepared", "delicious" Czech-International cuisine (including "hearty, traditional game dishes") is "augmented by an excellent wine list"; fans also "can't say enough good things about" the "gracious" service and "charming", "tiny space", insisting you're guaranteed a "most memorable" meal.

Essensia *Eurasian* 25 | 25 | 25 | VE

Little Quarter | Mandarin Oriental Hotel | Nebovidská 459/1 | (420) 233-088-888 | www.mandarinoriental.com

"A cut above the competition" and "one of the best" "places to take business clients" is this Eurasian in the Mandarin Oriental Hotel, which is housed in a converted 14th-century monastery and courtyard; "brilliant" cuisine is served in a series of five "beautiful", softly lit vaulted rooms by an "attentive staff"; it's pricey, but pragmatists point out "expensive eating in Prague would be considered cheap in London or Paris."

Fish ◐ *Czech/Seafood* 23 | 21 | 20 | E

Little Quarter | U Luzického semináre 42 | (420) 257-531-799 | www.kolkovna.cz

"The name doesn't lie" at this Czech seafooder in the Little Quarter with its "well-presented" and "delicious upscale" fin fare, particularly the *plateau des fruits de mer*; the "snazzy" underwater-like setting with its enormous circular aquarium and silver vaulted ceiling is "uptempo", and in summer its "lovely" riverside garden offers views of the Old Town and Charles Bridge.

Flambée *International* 24 | 25 | 26 | E

Old Town | Husova 5 | (420) 224-248-512 | www.flambee.cz

"Truly a treasure", this "gem" of an International in Old Town is manned by a "hospitable", "attentive staff" that "puts you at ease" the moment you descend to its "distinctive Gothic cellar", which "dates back to the 11th century" but has been updated with modern accents; "great chef" Dušan Jakubec's "culinary art reaches the highest standards" and when coupled with the "impeccable service" and "striking" setting more than justifies the "astronomical" prices.

Kampa Park *International/Seafood* 23 | 24 | 22 | E

Little Quarter | Na Kampe 8B | (420) 296-826-102 | www.kampapark.com

Perennially "popular", this "renowned" "favorite" "beautifully located" on the Little Quarter's "historic Kampa Island" (right "under the famous Charles Bridge") offers two terraces for "contemporary fine dining at the water's edge"; loyalists also laud the "lovely" interior and "inventive", "top-quality" International menu, but surveyors are split on the "efficient" staffers, with some swearing they "couldn't be more friendly" and others opining that they "need an attitude adjustment."

La Perle de Prague ☒ *French* 23 | 25 | 22 | VE

New Town | Tancící Dum | Rašínovo nábrezí 80 | (420) 221-984-160

"Both the beautiful views and good cocktails will make you giddy" at this "fantastic location atop" 'The Dancing House', architect Frank "Gehry's whimsical" creation in New Town; some say the "surroundings are far better than" the "overpriced" fare, but more insist the "excellent" New French cuisine - offered in a "funky", "contemporary" interior with "pampering service" - "matches the splendor of" the "amazing" vistas of the winding river, Old Town and Prague Castle on the horizon.

Maze *French* 23 | 20 | 21 | E

Old Town | Hilton Prague Old Town | V Celnici 7 | (420) 221-822-300 | www.gordonramsay.com/mazeprague

The latest offshoot of one of Gordon Ramsey's London establishments is this new contemporary French, in the refurbished Hilton Prague Old Town, with "excellent" à la carte and small-plates tasting menus and "attentive service"; even those who object to the "antiseptic decor" and "premium prices" admit that those criticisms do not keep it from being a "superb business-meal venue."

Mlýnec *International* 23 | 21 | 21 | E

Old Town | Novotného Lávka 9 | (420) 221-082-208 | www.zatisigroup.cz

With its "great location" on a pier "at the foot of the Charles Bridge" in Old Town, this "superb" spot offers "very nice views" along with "wonderful food" and "top-flight service"; the "interesting" International menu includes some local dishes, and the "good-quality wine list" features some Moravian selections.

Oliva ☒ *Mediterranean* 23 | 21 | 22 | M

New Town | Plavecká 4 | (420) 222-520-288 | www.olivarestaurant.cz

In-the-know locals have taken to this "stylish" Mediterranean in New Town that, like the name says, pays homage to the olive and its oil in some of its "delicious" dishes and also in the pale-green color on its walls; "fresh food", "friendly owners" and fair prices make many say they "wish this favorite were in their neighborhood."

Pravda *International* 22 | 23 | 22 | E

Old Town | Parízská 17 | (420) 222-326-203 | www.pravdarestaurant.cz

Set "on smart" "Parízská Street, next to the Old-New Synagogue" "in the Jewish Quarter" of Old Town, this "classy" International "celebrates tastes from all over the world"; the "simple", "modern, open space offers views of the bustling" thoroughfare ("during the summer months the outdoor tables" provide particularly "great people-watching"), and "excellent cocktails" add to the "lively", "trendy" vibe.

	FOOD	DECOR	SERVICE	COST
Rybí trh	24	19	23	E
U Modré Kachnicky	23	23	21	E
U Modré Ruze	24	21	22	E
U Zlaté Hrušky	24	23	21	M
V Zátiší	25	20	23	E

Rybí trh *International/Seafood*

Old Town | Týnský Dvur 5 | (420) 224-895-447 | www.rybitrh.cz

You might not expect "simply divine" "seafood in a land-locked country", but you'll find it at this Old Town "fish market/restaurant"; its "excellent" International menu offers a "great choice" of "creatively prepared" fin fare, the savvy staff has a knack for "fulfilling unspoken wishes" and the "understated" interior is appropriately decorated with "nice aquariums"; as for the cost, surveyors wax philosophical, saying "what can you do? - quality is expensive."

U Modré Kachnicky *Czech*

Little Quarter | Nebovidská 6 | (420) 257-320-308

U Modré Kachnicky II *Czech*

Old Town | Michalská 16 | (420) 224-213-418

www.umodrekachnicky.cz

"Those wanting to taste the true local flavor" of Prague "must stop" for a "cultural experience" 'At the Blue Duckling' (the English translation of this "quaint" and "cozy" Little Quarter "stalwart's" name); like "someone's grandmother's house", its "rustic" rooms are "quirky" but "comfortable", providing a "charming" setting in which to "relish" "exceedingly well-done" "homestyle Czech cooking" with "an emphasis on game" and "regional specialties", proffered by a "warm, gracious" staff; N.B. there's a newer offshoot in Old Town.

U Modré Ruze *Czech/International*

Old Town | Rytírská 16 | (420) 224-225-873 | www.umodreruze.cz

"Step down into" the "lovely subterranean setting" of this "first-class establishment" (whose name means 'At The Blue Rose') "located in a 15th-century cellar" in Old Town, where "authentic Czech cuisine" and some International offerings are backed up by a "small but reliable wine list" with "good [domestic] selections" at "moderate prices"; the "charming" barrel-vaulted stone walls lend "a medieval feel" to the setting, which is made all the more "romantic" by "a great piano player."

U Zlaté Hrušky *Czech/International*

Castle Quarter | Nový svet 3 | (420) 220-514-778 | www.uzlatehrusky.cz

"A golden find", this "cozy, quaint" "sleeper a little off the beaten track" in the Castle Quarter, "on a beautifully picturesque and quiet cobbled street", boasts a "menu offering traditional Czech food" (including "wonderful game and fish") as well as some International fare; the "pleasantly furnished, comfortable" interior "immediately transports one to another century" and is peopled by "lots of locals", all enjoying the "authentic" cuisine and "gracious service."

V Zátiší *Czech/International*

Old Town | Liliová 1 | (420) 222-221-155 | www.zatisigroup.cz

Think all Czech "cuisine is heavy"? - you'll "think again" after sampling the "excellent local specialties" "exquisitely cooked" with an International, "modern take" at this "lovely restaurant" "just off Betlemska Square" in the Old Town; its "feasts are fit for bohemian royalty" thanks to "creative" cuisine, "first-rate wines", "impeccable service" and an "intimate" setting; a few feel "there are equally good places" charging "much less money", but most insist it's "a truly wonderful dining experience" worthy of "a prompt return visit."

FOOD | DECOR | SERVICE | COST

Rome

TOP FOOD RANKING

	Restaurant	Cuisine
26	Vivendo	Italian
	La Pergola	Italian/Mediterranean
	Alberto Ciarla	Seafood
	La Rosetta*	Seafood
	Agata e Romeo	Roman
	Mirabelle	Italian
	Sora Lella*	Roman
25	Al Vero Girarrosto	Tuscan
	Quinzi e Gabrieli	Seafood
	Antico Arco	Italian
	L'Altro Mastai*	Mediterranean
	Baby	Neapolitan/Mediterranean
24	Il San Lorenzo	Neapolitan/Seafood
	Il Convivio Troiani	Italian
	Piperno	Roman/Jewish
	Da Tullio	Tuscan
	I Sofa' di Via Giulia	Italian/Mediterranean
	Antica Pesa	Roman
	Camponeschi	Italian
	Glass Hostaria	Italian
	Vecchia Roma*	Roman
	Mamma Angelina	Italian/Seafood

Agata e Romeo ⊠ *Roman* 26 | 22 | 24 | VE

Esquilino | Via Carlo Alberto 45 | (39-06) 446-6115 | www.agataeromeo.it

"Superior ingredients" help make for "brilliant" "creative" interpretations of Roman cuisine at this tiny, "family-run delight" where wife Agata Parisella is the chef, husband Romeo Caraccio is the host-sommelier and daughter Mariantonietta delivers the delicious goods; "a perfect meal" is complemented by an "outstanding wine list" and a "chic but cozy setting", so other than the expensive tabs, the only downside is the near-the-train-station locale in Esquilino; N.B. closed Saturdays and Sundays.

Alberto Ciarla ◐⊠ *Seafood* 26 | 20 | 24 | VE

Trastevere | Piazza San Cosimato 40 | (39-06) 581-8668 | www.albertociarla.com

The "food practically flops off your plate and into your mouth it's so fresh" at this "great", old famous seafooder that specializes in raw fish (*crudo*) in Trastevere; some pickier surveyors find the decor - with its black walls, sofas and mirrors - "tacky", but proponents counter that the space has been updated and insist "if you get the right spot it can be romantic", or alternatively, just head for the outdoor area.

* Indicates a tie with restaurant above

Al Vero Girarrosto Toscano ◐ *Tuscan*

FOOD	DECOR	SERVICE	COST
25	20	23	E

Via Veneto | Via Campania 29 | (39-06) 482-1899 | www.alverogirarrostotoscano.com

This "wonderful" Tuscan right behind the Via Veneto and only steps from Villa Borghese is "a true classic" that's been serving "abundant antipasti" and "the best steak Florentine" since 1969; "gracious service" and a "warm" and "cozy" basement setting combine to make customers feel "at home the minute they walk in."

Antica Pesa ◐ *Roman*

FOOD	DECOR	SERVICE	COST
24	20	20	E

Trastevere | Via Garibaldi 18 | (39-06) 580-9236 | www.anticapesa.it

"Be sure to bring an empty stomach" to this "terrific" Roman "taste treat" in Trastevere; though it dates back to 1922, its menu focuses on "excellent" modern interpretations of traditional ingredients like lamb; the "wonderfully romantic" setting - contemporary frescoes on the walls, a fireplace, enchanting garden and exceptional wine cellar - has become a celebrity hang since its recent association with Robert De Niro's Tribeca Film Festival and the new Rome Film Fest.

Antico Arco ◐ [S] *Italian*

FOOD	DECOR	SERVICE	COST
25	20	23	E

Gianicolo | Piazzale Aurelio 7 | (39-06) 581-5274 | www.anticoarco.it

It's "off the beaten path", up in the Janiculum Hill near the American Academy, but the "young and the beautiful are all here" at this popular, "innovative" Italian with "decently priced" "divine food", "exceptional wines" and "gracious service"; it's "minimalist in a NYC Village kind of way", there's a "hip vibe" and the experience is "special from entrance to exit."

Baby [M] *Neapolitan/Mediterranean*

FOOD	DECOR	SERVICE	COST
25	24	25	E

Parioli | Aldrovandi Palace Hotel | Via Ulisse Aldrovandi 15 | (39-06) 321-6126 | www.aldrovandi.com

This "great" Neapolitan-Med in the Aldrovandi Palace Hotel in Parioli is the baby of star chef Alfonso Iaccarino, whose celebrated flagship restaurant, Don Alfonso 1890, is near the Amalfi Coast; "excellent", "creative" cuisine is "enriched by the finest ingredients" and served by a "great staff" in a "fantastic setting", whose "crisp white decor" and "view of a swimming pool" "make it feel like the Caribbean" and a "great date place."

Camponeschi ◐ [S] *Italian*

FOOD	DECOR	SERVICE	COST
24	23	23	VE

Piazza Farnese | Piazza Farnese 50 | (39-06) 687-4927 | www.ristorantecamponeschi.it

"*Bella Italia* at its very best" is found at this "top-class", "they-do-everything-well", expensive Italian facing Michelangelo's Palazzo Farnese; there's "excellent food" and "superb service", and the "elegant setting", with hand-painted boiserie, is one of the most "romantic" rooms in Rome, but sitting outside looking at the exquisite square is also appealing; N.B. their wine bar next door serves the family's own wines along with about 500 others.

Dal Bolognese [M] *Emilian*

FOOD	DECOR	SERVICE	COST
23	19	20	E

Piazza del Popolo | Piazza del Popolo 1 | (39-06) 361-1426

"All of Rome passes through" this 65-year-old Emilian "classic" and its alfresco patio "perfectly positioned" on the Piazza del Popolo; "great" traditional food like *tagliatelle al ragu* and the trolley of boiled meats merits almost as much attention as the "wonderful people-watching"; a few snipe that "service can be snippy", but for most it's a "must."

Da Tullio ☒ *Tuscan* 24 | 18 | 23 | E

Piazza Barberini | Via San Nicola da Tolentino 26 | (39-06) 474-5560 | www.tullioristorante.it

The "simple" Tuscan near Piazza Barberini, that's "been in business forever for good reason", serves well-prepared" "authentic" dishes like *ribollita* and *bistecca alla fiorentina,* which are complemented by a "great" regional wine list.

Glass Hostaria Ⓜ *Italian* 24 | 21 | 21 | E

Trastevere | Vicolo del Cinque 58 | (39-06) 5833-5903 | www.glass-hostaria.com

Foodies hit this modern Italian "hot spot" in Trastevere for chef Cristina Bowerman's "outstanding" "inventive" cuisine, which ranges from pasta stuffed with crispy cured pork cheeks to a foie gras burger; it's also "trendy" because it's "immensely design oriented", with "great-looking" ultramodern glass and metal elements combined with the antique brick and wood of its original 17th-century structure.

Harry's Bar ◐☒ *International/Mediterranean* 18 | 21 | 20 | VE

Via Veneto | Via Veneto 150 | (39-06) 484-643 | www.harrysbar.it

"Bellini, panini and people-watching on the Via Veneto" are the point at this "clubby", 1958 International-Med "watering hole" "where you can feel the history"; it's "overpriced", "there are loads of Yanks" and some say "it's lost some of its charm", but most maintain "everyone has to go here at least once just to say they've been."

Il Convivio Troiani ☒ *Italian* 24 | 22 | 23 | VE

Piazza Navona | Vicolo dei Soldati 31 | (39-06) 686-9432 | www.ilconviviotroiani.com

The brothers Troiani "have consistently had one of Rome's best restaurants" is what surveyors say about this Italian near Piazza Navona; "outstanding" traditional and creative dishes, "attentive service" and a "soigné setting" - three rooms with frescoes or paintings - add up to a "pleasurable" evening; of course, the bill adds up to "very expensive."

Il San Lorenzo ◐☒ *Neapolitan/Seafood* 24 | 20 | 21 | E

Campo dei Fiore | Via dei Chiavari 4/5 | (39-06) 686-5097

This Neapolitan seafood specialist "conveniently located" near Campo dei Fiore "wins a lot of points" for its "excellent food", "respectful service" and "very pretty" multilevel dining rooms dotted with modern art, as well as an oyster-shell-studded bar where you can sip a glass of champers with your crustaceans; no wonder most maintain it's a mainstay "when you are in Rome."

Imàgo *International/Italian* 24 | - | 25 | VE
(fka Hassler Rooftop)

Trinitá dei Monti | Hotel Hassler | Trinità dei Monti 6 | (39-06) 699-34726 | www.hotelhasslerroma.com

"A must for everyone who can afford it" declare devotees of the Hotel Hassler's International-Italian with "a commanding rooftop view of the Eternal City" from its "perch atop the Spanish steps"; "delicious" "creative food, an impressive wine list" and "wonderful service" also add to the "romantic", "rarefied experience"; it's a "super-swank" hang for "the glitterati", so be prepared for "over-the-top prices for an over-the-top" evening; N.B. a post-Survey redo and name change make for a more modern and luminous setting, but the rest remains the same.

I Sofa' di Via Giulia ◐ *Italian/Mediterranean* 24 | 22 | 22 | E

Piazza Farnese | St. George Hotel | Via Giulia 62 | (39-06) 686-611 | www.stgeorgehotel.it

"Great food" is found at this Italian-Mediterranean in the luxury St. George Hotel, "excellently located" on central Rome's loveliest street, Via Giulia; a "wonderful staff" presides over an elegant setting that mixes minimalist modern decor with classic touches in travertine, plus there's a tranquil courtyard garden for warm-weather dining.

L'Altro Mastai 🅂🄼 *Mediterranean* 25 | 24 | 24 | E

Piazza Navona | Via Giraud 53 | (39-06) 6830-1296 | www.laltromastai.it

Supporters of rising star chef Fabio Baldassarre, a former protégé of La Pergola's acclaimed Heinz Beck, say his Mediterranean near Piazza Navona is among "the best in Rome today"; a "formal" setting with modern art, marble and mosaics is the backdrop for his brand of innovative fine dining; N.B. a move to a new location at Via delle Terme di Traiano, 4a, in the Colosseum area, is scheduled for spring 2009.

La Pergola 🅂🄼 *Italian/Mediterranean* 26 | 26 | 26 | VE

Monte Mario | Cavalieri Hilton | Via Alberto Cadlolo 101 | (39-06) 3509-2152 | www.cavalieri-hilton.it

"A German chef in an American hotel serving Italian-Med food results in one of the finest dining experiences imaginable" assert admirers of Heinz Beck and his "exceptional cuisine" at the Cavalieri Hilton; there's also an "impressive wine list", "outstanding staff" and "beautiful" rooftop room with "an amazing view of Rome"; a few mutter about its "out-of-the-way" Monte Mario locale and "tad-over-the-top" ways - gold cutlery and a "mineral water list with 40 choices" - but they're outvoted.

La Rosetta 🅂 *Seafood* 26 | 20 | 23 | VE

Pantheon | Via della Rosetta 8 | (39-06) 686-1002 | www.larosetta.com

For "mind-blowing" fish with a Sicilian accent, finatics urge you to try this family-owned stalwart with a "wonderful location near the Pantheon", where a "solicitous staff" presides over a "cozy, convivial" setting with frescoes; "prices are insane", but that doesn't prevent a jet-set crowd from streaming through the door.

La Terrazza *Italian/Mediterranean* 23 | 26 | 24 | VE

Trinitá dei Monti | Hotel Eden | Via Ludovisi 49 | (39-06) 4781-2752

There's a "romantic" and "unbelievable" "knockout view of Rome" from this Italian-Mediterranean on the Hotel Eden's rooftop; there's also "wonderful food, wine and service" as well as a "lovely piano bar with great cocktails", so "although prices are as lofty" as the vista, most maintain "it's worth the splurge."

Mamma Angelina *Italian/Seafood* 24 | 18 | 21 | E

Trieste-Salario | Viale Arrigo Boito 65 | (39-06) 860-8928

"*Mamma mia*" exclaim enthusiasts of this long-standing, family-run, "homestyle" Italian, just outside the City Center toward the Salaria, who come for "about-as-good-as-it-gets pasta" and "well-prepared seafood" dishes that are fairly priced for the quality; its classic trattoria decor - mahogany woodwork and marble floors - exudes "the ambiance of *Roma*."

Mirabelle *Italian* 26 | 24 | 24 | VE

Via Veneto | Hotel Splendide Royal | Via di Porta Pinciana 14 | (39-06) 4216-8838 | www.mirabelle.it

An "absolutely spectacular" "view over Rome" and the Villa Medici gardens "caps what is an excellent evening" sigh sybarites about this Italian atop the Hotel Splendide Royal; chef Giuseppe Sestito's "superb" cuisine, "first-class service" and a "beautiful" room make for a "perfect" and "extremely expensive" "marriage."

Piperno Ⓜ *Roman/Jewish* 24 | 18 | 21 | E

The Ghetto | Monte de' Cenci 9 | (39-06) 6880-6629 | www.ristorantepiperno.it

"For the best fried artichokes and stuffed zucchini blossoms", "forget your cholesterol problems" and head for this 1860 Roman-Jewish "must" that's a "bit hard to find" in The Ghetto; the rooms are a "bit worn", but dining out on the small piazza is pleasing.

Quinzi e Gabrieli Ⓢ *Seafood* 25 | 18 | 19 | VE

Pantheon | Via delle Coppelle 5/6 | (39-06) 687-9389 | www.quinziegabrieli.it

"The freshest seafood money can buy in Rome" is found at this "fashionable" fish house, near the Pantheon, where "exquisite", "unbelievably expensive" dishes are served raw or lightly cooked at the table; a "serene" room is decorated with murals of three seaport cities, and there's also appealing outdoor eating for the alfresco-oriented.

Sora Lella Ⓢ *Roman* 26 | 20 | 21 | E

Isola Tiberina | Via di Ponte Quattro Capi 16 | (39-06) 686-1601 | www.soralella.com

This long-standing, "family-run" Roman is set on Isola Tiberina, an island on the Tiber River, and features traditional dishes such as *rigatoni all'amatriciana* as well as more creative ones like leg of lamb with artichokes and pecorino cheese - all backed up by an extensive wine list.

Vecchia Roma *Roman* 24 | 21 | 21 | E

The Ghetto | Piazza Campitelli 18 | (39-06) 686-4604 | www.ristorantevecchiaroma.com

"To feel like you are really in 'Old Rome'", which is what the name means, "come here" to this "wonderful" stalwart, on the edge of the Ghetto, and order "delicious" dishes like "grilled baby calamari"; the interior boasts "beautiful hand-painted murals", but romantics revel in the softly lit, "quiet" piazza where "eating outside is a joy"; N.B. closed Wednesdays.

Vivendo Ⓢ *Italian* 26 | 27 | 25 | VE

Piazza della Repubblica | St. Regis Grand Hotel | Via Vittorio Emanuele Orlando 3 | (39-06) 4709-2736

Voted No. 1 for Food in Rome is this Italian in the "magnificent" St. Regis Grand Hotel, where "exceptional" "creative" cuisine is served by a "flawless staff" in a "lovely", quietly "lavish" room with satin fabrics and contemporary paintings; it all adds up to an experience that's quite expensive and "exquisite in every way."

FOOD | DECOR | SERVICE | COST

Stockholm

TOP FOOD RANKING

	Restaurant	Cuisine
28	Paul & Norbert	French/Swedish
	Wedholms Fisk	Swedish/Seafood
27	Restaurant Mathias Dahlgren	Swedish
	F12	International
26	Lux Stockholm	International/Swedish
	Ulriksdals Wärdshus	Swedish/International
	Vassa Eggen	International
25	Eriks Bakficka	International/Swedish
24	Operakällaren	French/International
	Pontus!	Seafood/Swedish
	Leijontornet	Scandinavian
23	Prinsen	Swedish/French
22	Kungsholmen	International
	Aquavit Grill	Swedish/American
	Den Gyldene Freden*	Swedish
	Eriks Gondolen	French/Swedish

Aquavit Grill & Raw Bar *Swedish/American* 22 | 21 | 20 | VE

City Center | Clarion Hotel Sign | Östra Järnvägsgatan 35 | (46-8) 676-9800 | www.aquavitgrillrawbar.se

Surveyors are split on this newcomer in the Clarion Hotel Sign, an offshoot of Swedish-born chef Marcus Samuelsson's NYC Aquavit original; enthusiasts exclaim over the "excellent" Swedish-New American food and long, sleek "Scandinavian chic setting" that attract the "beautiful people" and make for "a perfect evening", but critics cite "expensive" tabs, "noisy" surroundings and "service that needs to shape up."

Berns Asian *Asian* 19 | 24 | 18 | E

Norrmalm | Berns Hotel | Berzelii Park | (46-8) 5663-2222 | www.berns.se

"You have to love" the "fabulously over-the-top" interior of "this massive place" in Norrmalm; its "trendy, aristocratic" crowd ensures there's always "excitement in the air", but even they admit you "go for the drinks" and "scene", as service is only "adequate" and the "competent" kitchen's Asian fare can sometimes be "an afterthought."

Den Gyldene Freden ☒ *Swedish* 22 | 24 | 23 | E

Gamla Stan | Österlånggatan 51 | (46-8) 249-760 | www.gyldenefreden.se

"Beautiful old-world" 18th-century surroundings define this "charming, historic" Gamla Stan "favorite"; almost "everyone loves this place" for its combination of "cozy" ambiance, traditional local dishes (plus some International offerings) and "efficient service", even if some say it's "too bad" it's "getting a little staid" and "somewhat touristy" of late; P.S. "the Swedish Academy dines there on Thursdays."

* Indicates a tie with restaurant above

Eriks Bakficka ⊠ *International/Swedish* 25 | 17 | 24 | E

Östermalm | Fredrikshovsgatan 4 | (46-8) 660-1599 | www.eriks.se

"Owned by one of Sweden's best chefs", Erik Lallerstedt, "this charming bistro" is "a favorite haunt of locals" in the "expensive residential quarter" of Östermalm - indeed, the "well-heeled" guests seem to "all know each other" as they gather within its "more formal dining room" or "cozier bar section" to enjoy "fine" Swedish-International cuisine; true, it's "a little pricey", but insiders insist it offers "excellent value."

Eriks Gondolen ⊠ *French/Swedish* 22 | 26 | 22 | VE

Södermalm | Stadsgården 6 | (46-8) 641-7090 | www.eriks.se

Though it's the "fantastic atmosphere" and "breathtaking view of Stockholm" (including "spectacular" vistas of "the harbor" and "Old Town") that "really make it stand out", advocates avow you'll also "enjoy a fine meal" of "wonderful" Swedish-French cuisine and "excellent service" at this "great place to watch the sunset", suspended high above Södermalm; even those who feel the "very expensive" fare is "not outstanding" and "only secondary to" the venue's visual delights declare do "come for a drink" and "mingle at the nice bar."

F12 ⊠ *International* 27 | 22 | 24 | VE

Norrmalm | Fredsgatan 12 | (46-8) 248-052 | www.f12.se

A "favorite" for many, this "consistently excellent and stylishly" "mod locale" in Norrmalm is run by "people who care about food" - namely "talented" chef-owners Melker Andersson (a "god in Stockholm") and Danyel Couet, whose "flavorful", albeit very expensive, International fare is served by an "incredibly friendly and helpful staff" in a "first-rate setting"; those who are intimidated by their "innovative" tasting menu can now choose a traditional one or opt for ordering à la carte.

Kungsholmen *International* 22 | 22 | 20 | E

Kungsholmen | Norr Mälarstrand | (46-8) 5052-4450 | www.kungsholmen.com

Swedish restaurant guru Melker Andersson of the highly rated F12 "has done it again" with this "trendy" International in Kungsholmen, right on the waterfront, where patrons mix and match their meal from a variety of seven "upmarket" "gourmet food courts" serving everything from sushi to soups and salads; throw in a "delightful setting" that includes a floating terrace where you can have "drinks by the sea where the sun never seems to set", and it's no wonder a "hip crowd congregates" here.

Leijontornet ⊠ *Scandinavian* 24 | 27 | 23 | VE

Gamla Stan | Victory Hotel | Lilla Nygatan 5 | (46-8) 5064-0080 | www.leijontornet.se

An "authentic medieval room" in an "Old Town cellar" is the "wonderful setting" of this "great place to eat" in Gamla Stan's "small, high-class" Victory Hotel ("don't just eat at the restaurant - stay at the hotel too"); as if the "fabulous" environment weren't enough, you can also expect "splendid art from the kitchen" in the form of "superb" Scandinavian cuisine, served by a "staff that tries hard to please"; no wonder most predict you'll "enjoy the experience."

FOOD	DECOR	SERVICE	COST

Lux Stockholm S M *International/Swedish* 26 | 19 | 22 | E

Lilla Essingen | Primusgatan 116 | (46-8) 619-0190 | www.luxstockholm.com

Set "in a tastefully redone" "old Electrolux building" (hence the name) on Lilla Essingen island, "just outside central Stockholm", this "amazing" venue peopled by a "hip, beautiful staff and clientele" is "so trendy it hurts", but even the "cool atmosphere" "can't match the fabulous", "first-class modern Swedish"-International fare or "warm", "attentive service"; its "spacious dining room" is "beautifully minimalist" to some, "a bit too austere" for others, but all adore the "gorgeous view."

Operakällaren S M *French/International* 24 | 27 | 23 | VE

Kungsträdgården | The Royal Opera House | Karl XII:S Torg | (46-8) 676-5801 | www.operakallaren.se

"One can only say bravo!" about this "magnificent" "landmark" "in the lovely" Royal Opera House that's "so popular it's almost a cliché now" thanks to the hordes of "hip see-and-be-seen" people who "go for the scene" and to "check out the latest fashions"; most report the "grand" "opulent" interior, "delicious" French-International fare and "classic", "formal" service are also "superb", and "worth every penny" of the "astronomical price" here ("no, you can't sing for your supper").

Paul & Norbert S *French/Swedish* 28 | 23 | 25 | VE

Östermalm | Strandvägen 9 | (46-8) 663-8183 | www.paulochnorbert.se

"Truly" a "favorite", this "dining delight" in Östermalm is rated No. 1 for Food in Stockholm on the strength of its "superb" French-Swedish cuisine created by "excellent chef" Norbert Lang; you'll also "enjoy wonderful service" from an "exceptional" staff, a "nice atmosphere" and a "great wine selection", making it a "satisfying" "place for a private, romantic" "meal of a lifetime" - "but bring a lot of krona because you'll need them"; N.B. if you'd like an interactive evening, you can be a cook for the night and prepare your own meal alongside Lang.

Pontus! S *Seafood/Swedish* 24 | - | 23 | VE

(fka Pontus in the Green House)

Norrmalm | Brunnsgatan 1 | (46-8) 5452-7300 | www.pontusfrithiof.com

"Relax and enjoy" a "fantastic" experience at this Swedish seafooder, a bastion of "great dining" whose habitués "humbly bow to owner" Pontus Frithiof and his "artful kitchen" for delivering "delicious" dishes; other pluses are some "reasonably priced gems on the wine list" and a "friendly staff", so admirers advise "if you have the money to spare", "don't miss it"; N.B. post-Survey, the restaurant moved from Gamla Stan to this new location in Norrmalm.

Prinsen *Swedish/French* 23 | 22 | 23 | E

Norrmalm | Mäster Samuelsgatan 4 | (46-8) 611-1331 | www.restaurangprinsen.se

"The food is excellent and the service is accommodating" at this Norrmalm "classic that never disappoints" with its "innovative" Swedish-French fare, whether enjoyed "at one of the outside tables" or within the "impressive interior" of its "more formal" "wood-paneled dining room"; it's a "power-lunch" favorite for "the cognoscenti of the financial industry" as well as a "terrific evening" haunt of "tourists", and though it's "a bit on the expensive side", most insist it "always gives you value for your money."

Restaurant Mathias Dahlgren ☒ *Swedish* 27 | 24 | 26 | VE

City Center | Grand Hôtel | Södra Blasieholmshamnen 6 | (46-8) 679-3584 | www.mathiasdahlgren.com

"The best newcomer in Stockholm" pronounce proponents of this dual venue in the Grand Hôtel from "one of the top chefs in Sweden", Mathias Dahlgren (ex Bon Lloc); the dinner-only main dining room, Matsalen, offers "outstanding" "innovative" cuisine served by a "wonderful" staff in a "sophisticated" yellow-and-gray setting with views of the Royal Palace, and can cost "a little more than you paid for your first car"; "his attention to detail and perfection also apply" to Matbaren, the "less-expensive" bistro that's "an excellent choice for a business lunch or casual dinner."

Sturehof ◐ *Swedish/Seafood* 20 | 18 | 18 | E

Stureplan | Sturegallerian 42 | Stureplan 2 | (46-8) 440-5730 | www.sturehof.com

A "smart", "stylish crowd" of locals and "hip tourists" hails this "huge, fun place" "conveniently located" "in the hub of Stockholm's cool Stureplan district" for its "high-quality" "traditional Swedish" menu with a "seafood specialty" and "friendly, professional" staff (including "sommeliers knowledgeable" about the "nice wine list"); three "lively" bars and a generally "buzzing atmosphere" mean it's "too bustling" "for those who like quiet dining", but "lively" sorts love the "great people-watching" - especially from the "wonderful terrace in summertime."

Ulriksdals Wärdshus *Swedish/International* 26 | 23 | 26 | VE

Solna | Ulriksdals Slottspark | (46-8) 850-815 | www.ulriksdalswardshus.se

"Worth every minute of travel" to its "out-of-the-way" but "choice location" - "in the country by a bay" in the "peaceful" park of Ulriksdals Castle in Solna - this "gem" is "a rite of passage" "when visiting Stockholm" thanks to "excellent" Swedish-International cuisine (including a "fine smörgåsbord" served weekends and holidays); throw in a "superb wine cellar" and "formal" service from a "thoughtful staff" and no wonder enthusiasts insist it's "perfect for festive occasions."

Vassa Eggen ☒ *International* 26 | 17 | 23 | VE

Stureplan | Elite Hotel Stockholm Plaza | Birger Jarlsgatan 29 | (46-8) 216-169 | www.vassaeggen.com

Named after W. Somerset Maugham's novel *The Razor's Edge,* this "egg-stravagant" venue in the Elite Hotel Stockholm Plaza in Stureplan showcases "stunning" International cuisine (gourmets "strongly recommend the five-course dinner with corresponding wines - a rare experience"); still, some find the food "overly fancy", even "a little pretentious", and the service somewhat "impersonal."

Wedholms Fisk ☒ *Swedish/Seafood* 28 | 21 | 26 | VE

Norrmalm | Arsenalsgatan 1 | (46-8) 611-7874 | www.wedholmsfisk.se

"Do not leave Stockholm before" visiting this "old-school" Swedish seafooder on Norrmalm's Nybrokajen wharf, where the "first-rate" "chef rightly trusts his ingredients" (namely, "fresh", "fantastic fish"), which results in "superb, simply prepared" "traditional dishes" that are "not too elaborate" but truly "exceptional"; perhaps "the decor is rather plain" and the "atmosphere quiet" (like a "hospital waiting room" some quip), but the "efficient" staff provides "excellent service" - yet another reason to "book in advance."

FOOD | DECOR | SERVICE | COST

Venice

TOP FOOD RANKING

	Restaurant	Cuisine
27	Vini da Gigio	Venetian
26	Da Ivo	Tuscan/Venetian
	Osteria Da Fiore	Italian/Seafood
	Corte Sconta	Venetian/Seafood
25	Fortuny	Italian
	Club del Doge	Venetian/Mediterranean
	De Pisis*	Italian
	Osteria alle Testiere*	Italian/Seafood
	Al Covo	Seafood
24	Do Leoni	Italian/Seafood
	Fiaschetteria Toscana	Venetian
	La Cusina	Venetian/International
	Cip's Club	Venetian
	Hostaria da Franz	Venetian
	Ai Gondolieri	Venetian
	Antico Pignolo	Venetian/Seafood
	Al Paradiso	Venetian
23	La Terrazza	Italian/International
	Vecio Fritolin	Venetian/Seafood

Ai Gondolieri *Venetian* 24 | 19 | 23 | E

Dorsoduro | Fondamenta de l'Ospedaleto 366 | (39-041) 528-6396 | www.aigondolieri.com

Carnivores who can't catch a break in this seafood-loving city head to this Venetian in residential Dorsoduro, near the Guggenheim foundation, where "only land creatures are served" like the signature calf's liver, plus pork, lamb and "wonderful risottos"; an "impeccable yet warm" staff presides over a "low-key" rustic setting; N.B. closed Tuesdays.

Al Covo *Seafood* 25 | 20 | 23 | E

Castello | Campiello della Pescaria 3968 | (39-041) 522-3812

"Amazingly fresh" and "superb" Adriatic seafood is the focus at this "warm-and-welcoming" stalwart in Castello that's run by a "great" Italo-American couple with "high standards", chef Cesare Benelli and his wife, hostess and pastry chef, "delightful Diane"; the room is small but flower-filled, and there's a dining terrace with a sweet view of the square; N.B. closed Wednesdays and Thursdays.

Al Paradiso *Venetian* 24 | 20 | 21 | E

Rialto | Calle del Paradiso 767 | (39-041) 523-4910

Hidden in the *calli* among the many restaurant tourist traps near the Rialto Bridge is this heavenly little Venetian with "excellent" "authentic" cooking including "wonderful seafood", "great local wines" and "kind service"; the wood-beamed interior is "charming", and a small blue veranda with rattan chairs also appeals.

* Indicates a tie with restaurant above

FOOD | DECOR | SERVICE | COST

Antico Pignolo *Venetian/Seafood*

24 | 22 | 25 | E

San Marco | Calle dei Specchieri 451 | (39-041) 522-8123

"Convenient to St. Mark's Square" is this "good, dependable" Venetian seafooder with a "fantastic wine list", "outstanding service" and a big, beautiful garden for "delightful" outdoor dining; while wallet-watchers warn "bring buckets of euros", the philosophical simply shrug "but that's Venice."

Cip's Club *Venetian*

24 | 25 | 26 | VE

Giudecca | Hotel Cipriani | Isola della Giudecca 10 | (39-041) 520-7744 | www.hotelcipriani.com

Everyone wants to join this "wonderful", dinner-only club in the Cipriani with its "great view of St. Mark's Square" and the lagoon; "go only when the weather is good", "take the hotel's private power boat over" to the Isola della Giudecca, "sit outside on the terrace" and order something from the "tasty" Venetian menu along with "a glass of champagne"; of course, you'll "need a big bank roll", but for most it's a "must."

Club del Doge *Venetian/Mediterranean*

25 | 26 | 26 | VE

San Marco | Hotel Gritti Palace | Campo Santa Maria del Giglio 2467 | (39-041) 794-611 | www.starwoodhotels.com

"Why die when you can go to heaven here?" at this "stunning and elegant" Venetian-Med in the "grand" Hotel Gritti Palace that's "beautifully situated on the Grand Canal"; the "glorious view" from the veranda, "great food" and the "best service" add up to an extremely "expensive" but "transporting experience."

Corte Sconta [S] [M] *Venetian/Seafood*

26 | 17 | 20 | E

Castello | Calle del Pestrin 3886 | (39-041) 522-7024 | www.veneziaristoranti.it

"Unfussy" but "exceptional seafood" from "passionate owners" is the lure at this "off-the-beaten-path" Venetian near the Arsenale, the city's historic shipyard; the round of briny appetizers is legendary and the *moeche* (soft-shell crab) "sublime", leading surveyors to say a "first-rate meal" makes for a "memorable" and expensive evening.

Da Ivo [S] *Tuscan/Venetian*

26 | 21 | 23 | VE

San Marco | Ramo dei Fuseri 1809 | (39-041) 528-5004

It's "cool to arrive by gondola", but this "top" Tuscan-Venetian is also just a five-minute walk from St. Mark's Square; "gracious" chef-owner Ivo Natali prepares "wonderful" dishes like "huge, excellent *bistecca alla fiorentina*" or fresh Adriatic seafood, "pops out of the kitchen to ensure your pleasure" and presides over a "tiny, atmospheric, low-lit" "romantic" room that leads devotees to decree "just leave me here forever."

De Pisis *Italian*

25 | 24 | 25 | VE

San Marco | Il Palazzo at the Hotel Bauer | San Marco 1459 | (39-041) 520-7022 | www.bauervenezia.com

"The view, the food, the romance" and "the gracious service" leave sybarites sighing over this über-"expensive" Italian in the "grand" 18th-century Il Palazzo at the Hotel Bauer; the interior is opulent, and the "breathtaking terrace" vista of the Grand Canal and St. Mark's basin is better than namesake Italian artist De Pisis might have ever imagined.

Do Leoni *Italian/Seafood* 24 | 23 | 23 | E

Castello | Hotel Londra Palace | Riva degli Schiavoni 4171 | (39-041) 520-0533 | www.hotelondra.it

"Excellent cuisine and high-quality service" are the hallmarks of this Italian seafooder in the Hotel Londra Palace; the "beautiful" contemporary interior is stylish but soothing, and in warm weather the terrace is great for "people-watching" and a panoramic view that goes from the Grand Canal to the Lido.

Fiaschetteria Toscana *Venetian* 24 | 17 | 21 | E

Cannaregio | San Giovanni Grisostomo 5719 | (39-041) 528-5281 | www.fiaschetteriatoscana.it

Name to the contrary (it was once an outlet for Tuscan wines), this is a true, family-run Venetian in Cannaregio, and one of the tops in the city, serving "divine dishes" like tagliolini with lobster, risottos and other "fantastic" fish-oriented appetizers and entrees; "the decor is better downstairs, but the staff is charming no matter where you sit" in the "warm", "winning" place; N.B. closed Tuesdays.

Fortuny *Italian* 25 | 26 | 25 | VE
(fka Cipriani)

Giudecca | Hotel Cipriani | Isola della Giudecca 10 | (39-041) 520-7744 | www.hotelcipriani.com

This "fabulous, famous" and "formal" Italian in the Hotel Cipriani recently changed its name but still "has everything that makes Venice memorable - the view, the water, the romance"; the "impressive" experience starts with the "short private shuttle-boat ride from St. Mark's Square" and goes on to an "excellent staff" serving "exquisite" Italian cuisine in a "beautiful" room with mirrors or out on a "magical" terrace; even those who complain about "outrageous prices" urge "eat here once before you die just to say you did."

Harry's Bar *International/Venetian* 19 | 19 | 18 | VE

San Marco | Calle Vallaresso 1323 | (39-041) 528-5777 | www.cipriani.com

It's Cipriani's 1931 "mythic bar", the birthplace of the Bellini and former Hemingway hang in San Marco, and it's still packing "tourists" in, however controversially: the mellow cite the International-Venetian's "history and scene" and say just stick to the signature cocktail, but those no longer wild about Harry hiss "what a disappointment - we came in search of the legendary, found the ordinary and paid stratospherically."

Hostaria da Franz *Venetian* 24 | 18 | 25 | E

Castello | Fondamenta San Giuseppe 754 | (39-041) 522-0861 | www.hostariadafranz.com

"They serve wonderful food and treat you like long-lost rich relatives" at this father-and-son-run Venetian "gem" in Castello, near the Biennale Gardens; "fresh, delicious" dishes, "superb service" and a "great" summertime setting with outdoor tables along a tiny canal make it a "pleaser"; N.B. closed mid-November through mid-February.

La Cusina *Venetian/International* 24 | 24 | 23 | VE

San Marco | The Westin Europa & Regina | Larga XXII Marzo 2159 | (39-041) 240-0001 | www.westin.com/europaregina

This "very good" Venetian-International in The Westin Europa & Regina boasts a "beautiful" backdrop - a "grand view of the Grand Canal" from its terrace and an interior that's a series of elegant, intimate rooms filled with marble and Murano glass.

La Terrazza *Italian/International* 23 | 26 | 24 | VE

San Marco | Hotel Danieli | Riva degli Schiavoni 4196 | (39-041) 522-6480 | www.starwoodhotels.com

Romantics say "request a window table" or eat outside on the terrace at this "absolutely stunning" Italian-International with "spectacular views" of the Grand Canal, the lagoon and the Island of San Giorgio from the rooftop of the "opulent Hotel Danieli"; opinions on the food ("wonderful" vs. "average") and service ("terrific" vs. "stuffy") vary, but there's consensus that the astronomical tab would be "VE even for Bill Gates."

Osteria alle Testiere S M *Italian/Seafood* 25 | 18 | 24 | E

Castello | Calle del Mondo Novo 5801 | (39-041) 522-7220 | www.osterialletestiere.it

An "outstanding" "place for lovers of good fish" is this popular, "minuscule" Italian off Campo Santa Maria Formosa; "wonderfully prepared", "intriguingly flavored" dishes are served by a "top-notch" staff in a casual setting, making enthusiasts exclaim it's "not to be missed."

Osteria Da Fiore S M *Italian/Seafood* 26 | 22 | 24 | VE

San Polo | Calle del Scaleter 2202A | (39-041) 721-308 | www.dafiore.net

Among the very "best in Venice" is the Martin family's "innovative" Italian piscine palace in San Polo that some wish could be the "location of their last meal on earth"; "wonderful" cuisine that's "all about the ingredients", "gracious service" and a "comfortable yet elegant setting" add up to a feeling of "pure joy" for most; N.B. not to be confused with the similarly named Trattoria da Fiore near San Marco or Ristorante Osteria da Fiore in Santa Croce.

Vecio Fritolin M *Venetian/Seafood* 23 | 22 | 23 | E

Rialto | Calle della Regina 2262 | (39-041) 522-2881 | www.veciofritolin.it

They are famous for their *fritolini* (little deep-fried fish) at this "top-notch", "classic" Venetian seafooder near the Rialto bridge, but there are also "delicious pastas", homemade breads and desserts, all served by a "helpful staff"; a "great" Northern Italian wine list and warm, wood-lined 16th-century interior add to the "always-a-pleasure" experience.

Vini da Gigio M *Venetian* 27 | 19 | 25 | E

Cannaregio | Fondamenta San Felice 3628A | (39-041) 528-5140 | www.vinidagigio.com

A "little difficult to find" but "oh what a find" is this family-run Venetian in Cannaregio that's Voted No. 1 for Food in the city; "terrific" "simply and honestly prepared" meat and fish dishes and an "out-of-this-world wine list" are proffered in a "down-to-earth" setting by a "friendly" staff; it's "not the fanciest or most expensive" spot, but it is a "wonderful experience"; N.B. closed Mondays and Tuesdays.

FOOD | DECOR | SERVICE | COST

Vienna

TOP FOOD RANKING

	Restaurant	Cuisine
28	Steirereck	Austrian/International
26	Imperial	Austrian/International
25	Coburg	Austrian/International
24	Demel	Austrian/International
	Walter Bauer	Austrian/International
	Mraz & Sohn	Austrian/International
	Korso bei der Oper	International
	Kim Kocht	Asian/International
	Drei Husaren	Austrian/International
23	Julius Meinl am Graben	Austrian/International
	Zum weissen Rauchfangkehrer	Austrian
22	Österreicher im MAK	Viennese
	DO & CO	Austrian/International
	Plachutta	Austrian
	Goldene Zeiten	Chinese
21	Little Buddha	Asian
	Fabios	Italian/Mediterranean
	Indochine 21*	French/Vietnamese

Coburg *Austrian/International* 25 | 22 | 23 | VE

Innere Stadt | Palais Coburg | Coburgbastei 4 | (43-1) 5181-8800 | www.palaiscoburg.at

"Expensive, but justifiably" so, this Austrian-International in Innere Stadt's "breathtaking" Palais Coburg hotel showcases chef Christian Petz's "excellent" cuisine, paired with "outstanding" selections from an "incredible wine cellar"; a "young but well-trained" staff provides "courteous" service amid an "elegant" setting, and for many, dining on the "beautiful" terrace overlooking the Stadtpark is "unparalleled."

Demel *Austrian/International* 24 | 22 | 18 | E

Innere Stadt | Kohlmarkt 14 | (43-1) 5351-7170 | www.demel.at

"Expand your waistline, thin your wallet" at this "pastry nirvana" on the Innere Stadt's tony Kohlmarkt, where a "fantastic array" of "beautifully decorated" cakes (some 50 kinds) and desserts are shown in "famous window displays"; the Austrian-International menu, by contrast, is "unimpressive", and service can be "iffy", so many prefer to sit back with some "fabulous" "*kaffee und kuchen*" and "watch master bakers at work."

DO & CO Albertina *Austrian/International* 22 | 21 | 20 | E

Innere Stadt | The Albertina | Albertinaplatz 1 | (43-1) 532-9669

DO & CO Stephansplatz *Austrian/International*

Innere Stadt | Stephansplatz 12 | (43-1) 535-3969

www.doco.com

A "reliable mix of Austrian and International cuisine" (including "superb Japanese" dishes) "prepared in front of you", along with "stun-

* Indicates a tie with restaurant above

ning views of St. Stephan's Cathedral" and the beautiful Stephansplatz, attracts a "well-dressed crowd" to this "see-and-be-seen" spot atop the contemporary glass Haas Haus building in Innere Stadt; the "modern, urban" interior has a "NY feel" and the service is "competent" and "friendly"; N.B. it has a younger sibling in the Albertina museum.

Drei Husaren *Austrian/International* 24 | 23 | 23 | VE

Innere Stadt | Weihburggasse 4 | (43-1) 5121-0920 | www.drei-husaren.at

"Everything is top-drawer" at "Vienna's most famous" venue (circa 1933) in Innere Stadt near Stephansplatz, where you "feel like a Kaiser" (but you also better "have his bank account") thanks to "terrific" Austrian-International cuisine, including an "incredible hors d'oeuvre cart", "polite", "efficient" service and a "refined", "old-fashioned" setting with live music; while some find it "stuffy" and "not what it once was", for others it's still a "real experience."

Fabios ☒ *Italian/Mediterranean* 21 | 21 | 20 | VE

Innere Stadt | Tuchlauben 6 | (43-1) 532-2222 | www.fabios.at

"You can always meet the people who count" at this "hot spot" in Innere Stadt, just a short walk from Graben, where "authentic" Italian-Med cuisine is served by a "friendly" staff in a "trendy, modern" space with "large tinted windows", lots of "dark wood", leather and a "simple but elegant" lounge; still, some find the "masculine" setting "oppressive" and the service "overbearing", while wallet-watchers warn you're "paying for the atmosphere" and "good location."

Goldene Zeiten *Chinese* 22 | 21 | 20 | E

Innere Stadt | Dr. Karl Lueger-Platz 5 | (43-1) 513-4747 | www.goldenezeiten.at

This Chinese may be the "best there is in Vienna" say supporters who praise the chef-owner, who peppers his "authentic" menu with elaborate Shanghainese and Sichuan dishes, which are complemented by an extensive wine list that sparkles with some rare Austrian vintages; relocated from the suburbs to Innere Stadt, the bright modern digs feature butter-yellow walls and soaring ceilings that are punctuated by enormous red lamps.

Imperial *Austrian/International* 26 | 26 | 27 | VE

Innere Stadt | Hotel Imperial | Kärntner Ring 16 | (43-1) 5011-0356 | www.starwoodhotels.com

"You're treated like an emperor" at this Austrian-International housed in Innere Stadt's "grand" Hotel Imperial that provides "friendly", "flawless" service and "outstanding" cuisine in a "plush", wood-paneled Victorian room with Hapsburg portraits; a "marvelous pianist adds to the mood" of "old-world elegance and charm", making it a "slice of heaven on earth" for many - albeit at "hellish prices."

Indochine 21 ◐ *French/Vietnamese* 21 | 19 | 19 | E

Innere Stadt | Stubenring 18 | (43-1) 513-7660 | www.indochine.at

Across the street from the Museum für Angewandte Kunst (MAK) in Innere Stadt, this French-Vietnamese is a "nice change of pace" "from Viennese cooking", offering "delectable" dishes with "unusual taste combinations" and "competent" service in a "trendy" yet "comfortable" "cafelike" room with bamboo accents and Buddhist icons; the only complaint is that it's "overpriced."

Julius Meinl am Graben ☒ *Austrian/Mediterranean* | 23 | 17 | 21 | E

Innere Stadt | Graben 19 | (43-1) 532-3334 | www.meinlamgraben.at
For a "culinary adventure", a "cosmopolitan clientele" gravitates to Graben and this "upmarket" Austrian-Med on the second floor of "Vienna's leading gourmet store", which carries nearly "everything the heart desires"; a "courteous staff" serves chef Joachim Gradwohl's "innovative" fare in a "lovely" room with "stunning views" of the street, though some find it hard to "escape the fact that it is a supermarket."

Kim Kocht ◐☒M *Asian/International* | 24 | 18 | 20 | E

Alsergrund | Lustkandlgasse 4 | (43-1) 319-0242 | www.kimkocht.at
A "gourmet experience" awaits at this boîte in Alsergrund near the Volksoper, where chef-owner Sohyi Kim's "inventive" Asian-International cuisine emphasizing organic ingredients is "unbelievably tasty and healthy", and "needs are fulfilled immediately" by a "courteous" staff; "even first-time visitors feel at home" here - those who can get into the "mini" (24-seat) space, that is, which leads some to gripe that it's "impossible to get a table unless you know her well."

Korso bei der Oper *International* | 24 | 25 | 25 | VE

Innere Stadt | Hotel Bristol | Mahlerstr. 2 | (43-1) 5151-6546 | www.luxurycollection.com
For the "best bet after the opera", try this "classic, opulent" nearby venue in Innere Stadt's Hotel Bristol, which showcases celeb chef Reinhard Gerer's "superb" International creations; service is "polished and professional", the wine list is "excellent" and the "beautifully appointed" room evokes "old Vienna" in all its "elegance" - so "don't look at the prices and enjoy a special evening."

Little Buddha ◐ *Asian* | 21 | 23 | 18 | E

Innere Stadt | Lugeck 4 | (43-1) 512-1111 | www.littlebuddhavienna.com
The city recently got its own franchised version of the Paris-based Buddha Bar eatery/nightclub in Innere Stadt; most maintain "the food quality and service vary quite a bit", but the decor - a red, gold and black backdrop dominated by a plethora of baby buddhas and a giant 15-ft. one - is "stunning"; just "bring night-vision goggles, as it's like a cave" in here.

Mraz & Sohn ☒ *Austrian/International* | 24 | 21 | 19 | E

Brigittenau | Wallensteinstr. 59 | (43-1) 330-4594 | www.mraz-sohn.at
This "excellent, high-quality" Austrian-International may be located in the downscale neighborhood of Brigittenau, but foodies flock to the 45-seater to sample the creations of chef Markus Mraz, a molecular gastronomy pioneer in Vienna; the "casual" setting belies such sophisticated touches as a legendary wine list and choice selection of cheeses.

Österreicher im MAK *Viennese* | 22 | 23 | 21 | E

Innere Stadt | Museum für Angewandte Kunst | Stubenring 5 | (43-1) 714-0121 | www.oesterreicherimmak.at
"One of the best chefs in Austria", Helmut Österreicher (ex the highly rated Steirereck), brings *his* culinary art to The MAK (Museum for Applied Arts) at this expansive venue, and the result is "well-done" "traditional and slightly modernized" Viennese food; the "wonderful

location" is only exceeded by the "even greater interior design", which includes soaring ceilings and a chandelier made from 200 wine bottles.

Plachutta *Austrian* 22 | 14 | 19 | E

Hietzing | Auhofstr. 1 | (43-1) 877-7087
Innere Stadt | Wollzeile 38 | (43-1) 512-1577
Nussdorf | Heiligenstädterstr. 179 | (43-1) 370-4125
www.plachutta.at

"If you like *tafelspitz,* you can't go wrong" at this "dependable", "authentic" trio of Austrians where that signature Viennese dish and other "varieties of traditional boiled beef" are "unbeatable", if a bit "expensive"; you feel "like you're in good hands" with a "charming", "helpful" staff that presides over "simple", "bourgeois" digs that are "comfortable" even when they get "noisy and crowded."

Steirereck ☒ *Austrian/International* 28 | 25 | 26 | VE

Landstrasse | Im Stadtpark | Am Heumarkt 2A | (43-1) 713-3168 | www.steirereck.at

"By far the best" restaurant in the city and voted No. 1 for Food here, this Landstrasse landmark is a "fairy-tale" experience, featuring chef Heinz Reitbauer's "exquisite" Austrian-International cuisine, "cheese and bread carts that put others to shame", an "excellent" wine cellar and "first-class" service; the move to its current Stadtpark address "has been a fantastic success", thanks to the "exquisite" renovation of a century-old pavilion into a "knockout" setting with "no shortage of space."

Walter Bauer ☒ *Austrian/International* 24 | 18 | 26 | E

Innere Stadt | Sonnenfelsgasse 17 | (43-1) 512-9871

Regulars have "never been disappointed" by this "hidden gem" in a small medieval house (circa 1505) "on a quiet street" near Stephansplatz in one of the oldest parts of Innere Stadt; a "wide-ranging" Austrian-International menu is complemented by a "superb wine list", an "attentive staff" and an "intimate" setting.

Zum weissen Rauchfangkehrer ☒ M *Austrian* 23 | 20 | 23 | E

Innere Stadt | Weihburggasse 4 | (43-1) 512-3471 | www.weisser-rauchfangkehrer.at

For a "taste of Vienna", fans tout this "lovely old place" (circa 1844) near Stephansplatz offering "outstanding", mostly organic "takes on traditional Viennese fare"; "personable service" and a "classic setting" with lots of "country-style" "charm" also make it "worth a return visit."

Warsaw

TOP FOOD RANKING

	Restaurant	Cuisine
25	Restauracja Polska Tradycja	Polish
	Dom Polski	Polish
23	Restauracja Rubikon	Italian
	U Kucharzy	Polish
	Parmizzano's	Italian
22	Malinowa	Polish
	Michel Moran	French
	Belvedere	International/Polish
21	Qchnia Artystyczna	International
	Boathouse	Italian/Mediterranean
	Oriental	Asian/Sushi
19	Chianti	Italian
	La Bohème	Polish
18	Santorini	Greek

Belvedere *International/Polish* 22 | 26 | 23 | E

Srodmiescie | ul. Agrykola 1 | (48-22) 841-2250 | www.belvedere.com.pl

After "a welcome revamp" of its "stupendous location" - a "grand", "glass-facaded" 19th-century "orangery in Lazienki Park" with an "adjacent open-air terrace" overlooking "lush grounds" - this "classic" "fine-dining" venue in Srodmiescie is now not only "posh but trendy", attracting those who "enjoy people-watching" while "indulging" in "well-executed" Polish-International fare; it's an "excellent" place "for that special dinner", as long as "you have money to throw around."

Boathouse *Italian/Mediterranean* 21 | 17 | 17 | E

Saska Kepa | Wal Miedzeszynski 389a | (48-22) 616-3223 | www.boathouse.pl

"Ideal for larger groups", this spacious ground-floor "haven" "right on the river" in Saska Kepa is "a lovely place to dine" on "excellent" Italian-Med fare; it's especially "noteworthy" "in the summer" when you can choose the "charming outdoor seating" - just "beware the mosquitoes!"

Chianti *Italian* 19 | 19 | 20 | M

Srodmiescie | ul. Foksal 17 | (48-22) 828-0222 | www.kregliccy.pl

"Run by well-known restaurateurs" Agnieszka Kreglicka and Marcin Kreglicki, this "reliable", "simple trattoria" "conveniently located" in Srodmiescie is "still providing quality Italian fare" such as "good home-made pastas"; still, a few sigh that it "has run out of steam", saying there are now "better" venues in Warsaw for food from The Boot.

Dom Polski *Polish* 25 | 21 | 21 | E

Saska Kepa | ul. Francuska 11 | (48-22) 616-2488 | www.restauracjadompolski.pl

"If you want to taste real", "traditional Polish" fare, "look no further" than this "fabulous restaurant" in Saska Kepa, a beautiful residential area on the Vistula River's right bank; it's "still one of the best" of its kind and a "great place to get to know" the cuisine thanks to a kitchen that "excels at old", "tried-and-true recipes" - just "be hungry when you come, as the portions are big"; N.B. an expansion and the addition of a winter garden may outdate the above Decor score.

La Bohème *Polish* 19 22 19 E

Srodmiescie | Plac Teatralny 1 | (48-22) 692-0681 | www.laboheme.com.pl

Blessed with a "spectacular location" in the same building as the National Theatre, a "sophisticated" setting and a "nice terrace", this Srodmiescie "oasis" "crowded with businessmen, politicians" and artists offers "satisfying" Polish fare and an "extensive wine list"; supporters say it's "simply one of the finest overall dining experiences" around, but cynics snipe it's "too expensive for the quality of food."

Malinowa *Polish* 22 21 27 VE

Srodmiescie | Le Méridien Bristol | ul. Krakowskie Przedmiescie 42/44 | (48-22) 551-1000 | www.starwoodhotels.com

An "intelligent staff" oversees this "very expensive", "elegant restaurant in the famous" Le Méridien Bristol hotel in Srodmiescie, where the mostly "traditional" Polish menu features "some modern variations"; a few find it "a bit unexciting", saying "Warsaw has developed more interesting [venues] in recent years", but a majority reports an experience "worth repeating"; P.S. "Sunday brunch is fabulous."

Michel Moran Bistro de Paris ☒ *French* 22 16 19 E

Srodmiescie | pl. Pilsudskiego 9 | (48-22) 826-0107 | www.restaurantbistrodeparis.com

Amis assert "*mercis beaucoup*" are due to this Srodmiescie French in the rear of the National Theatre, where "talented" chef Michel Moran prepares "very good" cuisine that emphasizes seafood and relies on "excellent ingredients"; the "elegant" wood-paneled setting provides a view of Norman Foster's Metropolitan building, and in season the impressive, columned terrace makes for a prestigious perch that comes with a "charming summer menu."

Oriental, The *Asian/Sushi* 21 19 22 E

Srodmiescie | Sheraton Warsaw Hotel | ul. B. Prusa 2 | (48-22) 450-6705 | www.sheraton.pl

The "most-attentive service" from a "staff that couldn't be more helpful" "makes meals exceptional" at this "good bet" situated in Srodmiescie's Sheraton Hotel; folks who "walk in to see what smells so delicious" usually "stay" for the "authentic", "quality" Asian fare (as well as sushi) served in a "pleasant", "atmospheric" space.

Parmizzano's *Italian* 23 18 21 E

Srodmiescie | The Marriott Warsaw | al. Jerozolimskie 65/79 | (48-22) 630-5096 | www.marriott.com/wawpl

"Forget the usual hotel-type places" - this Srodmiescie spot "is a true gem of an Italian restaurant", "in spite of being located" on the second floor of The Marriott Warsaw, thanks to a staff providing "great service", a "chef who's really passionate" about turning out "heavenly" dishes and a setting that reminds some of "a quiet place in Sicily"; P.S. business sorts also say "it's a safe choice" for an "excellent light lunch."

Qchnia Artystyczna *International* 21 | 21 | 17 | E

Srodmiescie | al. Ujazdowskie 6 | (48-22) 625-7627 | www.qchnia.pl
Supporters of this "stylish" Srodmiescie venue "set in Ujazdowskie Castle" (home to the Center for Contemporary Art) say it produces "imaginative" International dishes within a "vibrant" space with "a great view of the park"; it's "popular with the hip and wealthy" for a "lovely lunch" or "a romantic dinner", even though some say "the service should be more professional and less arty."

Restauracja Rubikon *Italian* 23 | 21 | 22 | M

Mokotów | ul. Wróbla 3/5 | (48-22) 847-6655 | www.rubikon.waw.pl
"One of the best Italians in Warsaw" is what loyalists say about this bi-level Mokotów spot with a moderately priced, seasonally changing menu and "very polite service"; the ground floor is casual, while the more elegant upstairs has an art deco accent, plus there's a "lusciously green patio" for summer dining.

Restauracja Polska Tradycja *Polish* 25 | 25 | 25 | E

Mokotów | ul. Belwederska 18a | (48-22) 840-0901 | www.restauracjatradycja.pl
"Outstanding in every way", "this fabulous find on a quiet little street" in Mokotów, "an elegant residential area", is rated No. 1 for Food in Warsaw on the strength of its "authentic and oh-so-good" "traditional Polish cuisine", which is complemented by a "great wine list" and "first-class" staff; its "magical setting", "a beautiful old" renovated "villa close to Lazienki Park", is always "bustling with people enjoying themselves", making it "a wonderful place for a romantic dinner, business" gathering or any "special-occasion" "celebration."

Santorini *Greek* 18 | 18 | 19 | M

Saska Kepa | ul. Egipska 7 | (48-22) 672-0525 | www.kregliccy.pl
"If you've a hankering for" Hellenic fare, "check out this" "charming", "established" spot in Saska Kepa that offers "a real taste of Greece" that includes a "good choice of meze"; insiders advise looking past the facade of its "ugly communist-style building", as "inside" awaits a "nice" blue-and-white taverna that brings "a touch of the Mediterranean to Eastern Europe."

U Kucharzy ◐ *Polish* 23 | 20 | 21 | E

Srodmiescie | Hotel Europejski | ul. Ossolinskich 7 | (48-22) 826-7936 | www.gessler.pl
At this Polish venue set in the vast kitchen of the Hotel Europejski, which is currently closed for renovation, the chefs not only prepare "delicious" meals out in the open (using organic ingredients from the restaurant's own farm), they serve them in a series of white-tiled rooms as well; but surveyors are split on whether they find the overall experience here "unique" or "uneven."

	FOOD	DECOR	SERVICE	COST

Zurich

TOP FOOD RANKING

	Restaurant	Cuisine
27	Petermann's Kunststuben	French
26	Rest. Français/Le Pavillon	French/Mediterranean
	Lindenhofkeller	Swiss/International
24	Ginger	Japanese
	Casa Aurelio	Spanish/Swiss
	Ristorante Orsini	Italian
23	Casa Ferlin	Italian
	Sala of Tokyo*	Japanese
	Asian Place	Asian
	Sein	International
	Accademia	Italian
	Emilio*	Spanish
	Il Giglio	Italian
22	Widder	International
	Rive Gauche	Mediterranean
	Zentraleck	International
	Ristorante Bindella	Italian
	Haus Hiltl	Vegetarian/International
	Veltliner Keller	Swiss/French
	Kronenhalle	Swiss/French

Accademia ⊠ *Italian* — 23 | 18 | 23 | VE

Kreis 4 | Rotwandstr. 62 | (41-44) 241-4202

"One of Zurich's stalwarts", this "classic Italian" in Kreis 4 features "superb food" (including "extremely good pastas") made from "fresh ingredients" and offered amid "authentic decor"; expect "excellent service as well", even if a few feel "the formal staff" is "a little stuffy" and perhaps "slightly supercilious if you don't arrive dressed in an Armani suit"; just be warned that the "exceptional food comes at an exceptional price" – leading the cost conscious to exclaim "ouch!"

Asian Place ⊠ *Asian* — 23 | 17 | 20 | E

Glattbrugg | Renaissance Zurich Hotel | Thurgauerstr. 101 | (41-44) 874-5721 | www.asianplace.ch

Its descriptive "name says it all" at this "delightful surprise" "in the Renaissance Zurich Hotel, near the airport" in Glattbrugg, that makes "you feel as if you were in Asia" with its "wide selection" of "exciting", "exotic dishes" from Japan, China and Thailand, all "graciously served" by a "friendly" staff; some call the prices "inflated", but others say they're "justified by the quality of the food" and the "tranquil" location.

Brasserie Lipp *French* — 18 | 17 | 16 | E

Kreis 1 | Uraniastr. 9 | (41-43) 888-6666 | www.brasserie-lipp.ch

Like its famed Parisian namesake, this Kreis 1 spot is "a true French brasserie" in every respect – from its "authentic" decor, "suitable fur-

* Indicates a tie with restaurant above

nishings" and "high noise level" to its "nostalgic bar", "big wine list" and "dependable" (if "expected") menu sporting "specialties from *plateau de fruits de mer* to Alsatian choucroute"; most find it "enjoyable", even if the fact that it's "always crowded" means you may "have to wait and wait."

Casa Aurelio ⊠ *Spanish/Swiss* 24 17 18 E

Kreis 5 | Langstr. 209 | (41-44) 272-7744 | www.casaaurelio.ch

"There's always something special about eating at this Spanish-Swiss place in Zurich's" Kreis 5, which is perennially "popular" with an interesting mix of locals and celebrities for its "substantial portions" of "outstanding food" and "nice wine list" offered by an "obliging staff"; some say the environment is "somewhat noisy" and "slightly worn out", but then sometimes "patrons are the best decor."

Casa Ferlin ⊠ *Italian* 23 16 21 E

Kreis 6 | Stampfenbachstr. 38 | (41-44) 362-3509 | www.casaferlin.ch

"It's been around a long time, but it holds up well" is the consensus on this family-owned Italian in Kreis 6, where "large portions" of "excellent traditional dishes", particularly "fresh pasta" like "the best homemade ravioli", are served by an "attentive" staff; some find the decor "dark and dated", but devotees declare "that's just part of the charm."

Emilio *Spanish* 23 9 18 E

Kreis 4 | Zweierstr. 9 | (41-44) 241-8321 | www.restaurant-emilio.ch

A genuine "Spanish feel" pervades this Kreis 4 spot that "always delivers the same good quality" with its authentic fare, including "paella that can't be beat" and some of "the best chicken in the world" (which "is worth the nearly obscene price"); still, the "sometimes not-so-attentive service" "could be better" – and as for the "rather poor" decor, "well . . ."

Ginger ⊠ *Japanese* 24 18 19 VE

Kreis 8 | Seefeldstr. 62 | (41-44) 422-9509 | www.shinsen.ch

Some of the "very best and freshest sushi in town" can be found at this "small", "cool" Japanese venue in Kreis 8, where "creative" chefs fashion "great" "authentic" fare; sit at the H-shaped bar and choose from the fin fare that "revolves before you" on a carousel or is "obligingly served" to you in one of the few booths; remember, though, that it all comes "at a premium price", and those "little plates add up quickly."

Haus Hiltl *Vegetarian/International* 22 12 16 M

Kreis 1 | Sihlstr. 28 | (41-44) 227-7000 | www.hiltl.ch

Said to be "Europe's first vegetarian restaurant", this "definite don't-miss" "institution" with an International accent in Kreis 1 "opened its doors in 1898" and has since been serving a "marvelous selection" of "healthy" dishes that "make eating without meat a pleasure"; the "approachable staffers" help novices navigate the "reasonably priced" International menu, even though they're "often stressed" by the "hectic", crowded setting; N.B. a recent renovation may outdate the above Decor score.

Il Giglio ☒ *Italian* 23 | 16 | 19 | E

Kreis 4 | Weberstr. 14 | (41-44) 242-8597 | www.ilgiglio.ch

Locals "love this small, intimate Italian place" in Kreis 4 for its "nice, clean" dishes, many of which are accented with tomatoes imported from Calabria; the decor may be "nothing special", but the "pleasant" staff always provides "polite service"; P.S. look for "excellent wines of the month at moderate prices."

Kronenhalle *Swiss/French* 22 | 24 | 22 | VE

Kreis 1 | Rämistr. 4 | (41-44) 262-9900 | www.kronenhalle.com

"The owner's splendid collection" of "genuine" art treasures including "original works by Picasso, Chagall and Matisse" "makes for a wonderful atmosphere" at this "pricey" "perennial favorite" "centrally located" in Kreis 1, but there are "masterpieces on the plate" as well, in the form of "fabulous Swiss-French fare" "elegantly served" by an "expert" staff; P.S. for the best celeb spotting, "get a seat on the main floor."

Lindenhofkeller ☒ *Swiss/International* 26 | 20 | 24 | E

Kreis 1 | Pfalzgasse 4 | (41-44) 211-7071 | www.lindenhofkeller.ch

"Outstanding meals" await at this "upmarket" venue in Kreis 1, where the "very good wine list" has "depth and breadth" and the "excellent" menu "changes with the seasons" but always features "imaginative nouvelle Swiss"-International fare that's "more sophisticated than the typical" indigenous cuisine; additionally, the "pleasant, competent" staff is "amenable to customers' wishes", leading some who love "to linger" within the "cozy, comfortable" interior or in the "beautiful garden" to ask "when can I move in?"

Petermann's Kunststuben ☒ Ⓜ *French* 27 | 24 | 26 | VE

Küsnacht | Seestr. 160 | (41-44) 910-0715 | www.kunststuben.com

"Absolutely one of the finest restaurants in Switzerland", this "splendid" French "classic" is "first rate in every way" and ranks No. 1 for Food in Zurich; "outstanding cook Horst Petermann" maintains the "highest standards", producing "unbelievably good culinary" creations that are "almost too beautiful to eat", while "his wife, Iris, a wonderful hostess", presides over the "special" staff and "intimate setting"; all told, it's "an unforgettable dining experience" that's "worth the short trip to Küsnacht" - just be warned that "the bill will also be unforgettable."

Restaurant Français/ Le Pavillon *French/Mediterranean* 26 | 23 | 26 | VE

Kreis 1 | Baur au Lac | Talstr. 1 | (41-44) 220-5020 | www.bauraulac.ch

"Top class all the way", these "exceptional" Kreis 1 venues, "in one of Europe's classiest hotels", are facets of a single "Zurich institution", offering "outstanding meals" of "grand" fare, along with an "excellent wine selection"; from October to April, an "extremely attentive staff" presides over the "relaxing, elegant" main dining room and its French cuisine, then from April to October guests order from the Med menu "in the heavenly pavilion" with "a view of the garden and canal"; yes, it's very "expensive", but "you get what you pay for and then some."

	FOOD	DECOR	SERVICE	COST
Ristorante Bindella *Italian*	22	17	21	E

Kreis 1 | In Gassen 6 | (41-44) 221-2546 | www.bindella.ch
"Centrally located" in Kreis 1, this venue is "convenient after shopping", "popular with the business crowd" and "always a good place for friends or couples" thanks to a "frequently changing menu" of "delicious" Northern Italian fare that's prepared "with Swiss attention to detail"; an "extensive wine list", "friendly" staff and "smart" surroundings with "subdued lighting" add to the experience.

	FOOD	DECOR	SERVICE	COST
Ristorante Orsini *Italian*	24	19	25	VE

Kreis 1 | Hotel Savoy Baur en Ville Paradeplatz | Am Münsterhof 25 | (41-44) 215-2727 | www.savoy-baurenville.ch
"Superb service" from an "attentive" "old-school" staff "satisfies" visitors to this "reliable" "businessman-and-banker hangout" in Kreis 1's Savoy Baur en Ville hotel, while "cuisine purists" praise the kitchen for its "no-nonsense" Italian fare, calling it nothing short of "splendid"; factor in the "excellent selections" on its "good wine list" and the "bright, classic decor" of its "formal" dining room and you'll see why patrons predict "you will not be disappointed."

	FOOD	DECOR	SERVICE	COST
Rive Gauche Ⓢ *Mediterranean*	22	22	22	VE

Kreis 1 | Baur au Lac | Talstr. 1 | (41-44) 220-5060 | www.agauche.ch
As "the informal restaurant for the very formal Baur au Lac hotel", this Mediterranean draws a mix of local professionals, affluent guests and celebrities to its "central location" in Kreis 1; with its "classic" clubby decor and an "excellent" selection of "inventive cuisine" that emphasizes light seasonal dishes and is "served with Swiss efficiency and grace", no wonder that for many it's a "favorite place to dine in Zurich."

	FOOD	DECOR	SERVICE	COST
Sala of Tokyo Ⓢ Ⓜ *Japanese*	23	15	19	VE

Kreis 5 | Limmatstr. 29 | (41-44) 271-5290 | www.sala-of-tokyo.ch
"Quality and presentation" "make lunch or dinner always a great experience" at this "traditional" spot in Kreis 5; of course there's "excellent sushi", but the "varied" menu also features "all the Japanese specialties (such as shabu-shabu, sukiyaki, robatayaki, tempura)"; even those who deem the decor only "ok" agree the "ever-so-charming presence of [chef/co-owner] Sala" Ruch-Fukuoka improves the ambiance.

	FOOD	DECOR	SERVICE	COST
Sein Ⓢ *International*	23	20	21	E

Kreis 1 | Schützengasse 5 | (41-44) 221-1065
"Innovative" International fare, "luxurious" tapas at the bar and "real Swiss service" cater to dueling crowds at this Kreis 1 restaurant/bar: "suits and ties" at lunch versus hip types at night; a "bold, beautiful and bright" vibe permeates this vibrant mirrored red space, luring in all who just want to be "Sein."

	FOOD	DECOR	SERVICE	COST
Veltliner Keller Ⓢ *Swiss/French*	22	23	23	E

Kreis 1 | Schlüsselgasse 8 | (41-44) 225-4040 | www.veltlinerkeller.ch
"Everything is just right" at this "charming" Kreis 1 venue "in a medieval townhouse" in Old Town: the "classy" dark-wood setting with "beautiful carvings" is matched by the "formal but warm service" from

its "professional" staff, and the "delicious, if heavy", "traditional Swiss-French food" "wins you over with its simple style", leading acolytes to assert that "the price is irrelevant."

Widder *International* 22 | 23 | 23 | VE

Kreis 1 | Widder Hotel | Rennweg 7 | (41-44) 224-2526 | www.widderhotel.ch

A "classy" hotel composed of a series of historic Kreis 1 townhouses that "blend modern and old superbly" provides the "lovely setting" for this "upmarket" "fine-dining" venue whose "true professionals" "take pride in what they do, and it shows" in the "discreet service" and "great menu" of "excellent" International dishes they provide; with such "all-around quality", it's no wonder the place is "popular" – and a visit to the Widder "Bar afterward", with its live piano music and "phenomenal jazz" concerts twice a year, is "the cherry on the cake."

Zentraleck ⊠ *International* 22 | 20 | 21 | E

Kreis 3 | Zentralstr. 161 | (41-44) 461-0800 | www.zentraleck.ch

The young chef/co-owner of this small Kreis 3 International concocts "creative" dishes that are matched with "excellent wines" and served by a "flawless" staff in a simple, "cozy" setting of polished wood set against a sea of white; in sum, most proponents pronounce it a "delight."

UNITED STATES RESTAURANT DIRECTORY

FOOD | DECOR | SERVICE | COST

Atlanta

TOP FOOD RANKING

	Restaurant	Cuisine
29	Bacchanalia	American
28	Quinones Room	American
	Rathbun's	American
	Restaurant Eugene	American
27	Aria	American
	Ritz-Carlton/Dining Room	French/Mediterranean
	Bone's Restaurant	Steak
	Park 75	American
	MF Sushibar	Japanese
	Tamarind Seed	Thai
	di Paolo	Italian
	Nan Thai	Thai
	Taka	Japanese
	Chops Lobster Bar	Seafood/Steak

Aria ☒ *American* — 27 | 25 | 26 | E

Buckhead | 490 E. Paces Ferry Rd. NE (Maple Dr.) | 404-233-7673 | www.aria-atl.com

Gerry Klaskala's "destination restaurant" in Buckhead "never misses", offering "sublime", "slow-cooked" New American cuisine, "fabulous" desserts, "killer wines" and "splendid", "knowledgeable" service in a "refined", "minimalist" space with a "secret romantic table in the wine cellar"; critics complain of a "noisy" scene, a "slightly superior attitude" from the staff and "very, very high prices", but most agree it's "worth a splurge for that special occasion."

Bacchanalia ☒ *American* — 29 | 26 | 28 | VE

Westside | Westside Mktpl. | 1198 Howell Mill Rd. (bet. 14th St. & Huff Rd.) | 404-365-0410 | www.starprovisions.com

The "French Laundry of the South" is what devotees dub this Westside New American, Atlanta's perennial No. 1 for Food that "lives up to its amazing reputation" with a prix fixe menu of "superb" cuisine crafted from the "freshest local ingredients", "right-on" "wine pairings" and "excellent", "personalized" service; the "industrial" space is "elegant without being stuffy" (a few find it "drafty"), but be prepared for tabs so "steep" that cronies quip "taking a date here says 'you are the one – because I can't afford anyone else.'"

Bone's Restaurant *Steak* — 27 | 22 | 27 | E

Buckhead | 3130 Piedmont Rd. (Peachtree Rd.) | 404-237-2663 | www.bonesrestaurant.com

Voted Atlanta's Most Popular, this Buckhead "bastion of big beef and business" "knows how to do cow", offering "peerless", "melt-in-your-mouth" steaks as well as a "phenomenal" wine list and "service out the wazoo" to a local "who's who" that gravitates here for "deals or romantic meals"; you can dine at the "power bar" or in the warren of "comfy" rooms where an "old boys' club" atmosphere rules, and while the "check can cause a coronary", bullish backers snort "prices be damned."

Chops Lobster Bar *Seafood/Steak* 27 | 24 | 26 | E

Buckhead | Buckhead Plaza | 70 W. Paces Ferry Rd. (Peachtree Rd.) | 404-262-2675 | www.buckheadrestaurants.com

A "magnificent venue", this Buckhead Life Group "staple" is a "classic carnivore's" and "seafood lover's delight", serving "mind-blowingly good" "beach-and-beast" fare with a "first-rate wine list" to match, at "expense-account" prices; the service is "phenomenal" in the "clubby" upstairs steakhouse and the "more intimate" downstairs piscatorium, and there's "great people-watching" on both floors plus a "hopping bar scene at happy hour"; while a few feel it's "hyped out of reality", others insist it "never fails" for a "special evening" or "high-powered business" dining.

NEW **Craft** *American* - | - | - | E

Buckhead | Mansion on Peachtree | 3376 Peachtree Rd. (Stratford Rd. NE) | 404-995-7580 | www.craftrestaurant.com

Renowned NYC toque and *Top Chef* star Tom Colicchio takes on Atlanta with this upscale New American in The Mansion on Peachtree offering straightforward, single-ingredient-driven dishes served family-style; booked since day one, it's set in a slick second-story space that's simply adorned with rich woods, metals and leather columns, with old-fashioned incandescent bulbs adding a sophisticated glow.

NEW **Cuerno** ◐ *Spanish* - | - | - | M

Midtown | 905 Juniper St. NE (8th St.) | 678-904-4584 | www.sottosottorestaurant.com

Riccardo Ullio (Beleza, Fritti and Sotto Sotto) takes the bull by the horns and places him at the entrance of his newest venture, this Midtown Spanish showcasing chef Ken Bouche's authentic tapas, paellas and entrees, with a black-hoofed leg of *jamon iberico,* the world's most prized pig, making the rounds; layers of dark slate, antique tiles and curtains evoking Spanish lace make for a moody setting suitable for dates or nibbles with friends at the bar.

di Paolo M *Italian* 27 | 20 | 24 | E

Alpharetta | Rivermont Sq. | 8560 Holcomb Bridge Rd. (Nesbit Ferry Rd.) | 770-587-1051 | www.dipaolorestaurant.com

A "suburban wonder" "with big-city flair" in Alpharetta, Atlanta's No. 1 Italian is "one of the few real gastronomic delights north of the perimeter", thanks to "superb" cuisine and a "fantastic wine list"; "impeccable" service, "low lights" and "cool yet homey" decor set the stage, but critics admonish the staff to "lose the attitude", and since the "small" space "can get busy" and "loud", insiders advise "make a reservation or go on a Sunday"; N.B. chef Darin Hiebel and his wife assumed ownership post-Survey.

MF Sushibar *Japanese* 27 | 22 | 21 | E

Midtown | 265 Ponce de Leon Ave. (Penn Ave.) | 404-815-8844 | www.mfsushibar.com

Atlanta's No. 1 Japanese, the Kinjo brothers' "world-class" Midtown sushi establishment is "worth the trip from wherever" for "amazingly fresh", "artfully presented" fare in a "quintessentially West Coast" space, where you "feel cool walking in the door"; though the staff delivers "attentive" (if "snooty") service, it still "can take a while for your food to arrive", and it's so "expensive" you "may have to decide whether to buy that piece of furniture" or dine here, but most agree "you get what you pay for"; P.S. "reservations are a must."

Nan Thai Fine Dining *Thai* 27 | 27 | 26 | E

Midtown | 1350 Spring St. NW (17th St. NW) | 404-870-9933 | www.nanfinedining.com

An "elegant place worthy of its stripes", Atlanta's No. 1 for Decor is this "sophisticated" Midtown Thai in a "stunning", "sensual" Johnson Studio-designed space that feels like "another universe", with "feng shui"-friendly bathrooms that are "worth the trip" "whether or not you have to use" them; "exquisite", "upscale" dishes come in "beautiful" presentations that rival the "gorgeous", "finely dressed" servers who make guests "feel like royalty", and while it's all predictably "pricey", it's the "complete package."

Park 75 *American* 27 | 25 | 27 | VE

Midtown | Four Seasons | 75 14th St. (bet. Peachtree & W. Peachtree Sts.) | 404-253-3840 | www.fourseasons.com

"Consistently excellent" in all respects, this "pleasure palace" in Midtown's Four Seasons hotel sets the "standard by which other high-end restaurants should be judged", with "divine" New American cuisine, including an "excellent brunch" and "outstanding" weekend chocolate bar ("break out the maternity pants"), service that almost "outshines the food" and an "elegant setting" that's "posh without feeling stuffy"; in sum, it's a "beautiful dining experience" that's "worth the bloated prices."

Quinones Room at Bacchanalia Ⓢ Ⓜ *American* 28 | 27 | 29 | VE

Westside | Courtyard of Bacchanalia | 1198 Howell Mill Rd. (bet. 14th St. & Huff Rd.) | 404-365-0410 | www.starprovisions.com

"Worth the raid on the wallet", this Westside "stunner" from the owners of Bacchanalia is Atlanta's No. 1 for Service thanks to an "extremely professional but friendly" staff that deftly delivers eight- to 10-course tasting menus of "inspired, world-class" American cuisine and "perfect" optional wine pairings; the "elegantly chic" room with "very few seats" is "like a jewel box", although the ambiance is "unpretentious" and the "antithesis of stuffy", all of which makes for an "exceptional dining experience" "from beginning to end."

Rathbun's Ⓢ *American* 28 | 25 | 25 | E

Inman Park | Stove Works | 112 Krog St. NE (bet. Edgewood Ave. NE & Irwin St. NE) | 404-524-8280 | www.rathbunsrestaurant.com

Just "throw a dart at the menu" when ordering, for "you cannot go wrong" at this "superb" Inman Park New American from a "genius" chef, where "everything feels right and tastes fabulous", "from little plates to 'mortgage' plates"; "wonderful wines" and "decadent desserts" also win praise, and a "stellar" staff works the "enormous" "industrial-chic" space with a "high-energy" bar and a "wine room" that offers sanctuary to those who find the scene too "loud"; still, expect to "wait", "even with a reservation."

Restaurant Eugene *American* 28 | 26 | 26 | E

South Buckhead | The Aramore | 2277 Peachtree Rd. NE (Peachtree Memorial Dr.) | 404-355-0321 | www.restauranteugene.com

"There aren't enough good things to say about" this "magnificent" South Buckhead establishment that draws "locavores" as well as "foodies" with "magical", "world-class" New American cuisine with a "sublime" Southern drawl, including a "fantastic" "Sunday supper" that "warms the heart and soul"; the wine list is "fabulous", and an "enthusiastic" "mixologist" "whips up" "don't-miss drinks", while "point-perfect" servers "pamper" guests in the "elegant", "wonderfully quiet" space; though it's "aggressively priced", most agree it's "worth it" for "absolute perfection" "without a lot of attitude."

Ritz-Carlton Buckhead Dining Room [S] [M] *French/Mediterranean* 27 | 26 | 28 | VE

Buckhead | Ritz-Carlton Buckhead | 3434 Peachtree Rd. NE (Lenox Rd.) | 404-237-2700 | www.ritzcarlton.com

This "crème de la crème" of the Ritz-Carlton Buckhead would be "a top restaurant anywhere" gush guests who are "blown away" by the "inventive", "delicious" French-Med cuisine and "awesome wine pairings", presented by an "extraordinary" staff that "cossets you from the outset" (maitre d' Claude Guillaume "is a god"); the "elegant" room is one of the "quietest" "in town", which makes for "relaxing" "romantic" meals and "celebrations", and while this "once-in-a-lifetime experience" "does not come cheap", most agree it's "worth the price tag."

Taka [S] *Japanese* 27 | 15 | 22 | M

Buckhead | 375 Pharr Rd. NE (Grandview Ave.) | 404-869-2802

Boosters of this Buckhead Japanese advise "put your trust in" "master" chef-owner Taka Moriuchi and "you won't be disappointed", since he's "fanatically devoted to freshness" and "delivers every time" with "flawless, inventive" sushi and sashimi, but just remember that "top-flight fresh fish costs real money"; the "friendly, quick" staff works the "small, unpretentious" space as well as the "cozy", "nicely landscaped" patio.

Tamarind Seed Thai Bistro *Thai* 27 | 21 | 23 | M

Midtown | Colony Sq. | 1197 Peachtree St. NW (14th St.) | 404-873-4888 | www.tamarindseed.com

"Thank God it's back" sigh supporters of Nan's "reserved" sibling (voted Atlanta's No. 1 Thai), which relocated to a "cheery" "new" space in Midtown's Colony Square just "down the street" from its former site; you can "throw a dart at the menu and no matter where it lands", you'll get "superb", "authentic" fare that's "actually worth the prices"; "flawless service" and a "modern" space with "lots of outdoor seating" and "validated" "parking" are also much "appreciated."

FOOD | DECOR | SERVICE | COST

Baltimore

TOP FOOD RANKING

	Restaurant	Cuisine
28	Charleston	American
	Sushi King	Japanese
27	Samos	Greek
	Sushi Sono	Japanese
	Tersiguel's	French
	Cynthia's	American
	Chameleon Cafe	American
	Prime Rib	Steak
	Linwoods	American
	Helmand	Afghan
26	Mari Luna	Mexican
	Peter's Inn	American
	Bicycle	Eclectic
	Matsuri	Japanese
	Trattoria Alberto	Italian

Bicycle, The Ⓢ Ⓜ *Eclectic* 26 | 22 | 24 | E

South Baltimore | 1444 Light St. (bet. Birckhead St. & Fort Ave.) | 410-234-1900 | www.bicyclebistro.com

Chef-owner Nicholas Batey may be focusing his attention on opening his next restaurant project, but the kitchen at his original South Baltimore eatery continues to turn out "innovative", "palate-pleasing" Eclectic food that's "surprisingly complex"; the "chic" row house space can be "tight" and the tab "costly", but "attentive service", a "beautiful patio" and a "varied wine list" (including 18 bottles priced at $18) make it "worth the money."

Chameleon Cafe Ⓢ Ⓜ *American* 27 | 17 | 25 | M

Northeast Baltimore | 4341 Harford Rd. (bet. Montebello Terr. & Overland Ave.) | 410-254-2376 | www.thechameleoncafe.com

Known as a "foodie's paradise", this "hidden gem" in an "unlikely" Northeast Baltimore locale offers up a "delicious", "seasonal" New American menu from "creative" chef/co-owner Jeffrey Smith, who "coaxes the absolute best" out of "fresh", "local ingredients"; the interior is "small" and "not much to look at", but the ambiance is "warm" and "comfortable", and there's also an "accommodating staff" and a "well-selected" yet "affordable wine list."

Charleston Ⓢ *American* 28 | 27 | 28 | VE

Harbor East | 1000 Lancaster St. (S. Exeter St.) | 410-332-7373 | www.charlestonrestaurant.com

"You'll be thrilled with every aspect" of this "extraordinary" Harbor East experience that's rated No. 1 for Food, Service and Popularity in the Baltimore area thanks to "culinary genius" Cindy Wolf's "innovative" Southern-style New American cuisine (create-your-own tasting menus "give you the opportunity to try many dishes") and a "flawless" staff that "does everything it can to make your night special"; you'll need "lots of money", but the "warm", "elegant decor" and "phenomenal wine list" are two more reasons it's "worth the splurge."

Cynthia's *American* 27 | 16 | 24 | E

Severna Park | Park Plaza | 552 Ritchie Hwy. (bet. McKinsey & Robinson Rds.) | 410-315-8088 | www.cynthiasseverna park.com

"Who woulda thunk it?" – "an undistinguished strip mall" in Severna Park is the setting for this "ambitious" "jewel", a "much-needed fine-dining addition" offering "exceptional", "cleverly presented" New American cuisine that "changes seasonally" ("save room for dessert"); a "warm staff" ensures you have a "pleasant experience", and while some say the "spartan yet tasteful" decor is "lacking", the "gratis muffin you get to take home" is "a nice touch."

Helmand *Afghan* 27 | 20 | 23 | M

Mt. Vernon | 806 N. Charles St. (bet. Madison & Read Sts.) | 410-752-0311 | www.helmand.com

"Still a culinary standout" after 19 years, this "must in Mt. Vernon" maintains a "loyal" following for its "flavorful" Afghan food, an array of "wonderful meat and vegetarian dishes" that are "seasoned perfectly" ("exotic but not intimidating") and "served promptly" by a "warm" staff; it can feel "cramped" at times, but it generally "buzzes with an eclectic crowd" that's "enthralled" by the "one-of-a-kind" cuisine, "cozy" setting and "affordable" prices.

Linwoods *American* 27 | 25 | 26 | E

Owings Mills | 25 Crossroads Dr. (McDonogh & Reisterstown Rds.) | 410-356-3030 | www.linwoods.com

A "class act" for over 20 years, this "upscale oasis" in Owings Mills "never disappoints", delivering "consistently excellent" New American cuisine in a "restrained" ("but not stuffy") setting that's perfect "for a business dinner or a special occasion"; the "attention to detail" extends to the "prompt" and "pampering" staff, and while the tabs can be "a little pricey", "you'll leave feeling like you got your money's worth."

Mari Luna Mexican Grill *Mexican* 26 | 13 | 23 | I

Pikesville | 102 Reisterstown Rd. (Seven Mile Ln.) | 410-486-9910 | www.mariluna.com

"Not your run-of-the-mill Mexican", this "unassuming" "oasis" in suburban Pikesville offers up "awesome, authentic" food that "goes far beyond tacos and burritos" to include some "imaginative" meat and seafood dishes; "friendly", "attentive service" and "reasonable prices" add to the experience, but given that it's set in a "tiny" converted Carvel space, locals now visit the "eagerly awaited" second location at 1010 Reisterstown Road, which opened post-Survey.

Matsuri *Japanese* 26 | 15 | 22 | M

South Baltimore | 1105 S. Charles St. (Cross St.) | 410-752-8561 | www.matsuri.us

"Small but mighty", this "cozy" Japanese nestled in a "snug corner space" near the Cross Street Market sends locals to "sushi heaven" via some of "the freshest raw fish" around; there's also "tasty" tempura and teriyaki, and if you find the downstairs dining room to be "crowded", you can always grab a sidewalk table or head to the "spacious" second floor for a "quieter", more "comfortable" meal overseen by the same "attentive" staff.

Peter's Inn *American* — 26 | 17 | 21 | M

Fells Point | 504 S. Ann St. (Eastern Ave.) | 410-675-7313 | www.petersinn.com

Combining a "unique", "biker-chic" ambiance and a "real appreciation for cuisine", this "funky" Fells Point "gem" is a "secret weapon for [entertaining] out-of-town guests", who'll "think all of Baltimore's this cool" as they select from a "small", "ever-changing menu" of "amazing" New American fare; the "carefree attitude" extends to an "extensive" list of beer and wines, and although it's "tiny" and "doesn't take reservations", insiders insist it's "worth the wait."

Petit Louis Bistro *French* — 25 | 22 | 23 | E

Roland Park | 4800 Roland Ave. (Upland Rd.) | 410-366-9393 | www.petitlouis.com

A "little piece of Paris" in "charming Roland Park", this "neighborhood jewel" turns out "reliably wonderful" "renditions of bistro classics" in a "warm, convivial" setting that gets "packed" with "crowds of loyal fans"; a "superb French wine list" and "attentive staff" enhance the "classy" experience, but marble-topped tables that are nearly "on top of each other" mean there's at least "one drawback: it's noisy"; P.S. a $20 prix fixe makes it "delightful for lunch."

Prime Rib *Steak* — 27 | 24 | 26 | VE

Downtown North | 1101 N. Calvert St. (Chase St.) | 410-539-1804 | www.theprimerib.com

"Indulge" in "a trip back to" "Sinatra-style" "class" at this steakhouse "institution" where "well-connected" types "splurge" on "phone book-sized slabs of perfect prime rib", "excellent crab" and "real gin martinis" served by "formal waiters" in "opulent", "dimly lit" digs; "piano-bass combos" "set the mood", and as there's "no bending to changeable fashion", "proper dress" is de rigueur.

Ruth's Chris Steak House *Steak* — 25 | 22 | 24 | E

Inner Harbor | 600 Water St. (bet. Gay St. & Market Pl.) | 410-783-0033
Inner Harbor | Pier 5 Hotel | 711 Eastern Ave. (S. President St.) | 410-230-0033
Pikesville | 1777 Reisterstown Rd. (Hooks Ln.) | 410-837-0033
www.ruthschris.com

These "premier" meat palaces have "the sizzle as well as the steak", serving their "massive", "perfectly cooked" cuts on a hot "platter with melting butter" alongside "wonderful wines" and "generous" sides that could "be meals in themselves"; their "dark, clubby" environs and "dependable service" work for a "special occasion", and notwithstanding critics who question the "value-to-price ratio", most maintain they're "worthy" of the "top-shelf" tabs.

Samos *Greek* — 27 | 12 | 21 | I

Greektown | 600 S. Oldham St. (Fleet St.) | 410-675-5292 | www.samosrestaurant.com

The "heavyweight champ of Greek food in Baltimore" is this "unpretentious" "treasure" "tucked away" in a Greektown row house, where owner Nick Georgalas "takes great care of his customers" and - with son Michael - cooks up "huge portions" of "traditional" fare; the "small" space "isn't fancy" and you can expect "long lines", but a "warm" staff and "modest prices" make it "worth the wait"; P.S. "don't forget to bring cash" and "your vino from home."

Sushi King *Japanese* 28 | 17 | 23 | M

Columbia | 6490 Dobbin Rd. (Rte. 175) | 410-997-1269 | www.sushikingmd.com

It may be hidden in a "so-so location next to the DMV", but this Columbia Japanese "surprises" with "some of the best sushi and sashimi" around, including "impeccably fresh fish" and "a wide variety" of "fabulous rolls"; the "intimate" setting has "little flair", but acolytes return "again and again" thanks to reasonable tabs and a "friendly staff" that "remembers your name" - and "won't laugh too loudly should you get taken out by the strong wasabi."

Sushi Sono *Japanese* 27 | 20 | 24 | M

Columbia | 10215 Wincopin Circle (Little Patuxent Pkwy.) | 410-997-6131 | www.sushisonomd.com

Be "blessed by the piscatorial gods" at Columbia's "soothing" "sushi heaven" where "beautiful views of Lake Kittamaqundi" are the backdrop for some of "the freshest, most creative" Japanese fin fare around, including specials that are "always interesting" ("ask for the imports from Tokyo"); what's more, the "seafood symphony" is accompanied by "contemporary decor" and a "polite staff" that "treats everyone like a regular."

Tersiguel's *French* 27 | 24 | 27 | E

Ellicott City | 8293 Main St. (Old Columbia Pike) | 410-465-4004 | www.tersiguels.com

"Every meal is a special occasion" at this "lovely family-run establishment" in Ellicott City, where chef-owner Michel Tersiguel turns out "flawless" "rustic French cuisine" made with "fresh ingredients" and served by an "exceptional", "well-trained" staff; it's all set in a "cute" "converted house" with several "small dining rooms" that are "cozy (but close)", and while it's "a tad pricey", the "wonderful", "old-world" experience is "worth every penny."

Trattoria Alberto *Italian* 26 | 18 | 25 | E

Glen Burnie | 1660 Crain Hwy. S. (bet. Hospital Dr. & Rte. 100 overpass) | 410-761-0922 | www.trattoriaalberto.com

"Don't be dissuaded by its location" "in a nondescript Glen Burnie strip mall", because this "unexpected treasure" treats diners to "fine Northern Italian food and drink" ("melt-in-your-mouth homemade pastas") in a "pleasant atmosphere"; you'll be "treated like royalty" by the "skillful" staff, but "hold onto your wallet" since the prices are "exorbitant" - "if you order items not on the menu", "ask how much they are" and then "expect to pay."

FOOD | DECOR | SERVICE | COST

Boston

TOP FOOD RANKING

	Restaurant	Cuisine
28	L'Espalier	French
	Aujourd'hui	French
	Oleana	Mediterranean
	o ya	Japanese
	La Campania	Italian
	No. 9 Park	French/Italian
27	Ten Tables	American/European
	Bistro 5	Italian
	Clio/Uni	French
	Neptune Oyster	Seafood
	Troquet	American/French
	Oishii	Japanese
	Hamersley's Bistro	French
	EVOO	Eclectic
	Meritage	American
	Taranta	Italian/Peruvian
	Catch	American/Seafood
	Sorellina	Italian

Aujourd'hui M *French* 28 | 28 | 28 | VE

Back Bay | Four Seasons Hotel | 200 Boylston St. (Charles St.) | 617-351-2037 | www.fourseasons.com/boston

Voted Boston's No. 1 for both Decor and Service, this "elegant", "luxurious" "room overlooking the Public Gardens" in the Back Bay's Four Seasons retains the "ne plus ultra" of staffs to deliver "divine" New French cuisine that "dazzles both the eye and the palate"; yes, it's "a bit stuffy", but "that's kind of the point", and true, you'll be "shocked by the bill", but it's "worth every penny" for such a "sublime experience."

Bistro 5 S M *Italian* 27 | 24 | 26 | E

West Medford | 5 Playstead Rd. (High St.) | 781-395-7464 | www.bistro5.com

An "unprepossessing exterior" hides this Medford "jewel" where chef-owner Vittorio Ettore takes "great pride" in his "consistently wonderful" "gourmet" Italian dishes bolstered by "local" ingredients with "explosive" flavors (he also "frequents" the "elegant" dining room to "chat" with his guests); adding to the "amazing" – and yes, "pricey" – experience are "fabulous" staffers who "offer great pairing" ideas from the "well-chosen wine list."

Blue Ginger *Asian Fusion* 26 | 23 | 25 | E

Wellesley | 583 Washington St. (Church St.) | 781-283-5790 | www.ming.com

"As good as the hype" suggests, this "Wellesley wonder" stars Ming Tsai's "palate-popping" "East-meets-West" Asian-Fusion "miracles" – and the best part is the "gifted" "star chef" is "actually there" ("what a novelty!"), further rendering it "well worth" the "expensive" tabs; the "calming blue" decor is "even more inviting" thanks to a recent "upgrade", and the addition of a "phenomenal new bar area" makes it "now possible to drop in for a light meal without having made a reservation a month in advance."

Catch 🅼 *American/Seafood* 27 | 20 | 23 | E

Winchester | 34 Church St. (bet. School St. & Waterfield Rd.) | 781-729-1040 | www.catchrestaurant.com

"Sublime", "astoundingly creative" and "attractively presented" New American seafood of "exceptional" "freshness" is the hook at this "cozy", "homey" Winchester spot whose daily-changing menu is proffered by a "friendly, knowledgeable staff"; "the one real drawback" is the "miniscule portions", which quantity-controllers deem "pricey for what you get."

Clio/Uni *French* 27 | 26 | 26 | VE

Back Bay | Eliot Hotel | 370A Commonwealth Ave. (Mass. Ave.) | 617-536-7200 | www.cliorestaurant.com

"In the gracious confines" of the Back Bay's Eliot Hotel, this "tranquil enclave" continues to make foodies "swoon" over both the "bold, complex flavors" of chef Ken Oringer's "exceptional" New French cuisine ("with touches of molecular gastronomy") and the "heavy blow dealt to the wallet"; "more casual" yet just as "outrageously expensive" neighbor Uni does "spectacular" sashimi, and though the entire venue's staffers seem "snooty" to some, most cheer them as "professional" escorts to "ethereal" "heights of expectation fulfillment."

EVOO 🅂 *Eclectic* 27 | 22 | 26 | E

Somerville | 118 Beacon St. (Washington St.) | 617-661-3866 | www.evoorestaurant.com

Devoted regulars say the "sophisticated" Eclectic fare with "great emphasis on local ingredients" served at this "comfy", "urbane" Somerville "gem" "scores every time", particularly with the assistance of the "stellar" servers' "helpful" explanations of the "unique combinations" and "wonderful wine" pairings; for "this caliber", the prices are "completely reasonable", especially the "incredible-bargain" three-course prix fixe, while the chef's tasting menu (Monday-Thursday) is a "lovely splurge."

Hamersley's Bistro *French* 27 | 23 | 25 | E

South End | 553 Tremont St. (Clarendon St.) | 617-423-2700 | www.hamersleysbistro.com

"Maestro" Gordon Hamersley remains "very visible" at this "light, airy" South End "institution", just as his "not-trendy", "seasonally changing" country French fare "still lives up to its well-deserved reputation", particularly the "luscious" "signature roast chicken" (rumored to trigger "out-of-body experiences"); the "top-notch" dinners, complete with "superior service", command upper-tier pricing, but the "thoughtful wine list" displays "some good buys."

La Campania 🅂🅼 *Italian* 28 | 25 | 26 | E

Waltham | 504 Main St. (bet. Cross & Heard Sts.) | 781-894-4280 | www.lacampania.com

For a "special" "event", "reserve well in advance" for this "sublime" Waltham "experience" where "wonderfully flavorful, well-plated and inventive Italian cuisine" is conveyed by an "exquisite, unobtrusive" staff in a "charmingly rustic", "romantic" dining room; a "stellar wine list" completes the nearly "flawless package", and though you may be "surprised at how expensive" it is, this is one "splurge" that's "worth every penny."

Legal Sea Foods *Seafood* 22 | 18 | 20 | E

Back Bay | Copley Pl. | 100 Huntington Ave. (bet. Dartmouth & Exeter Sts.) | 617-266-7775
Back Bay | Prudential Ctr. | 800 Boylston St. (Fairfield St.) | 617-266-6800
Park Square | 26 Park Plaza (Columbus Ave.) | 617-426-4444 ◐
Waterfront | Long Wharf | 255 State St. (Atlantic Ave.) | 617-227-3115
Harvard Square | 20 University Rd. (Eliot St.) | Cambridge | 617-491-9400
Kendall Square | 5 Cambridge Ctr. (bet. Ames & Main Sts.) | Cambridge | 617-864-3400
Braintree | South Shore Plaza | 250 Granite St. (I-95, exit 6) | 781-356-3070
Chestnut Hill | Chestnut Hill Shopping Ctr. | 43 Boylston St. (Hammond Pond Pkwy.) | 617-277-7300
Peabody | Northshore Mall | 210 Andover St./Rte. 114 (Rte. 128) | 978-532-4500
Framingham | 50-60 Worcester Rd./Rte. 9 (bet. Concord & Speen Sts.) | 508-766-0600
www.legalseafoods.com

"Chain shmain!" - this seafood "institution" once again earns Boston's Most Popular restaurant slot not (only) due to its "ubiquity", but because of its "consistent" "delivery" of "guaranteed-fresh, well-prepared" fish, from the "basic" to the "ambitious", plus a "surprisingly decent wine list"; the "big, bustling" settings swing from "mall hideous" to "upscale" ("service varies" too), and while even admirers admit it's "perhaps a little overpriced", at least they're getting "the whole package."

L'Espalier *French* 28 | 28 | 28 | VE

Back Bay | 774 Boylston St. (bet. Exeter & Fairfield Sts.) | 617-262-3023 | www.lespalier.com

"An extraordinary culinary adventure" awaits at this Back Bay "legend" where the "unforgettable textures, flavors and scents" of its "inventive" New French cuisine, once again "soaring above the rest" to earn Boston's No. 1 Food rating, are "matched" to "world-class wines" by "extremely well-informed", "never stodgy" staffers; at Survey time, it moved into "more spacious", "modern" digs connected to the Mandarin Oriental, and while "the jury's out as to how it translates" ("how can a hotel have the warmth and charm of the old brownstone?"), "as long as" "genius" chef Frank McClelland's "in the kitchen", longtime fans with "fat wallets" will "be in the dining room."

Meritage Ⓜ *American* 27 | 27 | 26 | VE

Waterfront | Boston Harbor Hotel | 70 Rowes Wharf (High St.) | 617-439-3995 | www.meritagetherestaurant.com

"Fabulous harbor views" are only part of the package at this "special" Waterfront "wine-lover's paradise" via chef Daniel Bruce, whose "innovative" New American dishes are available in "small and large" portions ("enabling those with smaller appetites to sample more") and designed to be paired with a "perfect" selection of "terrific" *vini*; true, it's "expensive, but totally worth it" given the "polished service", "sumptuous surroundings" and overall "exquisite dining experience."

	FOOD	DECOR	SERVICE	COST
Neptune Oyster	27	20	22	E

Neptune Oyster *Seafood*
North End | 63 Salem St. (Cross St.) | 617-742-3474 | www.neptuneoyster.com
"Escape the typical Italian fare in the North End" at this "sardine"-sized, perennially "packed" seafooder famed for its "magnificent" raw bar selection and "vaunted hot lobster roll", served in a "little-bit-of-Paris" setting; the "cramped conditions" aren't helped by the "no-reservations" policy, so savvy shuckers snag seats by "arriving early" and "checking their bank account" before digging in - it's a tad on the "pricey" side.

	FOOD	DECOR	SERVICE	COST
No. 9 Park	28	24	27	VE

No. 9 Park [S] *French/Italian*
Beacon Hill | 9 Park St. (bet. Beacon & Tremont Sts.) | 617-742-9991 | www.no9park.com
Barbara Lynch still "dazzles" at her "jewel box" Beacon Hill flagship where "movers and shakers" for whom "money is no object" "celebrate in style" with "elegant", "intriguing" French-Italian creations that "marry unexpected tastes and textures" with "decadent" results; if the "smaller-than-small portions" can be balloon-bursters, the "savvy", "polished" servers and "superior" bartenders ("mixology is an art here", as is wine selection) "heighten the experience" - right back up to "cloud 9."

	FOOD	DECOR	SERVICE	COST
Oishii	27	17	21	E

Oishii [M] *Japanese*
Chestnut Hill | 612 Hammond St. (Boylston St.) | 617-277-7888
Sudbury | Mill Vill. | 365 Boston Post Rd./Rte. 20 (Concord Rd.) | 978-440-8300

Oishii Boston ◐ [M] *Japanese*
South End | 1166 Washington St. (E. Berkeley St.) | 617-482-8868 | www.oishiiboston.com
"Pristine" "flavors come shining through" thanks to "chefs who care about the fundamentals" at this "sublime" sushi set that provides "aesthetic" as well as "culinary treats" with "fantastical", "innovative presentations"; the staff can be "quite helpful" in their "recommendations" at all locations, which are comprised of the original Chestnut Hill "shoebox" ("always a wait", "expensive"), the more "modern" Sudbury branch (less "frenetic", "expensive") and the "hoity-toity" South End offshoot ("dark, romantic", "insanely expensive").

	FOOD	DECOR	SERVICE	COST
Oleana	28	23	25	E

Oleana *Mediterranean*
Inman Square | 134 Hampshire St. (bet. Elm & Norfolk Sts.) | Cambridge | 617-661-0505 | www.oleanarestaurant.com
"Attention to detail" is the hallmark of this "compelling" Inman Square "foodie attraction", where a "coveted reservation" allows the opportunity to sample chef-owner Ana Sortun's "unrivaled" Arabic-Mediterranean cooking (and simultaneously get an "education in spices" from the "enthusiastic" staffers); though seating is a little "cramped" and the pricing decidedly "upscale", diehards declare "there's no other restaurant like it"; P.S. a meal on the "first-come-first-served" patio is as "close to heaven" as you'll find in these parts.

	FOOD	DECOR	SERVICE	COST
o ya	28	23	26	VE

o ya [S] [M] *Japanese*
Leather District | 9 East St. (South St.) | 617-654-9900 | www.oyarestaurantboston.com
"Oh yeah", "the accolades are warranted!" - this "tiny" Leather District firehouse-turned-"sleek" izakaya provides culinary "transcendence"

via "wildly creative Japanese-fusion morsels" bursting with "extraordinary" "flavors not found elsewhere"; "put yourself in the capable hands" of the "enthusiastic" staff by ordering the "knockout omakase" - but bear in mind those 15 courses yield about "17 bites of food", which causes the "still hungry" to cry "o ya gotta be kidding me" when handed the "mortgage payment"-worthy, "nosebleed"-triggering bill.

Sorellina *Italian* 27 | 28 | 26 | E

Back Bay | 1 Huntington Ave. (Dartmouth St.) | 617-412-4600 | www.sorellinaboston.com

"Luxurious", "modern", "perfectly lit" black-and-white decor makes for a "visually stunning" setting at this "awesome experience" in the Back Bay, while just as "wow"-worthy is Italian fare filled with "contemporary" "twists" and "sumptuous combinations of fresh ingredients"; "caring, professional service" helps to create a "terrific ambiance" overall that leaves admirers "wishing" they "could afford to go more often."

Taranta *Italian/Peruvian* 27 | 21 | 23 | E

North End | 210 Hanover St. (Cross St.) | 617-720-0052 | www.tarantarist.com

A "breath of fresh air" blows through the North End courtesy of chef-owner Jose Duarte's "creative" "fusion" of Peruvian and Southern Italian cuisines (the "surprising mix of flavors works incredibly well") at this "charming" spot with three "lovely", "traditional" levels and a "lively", "knowledgeable" staff; it's "a little expensive, but worth it", especially to environmentalists who award it bonus points for having "gone completely green."

Ten Tables *American/European* 27 | 20 | 25 | E

Jamaica Plain | 597 Centre St. (Pond St.) | 617-524-8810

Ten Tables Cambridge *American/European*

Harvard Square | 5 Craigie St. (Berkeley St.) | Cambridge | 617-576-5444 www.tentables.net

"Locals are lucky" to have this "homey" spot in Jamaica Plain, as its European-New American fare is "prepared with love", served with "gusto" by a "knowledgeable" staff and loaded with "spectacular", "surprising tastes and textures"; those "loathe to give it a good review" because, "true" to its name, "it's you and nine other tables" and "10 times as good as" many other expensive competitors now send their friends to Harvard Square, where an offshoot opened post-Survey.

Troquet S M *American/French* 27 | 22 | 25 | E

Theater District | 140 Boylston St. (bet. Charles & Tremont Sts.) | 617-695-9463 | www.troquetboston.com

"Amazing by-the-glass pairings" in either "2- or 4-oz. servings" from a "deep wine list" that's "priced to enjoy" make this "classy" Theater District haunt "an oenophile's delight" - and the French-New American cuisine, featuring "incredible cheeses", "rises to the occasion" with "fantastic, creative" preparations (this is where the "expense" comes in); while the second-floor space gets "noisy" "when full", "great views of the Commons" appeal to "romantics", as do staffers who "anticipate every need without being obtrusive."

FOOD DECOR SERVICE COST

Chicago

TOP FOOD RANKING

Rank	Restaurant	Cuisine
29	Alinea	American
	Tallgrass	French
28	Carlos'	French
	Les Nomades	French
	Topolobampo	Mexican
	Vie	American
	Le Titi de Paris	French
	Niche	American
27	Tru	French
	Spring	American/Seafood
	Charlie Trotter's	American
	Everest	French
	Seasons	American
	Arun's	Thai
	Blackbird	American
	Spiaggia	Italian
	Frontera Grill	Mexican

Alinea M *American* — 29 | 28 | 29 | VE

Lincoln Park | 1723 N. Halsted St. (bet. North Ave. & Willow St.) | 312-867-0110 | www.alinearestaurant.com

"Visionary" chef Grant Achatz is "back in full swing" after a much-publicized health scare and offers an "adventure in amazement" at this Lincoln Park "gastronomic theater for all five senses", rated No. 1 for Food in Chicago thanks to "delicate", "witty" New American dishes exhibiting "staggering" "innovation" (some "come with instructions" and "creative tableware"); a "flawless", "surprisingly unpretentious" staff (ranked No. 1 for Service), "thoughtful wine pairings" and "quiet, minimalist" surroundings are more reasons why "anyone who cares about food" "must visit" - just brace for "astronomically expensive" tabs.

Arun's M *Thai* — 27 | 22 | 26 | VE

Northwest Side | 4156 N. Kedzie Ave. (bet. Irving Park Rd. & Montrose Ave.) | 773-539-1909 | www.arunsthai.com

"There are no menus" at Arun Sampanthavivat's "peaceful" Thai - instead, this Northwest Side standout offers an "original", "unbelievably artistic" 12-course prix fixe feast "fit for royalty" (with "royal prices" to match) backed by an "exceptional wine list" and "polite, efficient service" that "accommodates" spice-level preferences (peaking at "surface-of-the-sun hot"); diehards insist the "strange location" and somewhat "sterile dining room" "do not detract" from the experience.

Blackbird S *American* — 27 | 22 | 24 | E

West Loop | 619 W. Randolph St. (bet. Desplaines & Jefferson Sts.) | 312-715-0708 | www.blackbirdrestaurant.com

Paul Kahan and Mike Sheerin's "exceptional, seasonal" cuisine "sings", "releasing the inner spirit" of every ingredient at their West

Loop New American that's "still in top form" after 10 years; other assets include a "superb wine list", "attentive, personable service" and "hip", "minimalist", "not-for-romantics" decor that "makes the food the star" - just know that it's "pricey" and one diner's "lively" is another's "deafening", as "beautiful people" and "enthusiastic foodies" chatter away at "tight tables."

Carlos' *French* 28 | 25 | 27 | VE

Highland Park | 429 Temple Ave. (Waukegan Ave.) | 847-432-0770 | www.carlos-restaurant.com

Carlos and Debbie Nieto's "venerable" North Suburban Highland Park "dining institution" - long an "incubator for many top chefs in the region" - has faithful followers fawning over its "outstanding" New French fare, "attentive" service and "astounding" wine list that's "biased toward France"; it may be "very expensive" and, to some, a soupçon "pretentious", but the majority ranks it a "romantic" "classic", "perfect for anniversaries, birthdays, Valentine's Day" or any "special occasion"; N.B. jackets required.

Charlie Trotter's S M *American* 27 | 25 | 27 | VE

Lincoln Park | 816 W. Armitage Ave. (Halsted St.) | 773-248-6228 | www.charlietrotters.com

Lincoln Park's jackets-required "nirvana on Armitage" showcases the "boundless imagination" of its namesake "master chef" and his "daring" prix fixe seasonal American menus, which are "perfectly paired" with an 1,800-bottle wine list and served by a "highly trained", "gracious" staff in "quiet" environs; though querulous types quibble it's "no longer the novelty it once was" and balk at the "pretentious" air and "essence-of-expense-account" prices, supporters swear that this "world-class" "landmark" is "still the gold standard"; P.S. "the kitchen table is a must" for a "special night out."

Everest S M *French* 27 | 26 | 27 | VE

Loop | One Financial Pl. | 440 S. LaSalle St., 40th fl. (Congress Pkwy.) | 312-663-8920 | www.everestrestaurant.com

Ascend to the "top of the mountain" for a "heavenly view" at Jean Joho's Loop showcase boasting "phenomenal", "high-end" New French-Alsatian cuisine and a "mind-blowing" 1,700-bottle wine list that includes a "good choice of half bottles"; the "swank new interior" is presided over by a "first-rate" staff, and while a few modernists maintain it's "stuffy" and "no fun", partialists proclaim this "peak experience" "well worth" the "high-in-the-sky prices"; N.B. jackets suggested.

Frontera Grill S M *Mexican* 27 | 22 | 23 | E

River North | 445 N. Clark St. (bet. Hubbard & Illinois Sts.) | 312-661-1434 | www.fronterakitchens.com

"Master of his kitchen" Rick Bayless concocts "authentic regional" Mexican "flavors that jump off the plate" ("even the usual choices have an unusual spin") at this River North "classic" where the "mouth-watering margaritas are shaken tableside"; it's more "noisy", "festive" and "affordable" than sibling Topolobampo, though several suppers cite surprisingly "slow", even "surly" service, perhaps because it's "so crowded" and takes only limited reservations; P.S. "Saturday brunch is divine."

Restaurant	FOOD	DECOR	SERVICE	COST
Gibsons Bar & Steakhouse	25	20	23	E
Les Nomades	28	25	27	VE
Le Titi de Paris	28	24	27	E
Mercat a la Planxa	-	-	-	M
Niche	28	26	28	E

Gibsons Bar & Steakhouse ◐ *Steak*

Gold Coast | 1028 N. Rush St. (Bellevue Pl.) | 312-266-8999
Rosemont | Doubletree Hotel | 5464 N. River Rd. (bet. Balmoral & Bryn Mawr Aves.) | 847-928-9900
www.gibsonssteakhouse.com

"Bigger is better" at this "primal", "popular" Gold Coast purveyor of a porterhouse that "should have its own zip code", "jumbo drinks" and sweets "so large you need a forklift"; service is "professional" and the "packed" piano bar is a "spectacle" ("see the old men with their nieces", "cougars on the prowl" and "local celebs") - just expect "expense-account" prices and frequent "waits", "even if you have reservations"; P.S. the Rosemont rerun is a "welcome respite near the airport."

Les Nomades [S] [M] *French*

Streeterville | 222 E. Ontario St. (bet. Fairbanks Ct. & St. Clair St.) | 312-649-9010 | www.lesnomades.net

This 30-year-old "oasis" of "good taste" delivers "top-notch", "high-end" "modern French" fare alongside an "excellent" France-heavy wine list (including a "good half-bottle selection") served in a "staid" Streeterville "townhouse setting" with a "real wood fireplace" and "beautiful flowers" ("ask to be upstairs"); some find the "polished" service "haughty" and note the experience "comes at a price", but fans feel it's "worth every penny"; P.S. "jackets are required, not just suggested."

Le Titi de Paris [M] *French*

Arlington Heights | 1015 W. Dundee Rd. (Kennicott Ave.) | 847-506-0222 | www.letitideparis.com

Four years into their ownership, Michael and Susan Maddox "continue the tradition" at this longtime Northwest Suburban "temple" of "exceptional" New French fare that's "not as fancy" as it used to be (though the "robust sauces and desserts" evoke "old Paris"); the staff remains "courteous and pleasant" ("gone are the silver-haired servers"), a "knowledgeable sommelier" oversees the "excellent" wine list and while the tabs are still "pricey", it's "not pretentious" - just a "great place to celebrate."

NEW Mercat a la Planxa *Spanish*

South Loop | Blackstone Hotel | 638 S. Michigan Ave. (Balbo Ave.) | 312-765-0524 | www.mercatchicago.com

Chef Jose Garces (Philly's Amada and Tinto) serves classic Catalan tapas and *a la planxa* (grilled-to-order) seafood and steaks from an open kitchen in the South Loop's renovated Blackstone Hotel; the hip setting channels Barcelona with a winding central staircase, Gaudí-esque tile mosaics and views of Lake Michigan - a mood further fueled by seasonal sangrias and 40 wines by the bottle or glass.

Niche [S] [M] *American*

Geneva | 14 S. Third St. (State St.) | 630-262-1000 | www.nichegeneva.com

"Amazingly fresh, seasonal and unique" New American cuisine "paired with awesome wines" "at all price ranges" has voters convinced that this "worthy" West Suburban "successor to 302 West" (chef-owner Jeremy Lycan, sommelier-owner Jody Richardson and most of the staff hail from that late pioneer) "rivals its big-city competition"; the service is "knowledgeable" and has a "genuine sense of caring", the dining room boasts a "beautiful urban feel" and though prices qualify as "expensive", you "don't have to break the bank."

Seasons *American* 27 | 26 | 27 | VE

Gold Coast | Four Seasons Hotel | 120 E. Delaware Pl., 7th fl. (bet. Michigan Ave. & Rush St.) | 312-649-2349 | www.fourseasons.com

"Pure elegance" describes this "outstanding" Gold Coast hotel restaurant where Kevin Hickey's "inspired" seasonal New American prix fixe menus are matched by "sensitive service" and "expensive" tabs; the "spacious", "beautiful" and some say "slightly stuffy" setting features a "great view of the lake" and Michigan Avenue, drawing in supporters for a "special night out", "business or shopper's lunch" or an "impressive Sunday brunch"; N.B. jackets suggested.

Spiaggia *Italian* 27 | 26 | 26 | VE

Gold Coast | One Magnificent Mile Bldg. | 980 N. Michigan Ave., 2nd fl. (Oak St.) | 312-280-2750 | www.spiaggiarestaurant.com

Ranked the "best Italian in the city", this "haute" Gold Coast "institution" gets gold stars for Tony Mantuano's "exquisite compositions", a "deep" and "wide" Cal-Ital wine list, "personalized, knowledgeable service" (including a "fromagier who helps you select" from the cheese cart) and a jackets-required "tiered dining room" that provides "gorgeous views of the lake"; yet still surveyors are split on whether it's worth the "ginormous bucks", and some who find it "too fussy" and "serious" prefer the adjacent cafe.

Spring M *American/Seafood* 27 | 23 | 25 | E

Wicker Park | 2039 W. North Ave. (Damen Ave.) | 773-395-7100 | www.springrestaurant.net

At this "oasis of calm in frenetic Wicker Park", Shawn McClain turns out "delicate", "fresh" New American seafood with Asian "flair" that devotees deem "exceptional both in taste and presentation"; adding to the allure, its "Zen-spa" setting features "original" tiles from its former incarnation as a bathhouse, the servers are "never intrusive but always there when you need them", and there's a "carefully chosen wine list" and "powerful, original cocktails"; as for the value, diners differ over whether it's "overpriced" or "reasonable" for the "excellent quality."

Tallgrass M *French* 29 | 25 | 29 | VE

Lockport | 1006 S. State St. (10th St.) | 815-838-5566 | www.tallgrassrestaurant.com

"Spectacular" rave satisfied surveyors who "can't help but feel that they are dining in a different, more refined era" at this top-rated Suburban Southwest "diamond" that's so "high-end" you'd "expect to find it only in a major metropolis"; a staff that "picks up on the little things" serves "impeccably, imaginatively prepared" New French fare that is rife with "rich sauces"; add in a "highly sophisticated wine list" and a "cozy", "vintage" setting, and it's "worth the ride and the price."

Topolobampo S M *Mexican* 28 | 23 | 25 | E

River North | 445 N. Clark St. (bet. Hubbard & Illinois Sts.) | 312-661-1434 | www.rickbayless.com

Surveyors swear you get the "best high-end Mexican food in Chicago" (or perhaps "anywhere"), "crafted from the freshest ingredients", at "creative" "celebrity chef" Rick Bayless' "must-go" River North "treasure", the "upscale sister to Frontera Grill" ("with prices to match"); its "cheerful" servers are "extremely knowledgeable", and the "fantastic wine pairings" and "awesome" margaritas are "standouts" as well; just know that the "intimate", art-filled "white tablecloth" setting is "always crowded", so "make your reservations early."

Tru ☒ *French* 27 | 26 | 27 | VE

Streeterville | 676 N. St. Clair St. (bet. Erie & Huron Sts.) | 312-202-0001 | www.trurestaurant.com

"Still one of the best" despite Rick Tramonto and Gale Gand "not being there full-time", Streeterville's "superb", "over-the-top" New French has fans swooning over its "subtle but distinctive flavor combinations" and "sense of whimsy" ("chemistry or artistry? who cares!"), plus "out-of-this-world wines", "incredible personal attention" from "eerily clairvoyant" servers and a "hushed", "Zen-like" (if "austere") "art-gallery" atmosphere; it all adds up to a "tru-ly" "memorable" event that's "a must for foodies", at an "outrageous" ("dip into the kids' college fund") but "worth-it" price; N.B. jackets required.

Vie ☒ *American* 28 | 21 | 25 | E

Western Springs | 4471 Lawn Ave. (Burlington Ave.) | 708-246-2082 | www.vierestaurant.com

"Outstanding" "fine dining" hits home in Western Springs with chef Paul Virant's "artfully prepared" New American cuisine that "highlights local producers/growers" (with "sources prominently featured on the menu") in meals rife with "wonderful tastes and textures", delivered by "down-to-earth", "professional" servers; the "super-chic" atmosphere seems "stark" to some, and a few habitués flinch at the "high price tag", but most insist the tabs would be far larger "in the city", so it's "well worth the drive" - or the Metra ride, since "it's near the train station."

Wildfire *Steak* 24 | 22 | 21 | E

River North | 159 W. Erie St. (bet. LaSalle Blvd. & Wells St.) | 312-787-9000
Lincolnshire | 235 Parkway Dr. (Milwaukee Ave.) | 847-279-7900
Glenview | 1300 Patriot Blvd. (Lake Ave.) | 847-657-6363
Schaumburg | 1250 E. Higgins Rd. (National Pkwy.) | 847-995-0100
Oak Brook | Oakbrook Center Mall | 232 Oakbrook Ctr. (Rte. 83) | 630-586-9000
www.wildfirerestaurant.com

"Lettuce Entertain You's" "flamingly successful" (Chicago's Most Popular) city-and-suburban steakhouse chain remains the "place to go" for "wood-fire-grilled meats", "good" Traditional American "basics" ("cedar plank salmon" and "chopped salad"), "divine desserts" and a "whole page of martinis in the menu", all arrayed in an atmosphere evocative of "a '40s supper club"; "service level can vary", "reservations are a must" and some participants "don't get the attraction", considering the "noise" and "ridiculous waits"; N.B. River North serves dinner only.

FOOD | DECOR | SERVICE | COST

Dallas/Ft. Worth

TOP FOOD RANKING

	Restaurant	Cuisine
28	French Room	American/French
	Tei Tei Robata	Japanese
	Local	American
	Teppo Yakitori	Japanese
	Abacus	Eclectic
27	York Street	American
	Saint-Emilion	French
	Yutaka Sushi	Japanese
	Bonnell's	Southwestern
	Lanny's	Eclectic/Mexican
	Aurora	American
	Bijoux	French
	Stephan Pyles	Southwestern
	Del Frisco's	Steak
	Mercury Grill	American
	Amici	Italian
	Nana*	American
	Lola	American

Abacus 🅂 *Eclectic* 28 | 26 | 27 | VE

Knox-Henderson | 4511 McKinney Ave. (Armstrong Ave.) | Dallas | 214-559-3111 | www.kentrathbun.com

"Hands down one of the best restaurants in town" hail fans of this "inventive" Knox-Henderson Eclectic (indeed it's Dallas/Ft. Worth's Most Popular) helmed by Kent Rathbun, whose "truly memorable" "Californian, French and Asian"-style dishes - including signature lobster shooters that "deserve the hype" - "never fail to delight or impress"; service is "meticulous" as well, so the only downside is that it's so "expensive", you may "need an abacus to total the bill"; N.B. the Decor score does not reflect a recent redo.

Amici 🅂 Ⓜ *Italian* 27 | 17 | 24 | E

Carrollton | 1022 S. Broadway Rd. (Belt Line Rd.) | 972-245-3191 | www.amicisignature.com

A "delightful find" rave fans of this Carrollton "hideaway" overseen by a "charming chef-owner" who sends out "first-class" French-inflected Italian cuisine with "excellent game specials"; the dining room is "dark" and modern (and, it's worth noting, located up a "steep flight of stairs"), and because it's BYO, prices are a relative "bargain."

Aurora 🅂 *American* 27 | 24 | 27 | VE

Oak Lawn | 4216 Oak Lawn Ave. (Wycliff Ave.) | Dallas | 214-528-9400 | www.auroradallas.com

Diners don't hesitate to "max out [their] credit cards" at this "over-the-top" Oak Lawn New American that "stands out among the many temples

* Indicates a tie with restaurant above

of haute cuisine" thanks to "master" chef Avner Samuel, who serves up "beautifully presented" plates matched with wine from an "outstanding" 600-label list; bejeweled cognoscenti fill the art deco-inspired space and coo over its "luxury, sophistication and polish", though some find the "strip-center" drive-up an incongruous welcome.

Bijoux *French* — 27 | 25 | 25 | VE

West Lovers Lane | Inwood Vill. | 5450 W. Lovers Ln. (Inwood Rd.) | Dallas | 214-350-6100 | www.bijouxrestaurant.com

Expect "impeccable everything" at Scott Gottlich's "superb" West Lovers Lane "star that has not lost its luster", luring foodies and "special-occasion" celebrators with "ultra-refined" French food and "fabulous, attentive service"; the "tables are spaced nicely" in the artful, "sedate" space, so your conversation is your own, just know that prix fixe menus (which can be paired with "affordable wines") are the only dining option.

Bonnell's *Southwestern* — 27 | 23 | 26 | E

Southwest | 4259 Bryant Irvin Rd. (Southwest Blvd.) | Ft. Worth | 817-738-5489 | www.bonnellstexas.com

"A safari of fine foods" is rounded up by "wonderfully inventive" chef-owner Jon Bonnell, who is "true to Texas cuisine" at this moderately priced Southwestern "favorite" where "innovative" wild game preparations wow "adventurous" and timid types alike; "don't be fooled by the outside appearance", "next to the freeway" on the Southwest side of town - "inside is cozier", trimmed in stylish "cowboy and Western motifs", and serviced by a "top-quality" staff.

Charlie Palmer at the Joule *American* — - | - | - | VE

Downtown Dallas | Joule Hotel | 1530 Main St. (bet. Akard & Ervay Sts.) | Dallas | 214-261-4600 | www.charliepalmer.com

Acclaimed chef Charlie Palmer adds star power to this vibrant Downtown venue in the Joule Hotel; though the Adam Tihany-designed decor is themed on wind energy (with an earthy color scheme and turbine ceiling features to convey the message), it's the New American food that makes the bolder statement, along with an exceptional wine list that comes to the table in an electronic tablet; prices are high, but appropriate, given the top-tier experience; N.B. the adjacent wine shop and bar features selections from the restaurant.

Del Frisco's Double Eagle Steak House *Steak* — 27 | 24 | 25 | VE

North Dallas | 5251 Spring Valley Rd. (Dallas N. Tollway) | Dallas | 972-490-9000

Downtown Ft. Worth | 812 Main St. (8th St.) | Ft. Worth | 817-877-3999

www.delfriscos.com

Born in Dallas, this "high-end" franchise attracts a "see-and-be-seen" crowd with its "Texas-size" steaks and sides backed up by a "fantastic wine list"; sure, it's "way expensive", but in return you get sleek settings, "flawless service" from "attractive" staffers and a "no-chain feeling."

French Room *American/French* — 28 | 29 | 29 | VE

Downtown Dallas | Hotel Adolphus | 1321 Commerce St. (Field St.) | Dallas | 214-742-8200 | www.hoteladolphus.com

"Smitten" surveyors salute an "off-the-charts experience" at this Downtown "icon", voted No. 1 for Food, Decor and Service in Dallas/

Ft. Worth, where "stupendous" French-New American cuisine is served with "unparalleled attention to detail" inside the "opulent" crystal-chandeliered dining room of the Hotel Adolphus; sure, it's "expensive", but "close to perfect" for an "old-fashioned splurge" - especially if you opt for the tasting menu with "excellent" wine pairings.

Lanny's Alta Cocina Mexicana ⓢⓜ *Eclectic/Mexican* 27 | 25 | 26 | E

Cultural District | 3405 W. Seventh St. (Boland St.) | Ft. Worth | 817-850-9996 | www.lannyskitchen.com

"Simply awesome" declare those dazzled by chef Lanny Lancarte's "haute" Eclectic-Mexican eatery in Ft. Worth's Cultural District offering "clever takes" on south-of-the-border classics (like elk mole and pomegranate margaritas) plus "inventive" international dishes all served by a "friendly and efficient" staff; yes, it's "expensive", but an "inviting" atmosphere with a "beautiful patio" makes it all "worth it."

Local ⓢⓜ *American* 28 | 24 | 25 | E

Deep Ellum | 2936 Elm St. (1 block west of Hall St.) | Dallas | 214-752-7500 | www.localdallas.com

A "hidden gem" in Deep Ellum, chef Tracy Miller's "funky, modern" venue set in the historic Boyd Hotel building charms connoisseurs with "great wines" and a "zingy, fresh-flavored" New American menu that utilizes "local, seasonal ingredients", with fans calling it "one of the few places in Dallas where it's possible to eat both healthy and well"; solid service is a plus, though some find the tabs "pretty pricey" for the area; N.B. there's private parking adjacent to the restaurant.

Lola ⓢⓜ *American* 27 | 23 | 25 | VE

Uptown | 2917 Fairmount St. (Cedar Springs Rd.) | Dallas | 214-855-0700 | www.lola4dinner.com

"Romantics", "out-of-towners" and business execs all adore this "quaint old house" Uptown where "outstanding" New American cuisine is presented in "exquisite" prix fixe menus and matched with wines from an "incredible", "reasonably priced" list; add in high-level service, and it's the "perfect spot for a special evening"; P.S. the separate chef's tasting room with a 10-course menu is "one of the city's great fine-dining experiences."

Mercury Grill *American* 27 | 23 | 24 | E

Preston Forest | 11909 Preston Rd. (Forest Ln.) | Dallas | 972-960-7774 | www.mcrowd.com

"Talented" chef Chris Ward "gets it right" at this "fashionable" Preston Forest "place to be seen" with his "sublime" New American menu from which loyalists recite their litany of "favorites" ("heavenly mushroom risotto", braised short ribs); despite the fact that it's "tucked into a strip center", this is "one happening spot", with a staff so personable "we wished our waiter could have joined us for the meal" - just "watch out for the tab"; N.B there's a spacious lounge and rooms for private groups.

Mi Cocina *Tex-Mex* 21 | 19 | 20 | I

Galleria | Galleria | 13350 N. Dallas Pkwy. (Lyndon B. Johnson Frwy.) | Dallas | 972-239-6426

Lake Highlands | 7201 Skillman St. (Kingsley Rd.) | Dallas | 214-503-6426

(continued)

Mi Cocina

Park Cities | Highland Park Vill. | 77 Highland Park Vill. (bet. Mockingbird Ln. & Preston Rd.) | Dallas | 214-521-6426
Preston Forest | Preston Forest Vill. | 11661 Preston Rd. (Forest Ln.) | Dallas | 214-265-7704
West Village | West Vill. | 3699 McKinney Ave. (Lemmon Ave.) | Dallas | 469-533-5663
Las Colinas | 7750 N. MacArthur Blvd. (Lyndon B. Johnson Frwy.) | Irving | 469-621-0452
Plano | Lakeside Mkt. | 4001 Preston Rd. (Lorimar Dr.) | 469-467-8655
Plano | Shops at Legacy | 5760 Legacy Dr. (Bishop Rd.) | 972-473-8745
Sundance Square | Sundance Sq. | 509 Main St. (bet. 4th & 5th Sts.) | Ft. Worth | 817-877-3600
Southlake | Southlake Town Sq. | 1276 S. Main St. (Carroll Ave.) | 817-410-6426
www.mcrowd.com

Admirers assert this "upscale" chain with locations in Highland Park, North Dallas and all the nearby suburbs is the "standard setter" for Tex-Mex cuisine, with "light", "fresh-tasting" "contemporary" fare and "killer 'ritas" attracting a "noisy" crowd of "pretty folk" and their off-spring; "modern" atmosphere (no "south-of-the-border clichés" here) and "solid value", even considering the "expensive drinks", mean you can "go to any of them and leave satisfied."

Nana *American* — 27 | 27 | 27 | VE

Market Center | Hilton Anatole Hotel | 2201 Stemmons Frwy. (Market Center Blvd.) | Dallas | 214-761-7470 | www.nanarestaurant.com

It's tough to compete with "absolutely stunning" "panoramic" views of Downtown Dallas, yet chef Anthony Bombaci captivates diners with equally "amazing" New American dishes prepared in "imaginative" ways (think ahi tuna tartare with wasabi ice cream) at this elegant aerie atop the Hilton Anatole Hotel in Market Center; prices are "expen-sive", but the "superb" staff "executes at a high level", making it a top ticket for "special occasions."

Saint-Emilion [S] [M] *French* — 27 | 24 | 27 | E

Cultural District | 3617 W. Seventh St. (Montgomery St.) | Ft. Worth | 817-737-2781

A "country French delight" in Ft. Worth's Cultural District, this "jewel" warmed by brick walls and a wood-beamed ceiling is "perfect for dates", presenting "amazing" "blackboard specials" matched by a "fabulous" wine list and "hospitality on the same delicious level as the food"; fans say the prix fixe option offers a real "value in dining" and, as tables are limited, recommend making "reservations."

Stephan Pyles [S] *Southwestern* — 27 | 28 | 26 | E

Arts District | 1807 Ross Ave. (St. Paul St.) | Dallas | 214-580-7000 | www.stephanpyles.com

"Father of Southwestern cuisine" Stephan Pyles "has his groove back" say fans of this "elegant but relaxed" Dallas Arts District "hot spot" where he reprises some of his "classic" menu items while also "branching out into newer territory", mixing ingredients "you never expect to mesh"; though some say it can get "way too noisy", most concur that the "great lighting and architecture" create a "beyond phenomenal" package that's "classy down to the waiter's attire", making it "worth every cent and more."

Tei An *Japanese* — - | - | - | M

Arts District | 1 Arts Plaza | 1722 Routh St. (Flora St.) | Dallas | 214-220-2828
Chef-owner Teiichi Sakurai, who introduced Dallas to top-drawer sushi and robata at Teppo and Tei Tei, brings another Japanese first to town, this Arts District soba house crafting slurpilicious strands of buckwheat pasta served hot or cold with an array of dipping sauces and broths; a limited lineup of sushi and tempura plus shochu, sake and cocktails complete the offerings, which are presented in a tranquil dining room with a window peeking onto the noodlemakers in action.

Tei Tei Robata Bar *Japanese* — 28 | 23 | 23 | E

Knox-Henderson | 2906 N. Henderson Ave. (Willis Ave.) | Dallas | 214-828-2400 | www.teiteirobata.com
"Some of the best sushi in Dallas" shout aficionados at this "noisy" Knox-Henderson Japanese catering to a "hip" crowd with "fantastic" fish and a "wonderful" selection of grilled dishes served by a "warm" staff; it's "often very crowded", but fans find it's "worth the wait" and the somewhat "pricey" tabs.

Teppo Yakitori & Sushi Bar *Japanese* — 28 | 22 | 25 | E

Greenville Avenue | 2014 Greenville Ave. (Prospect Ave.) | Dallas | 214-826-8989 | www.teppo.com
It's "like a top yakitori restaurant in Tokyo" rave devotees of this "real-deal" Greenville Avenue Japanese that dishes out "killer sushi" and "great grilled" meats by chefs who clearly show "care in the preparation" of "fresh, fresh, fresh" food; adding to the "wonderful experience", its minimally decorated space (with semi-private tatami rooms for parties) feels "swanky yet comfortable", prices are "reasonable" and the staff is "welcoming" - just "be prepared for a long wait."

York Street *American* — 27 | 20 | 26 | E

Lakewood | 6047 Lewis St. (Skillman St.) | Dallas | 214-826-0968 | www.yorkstreetdallas.com
Chef-owner Sharon Hage's "artistry" makes for "beautifully conceived and executed" New American dishes incorporating "locally fresh" ingredients at this "teeny-tiny", hard-to-find "old house" on the outskirts of Lakewood; while some find the space "sparse" and "cramped", most agree the servers are "wonderful" (even if they sometimes "concentrate on regulars") and the food offers "substantial rewards" at "fair prices" to those willing to "reserve well in advance."

Yutaka Sushi Bistro *Japanese* — 27 | 19 | 22 | E

Uptown | 2633 McKinney Ave. (Boll St.) | Dallas | 214-969-5533 | www.yutakasushibistro.com
"Locals" lament "the secret is out" at this Uptown Japanese that's "packed" with fin-addicts feasting on "outstanding sushi" and "phenomenal grilled dishes", all best appreciated via an "omakase meal" that's "to die for"; the space is "small", but "down-to-earth prices" and a "friendly" staff compensate for occasional "waits."

FOOD | DECOR | SERVICE | COST

Denver Area & Mountain Resorts

TOP FOOD RANKING

	Restaurant	Cuisine
28	Mizuna	American
	Frasca	Italian
	Fruition	American
	Sushi Den	Japanese
27	Sushi Sasa	Japanese
	Six89	American
	Matsuhisa	Japanese
	Keystone Ranch	American
	Del Frisco's	Steak
	Restaurant Kevin Taylor	French
	Splendido at the Chateau	American
26	Sweet Basil	American
	Piñons	American
	Flagstaff House	American
	Luca d'Italia	Italian
	rioja	Mediterranean
	La Tour	French
	Barolo Grill	Italian

Barolo Grill S M *Italian* 26 | 23 | 25 | E

Cherry Creek | 3030 E. Sixth Ave. (bet. Milwaukee & St. Paul Sts.) | Denver | 303-393-1040 | www.barologrilldenver.com

"You'd have to travel to Tuscany to find better fare" than at this "elegant" Cherry Creek "favorite" where "beautiful people" sit by the "romantic fireplace" and savor "heavenly" Northern Italian cuisine that's "a study in flavor", especially when paired with selections from the "amazing wine list"; in fact, the staff itself "visits Italy every year", resulting in service that surveyors describe as "somewhat pretentious" but "knowledgeable and eager to help."

Del Frisco's Double Eagle Steak House *Steak* 27 | 24 | 26 | E

Greenwood Village | Denver Tech Ctr. | 8100 E. Orchard Rd. (I-25, exit 198) | 303-796-0100 | www.delfriscos.com

This "clubby" Greenwood Village "cow palace" corrals all types - from "power brokers" and "local sports celebrities" to "high rollers and those looking to hit on them" - for "consistently excellent" steaks plus "huge sides" and an "extensive wine list" that "reads like *War and Peace*"; "exceptional service" and a "separate cigar lounge" with nightly live entertainment add appeal, but be prepared - you'll need "some large bills" to pay the tab at this "carnivore's delight."

Flagstaff House *American* 26 | 27 | 27 | VE

Boulder | 1138 Flagstaff Rd. (on Flagstaff Mtn.) | 303-442-4640 | www.flagstaffhouse.com

"Make the drive up" Flagstaff Mountain to this "treasure in the sky" where "resplendent views" "overlooking Boulder and beyond" ("so beautiful at sunset!") are just the beginning: chef Mark Monette's "simply superb" New American cuisine, an "amazing wine list with incredible sommeliers to match" and "impeccable" service "timed to the second" also add to the "absolutely first-class" package; it's "not for the weak of wallet", but you should "go at least once in a lifetime."

Frasca Food and Wine [S] *Italian* 28 | 24 | 27 | E

Boulder | 1738 Pearl St. (18th St.) | 303-442-6966 | www.frascafoodandwine.com

"Words cannot adequately express how divine" Colorado's Most Popular restaurant really is, so you'll just have to "call two months ahead and pray" that you get a reservation at this "beacon in Boulder", where chef Lachlan Mackinnon-Patterson and master sommelier Bobby Stuckey (both French Laundry alums) "specialize in the food and wine of [Italy's] Friuli" region; what's more, there's a "knowledgeable staff" to help make this "truly world-class experience" "deserving of all the hype."

Fruition *American* 28 | 21 | 26 | E

Country Club | 1313 E. Sixth Ave. (bet. Lafayette & Marion Sts.) | Denver | 303-831-1992 | www.fruitionrestaurant.com

"Absolutely incredible" "plates that look like a Cézanne still life" are the hallmark of this "top-tier destination" situated between Capitol Hill and Country Club that has come to "fruition indeed" courtesy of "talented" chef/co-owner Alex Seidel, who "goes above and beyond" with his "fantastic", "expertly crafted" New American cuisine; "deft and friendly service" adds to the "sterling experience", and the "cozy" space has undergone post-Survey renovations that may outdate (and improve on) the above Decor score.

Keystone Ranch [S] *American* 27 | 27 | 26 | VE

Keystone | Keystone Ranch Golf Course | 1437 Summit County Rd. 150 (Rd. D) | 970-496-4161

"As good as it gets", this "rustic" "reminder of a time gone by" offers "consistently wonderful" regional New American cuisine and "superb service" amid the "spectacular" ambiance of an "elegant" 1930s-era Keystone ranch house; such a "memorable" evening could only end with dessert in a "cozy" sitting room "complete with roaring fire and overstuffed leather sofas"; in short, it may be "costly, but who cares?"

La Tour *French* 26 | 20 | 24 | E

Vail | 122 E. Meadow Dr. (I-70) | 970-476-4403 | www.latour-vail.com

Have your "French food and wine fantasy fulfilled" at this "hidden" "must-do in the Vail Valley", where chef/co-owner Paul Ferzacca offers "heaven on a plate" in the form of "creative", contemporary Gallic cuisine ("the Dover sole is truly inspired"); it's all served by a "friendly", "attentive staff that knows the menu" and can suggest the "perfect wine pairing", helping to make this both a "place to impress a date" and "a tough ticket in-season."

Luca d'Italia [S] [M] *Italian* 26 | 19 | 26 | E

Capitol Hill | 711 Grant St. (bet. 7th & 8th Aves.) | Denver | 303-832-6600 | www.lucadenver.com

Overseen by chef-owner Frank Bonanno ("the mind behind Mizuna"), this "splendid Italian noshery" on Capitol Hill is "a truly superior experience" offering "interesting culinary combinations" full of "unexpectedly wonderful flavors" plus homemade "pastas from the heavens"; although a few frown upon the "simple", "sterile" surroundings, they're outvoted by those who appreciate the "excellent tasting menu", "knowledgeable staff" and "great people-watching."

Matsuhisa *Japanese* 27 | 23 | 24 | VE

Aspen | 303 E. Main St. (Monarch St.) | 970-544-6628 | www.matsuhisaaspen.com

"A mile-high Nobu" that "lives up to its reputation", this Aspen eatery from the eponymous restaurateur is a "fabulous" "treat" delivering "jaw-dropping Japanese fusion" fare and "amazingly fresh" sushi; the "food outshines everything else", but the basement-level dining room has a "hip vibe" and the upstairs lounge is also a "happening" place to sip "chilled sake served in bamboo carafes"; still, "astronomical prices" have some insisting "it's not the lack of oxygen in the air that leaves you breathless - it's the bill."

Mizuna Ⓢ Ⓜ *American* 28 | 23 | 27 | E

Capitol Hill | 225 E. Seventh Ave. (bet. Grant & Sherman Sts.) | Denver | 303-832-4778 | www.mizunadenver.com

Rated No. 1 for Food in Colorado, this "consistently excellent" Capitol Hill "favorite" "still leads the pack" courtesy of "culinary genius" Frank Bonanno's "undeniably brilliant" New American menu (including "to-die-for lobster mac 'n' cheese"); it has "all the components of a wonderful evening" - a "well-rounded wine list", "impeccable service" and an "intimate" ambiance - so while prices are steep, it's "worth every penny" in order to "sweep a first date or longtime girlfriend off her feet."

Piñons *American* 26 | 24 | 26 | VE

Aspen | 105 S. Mill St. (E. Main St.) | 970-920-2021 | www.pinons.net

Still "an outstanding dining experience" after two decades, this "timeless" Aspen "favorite" draws "locals and VIPs" (hence there's "excellent people-watching") with its "superb" "Rocky Mountain haute cuisine", including meats that "practically 'moo' from your plate"; but whether you sit in the "elegant" interior or "outside on a perfect summer evening", be sure to take note of the "great mountain views" and take advantage of the "bargain", "early prix fixe dinner."

Restaurant Kevin Taylor Ⓢ *French* 27 | 25 | 26 | VE

Downtown Denver | Hotel Teatro | 1106 14th St. (Arapahoe St.) | Denver | 303-820-2600 | www.ktrg.net

Step into "a magical world where all your desires come true" at this "benchmark of excellence" in the Downtown theater district offering "exquisite" New French cuisine from "accomplished" and "uncompromising" chef-owner Kevin Taylor; situated in a "classic white-tablecloth" setting in the Hotel Teatro, it's an "elegant" (if "pricey") experience elevated by a "superior wine list" and "attentive but unobtrusive service."

rioja *Mediterranean* 26 | 23 | 23 | E

Larimer Square | 1431 Larimer St. (bet. 14th & 15th Sts.) | Denver | 303-820-2282 | www.riojadenver.com

Chef/co-owner Jennifer Jasinski "is nothing short of amazing", and her "cosmopolitan" restaurant in "hip Larimer Square" rewards its "loyal following" with "mouthwatering" Med cuisine that "makes use of seasonal and local ingredients" and is paired with "some fine

Spanish wines"; a "knowledgeable" staff that "goes above and beyond" adds to the "inviting" and "energetic" (if occasionally "noisy") ambiance; P.S. try to "get a seat at the chef's counter."

Six89 M *American* 27 | 22 | 25 | E

Carbondale | 689 Main St. (7th St.) | 970-963-6890 | www.six89.com

"Skip the scene in Aspen" and take a "trip down-valley" to this "swank" "favorite" that's "worth the drive" to Carbondale for "unusual", "truly creative" New American cuisine from chef-owner Mark Fischer, a proprietor who "knows no wrong"; the "food and wine combinations" are "coveted by locals", who also appreciate the "exceptional staff" and a "fantastic atmosphere" that includes a welcoming patio and a dining room "where you can carry on a conversation."

Splendido at the Chateau *American* 27 | 27 | 26 | VE

Beaver Creek | Beaver Creek Resort | 17 Chateau Ln. (Scott Hill Rd.) | 970-845-8808 | www.splendidobeavercreek.com

"An outstanding experience" "start to finish", this New American in the Beaver Creek Resort offers a "splendid blend of food, service and atmosphere": chef David Walford "runs a first-class kitchen" that turns out "imaginative" takes on local game, while a "fantastic" staff treats guests "like royalty" as they dine in the "elegant room" or sip cocktails in the "delightful piano bar"; yes, it's "expensive", but it's "worth it" "for a special occasion"; N.B. closed in the spring and on Mondays in summer.

Sushi Den *Japanese* 28 | 23 | 21 | E

South Denver | 1487 S. Pearl St. (E. Florida Ave.) | Denver | 303-777-0826 | www.sushiden.net

For "absolutely flawless" "fish so fresh you can't believe you're eating it in Colorado", set sail for this South Denver Japanese where "inspired sushi" and "unique rolls" are served in a "stylish" space that gets "crowded" with "local stars, sports celebrities" and other "beautiful people"; there are often "outrageous waits" and servers can be "snooty", but most agree it's "worth the suffering" to experience "the magic unfold"; P.S. "they don't take reservations" for parties of less than five.

Sushi Sasa *Japanese* 27 | 22 | 23 | E

Highlands | 2401 15th St. (Platte St.) | Denver | 303-433-7272 | www.sushisasadenver.com

At this "upscale" Japanese in the "increasingly popular Highlands neighborhood", chef-owner Wayne Conwell "is a magician" who will "tantalize your taste buds" with his "delicious seafood dishes" and "brilliantly crafted", "impeccably fresh sushi"; a "simple", "modern space" with "white everything" is a counterpoint to the "dynamic" cuisine, while a "friendly" staff adds to the "pleasant experience."

Sweet Basil *American* 26 | 23 | 24 | E

Vail | 193 E. Gore Creek Dr. (Bridge St.) | 970-476-0125 | www.sweetbasil-vail.com

"As sweet as ever", this "high-altitude gem" is "the gold standard of the Vail Valley" courtesy of "cutting-edge", "practically flawless" New American fare from chef Paul Anders plus a "killer wine list" and an "engaging staff"; a "glitzy crowd" gathers here "after a hard day in the powder", so though the "delightful setting" is newly expanded, it remains "tough to get a reservation"; P.S. "ask for a creekside window table."

Honolulu

TOP FOOD RANKING

	Restaurant	Cuisine
28	Alan Wong's	Hawaii Reg.
	Sushi Sasabune	Japanese
27	La Mer	French
	Le Bistro	French
26	Nobu Waikiki	Japanese
	Helena's Hawaiian	Hawaiian
	Hiroshi Eurasian	Eurasian
	Chef Mavro	French/Hawaii Reg.
	Sansei	Japanese/Pacific Rim
	Orchids	Pacific Rim
	Roy's	Hawaii Reg.
	Yohei Sushi	Japanese
25	Hoku's	Pacific Rim
	Akasaka	Japanese
	3660 on the Rise	Pacific Rim
	Pineapple Room	Hawaii Reg.

Akasaka ◐ *Japanese* 25 | 13 | 21 | M

Ala Moana | 1646B Kona St. (bet. Atkinson Dr. & Kaheka St.) | 808-942-4466

The "reasonably priced" "excellent nigiri sushi", "to-die-for butterfish" and other "tasty" Japanese "concoctions" keep "lots of regulars" returning to this "hard-to-find" Ala Moana "hole-in-the-wall", "tucked back behind a strip club" ("don't be put off by the location"); "late hours" and service "without pretentions" ensure that it's "always busy."

Alan Wong's *Hawaii Reg.* 28 | 22 | 27 | VE

McCully | McCully Ct. | 1857 S. King St., 3rd fl. (bet. Hauoli & Pumehana Sts.) | 808-949-2526 | www.alanwongs.com

"Your palate will thank you" gush gourmands of the "best restaurant" on the islands (voted No. 1 for Food in the state and Most Popular on Oahu), where the namesake chef turns out "ingenious" Hawaii Regional dishes "prepared to perfection" and "artfully presented" by a "superbly trained" staff; the "unusual setting in an inconspicuous business center" on McCully and the "understated decor" put the "clear focus on the food" - and it's "sensational", if expensive; P.S. "reservations are a must."

Chef Mavro M *French/Hawaii Reg.* 26 | 23 | 26 | VE

Moiliili | 1969 S. King St. (McCully St.) | 808-944-4714 | www.chefmavro.com

Chef George Mavrothalassitis "elevates dining in paradise to a higher level" at his namesake Hawaii Regional-French where the "first-class" "tasting menus with paired wines" are "brilliantly prepared" and "outstandingly presented" by "informative" servers in a "subtly sophisticated" space; even if the McCully/Moiliili location is a little out of the way and the fare so "sinfully expensive" "you'll melt down a credit card", connoisseurs consider it a "must" experience.

	FOOD	DECOR	SERVICE	COST

Duke's Canoe Club *American* 19 | 23 | 20 | M

Waikiki | Outrigger Waikiki | 2335 Kalakaua Ave. (bet. Dukes Ln. & Kaiulani Ave.) | 808-922-2268 | www.dukeswaikiki.com

It's all about "nostalgia" at the original Outrigger Waikiki Beach location of this "popular", "crowded" island institution named for "surfing legend" and Olympic champion swimmer Duke Kahanamoku; fittingly, surveyors say it's more about the "ultimate laid-back Hawaiian experience" with specialty drinks and "nightly music" than about the moderately priced "typical" American bar food; N.B. there are live concerts on the beach at the bar every weekend.

Helena's Hawaiian Food ⇏ *Hawaiian* 26 | 8 | 19 | I

Kalihi | 1240 N. School St. (Houghtailing St.) | 808-845-8044

The late Helen Chock (a James Beard Award winner) may no longer be in the kitchen at her namesake, family-run Hawaiian "hole-in-the-wall", but "you can still feel her presence" inside the "bare-bones" Kalihi space she opened in 1946, where her grandson now mans the stoves; you can also still taste her touch in the "broke da mouth" fare, so loyalists say go "early to beat the crowds" angling for a plate of "luscious pipikaula ribs", kalua pig, laulau and "onolicious haupia"; N.B. it's BYO and cash-only.

Hiroshi Eurasion Tapas *Eurasian* 26 | 21 | 25 | E

Restaurant Row | 500 Ala Moana Blvd. (Punchbowl St.) | 808-533-4476 | www.dkrestaurants.com

Chef Hiroshi Fukui's "delightfully creative tapas" featuring "local ingredients" are "small treasures of explosive taste" at this "casual-upscale" Eurasion in Restaurant Row; though a few foes find the tabs "too expensive for the bite-sized portions", fans say "the only thing better" than the food is the wine list maintained by Chuck Furuya, "one of two master sommeliers in the state"; P.S. the quarterly "seasonal" "kaiseki dinners are a must."

Hoku's *Pacific Rim* 25 | 26 | 25 | VE

Kahala | Kahala Hotel & Resort | 5000 Kahala Ave. (Kealaolu Ave.) | 808-739-8780 | www.kahalaresort.com

In a "romantic" locale with "jaw-dropping" views of the ocean, this "insanely expensive" Pacific Rim "classic" at the Kahala Hotel is a favorite for the "freshest" seafood and an "outstanding Sunday brunch buffet"; its "impeccable" and "unfailingly friendly" service also wins raves, although some detractors deem the atmosphere "a little formal for Hawaii."

La Mer *French* 27 | 28 | 28 | VE

Waikiki | Halekulani | 2199 Kalia Rd. (Lewers St.) | 808-923-2311 | www.halekulani.com

The No. 1 Decor and Service on Oahu are found at this "remarkable" New French "indulgence" in Waikiki's "famed Halekulani hotel", a "tasteful" room filled with "elegant Asian art", tables facing the "moonlit beach" and "exceptional" staffers who "treat you like royalty"; "world-class" chef Yves Garnier creates "flavors that will linger in your mind's eye forever", and while it's "frighteningly expensive", an "evening in paradise" "isn't supposed to be economical"; N.B. long-sleeve collared shirt or jacket required for gentlemen.

Le Bistro *French* — 27 | 20 | 24 | E

Niu Valley | Niu Valley Shopping Ctr. | 5730 Kalanianaole Hwy. (Halemaumau St.) | 808-373-7990

Reaching "levels unheard of in a neighborhood restaurant", this "quaint" bistro nearly "hidden in Niu Valley" Shopping Center is "always crowded" with "locals" cooing over the "glorious" French fare; the "sunny yellow" digs are just as "warm" as the "knowledgeable staff", and though it's "a little pricey", "large portions justify" it.

Nobu Waikiki *Japanese* — 26 | 25 | 25 | VE

Waikiki | Waikiki Parc Hotel | 2233 Helumoa Rd. (Lewers St.) | 808-237-6999 | www.noburestaurants.com

Sample "ambrosial" Japanese fusion in the Waikiki Parc Hotel at this "stylish" outpost of Nobu Matsuhisa's restaurant empire, where diners on "an all-out splurge" dig into "amazing" "edible art" and cry "wow!"; even though a few find the room "raucous" and the "innovative" menu too "complicated", the staff is "more than happy to recommend" one of the "mouthwatering" selections, including sushi, and suggest a "lovely pairing of sake" to boot.

Orchids *Pacific Rim* — 26 | 28 | 27 | E

Waikiki | Halekulani | 2199 Kalia Rd. (Lewers St.) | 808-923-2311 | www.halekulani.com

The Halekulani's "elegant" "oceanfront" Pacific Rim restaurant in Waikiki, appropriately decorated with the namesake flower, is "worth the splurge", especially for its "legendary Sunday brunch" (don't miss the "famous coconut cake") and "fabulous views of Diamond Head"; the "fantastic" service, "relaxing" vibe and "prix fixe lunch" also win praise, though many save dinner here for "special occasions only."

Pineapple Room *Hawaii Reg.* — 25 | 19 | 23 | M

Ala Moana | Macy's, Ala Moana Ctr. | 1450 Ala Moana Blvd. (bet. Atkinson Dr. & Piikoi St.) | 808-945-6573 | www.alanwongs.com

You "can't go wrong" with this "innovative" Hawaii Regional "pleaser" via Alan Wong that's "embedded" in the Ala Moana Center Macy's, where you can enjoy the "expert" chef's "gustatory delights" at "half" the price of his flagship; a "lovely wine list" helps make the "cleanly elegant room" "fine for dinner", but "marathon shoppers" say it's "best for lunch."

Roy's *Hawaii Reg.* — 26 | 22 | 24 | E

Hawaii Kai | 6600 Kalanianaole Hwy. (Keahole St.) | 808-396-7697
Waikiki | Waikiki Beach Walk | 226 Lewers St. (Helumoa Rd.) | 808-923-7697
www.roysrestaurant.com

They are "absolutely the best" gush groupies of chef Roy Yamaguchi's namesake Hawaii Regional eateries; it's a "bit of a drive" to the 20-year-old Hawaii Kai original, but the latest branch on Beach Walk boasts the same "outstanding" fare, and "nothing compares" to his melting hot chocolate soufflé; while most fans love the "lively" settings, a "disappointed" handful complain of "rushed service" and "lost excitement."

Sansei *Japanese/Pacific Rim* — 26 | 19 | 21 | E

Waikiki | Waikiki Beach Marriott Resort & Spa | 2552 Kalakaua Ave. (bet. Ohua & Paoakalani Aves.) | 808-931-6286 | www.sanseihawaii.com

Fans call this contemporary Japanese chainlet a "favorite", contending "there aren't enough superlatives for the mouthwatering" "new wave sushi" and Pacific Rim fare; kudos go to the "inventive rolls", "excellent" sashimi, "plate-lickin' sauces" and several "early-bird and late-night specials", but detractors are less enthused about the "loud and chaotic atmosphere" and iffy service at some locales.

NEW Stage ☒ *American/Pan-Asian* — | — | — | E

Ala Moana | Honolulu Design Ctr. | 1250 Kapiolani Blvd. (Pensacola St.) | 808-237-5429 | www.stagerestauranthawaii.com

With an urban, edgy look, this Pan-Asian-New American newcomer on the second floor of the Honolulu Design Center (furnished with pieces from the sales floor) is already on its second head toque - sous-chef Ron de Guzman (formerly of the Pineapple Room) has taken the reins from Jon Matsubara; the creative menu highlights local ingredients - Kona lobster, Kahuku corn, Hirabara Farm greens - and a six-course tasting menu is paired with sake and wine; N.B. barflys at the adjoining Amuse can sample some of this fare.

Sushi Sasabune ☒ *Japanese* 28 | 15 | 22 | VE

Makiki | 1419 S. King St. (bet. Keeaumoku & King Sts.) | 808-947-3800

Voted Oahu's No. 1 Japanese is this eatery located "on a nondescript street" in Makiki where "out-of-this-world sushi" is "carefully prepared by a master", aka Seiji Kumagawa, whose signature command to diners is 'trust me'; aficionados advise "sit at the bar" for the "omakase" meal and "do exactly as instructed or you'll be asked to leave", while critics gripe that for "all the hype" and the "sky-high prices", the "setting needs serious attention."

3660 on the Rise Ⓜ *Pacific Rim* 25 | 20 | 24 | E

Kaimuki | 3660 Waialae Ave. (Wilhelmina Rise) | 808-737-1177 | www.3660.com

Chef Russell Siu's flagship Pacific Rim restaurant is known for "locally sourced", "artfully presented" dishes like the signature ahi katsu (sushi-grade tuna wrapped in nori and deep-fried) and "incredible desserts", served by a "pleasant" staff; a "place to be seen", it's "popular" with locals for "special occasions and parties" despite its "bland decor" and "unimpressive" location in a Kaimuki office building.

Yohei Sushi ☒ *Japanese* 26 | 16 | 21 | M

Kapalama | 1111 Dillingham Blvd. (Kokea St.) | 808-841-3773

"Popular with both locals and Japan nationals", this "excellent" (and "expensive") sushi bar in an "industrial area" of Kapalama serves "traditional", "well-prepared" fin fare, as well as "meticulously presented" Japanese dishes; diners praise the "authentic flavors", but critics complain that it's in "the middle of nowhere" and the space is "small."

FOOD | DECOR | SERVICE | COST

Houston

TOP FOOD RANKING

	Restaurant	Cuisine
28	Mark's	American
	Da Marco	Italian
27	Tony's	Continental/Italian
	Kanomwan	Thai
	China View	Chinese
	Pappas Bros.	Steak
26	Cafe Annie	Southwestern
	Vic & Anthony's	Steak
	Japaneiro's	Japanese/S American
	Chez Nous	French
	Hugo's	Mexican
	Lynn's Steak	Steak

Bedford *American* — | - | - | - | E |

Heights | 1001 Studewood St. (Merrill St.) | 713-880-1001 | www.bedfordrestaurant.com

Taking its name from the birthplace of chef-owner Robert Gadsby (ex Noé), this swanky arrival is revving up to be another hot spot for the formerly forlorn Heights area; its global array of seasonal New American dishes can be served in the brick-accented dining area, at the emerald-studded bar or at Table One – the chef's restaurant-within-a-restaurant featuring seven- and nine-course tasting menus.

Cafe Annie ⊠ *Southwestern* — | 26 | 24 | 26 | E |

Galleria | 1728 Post Oak Blvd. (San Felipe St.) | 713-840-1111 | www.cafe-annie.com

Robert Del Grande "still has it" declare fans of his Galleria spot where "businessmen" and the "Chanel-clad" sup on "exquisite" Southwestern fare ferried by "impeccable" servers in an "elegant" room; though the less enthused call it "overpriced" and "overrated", most maintain that even with "occasional lapses", it's still among "the best in the city."

Carrabba's Italian Grill *Italian* — | 22 | 19 | 22 | M |

Briargrove | 1399 S. Voss Rd. (bet. San Felipe St. & Woodway Dr.) | 713-468-0868
Champions | Champions Vill. | 5440 FM 1960 W. (Champion Forest Dr.) | 281-397-8255
Northwest Houston | 7540 Hwy. 6 N. (Longenbaugh Dr.) | 281-859-9700
Upper Kirby District | 3115 Kirby Dr. (Branard St.) | 713-522-3131
West Houston | 11339 Katy Frwy. (bet. N. Kirkwood Rd. & N. Wildcrest Dr.) | 713-464-6595
Webster | 502 W. Bay Area Blvd. (I-45) | 281-338-0574
Kingwood | 750 Kingwood Dr. (Chestnut Ridge Dr.) | 281-358-5580
Sugar Land | 2335 Hwy. 6 S. (Southwest Frwy.) | 281-980-4433
The Woodlands | 25665 North Frwy. (Rayford Rd.) | 281-367-9423
www.carrabbas.com

For over 20 years these "dependable" "fixtures" have been "beloved by families with small children" for "solid", "midrange" Italian "without pretension" presented in "large portions"; insiders insist the Outback-controlled branches "can't compare" to the original "family-owned" outposts (Upper Kirby District and Briargrove), though all locations remain "noisy" and "crowded."

Chez Nous ⓢ *French* 26 | 21 | 26 | E

Humble | 217 S. Ave. G (Main St.) | 281-446-6717 | www.cheznousfrenchrestaurant.com

"A hidden treasure" that's "worth the drive to Humble" proclaim patrons of this "special-occasion" destination set in a converted home and serving "exceptional" "classic French cooking" featuring "fresh herbs and vegetables from their own garden"; the "charming" ambiance gets a boost from "top-notch" servers who lavish "personal attention" on diners, so even if a few lament it's "slipped just a bit", most maintain it's "still an all-time favorite"; N.B. jacket suggested.

China View *Chinese* 27 | 16 | 22 | I

West Houston | 11113½ Katy Frwy. (bet. Kirkwood Rd. & Wilcrest Dr.) | 713-464-2728 | www.chinaview.us

Helmed by "creative" and "caring" chef-owner Robin Luo, this West Houston "culinary pearl" "stands out", compensating for its somewhat "dismal setting" with "exquisite" Chinese dishes that utilize local produce and seafood; add in "very friendly service" and "bargain prices", and it's no wonder fans swear they "go there at least once a week."

Da Marco ⓢⓜ *Italian* 28 | 22 | 26 | E

Montrose | 1520 Westheimer Rd. (bet. Ridgewood & Windsor Sts.) | 713-807-8857 | www.damarcohouston.com

Aficionados "indulge" in "exemplary" Italian cuisine prepared from "the freshest ingredients" (including "superb pastas" "worth saving your carbs for") and sip wines from a "world-class" list at chef/co-owner Marco Wiles' pricey Montrose destination; its setting in a converted home cultivates a "cozy", "romantic" vibe, so even if "tables are too close together" and the "attentive" service sometimes feels "rushed", it still "stands out" as "one of Houston's finest."

Feast *British* - | - | - | M

Montrose | 219 Westheimer Rd. (Bagby St.) | 713-529-7788 | www.feasthouston.com

'Nose to tail' eating comes to Houston via this midpriced Montrose addition featuring a rustic, but modern, British menu with a focus on forgotten cuts, courtesy of co-chef James Silk, who trained under English offal-master Fergus Henderson; with its cheeky old cookbook photos, the tavernlike interior is an appropriately comfortable space for the hearty fare; N.B. closed Tuesdays.

Hugo's *Mexican* 26 | 23 | 22 | M

Montrose | 1600 Westheimer Rd. (Mandell St.) | 713-524-7744 | www.hugosrestaurant.net

This stylish Montrose "class act" provides "gourmet, designer Mexican" that's both "innovative and traditional", making it "a great alternative" for chile-hounds "who want Latin cuisine but are tired of the old Tex-Mex"; "excellent handmade margaritas", a "great wine list", a "cool setting" (though the noise-averse warn it has the "acoustics of an airplane hangar") and a capable staff add to the allure; P.S. Sunday brunch is the "best-kept secret here."

Japaneiro's Sushi Bistro & Latin Grill *Japanese/S American* 26 | 20 | 22 | I

Sugar Land | Sugar Land Town Sq. | 2168 Texas Dr. (Hwy. 59) | 281-242-1121 | www.japaneiro.com

"It works!" exclaim initiates impressed by the "fusion of Japanese and Latin" at this colorful original on the Town Square in Sugar Land, where the "interesting" "balance of tastes" yields "excellent" eating and "lots of things to choose from"; generous portions provide "value" for the quality, and the "service is great as well."

Kanomwan ☒ *Thai* 27 | 7 | 11 | I

Neartown | 736½ Telephone Rd. (Dumble St.) | 713-923-4230

Fans of this Neartown BYO (aka the 'Telephone Thai') fervently proclaim the "intensely flavored" Siamese eats "the best" in town, "hands down"; the "lackluster room" is "nothing to look at" and service is often "grumpy", but at least a trip here "won't break the bank."

Lynn's Steakhouse ☒ *Steak* 26 | 23 | 24 | E

West Houston | 955 Dairy Ashford St. (bet. I-10 & Memorial Dr.) | 281-870-0807 | www.lynnssteakhouse.com

Catering to "the expense-account crowd", this "high-end" West Houston meatery rewards the "well-heeled" with "delectable" prime beef and "first-rate" seafood complemented by "superior service" and an "extensive wine list" boasting over 900 labels; the office-park exterior belies a "warm", "intimate setting" suitable for "that romantic dinner."

Mark's American Cuisine *American* 28 | 26 | 27 | E

Montrose | 1658 Westheimer Rd. (bet. Dunlavy & Ralph Sts.) | 713-523-3800 | www.marks1658.com

"The old church still produces heavenly dishes" declare the faithful at this "upper-echelon" Montrose New American (voted Most Popular and No. 1 for Food in Houston) in a "beautifully converted" fane, where "master chef" Mark Cox fuses the finest in "fresh ingredients" into "exquisite" seasonal fare that's "expensive but so worth it"; "attentive" "but not stuffy" service and a "vibrant", upscale setting "truly bring the meal to the next level", marking this one as "tops" for "special occasions."

Pappas Bros. Steakhouse ☒ *Steak* 27 | 24 | 25 | E

Galleria | 5839 Westheimer Rd. (Bering Dr.) | 713-780-7352 | www.pappasbros.com

"The Pappas family does it right" at this "standout" meatery that keeps "packing them in" to its "sumptuous" quarters for a "phenomenal" combo of "awesome" beef, "killer wines" and "outstanding service" that's "worth every dollar" of the "high" prices; the "warm" ambiance is "great for business dinners or a night out with the guys", so expect a strong showing of "men in suits."

Perry's Steakhouse & Grille *Steak* 25 | 25 | 24 | E

Champions | 9730 Cypresswood Dr. (Cutten Rd.) | 281-970-5999
Memorial | 9827 Katy Frwy. (bet. I-10 HOV Ln. & Memorial City Way) | 832-358-9000
Clear Lake | 487 Bay Area Blvd. (Rte. 3) | 281-286-8800

(continued)

(continued)

Perry's Steakhouse & Grille

Sugar Land | Sugar Land Town Sq. | 2115 Town Square Pl. (Southwest Frwy.) | 281-565-2727

The Woodlands | 6700 Woodlands Pkwy. (Kuykendahl Rd.) | 281-362-0569

www.perryssteakhouse.com

"Superb for the suburbs", this locally based "chophouse chain" is a "classy but not stuffy" haven for those far from the city center that's "distinctive" for its "awesome meats" (including the "massive" "specialty" pork chop); the "sleek, stylish" space and "super service" make for a "top-notch" "night out", "especially on someone else's tab."

Textile S M *American/French* - | - | - | VE

Heights | 611 W. 22nd St. (bet. Lawrence St. & N. Shepherd Dr.) | 832-209-7177 | www.textilerestaurant.com

Chef-owner Scott Tycer (Gravitas) marks his return to the kitchen in this ambitious newcomer offering five- and seven-course French-American tasting menus, as well as a limited lineup of seasonal à la carte selections; it's located in a turn-of-the-century textile factory in the Heights, with sheer linen and beige burlap adorning the industrial space that fits just 10 tables.

Tony's S *Continental/Italian* 27 | 27 | 27 | E

Greenway Plaza Area | 3755 Richmond Ave. (Timmons Ln.) | 713-622-6778 | www.tonyshouston.com

An undisputed "Houston classic" installed in "knockout" Greenway Plaza digs, this "world-class" tribute to "formal dining" "caters to the elite" with "the total package": "exceptional" Continental-Italian fare, the "toniest" service around (rated No. 1 in Houston) and "smart, art-filled" surroundings; it's "expensive", but "you get what you pay for", and its "moneyed" clientele hardly objects if it's "a little stuffy."

Vic & Anthony's *Steak* 26 | 25 | 24 | E

Downtown | 1510 Texas Ave. (La Branch St.) | 713-228-1111 | www.vicandanthonys.com

It's "definitely pricey", but this "classic" Downtown steakhouse from "the Landry's empire" "ranks with the best", enticing a "power carnivore" crowd into its "opulent" "dark-oak" digs with "huge" cuts of "fabulous" beef, an "amazing wine list" and "top-of-the-line" service; sited "in the shadow of" Minute Maid Park, it's "perfect for the pre- or post-ball game" blowout.

NEW **Voice** *American* - | - | - | E

Downtown | Hotel Icon | 220 Main St. (bet. Congress & Franklin Sts.) | 832-667-4470 | www.hotelicon.com

Inside the revamped dining room in the Hotel Icon sits this tony destination where chef Michael Kramer (ex Mansion at Turtle Creek) offers up a varied, modern American menu that puts the focus on locally sourced ingredients; its striking setting features high ceilings, red banquettes and expansive windows that make it feel part of Downtown while still remaining pleasantly outside the fray.

FOOD | DECOR | SERVICE | COST

Kansas City

TOP FOOD RANKING

	Restaurant	Cuisine
27	Bluestem	American
26	Oklahoma Joe's	BBQ
	Le Fou Frog	French
	Tatsu's	French
	Plaza III	Steak
	Room 39	American
	American Restaurant	American
25	Danny Edwards'	BBQ
	Stroud's	American
	Fiorella's Jack Stack	BBQ
	Korma Sutra	Indian
	PotPie	French
	Café des Amis	French
	Starker's Restaurant	American
	Ruth's Chris	Steak
	Bristol Bar & Grill	Seafood
	André's	Swiss
	Pachamama's	Eclectic

American Restaurant 🅂 *American* 26 | 24 | 27 | E

Crown Center | Crown Ctr. | 200 E. 25th St. (Grand Ave.), MO | 816-545-8001 | www.theamericankc.com

Former executive chef Debbie Gold returned to this "formal" Crown Center stalwart post-Survey, and she's once again creating her "stellar" James Beard–award-winning New American food, which is, as always, complemented by "fantastic" service and a deep wine list showcasing 1,500 selections; the decor "could use an upgrade", but the interior setting is trumped anyway by the "amazing" city views.

André's Confiserie Suisse 🅂 *Swiss* 25 | 19 | 22 | I

Country Club Plaza | 5018 Main St. (bet. 50th & 51st Sts.), MO | 816-561-6484

Overland Park | 4929 W. 119th St. (Roe Ave.), KS | 913-498-3440

www.andreschocolates.com

A Kansas City "treasure" for 50+ years, this Alpine-designed, Country Club Plaza Swiss (along with its more modern Overland Park offshoot) delivers "sublime" pastries and chocolates that justify a "wait that's sometimes out the door"; at lunchtime, there are "tasty" savories.

Bluestem 🄼 *American* 27 | 22 | 24 | E

Westport | 900 Westport Rd. (Roanoke Rd.), MO | 816-561-1101 | www.bluestemkc.com

The "brilliant", "cutting-edge" dishes and their "remarkably" beautiful presentations add up to "high art" at this Westport New American (No. 1 for Food), a "nirvana" for gourmets that's guided by chef-owners Colby and Megan Garrelts, the latter the hand behind the "fabulous" desserts; it's a "big-city" experience where the urbane, "hip" space includes a lounge, the site of "delightful" libations and nicely priced fare.

Bristol Bar & Grill *Seafood* 25 | 23 | 24 | M

Downtown KCMO | 51 E. 14th St. (Main St.), MO | 816-448-6007
Leawood | Town Center Plaza | 5400 W. 119th St. (Nall Ave.), KS | 913-663-5777
www.bristolseafoodgrill.com

You "can't go wrong" with the "fabulously" "fresh" fish at this Leawood seafooder whose fare "competes" with what you'll find "miles away" on the "East Coast"; plus, the staff "goes overboard" to ensure smooth sailing; N.B. the Downtown KCMO branch opened post-Survey.

Café des Amis M *French* 25 | 21 | 25 | M

Parkville | 112½ Main St. (2nd St.), MO | 816-587-6767 | www.cafedesamiskc.com

Visitors "can't say enough" about this abundantly "charming" second-floor French in historic Parkville and its seriously "superb" Provençal selections that include "over-the-top" desserts that match the quality of the savories; the wooden deck is both the "perfect place to dine" and helps confirm its winning status among supporters.

Danny Edwards' Famous Kansas City Barbecue S *BBQ* 25 | - | 19 | I

Downtown KCMO | 2900 Southwest Blvd. (W. 29th St.), MO | 816-283-0880

"Now, this is what I'm talking about" echoes the sentiment of 'cue pros who've tried this Downtown eatery "living up to its rep" thanks to the "best" burnt ends and other "tasty", "messy" chow; in short, it's "what BBQ is meant to be."

Fiorella's Jack Stack *BBQ* 25 | 21 | 22 | I

Crossroads | 101 W. 22nd St. (Wyandotte St.), MO | 816-472-7427
Country Club Plaza | 4747 Wyandotte St. (Ward Pkwy.), MO | 816-531-7427
Overland Park | 9520 Metcalf Ave. (95th St.), KS | 913-385-7427
Martin City | 13441 Holmes Rd. (135th St.), MO | 816-942-9141
www.jackstackbbq.com

"Don't even think of going to KC without eating here" say regulars of this relatively "fancy" (Most Popular) quartet that proves barbecue "doesn't have to be eaten in a dive", especially when the vittles are all "downright fabulous", from the "best" babybacks to "to-die-for" burnt ends; the "amazing" quality makes the sometimes "long waits" no big deal.

Korma Sutra *Indian* 25 | 14 | 22 | I

Westport | 4113 Pennsylvania St. (Westport Rd.), MO | 816-931-7775
Overland Park | 7217 W. 110th St. (Metcalf Ave), KS | 913-345-8774
www.kckormasutra.com

The "modest" quarters may "not be fancy", but the food "awakens the taste buds" at these Overland Park and Westport Indians whose "earnest" servers tend to deliver "lots of tasty extra dishes"; the mood is "child-friendly", and even the kids will like the "fabulous" lunch buffet.

Le Fou Frog M *French* 26 | 19 | 22 | E

City Market | 400 E. Fifth St. (Oak St.), MO | 816-474-6060 | www.lefoufrog.com

Serving up "a little slice of Paris" in the "rugged" City Market area, this "funky" French "doesn't look like much on the outside", but "marvelous" food and a perpetually changing chalkboard menu put folks at ease; the "incredible" early-bird specials make the "tight" quarters palatable.

Lidia's *Italian* 23 | 26 | 23 | M

Crossroads | 101 W. 22nd St. (Baltimore Ave.), MO | 816-221-3722 | www.lidiasitaly.com

TV-celeb Lidia Bastianich is a "star" in KC too, "brightening the Italian scene" with her Crossroads venue (housed in a refurbed warehouse) that operates in "arguably the most beautiful" room in the city, thanks in part to the "gorgeous" chandeliers; the "gutsy", "high-quality" cooking is part of her trademark, made even better by "attentive" service.

McCormick & Schmick's *Seafood* 23 | 24 | 23 | E

Country Club Plaza | 448 W. 47th St. (Pennsylvania Ave.), MO | 816-531-6800 | www.mccormickandschmicks.com

"Great" seafood in a "land-locked town" means lots of customers show up at this Country Club Plaza standby also prized for its extensive selection of steaks and poultry; sit under the stained-glass ceiling, or opt for the outdoor patio - either way, the "good" servers "work pretty hard at making you forget" it's a chain.

Oklahoma Joe's Barbecue Ⓢ *BBQ* 26 | 12 | 18 | I

Roeland Park | Shamrock Gas Station | 3002 W. 47th Ave. (Mission Rd.), KS | 913-722-3366

Olathe | 11950 S. Strang Line Rd. (119th St.), KS | 913-782-6858

www.oklahomajoesbbq.com

No-nonsense types insist the "gas-station location is perfect" for enjoying "some of the world's best" pulled pork, "tender" ribs and other "amazing" low-cost cooking at this "great" barbecue joint in Roeland Park; if the Olathe spot's ambiance seems "less authentic", at least there's more space for gnawing.

Pachamama's Ⓜ *Eclectic* 25 | 25 | 23 | E

Lawrence | 800 New Hampshire St. (W. 8th St.), KS | 785-841-0990 | www.pachamamas.com

"Inventive" preparations, "artfully presented" are the forte of this Eclectic that "makes you think you're not in Lawrence"; the consensus: it's "worth a trip from the KC metro area", even if only for its "excellent" wine list; P.S. for diners prone to small plates, the "beautifully appointed" bar is the way to go.

Plaza III The Steakhouse *Steak* 26 | 22 | 25 | E

Country Club Plaza | Country Club Plaza | 4749 Pennsylvania Ave. (Ward Pkwy.), MO | 816-753-0000 | www.plazaiiisteakhouse.com

Packing "enough testosterone to make Chuck Norris blush" is this "quintessential" steakhouse in Country Club Plaza that gets props for "melt-in-your-mouth" meats; "be prepared to pay", and for those who can swing with the tabs, "check out the jazz" on weekends.

PotPie Ⓢ Ⓜ *French* 25 | 18 | 21 | M

Westport | 904 Westport Rd. (Roanoke Rd.), MO | 816-561-2702 | www.kcpotpie.com

You're as likely to see "someone with a tongue ring and pierced nose as you are to see someone in a suit and tie" at this homey, "funky" Westport French known for "delicious" homestyle cookery and a chalkboard menu that's updated regularly; modest prices and the "most friendly" service further guarantee "repeat" business.

Room 39 ☒ *American* 26 | 20 | 22 | M

39th Street | 1719 W. 39th St. (bet. Bell & Genessee Sts.), MO | 816-753-3939

Leawood | 10561 Mission Rd. (bet. W. 104th Terr. & W. 105th St.), KS | 913-648-7639

www.rm39.com

A "favorite" for breakfast and lunch but also offering "marvelous", "clever twists on American originals" at dinner, this "funky", affordable address has become a "staple" on 39th Street; it's "highly recommended", as one can see from "all the chefs in town eating there come Saturday morning"; N.B. the Leawood branch opened post-Survey.

Ruth's Chris Steak House *Steak* 25 | 21 | 23 | E

Country Club Plaza | Plaza Steppes | 700 W. 47th St. (Jefferson St.), MO | 816-531-4800 | www.ruthschris.com

The "butter-drenched" steaks are reserved for those who "throw caution to the wind" at this Country Club Plaza outlet whose "reputation precedes it as one of the best steakhouse chains"; thanks to the "predictably wonderful" chops, backers say visits here are "worth" the "pricey" outcome.

Starker's Restaurant ☒ *American* 25 | 24 | 26 | E

Country Club Plaza | 201 W. 47th St. (Wyandotte St.), MO | 816-753-3565 | www.starkersreserve.com

Get treated like "royalty" at this "romantic, secluded" "special-occasion" Country Club Plaza mainstay purveying chef-owner John McClure's "splendid" New American preparations that are "meticulously" executed and served; it's no secret that the restaurant is "favored" by oenophiles, who delight in the "incredible" 1,665-label wine list.

Stroud's *American* 25 | 16 | 21 | I

NEW **Mission** | 4200 Shawnee Mission Pkwy. (W. 55th St.), KS | 913-262-8500

Kansas City, North | 5410 NE Oak Ridge Dr. (Vivion Rd.), MO | 816-454-9600

www.stroudsrestaurant.com

"You haven't lived" till you've tried the "legendary" fried chicken and gravy, "mouthwatering" pork chops and the "best" chicken fried steaks all doled out at this North KC American in a roomy 19th-century homestead amid a "farm" setting; it's the "classic comfort-food" experience, and fans insist the restaurant makes a "major contribution" to the city every time a dish is served; N.B. the Mission locale opened post-Survey.

Tatsu's *French* 26 | 19 | 24 | E

Prairie Village | 4603 W. 90th St. (Roe Ave.), KS | 913-383-9801 | www.tatsus.com

"Reliably delicious" Classic French specialties set the tone for this "genteel" Prairie Village restaurant where meals are enhanced by "attentive" service; if you can abide the "staid", "granny's parlor" decor, you shouldn't have trouble enjoying this stalwart's "high standards."

	FOOD	DECOR	SERVICE	COST

Las Vegas

TOP FOOD RANKING

	Restaurant	Cuisine
28	L'Atelier de Joël Robuchon	French
	Joël Robuchon	French
	Rosemary's	American
	Nobu	Japanese
	Todd's Unique Dining	Eclectic
	Guy Savoy	French
27	Picasso	French
	Lotus of Siam	Thai
	Alex	French
	Tableau	American
	Michael Mina	Seafood
26	Del Frisco's	Steak
	André's	French
	B&B Ristorante	Italian

Alex *French* 27 | 28 | 27 | VE

Strip | Wynn Las Vegas | 3131 Las Vegas Blvd. S. (bet. Desert Inn & Spring Mountain Rds.) | www.wynnlasvegas.com

"No detail is left undone" at "genius" chef Alex Stratta's "foodie fantasy come true" in the Wynn, where "achingly delicious" prix fixe meals of New French cuisine "hit their mark perfectly", "exceptional" servers "treat everyone like a high roller" and "even your purse gets a fancy chair"; from the first step "down the grand staircase" into the "opulent" room to the last "sublime" bite of dessert, it's a "luxurious" "over-the-top experience" that has some "big spenders" swearing it's "worth repeating"; next time, "skip the gambling and invest your money here."

André's *French* 26 | 24 | 26 | VE

Downtown | 401 S. Sixth St. (bet. Bonneville St. & Bridger Ave.) | 702-385-5016 [S]

Strip | Monte Carlo Resort | 3770 Las Vegas Blvd. S. (bet. Harmon & Tropicana Aves.) | 702-798-7151

www.andrelv.com

"Old Las Vegas" comes alive at this Downtown "classic" from André Rochat that's "been here for decades" serving "rich" French fare ("even the butter is sautéed in butter") in a venerable converted house with plenty of "charm"; the newer Strip outpost offers the same "excellent" food but in more "elegant", "Louis XIV-style" quarters, while both pamper patrons with "impeccably polite service" that makes it all "worth the splurge"; N.B. the Decor score does not reflect a recent spruce-up at the Monte Carlo locale.

Aureole *American* 25 | 27 | 24 | VE

Strip | Mandalay Bay Resort | 3950 Las Vegas Blvd. S. (Mandalay Bay Rd.) | 702-632-7401 | www.charliepalmer.com

"It feels like walking into a dream" swoon surveyors "wowed" by chef Charlie Palmer's "NYC transplant" in Mandalay Bay where a "dramatic entranceway" opens into a "beautiful" room with a multistory wine tower famously attended to by "harnessed" "angels" who "elegantly ascend" to retrieve vintages from a "tremendous" collection; "first-class" New American cuisine "rises to new heights" as well in a "superb" prix fixe menu while near "flawless" service "makes you feel like a million bucks"; in all, it's an experience of "sensory overload" that "more than satisfies", especially if "someone else is paying" the "insanely expensive" bill.

B&B Ristorante *Italian* — 26 | 24 | 24 | VE

Strip | Venetian Hotel | 3355 Las Vegas Blvd. S. (bet. Flamingo & Spring Mountain Rds.) | 702-266-9977 | www.bandbristorante.com

"Finally", "just what Vegas was missing" declare "foodies" "delighted" with Mario Batali's pricey Venetian venture that mirrors the experience of NYC's Babbo with "phenomenal wines" and "ingenious" "twists on classic Italian dishes" like the "amazing" signature beef cheek ravioli; a "knowledgeable" staff and "intimate" digs decked out in dark woods also win raves, and if a few find "they still have a few kinks to work out", the majority is convinced this "exciting" arrival "will only get better."

Bellagio Buffet *Eclectic* — 24 | 19 | 19 | M

Strip | Bellagio Hotel | 3600 Las Vegas Blvd. S. (Flamingo Rd.) | 702-693-8111 | www.bellagio.com

"A certain diet destroyer" say the legions of surveyors who endure almost "constant lines" for what they call the "mac daddy" of all buffets, with a "vast" spread of Eclectic dishes from "Buffalo wings to wild boar", "bountiful quantities" of seafood, plus a "fantastic" brunch on Saturdays and Sundays, where the champagne "flows like the Bellagio fountains themselves"; some contend it's more "expensive" than competitors, though defenders justify the "high" prices, declaring "it's the only meal you need for the day."

Bouchon *French* — 25 | 24 | 24 | E

Strip | Venetian Hotel | 3355 Las Vegas Blvd. S. (bet. Flamingo & Spring Mountain Rds.) | 702-414-6200 | www.bouchonbistro.com

Thomas Keller's "relatively affordable" "outpost of gastronomy" in the Venetian is "true to his Yountville original" with "perfectly executed French bistro fare", from "heavenly breakfasts" ("light-as-a-feather waffles", a cheese Danish "to dream about") to "indescribably delicious" dinners; the "beautiful" Adam Tihany-designed dining area includes "relaxing" patio seating "overlooking a quiet, well-shaded pool" that "makes you forget where you are", so even if service is sometimes "a little lacking", patrons proclaim it all "thoroughly enjoyable" nonetheless.

NEW **Carnevino** *Italian/Steak* — - | - | - | VE

Strip | Palazzo Hotel | 3325 Las Vegas Blvd. S. (Sands Ave.) | 702-789-4141 | www.carnevino.com

From NY superstars Mario Batali and Joe Bastianich comes this new Italian steakhouse in the Palazzo that's a fine companion piece to their Enoteca San Marco and B&B Ristorante next door at the Venetian; fashioned like a Mediterranean villa with a liberal use of marble, crystal and wood, it serves pricey vittles that go beyond beef to include seafood, pasta and antipasti, all washed down with an impressive wine list.

	FOOD	DECOR	SERVICE	COST

NEW **CUT** *Steak* | - | - | - | VE |

Strip | Palazzo Hotel | 3325 Las Vegas Blvd. S. (Sands Ave.) | 702-607-6300 | www.palazzolasvegas.com

Wolfgang Puck puts a contemporary spin on the traditional steakhouse at this sleek addition to the Palazzo on the Strip; mirrored surfaces and modern art and furnishings in neutral hues set the scene for dramatic (and dramatically priced) cuts of beef, from rib eye to Wagyu, plus an edited selection of imaginatively prepared pork, lamb and fish; lesser appetites can hit the bar where the Rough Cuts nibbles menu features Kobe sliders, tuna tartare and the like.

Del Frisco's Double Eagle Steak House *Steak* | 26 | 23 | 25 | VE |

E of Strip | 3925 Paradise Rd. (Corporate Dr.) | 702-796-0063 | www.delfriscos.com

"A mix of locals and tourists" puts this east of the Strip chain beef bonanza "at the top of the list", saying "you can't go wrong" with its "divine" steaks, "extraordinary wines" and "remarkable" service, even if prices nearly "break the bank"; diners, however, take opposing sides on the mahogany wood and white-tablecloth decor, with some deeming it "classy" and others insisting it's "bland" and in need of an "update."

Delmonico Steakhouse *Steak* | 26 | 23 | 25 | VE |

Strip | Venetian Hotel | 3355 Las Vegas Blvd. S. (bet. Flamingo & Spring Mountain Rds.) | 702-414-3737 | www.emerils.com

"Emeril has it all together here" gush groupies of celebrity chef Lagasse, whose "absolute hunk-o-meat perfection" in the Venetian pleases with "fabulous cuts" of beef (including a "primo" bone-in rib eye), "wonderful Caesar salad" prepared tableside and an "amazing", "unending" wine list; in spite of a few "lapses", servers "take care of your every need", so the only complaint is the "monasterylike" atmosphere, which some say needs to be "kicked up a notch" - most would "prefer a little more grandeur" given the "high prices."

Guy Savoy M *French* | 28 | 26 | 27 | VE |

Strip | Caesars Palace | 3570 Las Vegas Blvd. S. (Flamingo Rd.) | www.caesarspalace.com

"How do you say 'beyond perfect' *en français*?" ask acolytes of "genius" chef Guy Savoy, who has "outdone himself" with this "gastronomic adventure" in Caesars Palace, which some say is "better than the three-star Paris original" with "brilliantly presented" New French cuisine served à la carte or from an "exquisite" tasting menu plus a "terrific" wine list with 1,500 labels; also "memorable" is "impeccable", "unpretentious" service (ladies like the "purse perches") and a "stylish" setting done up in dark, rich woods, while "breathtaking prices" are commensurate with the "once-in-a-lifetime" experience; N.B. the Bubbles Bar inside the restaurant offers a small-bites menu.

Joël Robuchon *French* | 28 | 27 | 28 | VE |

Strip | MGM Grand Hotel | 3799 Las Vegas Blvd. S. (Tropicana Ave.) | 702-891-7925 | www.mgmgrand.com

"Truly an experience for the ages" swoon surveyors "savoring each moment" of chef Joël Robuchon's "life-altering" New French in the

MGM Grand, where the "exquisite" tasting menus "build to a crescendo of amazing intensity", rendering "all other [meals] a mere blur"; so don a jacket, "buckle in" and revel in the "elegant lavender and cream interior" and "pampering" treatment (earning it Las Vegas' No. 1 score for Service) – and if you're daunted by the "three-hour-plus" meal (not to mention the "stratospheric prices"), gastronomes advise "pace yourself, breathe deeply and keep looking at the dessert cart for motivation."

L'Atelier de Joël Robuchon *French* 28 | 24 | 26 | VE

Strip | MGM Grand Hotel | 3799 Las Vegas Blvd. S. (Tropicana Ave.) | 702-891-7358 | www.mgmgrand.com

This downscaled (but still "staggeringly" expensive) sister to Joël Robuchon in the MGM Grand is "a less stuffy way" for "hard-core foodies" to experience "the master's" "stunning" New French cuisine, which earns it the No. 1 Food score in Las Vegas thanks to "memorable" small plates best appreciated from the U-shaped bar where "you can marvel at the action" in the open kitchen; refreshingly "unpretentious" service makes the black-and-red interior feel both "sleek" and "casual" at the same time, setting the scene for "one of the single best dining experiences in Vegas" – just bring your "sense of adventure."

Lotus of Siam *Thai* 27 | 10 | 20 | M

E Side | Commercial Ctr. | 953 E. Sahara Ave. (bet. Maryland Pkwy. & Paradise Rd.) | 702-735-3033 | www.lotusofsiamlv.com

"Hitchhike if you have to", but "don't leave town" without a stop at this "local treasure" east of the Strip that intrepid eaters rank as the "best Thai restaurant in the country", with a "dazzling" "affordable" array of "complex" dishes including "exquisite" Northern-style "gems" like jackfruit curry that pair well with sips from an "excellent list of German Rieslings"; "friendly service" helps you forget all about the "strip-mall" setting and "nondescript" decor; N.B. no lunch on Saturday or Sunday.

Michael Mina *Seafood* 27 | 24 | 26 | VE

Strip | Bellagio Hotel | 3600 Las Vegas Blvd. S. (Flamingo Rd.) | 702-693-8255 | www.michaelmina.net

"Easily the best seafood on the Strip" rave regulars who savor the "divine scallops three ways", a lobster pot pie that's either "to die for" or "a reason to live" and other tastings that "tickle the senses" at chef/co-owner Michael Mina's "romantic", "beautiful and relaxing" Bellagio destination; a "superb" wine list and "marvelous" service help justify the "third mortgage required to fund the extravagance."

Nobu *Japanese* 28 | 23 | 24 | VE

E of Strip | Hard Rock Hotel | 4455 Paradise Rd. (bet. Flamingo Rd. & Harmon Ave.) | 702-693-5090 | www.noburestaurants.com

"Exceptional raw fish in the desert" attracts seekers of the "absolute freshest" "sushi and sashimi creations" as well as "amazing cooked dishes" ("love the miso cod"), all served by a "superb" staff at Nobu Matsuhisa's outpost in the Hard Rock Hotel east of the Strip; sure, "they blast music like eardrums are going out of style" and you can expect a "flabbergasting bill", but many advise "just say omakase", "watch the masters at work at the bar" and "enjoy the ride."

Picasso *French* 27 | 29 | 27 | VE

Strip | Bellagio Hotel | 3600 Las Vegas Blvd. S. (Flamingo Rd.) | www.bellagio.com

"Perfection on a grand scale" comes via chef Julian Serrano's "lavish" New French palace in the Bellagio (voted tops for Decor as well as Most Popular in Las Vegas) where "high rollers" "live the luxe life" "surrounded by original Picassos" and an "abundance of fresh flowers" while tasting "transcendent" prix fixe meals paired with "fantastic" wines from an "extensive" European list; "polished" servers exhibit "pure finesse", making for a "sublime" experience that's sure to "break you out of your blue period" - at least until you get the check.

Rosemary's *American* 28 | 20 | 26 | E

W Side | West Sahara Promenade | 8125 W. Sahara Ave. (bet. Buffalo Dr. & Cimarron Rd.) | 702-869-2251 | www.rosemarysrestaurant.com

"A winner" that "hasn't lost its special touch", this West Sider proves "a tough act to follow", with chef-owners Michael and Wendy Jordan's "simply outstanding" New American cuisine showcasing "delicate flavors" and served à la carte or in an "excellent" $55 prix fixe meal available with "inspired" beer and wine pairings; "stellar" service makes the "pretty" (some say "dowdy") decor all the more "inviting", and though it's "quite a trip" from the Strip, most maintain they'd "go back in a heartbeat"; P.S. the "$28 three-course lunch may be the best deal in town."

Tableau *American* 27 | 25 | 27 | VE

Strip | Wynn Las Vegas | 3131 Las Vegas Blvd. S. (bet. Desert Inn & Spring Mountain Rds.) | 888-352-3463 | www.wynnlasvegas.com

"Exceptional breakfasts", "civilized lunches" and "delectable" dinners await at this French-influenced New American whose "exclusive" south tower location in the Wynn makes it feel like an "elegant" "private dining room", with poolside views and "flawless service" adding to the "appeal"; diehards decree that it "deserves more attention", though insiders insist the fact that it's "not so well known" is exactly what makes it "special."

Todd's Unique Dining ⊠ *Eclectic* 28 | 16 | 25 | E

Henderson | 4350 E. Sunset Rd. (Green Valley Pkwy.) | 702-259-8633 | www.toddsunique.com

One of Henderson's "best-kept secrets", chef-owner Todd Clore's "valley favorite" "shines" with "serious", "sophisticated" seasonal Eclectic dishes plus a wine list with "phenomenal values" (and no pouring charge on Wednesdays, should you decide to bring your own); factor in "accommodating service" and enthusiasts appraise it's "as good as any on the Strip", but at "half the price"; even if the decor "could use sprucing up", everything else "just keeps getting better."

	FOOD	DECOR	SERVICE	COST

Los Angeles

TOP FOOD RANKING

	Restaurant	Cuisine
28	Mélisse	American/French
	Asanebo	Japanese
27	Lucques	Californian/Mediterranean
	Nobu Malibu	Japanese
	Shiro	French/Japanese
	Derek's	Californian/French
	Matsuhisa	Japanese
	Leila's	Californian
	Mori Sushi	Japanese
	Water Grill	Seafood
	Katsu-ya	Japanese
	Sona	French
	Angelini Osteria	Italian
	Hatfield's	American
	Spago	Californian
	Piccolo	Italian
	Brandywine	Continental
	La Cachette	French

Angelini Osteria M *Italian* 27 | 16 | 22 | E

Beverly Boulevard | 7313 Beverly Blvd. (Poinsettia Pl.) | 323-297-0070 | www.angeliniosteria.com

The "perfect" "neighborhood trattoria" assert champions of "phenomenal chef" Gino Angelini's Beverly Boulevard "gem" that "always gets it right" with "lusty" Italian dishes that "straddle the line between elegance and rusticity" and a "thoughtful" selection of regional vintages that's "terrific" too; "dreamy" waiters "with thick accents" always "try their best" to "please", so even if the "sardine" seating means you'll "literally be rubbing elbows" with neighbors, that's all part of the "charm"; P.S. be sure to "reserve well in advance."

NEW **Anisette Brasserie** *French* - | - | - | E

Santa Monica | 225 Santa Monica Blvd. (3rd St. Promenade) | 310-395-3200 | www.anisettebrasserie.com

This hotly anticipated French arrival on the ground floor of Santa Monica's historic Clock Tower Building provides a dramatic backdrop for the return of chef Alain Giraud (last seen at Bastide), who's now serving authentic, steeply priced brasserie fare; located just a few feet from the Third Street Promenade, the multilevel space boasts high ceilings, gleaming tiles and an open kitchen.

A.O.C. *Californian/French* 26 | 22 | 23 | E

Third Street | 8022 W. Third St. (bet. S. Crescent Heights Blvd. & S. Fairfax Ave.) | 323-653-6359 | www.aocwinebar.com

Devotees find "nirvana" in the "exquisite" "little morsels" at this "foodie favorite" on Third Street from Suzanne Goin (Lucques) - a pioneer in the "small-plates revolution" - featuring a "marvelous" Cal-

French menu with "wonderful cheeses", housemade charcuterie and 50 wines by the glass; add in "expert" servers and an "energetic" "star-studded" room and it's easy to see why so many "swear by it", even if all that "grazing" can "add up to a big bill."

Asanebo 🅼 *Japanese* 28 | 15 | 24 | E

Studio City | 11941 Ventura Blvd. (bet. Carpenter & Radford Aves.) | 818-760-3348

Loyalists liken the "incredible" fish dishes to works of "art" (should you "look at it or eat it"?) at this Japanese in Studio City, where chef Tetsuya Nakao sends out "impressive" displays of "stellar" sushi and sashimi and "immaculately seasoned" daily specials that require a big appetite as well as a "big wallet"; given the "tiny" space jammed with "studio heads and industry players", "reservations" are recommended and insiders assert the bar seating is the way to go.

Brandywine 🅢 *Continental* 27 | 20 | 27 | E

Woodland Hills | 22757 Ventura Blvd. (Fallbrook Ave.) | 818-225-9114

A "charming owner" presides over this "sweet", "little" Woodland Hills "gem" that embodies "old-world elegance" with "lovingly prepared" Continental cuisine and "quaint" decor that makes you feel "swept away" to a "French countryside home"; it's certainly "not cheap", but the smitten swear it's "worth dressing up and paying a little bit extra" for such a "memorable", "romantic" meal.

Café Bizou *Californian/French* 23 | 19 | 21 | M

Pasadena | 91 N. Raymond Ave. (Holly St.) | 626-792-9923

Sherman Oaks | 14016 Ventura Blvd. (bet. Costello & Murietta Aves.) | 818-788-3536

www.cafebizou.com

"Longtime" patrons proclaim "you just can't miss" with these "bargain" Cal-French bistros in Pasadena and Sherman Oaks, which win "*bizoux*" thanks to a "tasty" "traditional" menu and a "$2 corkage fee" that "sweetens" the deal for "wine aficionados"; "unflappable" servers and a "bustling" atmosphere are part of the appeal, but given the constant "crowds", "don't expect to linger."

Derek's 🅢🅼 *Californian/French* 27 | 23 | 26 | E

Pasadena | 181 E. Glenarm St. (bet. Arroyo Pkwy. & Marengo Ave.) | 626-799-5252 | www.dereks.com

"Intimate dining in a strip mall" can be found at this "refined" Cal-French "special-event place" in Pasadena where the cooking is "superb" and the "tasting menu with wine pairings never misses"; despite the "off-putting" exterior, its "romantic" setting ("sit by the fireplace on a cold night") and "fine", "considerate" staff round out an experience that justifies the "expensive" tab.

NEW **XIV** *American* - | - | - | E

West Hollywood | 8117 Sunset Blvd. (bet. Crescent Hts. & Selma Ave.) | 323-656-1414 | www.xivla.com

For his 14th restaurant (hence the name), Michael Mina makes his LA debut adjacent to West Hollywood's Chateau Marmont with this New American featuring a retro design by Philippe Starck – think dark wood, richly colored carpets and understated lighting; the menu's many small plates can add up quickly at $8 a pop (Kobe beef and caviar cost more).

Hatfield's ☒ *American* 27 | 20 | 25 | VE

Beverly Boulevard | 7458 Beverly Blvd. (Gardner St.) | 323-935-2977 | www.hatfieldsrestaurant.com

"Hats off!" cheer champions of "husband-and-wife duo" Quinn and Karen Hatfield's Beverly Boulevard "jewel" presenting an "intelligent" New American menu showcasing "bold and clean flavors" from "farm-fresh" ingredients in "memorable" à la carte selections or in a "luxurious" seven-course tasting menu; the "graceful" staff provides "smooth service", and if some customers quibble about the "spare", "tiny" space, proponents proclaim it's just proof that "great things come in small packages."

Katsu-ya *Japanese* 27 | 15 | 19 | E

Encino | 16542 Ventura Blvd. (Hayvenhurst Ave.) | 818-788-2396
Studio City | 11680 Ventura Blvd. (Colfax Ave.) | 818-985-6976
www.sushikatsu-ya.com

Boasting "brilliant", "inventive" sushi and cooked dishes, these Encino and Studio City Japanese "gems" provide "exceptional" culinary quality while offering a "better deal" "without the attitude" of their "flashier" unhyphenated cousins; their "small" "nothing-to-look-at" digs are "always crowded" with a "cult" following and then some, so vets advise "make reservations" and "order from the board for a gastronomic treat."

La Cachette ☒ *French* 27 | 25 | 25 | VE

Century City | 10506 Little Santa Monica Blvd. (Thayer Ave.) | 310-470-4992 | www.lacachetterestaurant.com

"What fine dining should be", this "jewel box" in Century City treats fans to a "first-rate" "taste of France" by chef-owner Jean Francois Meteigner, who reinvents "classic" dishes with "imagination", "elegance" and a "light" touch; service is "seamless" too, and though the "spacious" Provençal-inspired dining room feels a bit "sedate" and "elite" to some, most find it "marvelous" enough to warrant the "hefty price tag."

Leila's ☒ Ⓜ *Californian* 27 | 19 | 24 | E

Oak Park | RE/MAX Plaza | 706 Lindero Canyon Rd. (Golden Eagle Dr.) | 818-707-6939 | www.leilasrestaurant.com

"Quite a surprise" considering its "strip-mall exterior", this "always fabulous" Californian in Oak Park provides "awesome", "frequently changing" seasonal fare by "superb" chef Richie DeMane, who "obviously loves food"; "reasonable" choices on the "outstanding" wine list and "personable" service add to the "positive" experience, though some feel the colorful, "eclectic" setting "could use some work."

Lucques *Californian/Mediterranean* 27 | 24 | 25 | E

West Hollywood | 8474 Melrose Ave. (La Cienega Blvd.) | 323-655-6277 | www.lucques.com

Dining is a "dream" at this "casually elegant" Cal-Med in West Hollywood where "brilliant" chef/co-owner Suzanne Goin (A.O.C.) continues to "surprise and delight" with "inventive" dishes highlighting the "farms' freshest" ingredients, served by a "spot-on" staff; "warm", with a "cozy fireplace" and "charming" patio, the converted carriage house has an "inviting", "grown-up" atmosphere to suit the "unpretentious" crowd; P.S. most nights it's a "splurge", but the prix fixe Sunday Supper still has it "goin' on" as one of the "best deals in town."

Matsuhisa *Japanese* 27 | 16 | 23 | VE

Beverly Hills | 129 N. La Cienega Blvd. (bet. Clifton Way & Wilshire Blvd.) | 310-659-9639 | www.nobumatsuhisa.com

"Raw fish guru" Nobu Matsuhisa "hasn't lost a step" at his first "home" in Beverly Hills, "turning out unbelievably fresh sushi" and "imaginative" Japanese dishes with Peruvian twists that "entice you to return" "even if you have to wait until your next paycheck" to afford it; the "helpful" staff "makes you feel welcome and at ease", and though some say the decor is "in need of a serious face-lift", most agree it still "sets the standard" for LA cuisine.

Mélisse [S] [M] *American/French* 28 | 25 | 27 | VE

Santa Monica | 1104 Wilshire Blvd. (11th St.) | 310-395-0881 | www.melisse.com

"Marvelous evenings" are made at Josiah Citrin's "sublime" French-New American in Santa Monica, renowned for "meticulously prepared" seasonal dishes and "exceptional" tasting menus that "open new vistas" of experience, earning it the No. 1 Food score in LA; rounded out by an "elegant", "quiet" atmosphere and "impeccable" (if "serious") service, it wins accolades as a "national treasure" - just "be prepared to pay for this pursuit of perfection."

Mori Sushi [S] *Japanese* 27 | 17 | 21 | VE

West LA | 11500 W. Pico Blvd. (Gateway Blvd.) | 310-479-3939 | www.morisushi.org

"Scintillating combinations of ingredients" showcasing "sparkling fresh" fish presented on "beautiful" "handcrafted" plates dazzle diners who say "splurge on the omakase" by "Mori-san" (chef-owner Morihiro Onodera) at this West LA Japanese; while the digs "feel a bit spartan", that hardly matters when you're savoring "sushi from the gods."

Nobu Malibu *Japanese* 27 | 20 | 22 | VE

Malibu | 3835 Cross Creek Rd. (PCH) | 310-317-9140 | www.nobumatsuhisa.com

"Near perfection" is how devotees describe Nobu Matsuhisa's Malibu Japanese "hot spot" where "A-listers abound" in the "casually luxe" setting, but the "food is the star", with "spectacular" sushi and "phenomenal carpaccio dishes" all delivered by a "warm crew"; though it thrives on a "laid-back" feel, don't let the "tacky strip-mall locale" fool you - this "spectacular culinary experience" is "not for the faint of wallet."

Piccolo *Italian* 27 | 17 | 24 | E

Venice | 5 Dudley Ave. (Spdwy.) | 310-314-3222 | www.piccolovenice.com

"A secret hideaway" just "steps from the beach", this "charming" Venice Italian showcases "big-flavored" cooking that's "always delicious, even with the changes in chefs", and "splendid vino" in a "postage-stamp"-sized setting; a no-reservations policy means you can "expect to wait", but once you snag a seat, regulars report you're in for a "treat", albeit a somewhat "expensive" one.

FOOD | DECOR | SERVICE | COST

Pizzeria Mozza *Pizza*

FOOD	DECOR	SERVICE	COST
26	19	21	M

Hollywood | 641 N. Highland Ave. (Melrose Ave.) | 323-297-0101 | www.mozza-la.com

The "hottest ticket in town", this "instant classic" in Hollywood from "rock-star chefs" Mario Batali and Nancy Silverton might just "change your worldview about pizza" with "ethereal" pies sporting perfectly "charred" crusts and "esoteric toppings" like squash blossoms and burrata; given the frequently "packed house", servers are "overwhelmed" and the noise level "much too loud", yet acolytes insist they "could eat here every night" if only they "could get in" (psst - "reserve well ahead" or "try the bar" for impromptu dining).

Shiro [M] *French/Japanese*

FOOD	DECOR	SERVICE	COST
27	18	26	E

South Pasadena | 1505 Mission St. (bet. Fair Oaks & Fremont Aves.) | 626-799-4774 | www.restaurantshiro.com

"Gotta love the deep-fried catfish" crow customers who find the seafood "addictive" at this "sensational", high-end South Pasadena destination where the "quality never fades" thanks to chef-owner Hideo Yamashiro's intrepid market-going and "memorable" French-Japanese cooking (no sushi); the staff is "helpful", so even given the "spartan" surroundings, many agree it's a winning "date place."

Sona [S] [M] *French*

FOOD	DECOR	SERVICE	COST
27	24	27	VE

West Hollywood | 401 N. La Cienega Blvd. (bet. Beverly Blvd. & Melrose Ave.) | 310-659-7708 | www.sonarestaurant.com

A "temple for food", this "minimalist" WeHo "favorite" from "wizard" David Myers showcases a "well-orchestrated" New French menu of "beautiful, delicate dishes with artfully combined flavors" matched by an "incredible" wine list; insiders recommend the "sublime" tasting menu, as it's "worth taking out a loan" just to "sit back and be pampered in every sense of the word" by the "unbeatable" team.

Spago *Californian*

FOOD	DECOR	SERVICE	COST
27	25	25	VE

Beverly Hills | 176 N. Cañon Dr. (Wilshire Blvd.) | 310-385-0880 | www.wolfgangpuck.com

"A permanent fixture in the LA culinary firmament", this Wolfgang Puck "flagship", voted the city's Most Popular restaurant, has "still got it in spades" thanks to chef Lee Hefter's Californian fare that's "artistically appointed and cooked to perfection", Sherry Yard's "extraordinary" desserts and a staff that "makes a nobody feel like a star"; add in prime Beverly Hills "people-watching" in the "fanciful" room and on the "beautiful" patio, and patrons would pony up the "crown jewels" for the "fabulous" feast.

Water Grill *Seafood*

FOOD	DECOR	SERVICE	COST
27	24	25	VE

Downtown | 544 S. Grand Ave. (bet. 5th & 6th Sts.) | 213-891-0900 | www.watergrill.com

A "perennial favorite" for "fabulous" feasts of "swimmingly delicious" fin fare, this Downtown seafooder proves "all around wonderful" for fans savoring some of "the finest fish in LA" backed by a "broad, creative" wine list and "gracious" service from the "attentive" staff; though the "elegant" yachtlike interior feels "a bit staid" to some, most maintain it's "always a pleasure" for "business lunches", "romantic" dinners and other "splurge"-worthy special occasions.

Miami

	FOOD	DECOR	SERVICE	COST

TOP FOOD RANKING

	Restaurant	Cuisine
28	Michy's	American/French
27	Palme d'Or	French
	Nobu Miami Beach	Japanese
	Romeo's Cafe	Italian
	Prime One Twelve	Seafood/Steak
	Pascal's on Ponce	French
26	Francesco	Peruvian
	Azul	Mediterranean
	Hiro's Yakko San	Japanese
	Cacao	Nuevo Latino
	Joe's Stone Crab	Seafood
	Tropical Chinese	Chinese
	Osteria del Teatro	Italian
	Oceanaire Seafood Room	Seafood
	Caffe Vialetto	Italian
	Quinn's Restaurant	Seafood

Azul *Mediterranean* 26 | 27 | 25 | VE

Brickell Area | Mandarin Oriental Hotel | 500 Brickell Key Dr. (8th St.) | 305-913-8358 | www.mandarinoriental.com

"Creative, amazing food" – officially Mediterranean, but with "a touch of Asia, a touch of France and a touch of the U.S." – "excellent" wines and staffers who "know what you want before you do" make dining at the Mandarin Oriental an "orgasmic experience"; "you'll want to devour the view too", and the "as-chic-as-they-come" surroundings are "a great place to go spotting local celebrities"; some sigh "prices rose after chef Michelle Bernstein left", but landing current toque Clay Conley "was quite a coup", and overall this remains "one of Miami's top innovative restaurants."

Barton G...The Restaurant *American* 22 | 26 | 23 | VE

South Beach | 1427 West Ave. (14th Ct.) | Miami Beach | 305-672-8881 | www.bartong.com

"Good for celeb spotting" and "celebrations" too, it's always "showtime!" at SoBe's "DisneyWorld for foodies" where, amid a "beautiful garden" setting, "ridiculously huge"-sized (and -priced) New American dishes are "served in an unusual manner" (e.g. "popcorn shrimp in movie popcorn boxes"); if foes fear "this once-novel restaurant is becoming a novelty", with cuisine and staff "sacrificed to the humor, pomp and circumstance of the presentation", stalwarts swear "there may be places with better food, service or decor, but this puts all three together."

Blue Door at Delano ◐ *French* 24 | 27 | 22 | VE

South Beach | Delano Hotel | 1685 Collins Ave. (17th St.) | Miami Beach | 305-674-6400 | www.chinagrillmgt.com

The "epitome of high-end SoBe decor", the Delano Hotel's "paradise in white" is a "fittingly swank location" for "checking out the rich and famous" as you consume "terrific" New French cuisine from *célébrité* chef Claude Troisgros, brought by "white-glove", if somewhat self-impressed, servers; skeptics sniff it's all "style over substance", but most deem the experience "worth it" - "even when they bring the check."

Cacao ☒ *Nuevo Latino* 26 | 23 | 24 | E

Coral Gables | 141 Giralda Ave. (bet. Galiano St. & Ponce de Leon Blvd.) | 305-445-1001 | www.cacaorestaurant.com

As its name suggests, "wonderful" chocolate desserts cap off Venezuelan chef-owner Edgar Leal's "gourmet riff on the best of Latin American fare"; "superb" service, "cosmopolitan" white/orange decor and a "wine cellar second to none" all enhance his "sophisticated" menu, and while some hesitate at the "high prices", few deny this is "a wonderful alternative to the tried-and-tired Coral Gables offerings."

Caffe Vialetto *Italian* 26 | 20 | 24 | E

Coral Gables | 4019 Le Jeune Rd. (bet. El Prado Blvd. & Malaga Ave.) | 305-446-5659

"A small restaurant, but a big restaurant taste and experience" gush groupies of this "simple storefront" in Coral Gables, where the Latin- and Caribbean-tinged Italian cuisine is both "excellent and consistent" and the staff "treats you like family"; the "jammed", "noisy" dining room is strictly small-time, though, as is the no-weekend-reservations policy, even if you do get "complimentary glasses of wine while you wait."

Francesco ☒ *Peruvian* 26 | 16 | 23 | E

Coral Gables | 325 Alcazar Ave. (bet. SW 42nd Ave. & Salzedo St.) | 305-446-1600 | www.francescorestaurant.com

"The best Peruvian north of Lima" say surveyors about this "quaint" Coral Gables eatery specializing in seafood that is "absolutely fresh and cooked perfectly" ("be sure to order the ceviche" too), brought by "cordial" servers; and even if the decor's "nondescript" and the quarters "cramped", most deem it a "good value", given the "unique" fare and "unusual South American wines."

Hiro's Yakko San ◐ *Japanese* 26 | 12 | 20 | M

North Miami Beach | 17040-46 W. Dixie Hwy. (bet. 170th & 171st Sts.) | 305-947-0064 | www.yakko-san.com

"A treasure hidden" in North Miami Beach, this "authentic Japanese" dishes up "superlative" cooked fare, including "innovative tapas" that pique the palates of "adventurous" diners who "like trying new and exotic foods"; it may be a "hole-in-the-wall" with "not-wonderful decor", but the "polite" staff, "great selection of sakes" and 2 AM closing time (3 AM on weekends) lead fish-o-philes to bubble "this is the real deal."

Joe's Stone Crab *Seafood* 26 | 19 | 23 | E

South Beach | 11 Washington Ave. (S. Pointe Dr.) | Miami Beach | 305-673-0365 | www.joesstonecrab.com

"Who doesn't love Joe's?" - no one, apparently, since this "South Beach classic", "a shrine to the stone crab", is voted Miami's Most Popular; the claws are simply "awesome", as are the "heavenly hash browns", and do "leave room for the best Key lime pie"; expect "excruciating" waits to get into the "cafeteria"-like dining room and, once inside, "astronomical" prices and "rushed", if "reponsive", service; even so, "you have to go once (then order takeout after that)."

Michy's ⓜ *American/French* 28 | 19 | 25 | E

Upper East Side | 6927 Biscayne Blvd. (bet. NE 69th & 70th Sts.) | 305-759-2001

Chef "Michelle Bernstein stars" at this "cozy, intimate" Upper Eastsider where a "sophisticated menu for real foodies" - voted No. 1 in Miami - lists a variety of tapas-style, New American-French dishes that "blend Latin, Southern, comfort food and just plain delicious flavors"; "warm, friendly" service is another plus, and though the "dodgy" neighborhood and "quirky" orange/blue decor "leave something to be desired", this place "would proudly hold its own with the best in New York."

Nobu Miami Beach ◐ *Japanese* 27 | 23 | 22 | VE

South Beach | Shore Club | 1901 Collins Ave. (20th St.) | Miami Beach | 305-695-3232 | www.noburestaurants.com

"It's noisy, it's expensive, it's young, it's fabulous" - it's the "swanky" SoBe outpost of Nobu Matsuhisa's empire, with "the same incredible", "addictive" Japanese-Peruvian fare that features the "freshest, best-prepared sushi on the planet"; some say the staff, while "knowledgeable", is "more interested in being seen than in serving", and you better "be there exactly when it opens to avoid killer waits" (reservations for six or more only), but most hail this "shining star" (indeed, "stay long enough and you may see a star").

Oceanaire Seafood Room *Seafood* 26 | 25 | 24 | VE

Downtown | Mary Brickell Vill. | 900 S. Miami Ave. (10th St.) | 305-372-8862 | www.theoceanaire.com

"Part of a chain, though it doesn't feel chain-y", this, "elegant" fish house blows a "welcome breath of fresh air into Downtown", dishing up an "amazing variety of seafood" "served steakhouse-style" (e.g. separately priced sides) in a dining room "that looks like a cruise ship"; to be sure, it's "pricey" and the "friendly staff is maybe too friendly", but the "super-sized portions" and super-"fresh" fare make those of the piscine persuasion want to "go back again and again."

Osteria del Teatro ⓢ *Italian* 26 | 16 | 24 | E

South Beach | 1443 Washington Ave. (Española Way) | Miami Beach | 305-538-7850 | www.osteriadelteatromiami.com

"There's no need to read the menu" at this "little bit of Italy in South Beach", but "you may want to take notes on the many specials" of "oh-so-simple, but oh-so-good" Northern Italian fare or risk "being overwhelmed with choices"; hungry throngs can swamp the "cramped" dining room, but servers who "anticipate your every need" help alleviate the pain of "paying dearly" for "food that reigns supreme."

Palme d'Or ⓢⓜ *French* 27 | 26 | 26 | VE

Coral Gables | Biltmore Hotel | 1200 Anastasia Ave. (Granada Blvd.) | 305-913-3201 | www.biltmorehotel.com

Francophiles fawn life "doesn't get better" than at this "luxurious", "sophisticated" Biltmore Hotel restaurant, a contemporary corner of the famed "shrine to turn-of-the-century Mediterranean architecture"; chef Philippe Ruiz's menu of New French small plates "brings new meaning to the word flavor", the wine list is "excellent" and the "formal, intelligent and well-trained personnel" are rated No. 1 for

Service in Miami; the experience "doesn't come cheap", but you'll "leave with a sense of well-being."

Pascal's on Ponce ☒ *French* — 27 | 18 | 24 | E

Coral Gables | 2611 Ponce de Leon Blvd. (bet. Almeria & Valencia Aves.) | 305-444-2024 | www.pascalmiami.com

The staff "treats you like VIPs" while the kitchen turns out "artistic", "classically inspired New French fare" at this "high-end bistro" run by "incredibly creative" chef Pascal Oudin; "*c'est magnifique!*" crows a contented Coral Gables crowd, whose "only gripe is that tables are oh-so-Parisian close."

Prime One Twelve ◐ *Seafood/Steak* — 27 | 23 | 23 | VE

South Beach | 112 Ocean Dr. (1st St.) | Miami Beach | 305-532-8112 | www.prime112.com

"The hottest restaurant south of the Mason-Dixon line" caters to celebrities from the "NBA to fashion to Hollywood and everyone in between" with "gargantuan" portions of "perfect seafood" and steaks that are "a religious experience"; "even with reservations, waits can be horrible" for a seat in the "crowded", "deafening" dining room, service swings from "surprisingly quick" to "standoffish" and critics crack it should be called "Crime One Twelve", given the "exceptionally expensive" tabs; nevertheless, this is "the ultimate SoBe" scene.

Quinn's Restaurant *Seafood* — 26 | 23 | 24 | E

South Beach | Park Central Hotel | 640 Ocean Dr. (bet. 6th & 7th Sts.) | Miami Beach | 305-673-6400 | www.quinnsmiami.com

To "enjoy the alfresco atmosphere without all the crowds" on Ocean Drive - and get in some "great people-watching" as well - "request a seat on the patio" of chef-owner Gerry Quinn's "pretty" seafooder, home of "the highly touted bam bam shrimp"; advocates attest that "everything about this place says 'winner'", from the "upbeat service" to the nightly guitarist.

Romeo's Cafe ☒ Ⓜ *Italian* — 27 | 18 | 26 | VE

Coral Way | 2257 SW 22nd St./Coral Way (bet. 22nd & 23rd Aves.) | 305-859-2228 | www.romeoscafe.com

For a "unique, romantic experience", get thee to this "jewel box" of a Northern Italian in Coral Way, where "there is no printed menu"; instead, namesake toque Romeo Majano "will visit your table to discern your likes and dislikes", then create an "incredible" multicourse meal; it's "like having your own personal chef", as well as your own "wonderful" staff for a "rich", elaborate and "expensive" evening - one that has "discerning diners" declaring "bravo Romeo!"

Tropical Chinese *Chinese* — 26 | 16 | 20 | M

Westchester | Tropical Park Plaza | 7991 SW 40th St. (SW 79th Ave.) | 305-262-7576

"A nonstop gastronomic parade" of "incredible, inexpensive dim sum" is the "real attraction" of this "gourmet" Chinese where the "gruff" but "competent" waiters, "glassed-in kitchen" and "lazy Susans on large tables" make you "feel like you're in Hong Kong", even though you're really in an "out-of-the-way" Westchester strip mall; P.S. at night, "you must get the Peking duck - more than a dish, it's an art form."

FOOD	DECOR	SERVICE	COST

New Orleans

TOP FOOD RANKING

	Restaurant	Cuisine
28	Brigtsen's	Contemp. Louisiana
	Stella!	American
	Bayona	American
	Dakota	American/Contemp. Louisiana
	Gautreau's	American/French
	August	Continental/French
27	Clancy's	Creole
	K-Paul's	Cajun
	Commander's Palace	Creole
	La Provence	Creole/French
	La Boca	Argentinean/Steak
	Cypress	Creole
	Galatoire's	Creole/French
26	Herbsaint	American/French
	Dick & Jenny's	Creole/Eclectic

Acme Oyster House *Seafood* 22 | 14 | 19 | I

French Quarter | 724 Iberville St. (bet. Bourbon & Royal Sts.) | 504-522-5973
Metairie | 3000 Veterans Memorial Blvd. (N. Causeway Blvd.) | 504-309-4056
Covington | 1202 N. Hwy. 190 (bet. Crestwood Blvd. & 17th Ave.) | 985-246-6155
www.acmeoyster.com

"There's a wait out the door for a reason" at this French Quarter "old faithful" (with less historic outposts in the 'burbs) whose "phenomenal" oysters ("raw, char-grilled and fried") as well as other "inexpensive", "off-the-boat" seafood is the stuff "you write about in postcards"; tourists "sit elbow-to-elbow with natives" in the "merry", "faux-divey" digs, while those in-the-know head to the bar's "marble counter" for a close-up of the shuckers' "floor show."

August *Continental/French* 28 | 27 | 27 | VE

Central Business Dist. | 301 Tchoupitoulas St. (Gravier St.) | 504-299-9777 | www.rest-august.com

"Exceptionally creative" celebrity chef/co-owner John Besh "impresses" guests with "attention to detail that's something to behold" at his CBD flagship, crafting an "exciting and satisfying" menu of Continental-New French cuisine that's "filled with fresh, local surprises"; both the "lovely" interior of "exposed brick and shimmering chandeliers" and "terrific" service by a "well-versed" staff complete the "sublime" meal, so "if you can stomach the prices", you'll make your stomach very "happy."

Bayona ☒ *American* 28 | 26 | 26 | E

French Quarter | 430 Dauphine St. (bet. Conti & St. Louis Sts.) | 504-525-4455 | www.bayona.com

"Culinary genius" Susan Spicer creates "imaginative", "delectable" New American dishes with "local flavor", which are delivered by her "crackerjack" staff at this "shining star" in a Creole cottage "tucked away from the craziness of the French Quarter"; its "picturesque" patio and "multiple, intimate" dining areas ("request the first floor") are equally "attractive", adding up to a "slice of heaven" that's "well worth the price"; P.S. "go for lunch" - it's a "bargain" and the "duck PB&J will make you glad you're an adult now."

Brigtsen's [S] [M] *Contemp. Louisiana* — 28 | 23 | 27 | E

Riverbend | 723 Dante St. (Maple St.) | 504-861-7610 | www.brigtsens.com

"Believe everything you've heard" about chef/co-owner Frank Brigtsen's "marvelous", "innovative" Contemporary Louisiana "comfort food with flair" presented at a "perfect pace" by a "delightful", "down-to-earth" staff (helmed by wife and manager Marna Brigtsen) at this Riverbend "winner", rated No. 1 in New Orleans for Food and Service; many "love the atmosphere" in a "quaint" cottage too (though critics call it "cramped"), finding the whole experience "New Orleans through and through" and a "great value" to boot.

Clancy's [S] *Creole* — 27 | 22 | 25 | E

Uptown | 6100 Annunciation St. (Webster St.) | 504-895-1111

"You can get lost finding" this "clubby" Uptown "institution" that's "among the last of the haute Creole houses", where "traditional waiters" serve "outstanding" dishes like oysters with Brie and smoked soft-shell crab at upscale but "fair" prices; boasting a "high-octane atmosphere", it plays host to plenty of "back-slapping" among the "old-guard" crowd and is still the "place you're most likely to see someone in seersucker."

Commander's Palace *Creole* — 27 | 28 | 27 | E

Garden District | 1403 Washington Ave. (Coliseum St.) | 504-899-8221 | www.commanderspalace.com

"To be the king", go to this Garden District "palace" for "culinary masterpieces" that "honor Creole tradition while being creative" at the same time; once again voted the city's Most Popular restaurant (a title it held for 17 consecutive years prior to an extended post-Katrina closure), it's also rated No. 1 for Decor following a "gorgeous" renovation by owners Lally Brennan and Ti Martin; the "old-style" service is "top-notch" too, and "Sunday jazz brunch in the garden room is a must"; P.S. try the "quarter-martini lunch if you're on a budget."

Cypress [S] [M] *Creole* — 27 | 21 | 25 | M

Metairie | 4426 Transcontinental Dr. (W. Esplanade Ave.) | 504-885-6885 | www.restaurantcypress.com

"A bit out of the way", this "unexpected" sleeper in a Metairie strip mall boasts the talents of chef/co-owner Stephen Huth, who "really knows his flavors" and uses "fresh, local ingredients" to craft "fabulous" contemporary Creole food; fans also appreciate the moderate prices, "funny" staff and "family-friendly" atmosphere, judging it a "jewel" that could "rival just about any establishment in the city"; P.S. "seating is limited" and reservations aren't taken, so "get there early."

Dakota, The [S] *American/Contemp. Louisiana* — 28 | 24 | 26 | E

Covington | 629 N. Hwy. 190 (¼ mi. north of I-12) | 985-892-3712 | www.thedakotarestaurant.com

From "crab and Brie soup to die for" to game, seafood and some of the "best steaks on the North Shore", this "long-standing" Covington destination dazzles diners with chef Kim Kringlie's "outstanding" New American-Contemporary Louisiana cuisines set off by an "excellent" 600-bottle wine list as well as "fabulous" service; despite its "suburban" highway location, most find the richly toned, flower-filled interior a "sophisticated" setting to indulge in an "expensive", "one-of-a-kind" meal.

Dick & Jenny's *Creole/Eclectic* 26 | 22 | 25 | E

Uptown | 4501 Tchoupitoulas St. (Jena St.) | 504-894-9880 | www.dickandjennys.com

As irresistable as a "Southern woman's open arms", this "charming", no-reservations Uptowner offers a "modern take on Crescent City flavors" with its "out-of-this-world" "haute" Creole-Eclectic fare served by an "engaging", "efficient" staff in a "funky" clapboard cottage; factor in prices that don't "break the bank", and diners "don't mind having a bottle of wine on the porch" while waiting for a table - a speed bump many view as part of the "wonderfully New Orleans" experience.

Galatoire's *Creole/French* 27 | 25 | 27 | E

French Quarter | 209 Bourbon St. (Iberville St.) | 504-525-2021 | www.galatoires.com

"It's not just a restaurant, it's an experience" effuse fans of this "cherished New Orleans tradition", a French Quarter "temple" of "superlative" Creole-French fare (especially seafood) served by "impeccable" waiters who look like they "stepped out of a painting"; so "dress your best" and "head over early for Friday lunch" - when local blue bloods feast and "get smashed" in the "classy" mirrored dining room downstairs, often carousing "till dinner" - or Sunday brunch among "beautiful ladies" and "gentlemen who looked like they enjoyed putting on a tie"; N.B. jackets required after 5 PM and on Sundays.

Gautreau's *American/French* 28 | 24 | 26 | E

Uptown | 1728 Soniat St. (Danneel St.) | 504-899-7397 | www.gautreausrestaurant.com

"Exquisite", "adventuresome" New American-New French dishes created by "up-and-coming" chef Sue Zemanick and served by an "outstanding" staff keep natives returning to this "old Uptown favorite", a "rarified" retreat "hidden" in a residential neighborhood with "no sign" out front; post-K, proprietor Patrick Singley gave the "civilized" converted-drugstore setting a face-lift by re-creating the "original hammered tin ceiling" and adding trompe l'oeil walls with a draping effect, so it feels as if you're dining "inside a very decadent tent."

Herbsaint *American/French* 26 | 22 | 24 | E

Warehouse District | 701 St. Charles Ave. (Girod St.) | 504-524-4114 | www.herbsaint.com

"Love it!" is still the word on this "brilliant" New American-New French bistro in the Warehouse District where "big-time" chef/co-owner Donald Link continues to coax "amazing flavors" from "local" ingredients in his "sophisticated" take on Big Easy cuisine; among the highlights are "wonderful", "well-priced" small plates and cocktails (including the "best" Sazerac), "courteous" service and a "clean, refreshing" setting with a "wall of windows" where you "see the streetcar go by", all adding up to a "real winner."

	FOOD	DECOR	SERVICE	COST
K-Paul's Louisiana Kitchen [S] *Cajun*	27	21	24	E

French Quarter | 416 Chartres St. (bet. Conti & St. Louis Sts.) | 504-596-2530 | www.kpauls.com

"Put this one on your A-list" affirm acolytes of "culinary legend" Paul Prudhomme's French Quarter shrine, a "well-oiled establishment" where exec chef Paul Miller continues to mesmerize "tourist" hordes (and a few "locals") with "authentic" Cajun cuisine boasting "incredible flavors" that "live up to the hype"; while it's "expensive", the "cozy", "understated" space and "talented" staff create just the right "laid-back" mood for savoring the "joyful, plentiful" meal.

	FOOD	DECOR	SERVICE	COST
La Boca [S] *Argentinean/Steak*	27	20	24	E

Warehouse District | 857 Fulton St. (St. Joseph St.) | 504-525-8205 | www.labocasteaks.com

Lovers of "red meat and red wine" say "run, don't walk" to this "tiny" Warehouse District Argentinean (a sib of RioMar) where the specialty is "superbly cooked" "unusual cuts" of steak escorted by "interesting" "homemade" sauces and "fantastic" sides, as well as "tasteful" vino from the same region; the staff "makes you feel at home", while soccer uniforms and photos of the "Boca Juniors team" lend a spirited touch to the "masculine" setting.

	FOOD	DECOR	SERVICE	COST
La Provence [M] *Creole/French*	27	27	26	E

Lacombe | 25020 Hwy. 190 (bet. Bremermann & Raymond Rds.) | 985-626-7662 | www.laprovencerestaurant.com

When celebrity chef/co-owner John Besh took over this "beautiful, rustic" Lacombe manor from "his mentor", the late Chris Kerageorgiou, he inherited "charming" premises evocative of a place "you would stumble upon in the French countryside" and made them gleam; in step with the surroundings are "extraordinary" Creole-Provençal dishes with a "home-cooked touch", enhanced by a "well-thought-out" wine list and "gracious" service that justify the 40-mile drive from New Orleans; N.B. the Food score does not reflect a post-Survey executive chef change.

	FOOD	DECOR	SERVICE	COST
Stella! *American*	28	26	27	VE

French Quarter | Hotel Provincial | 1032 Chartres St. (bet. St. Philip & Ursuline Sts.) | 504-587-0091 | www.restaurantstella.com

"The artistry and science that go into preparing the dishes is tops" at this "must-visit" New American in the French Quarter where "über"-chef-owner Scott Boswell creates "spectacular" dishes with an "avant-garde" "Asian backbeat"; "intelligent" wine choices, "engaged yet formal" servers who "knock themselves out to please" and a "soothing" setting pull together the "exceptional" meal, but "bring a fat wallet", since the check is equally "awe-inspiring."

FOOD	DECOR	SERVICE	COST

New York City

TOP FOOD RANKING

	Restaurant	Cuisine
28	Per Se	American/French
	Le Bernardin	French/Seafood
	Daniel	French
	Jean Georges	French
	Sushi Yasuda	Japanese
	Bouley	French
	Mas	American
	L'Atelier de Joël Robuchon	French
	Gramercy Tavern	American
27	Chanterelle	French
	Sasabune	Japanese
	Gotham Bar & Grill	American
	Sushi Seki	Japanese
	Café Boulud	French
	Degustation	French/Spanish
	Sugiyama	Japanese
	Nobu	Japanese
	Aureole	American
	Masa/Bar Masa	Japanese
	Babbo	Italian
	La Grenouille	French
	Union Square Cafe	American

Aureole ☒ *American* — 27 | 26 | 26 | VE

E 60s | 34 E. 61st St. (bet. Madison & Park Aves.) | 212-319-1660 | www.charliepalmer.com

A "foodie mecca", Charlie Palmer's "joyous" East Side New American is known for "paradise-on-a-plate", "chic people-watching" and blessedly "easy reservations"; "stellar" service and a "posh", flower-filled townhouse setting cushion the fact that the prix fixe–only dinners are priced like "Picassos"; N.B. it's set to relocate off Bryant Park in spring 2009.

Babbo ◐ *Italian* — 27 | 23 | 24 | VE

G Village | 110 Waverly Pl. (bet. MacDougal St. & 6th Ave.) | 212-777-0303 | www.babbonyc.com

Only "getting better with age", Mario Batali and Joe Bastianich's Village flagship offers "brilliant" repasts backed by an "unparalleled wine list" and "exemplary service" in a handsome carriage house setting; prices are high, but since it's NYC's No. 1 Italian, reservations are nearly "impossible"; to avoid waiting for a seat until the "next geological epoch", come early and "dine at the bar"; still, some say "overhyped."

Bouley ◐ *French* — 28 | - | 27 | VE

TriBeCa | 163 Duane St. (Hudson St.) | 212-964-2525 | www.davidbouley.com

Relocated around the corner from its former West Broadway digs, this "transcending" TriBeCa experience via David Bouley still features "fantastic" French cooking and an "unobtrusive" staff that "knows exactly what to do" and does it; sure, the tabs are as "splurge"-worthy as ever, but in return you can expect "special-occasion" meals every night of the week and a $48 prix fixe lunch that's an "all-time fave."

Café Boulud *French* 27 | 23 | 26 | VE

E 70s | Surrey Hotel | 20 E. 76th St. (bet. 5th & Madison Aves.) | 212-772-2600 | www.danielnyc.com

"Comfortable" yet "civilized", Daniel Boulud's "sophisticated" Upper East Side satellite provides "glorious" dining thanks to chef Gavin Kaysen's "exquisite" French cuisine, "interesting" wines and "seamless service"; though decidedly "costly", prices are "less astronomical" than at the flagship, especially for the "bargain" $24 lunch prix fixe.

Chanterelle *French* 27 | 26 | 28 | VE

TriBeCa | 2 Harrison St. (Hudson St.) | 212-966-6960 | www.chanterellenyc.com

"Adult perfection" sums up the scene at David and Karen Waltuck's 30-year-old French "destination", bringing "ethereal", "transcendent" cuisine to TriBeCa; "anticipatory" service and a "large", "flower"-filled room have diners "floating on air", though the "big", prix fixe-only bills may keep them tethered to earth; N.B. the set-price $45 lunch (when dishes are also available à la carte) is more affordable.

NEW Corton ☒ *French* - | - | - | VE

TriBeCa | 239 W. Broadway (bet. Walker & White Sts.) | 212-219-2777 | www.cortonnyc.com

Restaurateur Drew Nieporent (Nobu, Tribeca Grill) and avant-garde chef Paul Liebrandt (ex Atlas, Gilt) join forces at this New French in TriBeCa's former Montrachet space, now redesigned in an ultra-minimalist style; look for exotic takes on classical French cuisine - served in pricey, prix fixe-only menus starting at $79 - paired with a wine list concentrating on the Burgundy region.

Daniel ☒ *French* 28 | 28 | 28 | VE

E 60s | 60 E. 65th St. (bet. Madison & Park Aves.) | 212-288-0033 | www.danielnyc.com

Home to what could be "heaven's kitchen", Daniel Boulud's eponymous East Side "masterpiece" exudes "true class" with "matchless" staffers serving "incomparable" New French prix fixes and a "definitive" wine list in a newly renovated, jackets-required milieu (the lounge also offers à la carte dining); it may cost a "king's ransom", but appropriately enough, most who experience it "feel like royalty" at meal's end.

Degustation ☒ *French/Spanish* 27 | 21 | 24 | E

E Village | 239 E. Fifth St. (bet. 2nd & 3rd Aves.) | 212-979-1012

The "lucky" few parked at the 16-seat tasting bar at Jack and Grace Lamb's "unique" East Villager have the chance to observe "masterful chefs" concocting "heavenly" Franco-Spanish small plates from the best possible ingredients; it's an "unforgettable experience" for "serious foodies" who "only wish the space were bigger", and perhaps that the price was a bit lower.

	FOOD	DECOR	SERVICE	COST
Gotham Bar & Grill *American*	27	25	26	VE

G Village | 12 E. 12th St. (bet. 5th Ave. & University Pl.) | 212-620-4020 | www.gothambarandgrill.com

"Everything's just right" at this "amazingly consistent" Village "special-occasion spot" helmed by chef Alfred Portale, whose "architectural" New American "tall food" is "every bit as thrilling" as when it opened 25 years ago; the staff is "on its game", the room "majestic" and the prices as "sky-high" as ever (though the $31 prix fixe lunch is a "bargain"); in short, it "makes you glad you live in this great town."

	FOOD	DECOR	SERVICE	COST
Gramercy Tavern *American*	28	26	27	VE

Flatiron | 42 E. 20th St. (bet. B'way & Park Ave. S.) | 212-477-0777 | www.gramercytavern.com

A "not-to-be-missed restaurant experience", Danny Meyer's "special-occasion" Flatiron "powerhouse" still "fires on all cylinders" thanks to chef Michael Anthony's "heavenly" New American food, "treat-you-like-royalty" service and an "upscale rustic" ambiance right out of 18th-century New England; sure, the prix fixe-only tabs can "break the bank", but in return you "honestly get everything you pay for", and the "less expensive" upfront tavern is a "great alternative."

	FOOD	DECOR	SERVICE	COST
Jean Georges [S] *French*	28	26	27	VE

W 60s | Trump Int'l Hotel | 1 Central Park W. (bet. 60th & 61st Sts.) | 212-299-3900 | www.jean-georges.com

A "class act from start to finish", Jean-Georges Vongerichten's Columbus Circle flagship "continues to dazzle" with "top-rung", "ever-evolving" New French prix fixes that "simultaneously comfort and excite", served by a "read-your-mind" staff in a beautifully "understated", "modern" setting; jackets are required for this "practically perfect" dining experience, and though prices are "not for the weak of pocketbook", most agree it's "worth every cent" and say the $24 set-price lunch (in the "more casual" Nougatine Room) is the "best deal in town", rivaled only by the main room's $28 lunch "steal."

	FOOD	DECOR	SERVICE	COST
La Grenouille [S][M] *French*	27	27	27	VE

E 50s | 3 E. 52nd St. (bet. 5th & Madison Aves.) | 212-752-1495 | www.la-grenouille.com

The "second-best thing the French ever gave NYC" is this Midtown "archetype of fine dining", considered the "last" of the city's "great cathedrals of French food"; its "rich", "classic" cuisine "takes you to another plane of consciousness" but also "takes a bite out of your pocket", so make sure to "soak in" the "breathtaking" "flower-filled" room and the staff's "gracious hospitality"; N.B. jackets required.

	FOOD	DECOR	SERVICE	COST
L'Atelier de Joël Robuchon *French*	28	25	26	VE

E 50s | Four Seasons Hotel | 57 E. 57th St. (bet. Madison & Park Aves.) | 212-350-6658 | www.fourseasons.com

"Exquisite in every way", "genius" chef Joël Robuchon's "stunning" Japanese-influenced Midtown French outpost offers "sublime", "almost-too-beautiful-to-eat" small plates that achieve "absolute purity of flavor"; sit at the "sushi bar"-style counter and "watch the chefs at work" while being attended to by a "pleasant" pro staff - but "be prepared to mortgage your apartment" because "perfection doesn't come cheap."

	FOOD	DECOR	SERVICE	COST

Le Bernardin *French/Seafood* 28 | 27 | 27 | VE

W 50s | 155 W. 51st St. (bet. 6th & 7th Aves.) | 212-554-1515 | www.le-bernardin.com

"Absolute master" chef Eric Ripert continues to "dazzle the senses" with "final meal"-worthy "piscatorial revelations" at Maguy LeCoze's "matchless" Midtown French "seafood mecca"; "telepathic" service in an "elegant", "understated" setting are reasons why it's "worth dressing up" for (jackets required) and "fishing out your wallet" to settle the whale of a tab; P.S. the $64 prix fixe lunch is a "relative bargain."

Mas *American* 28 | 24 | 26 | VE

G Village | 39 Downing St. (bet. Bedford & Varick Sts.) | 212-255-1790 | www.masfarmhouse.com

"Close to dining perfection", this "elegant yet hip" New American Villager is an oasis of "casual" refinement where the "wonderful, market-fresh" cooking by Galen Zamarra is delivered by a "warm" crew in quarters that are "romantic" yet "not too quiet"; all this "pricey" sophistication means it's "like no *mas*" (farmhouse) most have encountered.

Masa *Japanese* 27 | 24 | 26 | VE

W 60s | Time Warner Ctr. | 10 Columbus Circle, 4th fl. (60th St. at B'way) | 212-823-9800

Bar Masa *Japanese*

W 60s | Time Warner Ctr. | 10 Columbus Circle, 4th fl. (60th St. at B'way) | 212-823-9800

www.masanyc.com

The "absolute best" sushi can be found at this Zen-like Time Warner Center Japanese, where "perfectionist" chef Masayoshi Takayama's "exquisite" kaiseki dinners feature course upon course of raw fish "like silk"; at $400 prix fixe, it's a major blowout, but it's also an "unforgettable experience", with otherwise hard-to-find ingredients flown in daily from Japan; mere mortals can indulge in "almost as good" à la carte offerings at next door's more casual, less expensive Bar Masa; either way, Masa spells *mecca*.

Nobu *Japanese* 27 | 22 | 23 | VE

TriBeCa | 105 Hudson St. (Franklin St.) | 212-219-0500

Nobu, Next Door *Japanese*

TriBeCa | 105 Hudson St. (bet. Franklin & N. Moore Sts.) | 212-334-4445 www.noburestaurants.com

"Still the gold standard", this TriBeCa "classic" named after founder Nobu Matsuhisa will "blow you away" with its "phenomenal" Japanese-Peruvian "creations", "terrific" service and "stratospheric prices"; an "A-list" assortment of "high rollers" and "celebs" (Robert De Niro is a partner) makes it "the place to be", and though reservations are "a nightmare", the "more reasonable" Next Door produces "the same quality" for walk-ins only - and lunch is always a good bet; N.B. if you're uptown try Nobu 57.

Per Se *American/French* 28 | 28 | 28 | VE

W 60s | Time Warner Ctr. | 10 Columbus Circle, 4th fl. (60th St. at B'way) | 212-823-9335 | www.perseny.com

"In a category by itself" - it's voted No. 1 for Food and Service in NYC - Thomas Keller's French-New American "paragon" presents an "unforgettable" "gastronomical marathon" via "transcendental" prix fixe spreads served by "impeccable" "synchronized" staffers in "world-class" surroundings with "majestic" Central Park and Columbus Circle views; though it's "stunningly expensive", there's "never a regret", since once past the "daunting" reservations system, "you're in for the treat of your life."

Sasabune *Japanese* 27 | 11 | 21 | VE

E 70s | 401 E. 73rd St. (bet. 1st & York Aves.) | 212-249-8583

"Sushi purists" "trust the master" at Kenji Takahashi's UES omakase-only "gem", where the "always-changing" offerings are "guaranteed to dazzle"; the digs are "tiny" and "minimalist" and the prices "high", but supporters say it's "not expensive considering the quality."

Sugiyama *Japanese* 27 | 19 | 26 | VE

W 50s | 251 W. 55th St. (bet. B'way & 8th Ave.) | 212-956-0670 | www.sugiyama-nyc.com

Chef Nao Sugiyama is the "king of kaiseki" declare "true lovers of Japanese" cuisine tucking in at his "transcendent" Midtown "jewel"; "memorable" dishes "perfectly prepared and presented" come via "classy" staffers in "simple surroundings", adding up to "one of NYC's magical experiences" - with accordingly "high prices."

Sushi Seki *Japanese* 27 | 13 | 22 | VE

E 60s | 1143 First Ave. (bet. 62nd & 63rd Sts.) | 212-371-0238

"Animated" chef Seki "will blow you away" with an "out-of-this-world" omakase at his UES Japanese "standout", where "attentive" service outweighs "nondescript" decor; "mortgage-the-house" prices are "commensurate" with the "excellent quality", and sushi bar service until 3 AM is another "selling point."

Sushi Yasuda *Japanese* 28 | 21 | 23 | VE

E 40s | 204 E. 43rd St. (bet. 2nd & 3rd Aves.) | 212-972-1001 | www.sushiyasuda.com

"If God were going out for sushi", chef Naomichi Yasuda's "peaceful" Grand Central-area "temple" - once again voted the No. 1 Japanese in NYC - might "be the place" thanks to its "pristine" bites of "pure piscatorial pleasure"; mortals enjoying the "heavenly" experience "relax" in a handsome "minimalist" space attended to by a "polite" staff, preparing to tithe for this experience.

Union Square Cafe *American* 27 | 23 | 26 | VE

Union Sq | 21 E. 16th St. (bet. 5th Ave. & Union Sq. W.) | 212-243-4020 | www.unionsquarecafe.com

Danny Meyer's Union Square "convivial classic" is once again "top of the heap" - it's voted NYC's Most Popular - with new executive chef Carmen Quagliata now overseeing the kitchen and its "beautifully composed" New American cuisine "honoring" "seasonal" ingredients; the experience of a "fundamentally perfect meal" is completed by the service ("top-tier but down-to-earth") and setting ("lovely", "comfortable" rooms "without pretense"); N.B. if you can't score reservations, "go spur-of-the-moment" and dine at the "lively" bar.

FOOD | DECOR | SERVICE | COST

Orlando

TOP FOOD RANKING

	Restaurant	Cuisine
28	Victoria & Albert's	American
	Le Coq au Vin	French
27	Primo	Italian/Mediterranean
	Chatham's Place	Continental
	Enzo's Restaurant	Italian
	California Grill	Californian
	Del Frisco's	Steak
26	Jiko	African
	Artist Point	Pacific NW
	K Restaurant	Eclectic
	Manuel's	Eclectic
	Palm	Steak
	Morton's	Steak
	Christini's Ristorante	Italian
	Ruth's Chris	Steak

Artist Point *Pacific NW* 26 | 26 | 25 | E

Magic Kingdom Area | Disney's Wilderness Lodge | 901 Timberline Dr. (Wilderness Way) | Lake Buena Vista | 407-824-1081 | www.disneyworld.com

"The northwest meets the southeast" at this Disney darling delivering "Oregon-chic food" in an "amazing" Wilderness Lodge setting that "feels like a genuine Frank Lloyd Wright retreat" with its "inviting views", "gorgeous ceiling murals" and "quiet" ambiance; whether you opt for the "best salmon ever" cooked on a cedar plank or try one of the "unusual game specials", be sure to pair it with an "interesting Pacific NW wine" and then "walk around the resort after dinner."

California Grill *Californian* 27 | 25 | 24 | E

Magic Kingdom Area | Disney's Contemporary Resort | 4600 N. World Dr., 15th fl. (Contemporary Resort Access Rd.) | Lake Buena Vista | 407-939-3463 | www.disneyworld.com

The "holy grail of restaurants" in the Disney domain (it's the Most Popular spot in the Orlando area), this Californian "favorite" offers an "enchanting" combination of "creative, seasonal" fare, "solicitous" service and "one of the most extensive wine lists east of Napa"; it also boasts a "fabulous location" on the 15th floor of the Contemporary Resort, so be sure to "time your reservation" to take advantage of the "killer view of the fireworks" over Cinderella Castle.

Chatham's Place *Continental* 27 | 20 | 28 | E

Bay Hill/Dr. Phillips | 7575 Dr. Phillips Blvd. (Sand Lake Rd.) | 407-345-2992 | www.chathamsplace.com

In a "hard-to-find" spot just "steps from Restaurant Row", this "cozy, comfortable" Dr. Phillips "charmer" is "where the locals eat", in part because they "always feel welcome" while indulging in "divine" Continental cuisine (the "flavors are bold yet well-balanced") accompanied by a "wonderful wine selection"; it's "pricey", but the "impeccable service" and nightly guitar "serenading" will have you feeling like you're eating at "your personal restaurant."

Christini's Ristorante Italiano *Italian* 26 | 22 | 25 | E

Bay Hill/Dr. Phillips | The Marketplace | 7600 Dr. Phillips Blvd. (Sand Lake Rd.) | 407-345-8770 | www.christinis.com

Be "blown away" by a meal at this "elegant" Dr. Phillips Italian where the "exceptional experience" includes "fabulous" old-world cuisine made with "the finest and freshest ingredients", a "gracious", "attentive" staff and a selection of "hard-to-find wines" (let the "knowledgeable sommelier" help you choose); female patrons "get a rose" as they're seated, but given the "high prices", some suggest "it turns out to be a very expensive rose."

Del Frisco's Prime Steak & Lobster [S] *Steak* 27 | 17 | 23 | E

Winter Park | 729 Lee Rd. (Alloway St.) | 407-645-4443 | www.delfriscosorlando.com

For some of "the best steaks in O-Town", head to this "clubby" Winter Park staple serving "sinfully delicious" beef that's "still sizzling when it hits the table", plus "perfectly cooked" rock lobster, a "killer wine list" and all "the requisite sides"; a few crabby carnivores suggest the "dark, bordello-style" decor is a bit "dated", but a staff that "goes the extra mile" is yet another reason your "business dinner" will be "worth every penny."

Emeril's Orlando *Creole* 24 | 21 | 23 | E

Universal Orlando | Universal Studios CityWalk | 6000 Universal Blvd. (Major Blvd.) | 407-224-2424 | www.emerils.com

"A welcome respite", this Creole "classic" from celebrity chef Emeril Lagasse "whisks you away" from the "Universal Studios hustle and bustle" with "imaginative" fare that's "beautifully prepared" and complemented by "premier presentation" and "friendly service"; it's "worth the price for a true foodie", although the "loud", "busy" ambiance has mellow types murmuring "the food is terrific, the tourists are annoying"; P.S. "if you can't get a seat, eat at the bar."

Enzo's Restaurant on the Lake [S] [M] *Italian* 27 | 23 | 24 | E

Longwood | 1130 S. Hwy. 17-92 (bet. Laura St. & Wildmere Ave.) | 407-834-9872 | www.enzos.com

As "reliable as a good Tuscan wine", this Longwood "gem" remains an "institution for special occasions" thanks to its "outstanding", "high-end" Italian cuisine and a "romantic atmosphere" that includes "beautiful" "lakeside dining"; it's equally "a pleasure" for "socializing with business colleagues", and the family of late founder Enzo Perlini continues in the tradition of "cordial, welcoming" service; P.S. be sure to "try the wonderful antipasti" bar.

Jiko - The Cooking Place *African* 26 | 27 | 26 | E

Animal Kingdom Area | Disney's Animal Kingdom Lodge | 2901 Osceola Pkwy. (Hwy. 192) | Lake Buena Vista | 407-938-4733 | www.disneyworld.com

Experience a "taste of Africa without the exorbitant airfare" at this "welcome departure" in Disney's Animal Kingdom Lodge, where the "unexpected flavors" - think comfort foods prepared with "exotic" sub-Saharan spices - "don't fail to exceed expectations"; the "wonderful experience" includes a "sleek, tranquil" setting, "impeccable" service and an "awesome" South African wine list that will make oenophiles "weep with excitement."

K Restaurant Wine Bar 🅂 *Eclectic* 26 | 21 | 23 | E

College Park | 2401 Edgewater Dr. (Vassar St.) | 407-872-2332 | www.krestaurantwinebar.com

"You can't go wrong" at this College Park "stalwart" that's "built a solid reputation for innovative" Eclectic fare that's "always fresh and always delicious"; the "upscale bistro" setting is "small but doesn't feel cramped" and benefits from "changing artwork on the wall", "great outdoor seating" and servers who "remember guests from past visits"; fans find it a "unique" treat and say "in this climate of chain restaurants, I hope K is here to stay."

Le Coq au Vin 🄼 *French* 28 | 19 | 25 | E

South Orlando | 4800 S. Orange Ave. (Gatlin Ave.) | 407-851-6980 | www.lecoqauvinrestaurant.com

"Where locals go to get away from the tourists", this "hidden delight" in South Orlando demonstrates its "commitment to quality and consistency" via chef-owner Louis Perrotte's French cuisine, a "spectacular" lineup of "food not to die for, but to live for!"; a few suggest it "can be noisy", but its "perfectly paired wines", "country ambiance", "warm service" and "moderate prices" are all reasons it's been a "perennial favorite" for over 25 years.

Manuel's on the 28th 🅂🄼 *Eclectic* 26 | 25 | 26 | E

Downtown Orlando | Bank of America Bldg. | 390 N. Orange Ave., 28th fl. (Robinson Ave.) | 407-246-6580 | www.manuelsonthe28th.com

"What a view! - and every table has one" exclaim acolytes of this "romantic", "special-occasion" Eclectic nestled on the 28th floor of the Bank of America Building; the "trademark" vistas are the backdrop for "innovative", "well-prepared" food, an "out-of-this-world" wine list and service from an "attentive, professional" staff, but while some suggest this is "as big-time as Orlando gets", others insist the "high cost" is proof it's "taking itself a little too seriously."

Morton's The Steakhouse *Steak* 26 | 22 | 25 | VE

Bay Hill/Dr. Phillips | The Marketplace | 7600 Dr. Phillips Blvd. (Sand Lake Rd.) | 407-248-3485 | www.mortons.com

"The poster boy of steakhouses", this Restaurant Row "classic" caters to carnivores with "gigantic" "steaks the way you would expect" accompanied by "flavorful" side dishes "the size of entrees"; "impeccable service" and a "manly club atmosphere" add to the "wonderful experience", and though it's "expensive", rest assured "you get what you pay for!"

Palm, The *Steak* 26 | 21 | 24 | E

Universal Orlando | Hard Rock Hotel | 5800 Universal Blvd. (Major Blvd.) | 407-503-7256 | www.thepalm.com

"Lipitor should be the corporate sponsor" of this "top-of-the-line" chain chophouse that lures "unabashed carnivores" to Universal's Hard Rock Hotel with its "perfectly done" steaks, "huge, wonderful lobsters" and "luscious martinis - what else do you need?"; a few find the "noisy", "caricature-filled" room to be "nothing special", but others suggest it's just like the original in NYC "but without the snob appeal and service attitude."

Primo *Italian/Mediterranean* 27 | 25 | 26 | VE

South Orlando | JW Marriott Orlando Grande Lakes | 4040 Central Florida Pkwy. (John Young Pkwy.) | 407-393-4444 | www.grandelakes.com

"Worth the extra drive" to South Orlando's JW Marriott Grande Lakes, this "elegant" option is "in a class of its own" thanks to "master" chef Melissa Kelly and her "unbelievable", "imaginative" Italian-Med cuisine that "transports you to food heaven" with its "freshness and taste" (much of the "all-organic" produce is grown on-site); plus, it's set in a "beautiful" space that "makes you forget you're in a hotel."

Ruth's Chris Steak House *Steak* 26 | 23 | 24 | E

Bay Hill/Dr. Phillips | 7501 W. Sand Lake Rd. (bet. Dr. Phillips Blvd. & Turkey Lake Rd.) | 407-226-3900

Lake Mary | 80 Colonial Center Pkwy. (Village Oak Ln.) | 407-804-8220

Winter Park | Winter Park Village | 610 N. Orlando Ave. (Webster Ave.) | 407-622-2444

www.ruthschris.com

"Steak doesn't get any better than Ruth's, baby" chime champions of these Central Florida outlets of the "upscale" chophouse chain revered for "sizzling, buttery" beef and "terrific sides" served in "exceptionally plush" dining rooms manned by "high-quality servers"; just "don't forget to bring cab fare, because you'll have to leave your car there to cover the bill."

Seasons 52 *American* 25 | 26 | 24 | E

Altamonte Springs | The Altamonte Mall | 463 E. Altamonte Dr. (Palm Springs Dr.) | 407-767-1252

Bay Hill/Dr. Phillips | Plaza Venezia | 7700 W. Sand Lake Rd. (bet. Della Dr. & Dr. Phillips Blvd.) | 407-354-5212

www.seasons52.com

"Sheer genius" say smitten surveyors of these Altamonte Springs and Dr. Phillips links in a local chain, whose "wonderful" New American menu offers "decadent food without the guilt": each "seasonally adjusted" savory is "under 475 calories" and "tempting, rational" "minidesserts are served in shot glasses"; they're "on the pricey side", but the "stunning" "modern" settings ("Frank Lloyd Wright-inspired") abet the feeling they're "well worth every penny"; P.S. "without reservations, there can be significant waits."

Victoria & Albert's *American* 28 | 27 | 28 | VE

Magic Kingdom Area | Disney's Grand Floridian Resort & Spa | 4401 Grand Floridian Way (bet. Maple Rd. & W. Seven Seas Dr.) | Lake Buena Vista | 407-939-3463 | www.disneyworld.com

"Want to know what dinner would be like in heaven?" - then "dress up" and tow "a boatful of money" to this "fantasy" in Disney's Grand Floridian Resort, where "meticulous" servers present "genius" chef Scott Hunnel's "inventive", "decadent" six-course, prix fixe-only New American menu, earning this "treat" the No. 1 rating for Food and Service in the Orlando area; "thankfully, no children [under 10] are allowed" in the "sophisticated" room, making it "wonderful for romance"; P.S. "book well in advance" and try for the "coveted chef's table."

Palm Beach

FOOD | DECOR | SERVICE | COST

TOP FOOD RANKING

	Restaurant	Cuisine
27	Chez Jean-Pierre	French
	Marcello's La Sirena	Italian
	L'Escalier	French
	Four Seasons	Floridian
	Little Moir's	Seafood
26	Cafe Chardonnay	American
	11 Maple Street	American
	Café Boulud	French
	Chops Lobster Bar	Seafood/Steak
	Kathy's Gazebo	Continental
25	Sushi Jo's	Japanese
	Café L'Europe	Continental
	New York Prime	Steak
	Trattoria Romana	Italian
	Abe & Louie's	Steak
	Bluefin Sushi	Japanese/Thai
	32 East	American

Abe & Louie's *Steak* 25 24 23 E

Boca Raton | 2200 W. Glades Rd. (Renaissance Way) | 561-447-0024 | www.abeandlouies.com

"Attractive" and "old school"-looking (though it opened in 2005), this Boston-based steakhouse beckons "Boca's rich and beautiful" with "yum-o" fillets, "superlative service" and "a fine wine list with fair prices"; but the "decibel level is like being on the Florida turnpike", and even with "huge portions", "prices are crazy", so it's "worth paying the hefty sharing charge" or "skipping the dinner scene" altogether (some feel it's "best for lunch or brunch" anyway).

Bluefin Sushi *Japanese/Thai* 25 18 20 M

Boca Raton | 861 Yamato Rd. (Congress Ave.) | 561-981-8986 | www.bluefinsushi.com

"Who needs to go to Nobu?" when "outstanding sushi" (including a "lobster bomb that's da bomb"), plus "solid Thai" fare, is on hand at this "small", "off-the-beaten-path" Boca spot; it's "almost impossible to get a table in season" however, and "ambiance is sadly lacking", so some say it's "not for fine dining - strictly eating."

Café Boulud *French* 26 27 25 VE

Palm Beach | Brazilian Court Hotel | 301 Australian Ave. (Hibiscus Ave.) | 561-655-6060 | www.danielnyc.com

Almost "as good as its NYC sister" declare devotees of Daniel Boulud's Brazilian Court Hotel bistro, a "beautifully serene" site with the "best courtyard dining room on Fantasy Island"; the food is a "French event" - "delicious and beautiful" - and service is "smooth as old silk", particularly the "pleasant" sommeliers; a "very 'old money' PB atmosphere" prevails, but many say "it's a pleasure to see men wearing jackets", and even those who "had to hock some jewelry" to pay the "astronomical prices" proclaim "it's worth it."

Cafe Chardonnay *American* — 26 | 22 | 24 | E

Palm Beach Gardens | Garden Square Shoppes | 4533 PGA Blvd. (Military Trail) | 561-627-2662 | www.cafechardonnay.com

"Don't be put off by the shopping-center" locale of this Palm Beach Gardens New American - still a "standout" after 23 years - where a "dynamite wine list" ("by the glass too!") and "well-trained staff" complement the "creative", "consistently excellent" food in a "beautiful setting"; it's "like New York in Florida" - read: "crowded in season" - so "reservations in advance are a must."

Café L'Europe *Continental* — 25 | 26 | 24 | VE

Palm Beach | 331 S. County Rd. (bet. Australian & Brazilian Aves.) | 561-655-4020 | www.cafeleurope.com

"The wealth of Palm Beach dines here" at the town's "most glamorous and well-decorated" place; "an oasis of flowers" sets the scene for "divine, luscious" Continental cuisine that "balances between old standbys and creative new dishes", backed by an "extensive" wine list and "genteel" service; the sensitive sense a "somewhat haughty" attitude toward non-regulars, but "if your budget can handle it", "this is the place to splurge"; P.S. for a "better deal", try the "late-week lunch" prix fixe.

Chez Jean-Pierre Bistro [S] *French* — 27 | 22 | 25 | VE

Palm Beach | 132 N. County Rd. (bet. Sunrise & Sunset Aves.) | 561-833-1171

"Simply the best in PB" (with the No. 1 Food rating to prove it), this "family-owned and -run jewel" of a Classic French furnishes a "fantasy dining experience" for the flush, with "fun", diversely decorated rooms and "professional" but "not stuffy" service to complement chef Jean-Pierre Leverrier's "fahbulous" fare; "reservations can be difficult, but persevere - you won't regret it."

Chops Lobster Bar *Seafood/Steak* — 26 | 27 | 24 | VE

Boca Raton | Royal Palm Pl. | 101 Plaza Real S. (SE Mizner Blvd.) | 561-395-2675 | www.chopslobsterbar.com

Boca's "beautiful" bi-parte "addition from Atlanta" has surveyors licking their chops over the "incredible steaks" - even "the smallest are huge" - and "to-die-for fried lobster" fetched from the "cool open kitchen" by an "obliging staff"; be braced for a "noisy" scene with nightly live entertainment, but "fortunately the food is so good, conversation isn't necessary"; P.S. if you forget to "bring bags of bucks", order from the bar's more affordable small-plates menu.

11 Maple Street [M] *American* — 26 | 24 | 25 | E

Jensen Beach | 3224 NE Maple Ave. (11th Ave.) | 772-334-7714 | www.11maplestreet.net

"Drive an hour each way if you have to" ("MapQuest it if you're not familiar with the area") for a "sublime dining experience" at this Jensen Beach veteran where converts "can't get enough" of chef-owner Mike Perrin's "towering edible constructions" of "imaginative" New American fare; there's also an "amazing rare wine list and amazing servers too (a rarity!)", all set in an "antiques-adorned house" that channels "charming Old Florida"; N.B. also closed Tuesdays.

	FOOD	DECOR	SERVICE	COST

Four Seasons – The Restaurant Ⓜ *Floridian* 27 | 27 | 27 | VE

Palm Beach | Four Seasons Resort | 2800 S. Ocean Blvd. (Lake Ave.) | 561-533-3750 | www.fourseasons.com

Exuding "the quality the wannabes should strive for", this "beautiful oasis" perched oceanside boasts "the best service" in Palm Beach (voted No. 1), as exhibited by a staff that'll "spoil you rotten"; while Hubert Des Marais, "the original chef", left a while back (not fully reflected in the Food score), the kitchen is still turning out "imaginative" Floridian favorites "layered with so many exquisite flavors" that, "even if you go broke, you must eat here once in your lifetime - this is heaven!"

Kathy's Gazebo Café Ⓢ *Continental* 26 | 22 | 24 | E

Boca Raton | 4199 N. Federal Hwy. (Spanish River Blvd.) | 561-395-6033 | www.kathysgazebo.com

"Jackets are not required, but everyone wears one" at this "romantic" "classic" Continental in Boca, where an "older crowd" delights in "Dover sole as it should be" and "old-fashioned European service"; it all may be "too traditional" for trendsetters, especially given the "tight quarters", but most enjoy this "elegant" experience.

Kee Grill *Seafood/Steak* 24 | 21 | 21 | E

Juno Beach | 14010 US Hwy. 1 (Donald Ross Rd.) | 561-776-1167

Boca Raton | 17940 N. Military Trail (bet. Champion Blvd. & Clint Moore Rd.) | 561-995-5044

Though they're technically surf 'n' turfers, the "seafood is king" at this pair voted the Most Popular in Palm Beach County; true, there's "too long a wait for a table" and some protest "your plate's cleared before the fork hits the china", but most concentrate on the "always-fresh fish", "awesome spinach side" and bamboo-walled "Florida atmosphere", declaring this duo "a real class act."

L'Escalier Ⓢ Ⓜ *French* 27 | 28 | 26 | VE

Palm Beach | The Breakers | 1 S. County Rd. (Breakers Row) | 561-655-6611 | www.thebreakers.com

The "breathtaking", "grand atmosphere of The Breakers is the setting" for the "finest" "flawlessly executed" French cuisine and "excellent wines", backed by "solicitous but discreet service"; "elegant" and "extraordinary", it's "expensive" of course - but also a "unique experience", so "bring out the jewels and sell some to eat here."

Little Moir's Food Shack Ⓢ *Seafood* 27 | 12 | 22 | M

Jupiter | Jupiter Sq. | 103 US Hwy. 1 (E. Indiantown Rd.) | 561-741-3626

Little Moir's Leftovers Café Ⓢ *Seafood*

Jupiter | Abacoa Bermudiana | 451 University Blvd. (Military Trail) | 561-627-6030

www.littlemoirsfoodshack.com

"It's all about the food" at this "kooky", "ultracasual" piscatorial place, since the decor's pure beach "shack-y", the wine's "severely lacking, as is the plastic stemware", and the "fast service" ensures "no lingering" at table (though you "wait . . . and wait . . . and wait" to get in); but oh, those "fantastic" fish choices with "unusual" coatings ("sweet potato is my favorite") - they cause even the initially skeptic to say "don't walk, run" to this Jupiter joint; N.B. don't worry - it's not really leftovers served at the new, more spacious Abacoa addition.

	FOOD	DECOR	SERVICE	COST
Marcello's La Sirena *Italian*	27	19	23	E

West Palm Beach | 6316 S. Dixie Hwy. (Forest Hill Blvd.) | 561-585-3128 | www.lasirenaonline.com

An "old-timer" "off the beaten path" in West Palm Beach, this Italian has a "chef-owner who can cook with the country's best" and backs up his *cucina* with a "great cellar of fine wines" from around the globe; the service is "refined", and, heeding pleas "to spruce the place up a little", they are making over the dining room (not reflected in the Decor score).

	FOOD	DECOR	SERVICE	COST
New York Prime *Steak*	25	21	21	VE

Boca Raton | 2350 Executive Center Dr. NW (Glades Rd.) | 561-998-3881 | www.newyorkprime.com

Expect "prime food" at "prime prices" at this "loud" "very Boca" meatery where "many celebs" and other "with-it" types nosh on the "top-quality" fillets after quaffing a few at the "old-world Euro bar"; if the bellicose beef there's "attitude everywhere" and you "have to wait even with a reservation", advocates argue it's "annoying but worth it."

	FOOD	DECOR	SERVICE	COST
Sushi Jo's *Japanese*	25	17	21	M

West Palm Beach | 319 Belvedere Rd. (S. Olive Ave.) | 561-868-7893
Palm Beach Gardens | PGA Commons | 5080 PGA Blvd. | 561-691-9811
Boynton Beach | Ocean Plaza | 640 E. Ocean Ave. (SE 6th Ct.) | 561-737-0606
www.sushijo.com

"Go for the food, stay for the hip scene" at this trio where "top-notch" "insanely fresh" sushi and a "fantastic selection of cold sake" are served in a "dim" "lounge-type atmosphere"; raw fish fans rave this is "not your typical 'clinical' Japanese restaurant", even if the "hip music" can be "too loud" and the prices - "well, just don't look."

	FOOD	DECOR	SERVICE	COST
32 East *American*	25	19	22	E

Delray Beach | 32 E. Atlantic Ave. (bet. SE 1st & Swinton Aves.) | 561-276-7868 | www.32east.com

Offering a "scene-o-rama" with "sexy atmosphere", this Delray Beach New American is where "the who's who of Palm Beach County hang", sampling "market-fresh cuisine" from "wildly creative chef" Nick Morfogen, who "changes the menu at whim" ("depending on what he finds" that day); so when this "cosmopolitan" place "is on, it's all the way", especially now that there's sound-absorbing paneling to dampen the "eardrum-splitting volume."

	FOOD	DECOR	SERVICE	COST
Trattoria Romana *Italian*	25	17	20	E

Boca Raton | 499 E. Palmetto Park Rd. (NE 5th Ave.) | 561-393-6715

"They take care of the regulars" at this "dependable" "old-time Italian" where the "spare-nothing" menu includes a "humongous veal chop" and "b-i-ggg" drinks; there's "not much atmosphere" and it gets quite "loud" (tip: the back room "has a lot less noise"), but believers bellow "*buonissimo!*" for this East Boca bit of The Boot.

	FOOD	DECOR	SERVICE	COST

Philadelphia

TOP FOOD RANKING

	Restaurant	Cuisine
29	Fountain Restaurant	Continental/French
28	Little Fish	Seafood
	Birchrunville Store	French/Italian
	Amada	Spanish
	Le Bar Lyonnais	French
	Gilmore's	French
	Lacroix/Rittenhouse	French
27	Vetri	Italian
	Le Bec-Fin	French
	Paloma	French/Mexican
	Restaurant Alba	American
	Tinto	Spanish
	Swann Lounge	American/French
	Blue Sage	Vegetarian
	La Bonne Auberge	French
	Sola	American

Alma de Cuba *Nuevo Latino* 25 | 25 | 23 | E

Center City West | 1623 Walnut St. (bet. 16th & 17th Sts.) | 215-988-1799 | www.almadecubarestaurant.com

For Cuban "flair" near Rittenhouse Square, follow the "fashionistas" and foodies to this "swanky" tri-level extravaganza from Stephen Starr and celeb chef Douglas Rodriguez, which fuses "fabulous" Nuevo Latino food and drink with a "sexy" "old-time" Havana ambiance complete with "attentive" waiters in white jackets; in-Fidels find it "noisy" and "expensive", but most maintain it's well "worth it."

Amada *Spanish* 28 | 24 | 25 | E

Old City | 217 Chestnut St. (bet. 2nd & 3rd Sts.) | 215-625-2450 | www.amadarestaurant.com

"Tapas of the heap" sums up the sentiment on Jose Garces' "sexy", "sublime" Spaniard in Old City, where armadas of amigos ("book way in advance") share small plates of "awesome", "cutting-edge" *comidas* and "primo" sangria served by an "informative" staff; it may be "pricey", but the $45 tasting menu helps contain costs, and if "noise" is a concern, come early (or for lunch) and pass on the "loud" though "super-fun" flamenco shows on Wednesdays and Fridays.

Birchrunville Store Cafe Ⓑ Ⓜ ≠ *French/Italian* 28 | 23 | 27 | E

Birchrunville | 1403 Hollow Rd. (Flowing Springs Rd.) | 610-827-9002 | www.birchrunvillestorecafe.com

"Book early" and bring cash along with your best BYO bottle to Francis Trzeciak's "charming" Franco-Italian – "if you can find it" – in rural Chester County; its "superb" cuisine (including a $65 six-course tasting menu served Wednesdays and Thursdays), "attentive" service and a historic "country-inn" setting make high tabs and "impossible"-to-land reservations "worth it"; N.B. closed Sunday–Tuesday.

	FOOD	DECOR	SERVICE	COST
Blue Sage Vegetarian Grille	27	15	23	M
Buddakan	26	27	24	E
Capital Grille, The	26	23	24	E
Fountain Restaurant	29	28	28	VE
Gilmore's	28	22	28	E

Blue Sage Vegetarian Grille [S] [M] *Vegetarian*

Southampton | 772 Second St. Pike (Street Rd./Rte. 132) | 215-942-8888 | www.bluesagegrille.com

"Come hungry" for "huge" portions of "insanely delicious", "unique" vegetarian vittles served by a "fun, helpful" staff at Mike and Holly Jackson's "small", "crowded" Bucks strip-mall BYO; fans who dub it "my blue heaven" say "whether you're a veggie or not", it's "total nirvana" - "if you can get in", that is ("reservations are a must" for dinner).

Buddakan *Pan-Asian*

Old City | 325 Chestnut St. (bet. 3rd & 4th Sts.) | 215-574-9440 | www.buddakan.com

"Everything you've heard" about Stephen Starr's "theatrical" "see-and-be-seen" "scene" in Old City is "true": expect "large portions" of "fabulous" Pan-Asian cuisine to "share" ("black cod? - cod bless you"), "cool", "streamlined" surroundings, "spot-on" service "under the smiling Buddha", a "who's who" crowd - and a "noise level" befitting "a construction site"; it's again Philly's Most Popular, so getting a reservation is "like scoring a date with Miss USA."

Capital Grille, The *Steak*

Avenue of the Arts | 1338 Chestnut St. (Broad St.) | 215-545-9588 | www.thecapitalgrille.com

"You get what you pay for" at this "swanky", "old-school" beefery (one of the "best chain steakhouses, hands-down"), a "Grand Central Station" near City Hall where Philly's "movers and shakers" gleefully "break out the platinum card" for "prime" cuts that "cost a car payment" and "professional" service that "meets expectations"; the "always-packed" bar attracts a "suit-and-briefcase" crowd that knows to "watch out" for the many specialty drinks.

Fountain Restaurant *Continental/French*

Center City West | Four Seasons Hotel | 1 Logan Sq. (Benjamin Franklin Pkwy.) | 215-963-1500 | www.fourseasons.com

"Ask and you shall receive" at this "staggeringly good" New French-Continental "splurge" (again rated No. 1 for Food in Philadelphia) in Center City's Four Seasons Hotel showcasing Martin Hamann's "exquisite" tasting menus that "bubble over" with "creativity"; the "sumptuous" quarters overlook the namesake fountain on Logan Square, and the "stately" though "nearly invisible" staff is "so attentive I expected a pedicure with dessert"; N.B. jacket required.

Gilmore's [S] [M] *French*

West Chester | 133 E. Gay St. (bet. Matlack & Walnut Sts.) | 610-431-2800 | www.gilmoresrestaurant.com

Francophiles in Downtown West Chester gush over Peter Gilmore's "fantabulous" BYO, citing "mouthwatering" Gallic fare served by a staff that "feels like family" (the chef often "comes out" to chat as well) in a "romantic", if "slightly cramped", setting; if you crave Gay Paree, "save yourself the flight time" - and the euros - and head here (just be sure to "book way in advance"); N.B. there's a $35 four-course prix fixe.

La Bonne Auberge [M] *French* — 27 | 26 | 27 | VE

New Hope | 1 Rittenhouse Circle (River Rd.) | 215-862-2462 | www.bonneauberge.com

"After all these years", Gerard Caronello's "formal" French "in the middle" of a condo development in New Hope still ranks among "the best" "special-occasion" venues in Bucks County; boosters note it's "priced accordingly", so "be prepared to open your wallet" for "perfect" eats in a country "dollhouse atmosphere" aided by a "professional" staff; N.B. dinner only, Thursday-Sunday.

Lacroix at The Rittenhouse *French* — 28 | 27 | 27 | VE

Center City West | Rittenhouse Hotel | 210 W. Rittenhouse Sq. (bet. Locust & Walnut Sts.) | 215-790-2533 | www.lacroixrestaurant.com

Ardent admirers find "a spot of heaven" overlooking the Square at the Rittenhouse's "handsome", "special-occasion" French, where chef Matthew Levin creates "memorable" tasting menus of "micro-gastronomic" feats that "explode on your taste buds" (plus a "divine" Sunday brunch), augmented by a "great wine list" and "impeccable" service; "bring your expense-account card", "sit near a window" and experience one of Philly's "wows"; N.B. jacket suggested.

Le Bar Lyonnais [S] *French* — 28 | 23 | 26 | E

Center City West | 1523 Walnut St. (bet. 15th & 16th Sts.) | 215-567-1000 | www.lebecfin.com

A "delight on all accounts", Georges Perrier's "cozy boîte" beneath Le Bec-Fin might be the "best bargain" around for "those who like the kitchen but not the prices upstairs"; with "top-notch" service and "clubby", "intimate" surroundings (including a small, "sexy" bar), it works for a "lovers' rendezvous", and though wine prices "can negate savings", for most it's "worth every penny."

Le Bec-Fin [S] *French* — 27 | 27 | 27 | VE

Center City West | 1523 Walnut St. (bet. 15th & 16th Sts.) | 215-567-1000 | www.lebecfin.com

Georges Perrier's "euphoric" French "gold standard" in a "fin de siècle"-style Center City brownstone got with the times and revamped to a lower-priced à la carte menu post-Survey (bring the "platinum card" now, not the "titanium"), while still serving "exquisitely crafted" prix fixe tasting menus at lunch (five courses, $55) and dinner (seven courses, $140); count on the "all-you-care-to-try" dessert cart (it "never disappoints") and "assiduous" service that "anticipates your every need."

Little Fish *Seafood* — 28 | 13 | 22 | M

South Philly | 600 Catharine St. (6th St.) | 215-413-3464 | www.littlefishphilly.com

Loyalists laud this "fintastic" South Philly BYO where the seafood "melts in your mouth" and "troubles disappear" thanks to the "heart"-felt cooking by new chef-owner Mike Stollenwerk; the Sunday five-course prix fixe is a "steal" in the small, "enticing" dining room.

Paloma [S] [M] *French/Mexican* — 27 | 20 | 27 | E

Northeast Philly | 6516 Castor Ave. (bet. Hellerman St. & Magee Ave.) | 215-533-0356 | www.palomafinedining.com

"It's always a pleasure" for fans of this "surprise" French-Mexican "sleeper" on an "unlikely" block in Northeast Philly, purveying "sublime", "magnificently presented" cuisine that's "worth the trip if you want a classy meal"; "wonderful" service (the owner "takes a personal interest in your satisfaction") and a "quaint" atmosphere add to the "wow" factor; N.B. open for dinner Thursday-Saturday.

Restaurant Alba *American*

Food	Decor	Service	Cost
27	22	25	E

Malvern | 7 W. King St. (Warren Ave.) | 610-644-4009 | www.restaurantalba.com

"Serious cooking" from Sean Weinberg's "wood-fired grill" attracts a "gourmet" crowd to this "warm" Malvern New American BYO for locally driven, "nuanced" cuisine (including a five-course tasting menu and "innovative" antipasti plates) proffered by "professionals"; quibbles about "noise" and "smoke" from the grill aside, "it doesn't get much better than this" in the 'burbs.

Sola *American*

Food	Decor	Service	Cost
27	19	24	E

Bryn Mawr | 614 W. Lancaster Ave. (Penn St.) | 610-526-0123

"Ex-sola-nt" exclaim enthusiasts about this "intimate" New American BYO in Bryn Mawr, regarded by some as "the best-kept secret on the Main Line", where "superb", "refined" "city food" is served by an "attentive" staff in a "jewel box-size" space; "suburban prices" make it easier to "bring your finest" wine to pour into the "high-end" Schott Zwiesel stemware.

Swann Lounge *American/French*

Food	Decor	Service	Cost
27	27	27	E

Center City West | Four Seasons Hotel | 1 Logan Sq. (bet. Benjamin Franklin Pkwy. & 18th St.) | 215-963-1500 | www.fourseasons.com

When you don't want to "brave" the Fountain's "formality", the Four Seasons' "bargain" "little sister" next door delivers "accessible elegance" in the form of "top-notch" New American cooking with a "French flair", "impeccable" service and "delicious views" of Swann Fountain; besides, it's fun to see the mix of "guests in their sweats and locals after a black-tie affair"; P.S. the $26 lunch buffet comes "highly recommended."

Tinto *Spanish*

Food	Decor	Service	Cost
27	22	24	E

Center City West | 114 S. 20th St. (Sansom St.) | 215-665-9150 | www.tintorestaurant.com

Basque-ing in superlatives such as "awesome" and "sublime", Jose Garces' "intimate" Spanish sibling of Amada near Rittenhouse Square offers an "ever-changing" assortment of "fantastic" small plates, backed by "pitchers of sangria" and "unusual wines"; the "knowledgeable" staff "makes solid suggestions", and even after an expansion of the "claustrophobia"-inducing space, some quip it'll still "cost your first born to get a reservation."

Vetri *Italian*

Food	Decor	Service	Cost
27	23	27	VE

Center City East | 1312 Spruce St. (bet. Broad & 13th Sts.) | 215-732-3478 | www.vetriristorante.com

Although "you're not under the real Tuscan sun", fans swear you're as good as there at Marc Vetri and Jeff Benjamin's "rustic" Italian "legend" in Center City, which "continues to amaze" with a menu of "sublime" "handmade everything" and "outstanding", "knowledgeable" service; it's "tough to get a table" in the "shoebox"-like space, and be prepared "to pay an arm and a leg"; N.B. there's no à la carte on Saturdays.

FOOD DECOR SERVICE COST

Phoenix/Scottsdale

TOP FOOD RANKING

	Restaurant	Cuisine
28	Kai	Eclectic
	Sea Saw	Japanese
	Binkley's Restaurant	American
27	Pizzeria Bianco	Pizza
26	Atlas Bistro	Eclectic
	T. Cook's	Mediterranean
	Vincent's on Camelback	French/Southwestern
	Rancho Pinot	American
	Cyclo	Vietnamese
	Barrio Cafe	Mexican
	Mastro's Steak	Steak
	Mastro's City Hall	Steak
	Tarbell's	American
25	Los Dos Molinos	New Mexican

Atlas Bistro Ⓑ Ⓜ *Eclectic* 26 | 14 | 24 | E

South Scottsdale | Wilshire Plaza | 2515 N. Scottsdale Rd. (E. Wilshire Dr.) | Scottsdale | 480-990-2433

"Heaven for foodies", this South Scottsdale BYO serves "imaginative" Eclectic fare with a Southwestern "kick" that "never disappoints" (unlike the "funky" and admittedly "cramped" digs, but "you'll forget" about all that "once you take a bite"); it's also "paradise" for oenophiles, as guests "select the perfect bottle to accompany a memorable meal" at the attached "discount wine store" and then "save a bundle" thanks to waived corkage fees (if you bring it from elsewhere, it's only $10).

Barrio Cafe Ⓜ *Mexican* 26 | 17 | 21 | M

Phoenix | 2814 N. 16th St. (Thomas Rd.) | 602-636-0240 | www.barriocafe.com

"No Tex-Mex here" declare fans who suffer a "lousy" Phoenix location with "difficult parking", a "no-reservations policy" and "long waits" for Silvana Salcido Esparza's "out-of-the-ordinary", "craveable" Southern Mexican fare featuring "fascinating blends" of lighter, less-spicy flavors (start off with the "outstanding" "tableside-prepped guacamole"); a "unique selection of wines", hundreds of tequilas and margaritas that "knock you on your *culo*" fuel the "noisy", "fun-filled" atmosphere.

Binkley's Restaurant Ⓜ *American* 28 | 20 | 26 | VE

Cave Creek | 6920 E. Cave Creek Rd. (Tom Darlington Dr.) | 480-437-1072 | www.binkleysrestaurant.com

"Napa Valley meets funky Cave Creek" at this "small" "foodie oasis" from "super-talented" French Laundry alum Kevin Binkley, whose "adventurous" French-influenced New American fare comes with "fresh local ingredients" and "molecular-gastronomy flourishes" that yield "magical flavor combinations"; "whether you order the [four-to-six-course] tasting menu or not", you'll "be blown away" by the "variety of amuse-bouche" "sprinkled" throughout the meal by "bend-over-backward" servers, not to mention the "expensive" tabs (still, they "would be twice as much in New York").

Cyclo [S][M] *Vietnamese* 26 | 13 | 21 | I

Chandler | 1919 W. Chandler Blvd. (Dobson Rd.) | 480-963-4490 | www.cycloaz.com

She may be the "hottest restaurant owner" in Chandler, but "sassy" Justina Duong delivers far more than "wisecracking" "personality" and "eye candy" at this Vietnamese BYO; the "authentic" fare "with gourmet flair" - "always fresh" and "inexpensive" - also makes it "worth the trip", despite the "unamusing strip-mall setting" and "depressing decor" (a post-Survey modernization should cheer things up).

Eddie V's Edgewater Grille *Seafood/Steak* 25 | 23 | 23 | E

North Scottsdale | 20715 N. Pima Rd. (E. Thompson Peak Pkwy.) | Scottsdale | 480-538-8468 | www.eddiev.com

"The freshest fish you'll find in the desert", "outstanding steaks" and "hearty sides" are "well-presented" in "exciting" preparations at this "clubby", "bustling" North Scottsdale surf 'n' turfer; sure, there's "lots of money" on display, but the "nice crowd" is not above a bargain, sometimes preferring to "make a great meal" out of the "yummy" half-price happy-hour appetizers in the "jazz bar" (if it's too "noisy" for you, the patio may be "quieter").

Kai [S][M] *Eclectic* 28 | 26 | 27 | VE

Chandler | Sheraton Wild Horse Pass Resort & Spa | 5594 W. Wild Horse Pass Blvd. (Loop Rd.) | 602-225-0100 | www.wildhorsepassresort.com

Situated on tribal land in Chandler, this "consistently phenomenal" resort restaurant earns Phoenix-Scottsdale's No. 1 Food rating with an "innovative", "exquisite" "blending of Native American" and Eclectic fare that utilizes "modern techniques" to turn "locally sourced ingredients from the reservation and nearby communities" into edible "artwork"; the "polished service" adds another "first-class" layer to the "worth-every-penny" experience, available in an "understated" contemporary interior and on a "quiet, romantic patio" exhibiting "spectacular sunset views."

Lon's at the Hermosa *American* 25 | 26 | 25 | E

Paradise Valley | Hermosa Inn | 5532 N. Palo Cristi Rd. (E. Stanford Dr.) | 602-955-7878 | www.lons.com

For "old time Arizona at its best", settle into this "romantic" New American in a "gorgeous" Paradise Valley hacienda that once "belonged to famous cowboy artist" Lon Megargee; Michael Rusconi's "exquisitely prepared" fare exhibits "innovative Southwestern" "flair", and though it's "pricey", "you get what you pay for", especially when you procure a table on the "magical" patio, which is "warmed by juniper-fueled" fireplaces and backed by "stunning views" of Camelback Mountain.

Los Dos Molinos [S][M] *New Mexican* 25 | 16 | 17 | I

South Phoenix | 8646 S. Central Ave. (Baseline Ave.) | Phoenix | 602-243-9113 | www.losdosmolinosaz.com

The desert "ain't as hot" as the New Mexican cuisine whipped up at this South Phoenix "icon" where "chileheads" put up with "horrendous waits", a "loud, brash" atmosphere and sometimes "rude" service for dishes that are "more spicy than [they] ever imagined"; "strong", "huge margaritas" to cool the "fiery" fare make "a designated driver and Pepto" necessities when they "walk out hallucinating."

Mastro's City Hall Steakhouse *Steak* 26 | 24 | 25 | VE
(fka Drinkwater's City Hall Steakhouse)

Scottsdale | 6991 E. Camelback Rd. (Goldwater Blvd.) | 480-941-4700 | www.mastrosoceanclub.com

Primo for "people-watching", this steakhouse in a "trendy area of Scottsdale" "impresses" with a "dynamic setting", dim lighting, "bar action" and "enjoyable entertainment"; more important, the "juicy, buttery" beef is joined by a "nice selection of other entrees and sides", plus "stiff cocktails" brought to table by "stellar" servers; in short, if "money's not a problem, this is the place for you."

Mastro's Steakhouse *Steak* 26 | 24 | 24 | VE

North Scottsdale | La Mirada | 8852 E. Pinnacle Peak Rd. (N. Pima Rd.) | Scottsdale | 480-585-9500 | www.mastrossteakhouse.com

The "whole package is great" at this "high-energy", "high-decibel" North Scottsdale steakhouse: from the "lush and seductive" "old supper-club feel" to the "massive" portions of "first-rate", "juicy steaks" and "yummy sides" to the "wonderful wine list" (if necessary, procure a "third mortgage" to experience it all); "attentive service" can be found both in the dining room and at the "crowded" bar, the milieu of "huge martinis" and "older"-people "pickups."

P.F. Chang's China Bistro *Chinese* 20 | 20 | 19 | M

Chandler | Chandler Fashion Ctr. | 3255 W. Chandler Blvd. (bet. Chandler Village Dr. & Rte. 101) | 480-899-0472
Fashion Square | The Waterfront | 7135 E. Camelback Rd. (N. Scottsdale Rd.) | Scottsdale | 480-949-2610
Mesa | 6610 E. Superstition Springs Blvd. (Power Rd.) | 480-218-4900
North Scottsdale | Kierland Commons | 7132 E. Greenway Pkwy. (N. Scottsdale Rd.) | Scottsdale | 480-367-2999
Tempe | 740 S. Mill Ave. (bet. E. 7th St. & E. University Dr.) | 480-731-4600
www.pfchangs.com

While "not for purists", the "Americanized" Chinese fare offered at these outposts of the "midpriced" chain is "remarkably consistent" and "delicious" (as always, you "can't go wrong" with the "super-fine lettuce wraps"), so surveyors cut them "some slack"; besides, the "fun atmosphere" "beats takeout" any day, even though they're "noisy" and often "hard to get into."

Pizzeria Bianco ☒ Ⓜ *Pizza* 27 | 19 | 20 | M

Downtown Phoenix | Heritage Sq. | 623 E. Adams St. (N. 7th St.) | Phoenix | 602-258-8300 | www.pizzeriabianco.com

Using "only the best fresh ingredients", "brilliant" Chris Bianco makes "glorious" wood-fired Neapolitan-style pizzas, deemed the "best in the known world" by Phoenix "locals and traveling foodies alike"; get in line "before they open" at 5 PM and you may get seated within "40 minutes" - as opposed to "horrendous"-"beyond-belief" "three-to-four hour" waits ("raise your spirits" at the "wine bar next door").

	FOOD	DECOR	SERVICE	COST
Rancho Pinot *American*	26	20	24	E
Sea Saw *Japanese*	28	18	25	VE
Tarbell's *American*	26	20	25	E
T. Cook's *Mediterranean*	26	28	26	E
Vincent's on Camelback *French/Southwestern*	26	22	24	E

Rancho Pinot *American*

Scottsdale | Lincoln Vill. | 6208 N. Scottsdale Rd. (bet. Lincoln & McDonald Drs.) | 480-367-8030 | www.ranchopinot.com

Although it's "hidden away" in a Scottsdale strip mall, this "neighborhood" "jewel" with "cowboy-chic" decor is a "real find" thanks to chef Chrysa Robertson (a "huge talent"), who lends an "Arizona accent" to her "sophisticated" New American "comfort food" by using "seasonal and locally grown" ingredients; praise also goes to her "gracious", "funny" partner Tom Kaufman, who oversees the "superb wine program" and the "charming", "well-informed" staff.

Sea Saw *Japanese*

Old Town | 7133 E. Stetson Dr. (E. 6th Ave.) | Scottsdale | 480-481-9463 | www.seasaw.net

For an "experience like no other", "make a reservation" for the "spectacular omakase" – chef Nobuo Fukuda's tasting menu of "traditional"-meets-"unique" Japanese tapas – "prepared before your eyes" at the bar of this "tiny", sparsely furnished space in Old Town Scottsdale (a few tables are also available for ordering à la carte); "sake that'll curl your toes" and a "tremendous wine selection" add to tabs "you will spend your paycheck" on, but "your taste buds will never be the same."

Tarbell's *American*

Camelback Corridor | Camelback East Shops | 3213 E. Camelback Rd. (N. 32nd St.) | Phoenix | 602-955-8100 | www.tarbells.com

"This is the way to run a neighborhood restaurant" cheer boosters of this "comfortable", "cosmopolitan" Camelback Corridor American bistro beloved for its "upbeat" atmosphere and "delicious", "seasonally current" "classic" dishes; Mark Tarbell (the "consummate host") manages a "brilliant wine list" as well as schmoozes "beautiful locals" who wish they "could eat here every night" (it's a bit "expensive" for that).

T. Cook's *Mediterranean*

Phoenix | Royal Palms Resort & Spa | 5200 E. Camelback Rd. (bet. N. Arcadia Dr. & 56th St.) | 602-808-0766 | www.royalpalmshotel.com

"Dripping with romance", this "gorgeous-in-all-seasons" "date-night" and "special-occasion" staple (voted Most Popular in Phoenix/Scottsdale) features "elegant", "enchanting" "Southwestern-style decor" and the Royal Palms' "beautiful grounds"; the "freshest ingredients are always the star" of the "far-from-ordinary", "gourmet" Med cuisine, which is "beautifully presented" by staffers who "know what professional service means"; P.S. while dinner is "expensive" (and "worth it"), lunch and Sunday brunch are relative "steals."

Vincent's on Camelback *French/Southwestern*

Camelback Corridor | 3930 E. Camelback Rd. (N. 40th St.) | Phoenix | 602-224-0225 | www.vincentsoncamelback.com

"Phoenix food legend" Vincent Guerithault crafts a "magnificent fusion" of French and Southwestern (the "menu's divided into classic and nouveau") at this "quaint" Camelback Corridor "oldie but goodie" also known for a "super array of wines", "out-of-this-world service" and "expensive" checks; while carpers contend that the whole endeavor "needs a creative kick in the pants" (particularly "tiresome" decor), the majority opines "it's hard to improve on perfection."

FOOD	DECOR	SERVICE	COST

San Diego

TOP FOOD RANKING

	Restaurant	Cuisine
28	Sushi Ota	Japanese
	WineSellar & Brasserie	French
27	El Bizcocho	French
	Karen Krasne's	French/Italian
	Pamplemousse Grille	American/French
	Market Restaurant	American
	Tapenade	French
	A.R. Valentien	Californian
26	Primavera Ristorante	Italian
	Morton's	Seafood/Steak
	Mille Fleurs	French
	Donovan's Steak	Steak

A.R. Valentien *Californian* 27 27 26 E

La Jolla | The Lodge at Torrey Pines | 11480 N. Torrey Pines Rd. (Callan Rd.) | 858-777-6635 | www.lodgetorreypines.com

"Exquisite Craftsman-style architecture", a study in gleaming woods and stained-glass light fixtures amid the "ethereal surroundings" of the Torrey Pines golf course and the Pacific, "amazes" the "high rollers" who habituate this "fantastical dining experience" in La Jolla, No. 1 for Decor in San Diego; just as "unforgettable" is chef Jeff Jackson's "amazing", "innovative" Californian cuisine, which utilizes "farm-fresh local produce" and is "presented with creative flair" by "impeccable" servers; P.S. "sitting outside is paradise" "for romance and business" alike.

Donovan's Steak & Chop House *Steak* 26 23 25 E

NEW **Gaslamp Quarter** | 570 K St. (6th Ave.) | 619-237-9700
Golden Triangle | 4340 La Jolla Village Dr. (Genesee Ave.) | 858-450-6666 S
www.donovanssteakhouse.com

"You simply can't go wrong" with any "hunk of mouthwatering beef" you order at this Golden Triangle "steakhouse extraordinaire", be it an "outstanding bone-in rib eye", a "spectacular filet mignon" or an "off-the-charts New York strip", all of which come with "luscious sides" ("unlike at others" of this ilk); in a manner befitting the "refined, wood-paneled" "gentleman's club-like" environs, the "superb" servers remain "unruffled" even when the "rather large" tabs (especially from the "overpriced wine list") draw protests; N.B. the Gaslamp locale debuted post-Survey.

El Bizcocho *French* 27 26 27 VE

Rancho Bernardo | Rancho Bernardo Inn | 17550 Bernardo Oaks Dr. (Francisco Dr.) | 858-675-8550 | www.ranchobernardoinn.com

"Firing on all cylinders", this Rancho Bernardo Inn "delight" zooms to the "top of the line" by utilizing "surprising flavor combinations" and "complex techniques" to create "challenging", "spectacular" French cuisine worthy of the "beyond-description" 1,600-label wine cellar;

"discreet" yet "responsive" servers and an "elegant" setting add to the "special-occasion" feel, so "bring the diamond ring to propose to your sweetie" (or hock it beforehand to pay for it all); N.B. post-Survey changes in chef and style (tasting menus only, no à la carte options) may outdate the above Food score.

George's Ocean Terrace *Californian* 24 | 24 | 23 | E

La Jolla | 1250 Prospect St. (bet. Cave St. & Ivanhoe Ave.) | 858-454-4244 | www.georgesatthecove.com

Feel like you're "sitting on top of the world" as you take in "wine, sunshine" and "incomparable ocean views" at this rooftop "tradition" "overlooking La Jolla Cove", the "perennial favorite for tourists and locals alike", voted San Diego's Most Popular restaurant; a "more casual", "less expensive version of George's California Modern downstairs", it offers the "same great quality", "inventive", "artistic" Californian fare for "languid lunches" or dinners; P.S. a post-Survey refresh that includes a new 12-seat ocean-view bar should add to the "wow" factor.

Karen Krasne's Extraordinary Desserts *Dessert* 27 | 21 | 17 | I

Bankers Hill | 2929 Fifth Ave. (bet. Palm & Quince Sts.) | 619-294-2132

Karen Krasne's Little Italy *French/Italian*

Little Italy | 1430 Union St. (bet. W. Ash & W. Beech Sts.) | 619-294-7001

www.extraordinarydesserts.com

"You'll moan in ecstasy" when tasting the "decadent" "über-desserts" at this "cozy cottage" in Bankers Hill and its Little Italy offshoot, which also offers a "savory menu" of "light" French and Italian "small plates", a "wide selection of wines" and a "techno-modern" design that's of definite "architectural interest"; everything at both is so "artfully crafted", you may forgive counter help that can be "lackadaisical" and somewhat "snobby" - that is, if they don't "ignore you."

Market Restaurant & Bar *American* 27 | 21 | 23 | E

Del Mar | 3702 Via de la Valle (El Camino Real) | 858-523-0007 | www.marketdelmar.com

"Well-trained" "creative" "genius" Carl Schroeder "raises the bar" at this Del Mar "star" with his "daily changing menu" of New American dishes "so fresh and carefully thought out", they yield an "absolutely mouthwatering", "near-perfect mix of flavors and textures"; persimmon walls and chocolate leather banquettes figure heavily into decor that's "hip but not tragically so", and while the floor staff is "well-trained" and "helpful", some report "rude" front-of-housers; N.B. there's also a sushi bar.

Mille Fleurs *French* 26 | 25 | 26 | VE

Rancho Santa Fe | Country Squire Courtyard | 6009 Paseo Delicias (Avenida de Acacias) | 858-756-3085 | www.millefleurs.com

You can just "smell the money around you" at this "world-class" exercise in "investment dining" where the "glitterati of Rancho Santa Fe" revel in chef Martin Woesle's "sublime" New French fare that's "fresh and exciting without being too off-the-wall"; the "impeccably presented" dishes are then conveyed by "utterly professional" servers through the "lovely", "formal" space.

Morton's The Steakhouse *Seafood/Steak* 26 22 24 E

Downtown | 285 J St. (3rd Ave.) | 619-696-3369 | www.mortons.com

"A guy's steakhouse that women love" too, this Downtown spot may be a "typical" representation of the chain, but it's "nonetheless great" for "piping-hot, juicy and tender" beef paired with "fine trimmings", served in "wow" sizes and "outrageously priced" (don't forget about the lobster, it "will thrill you as well"); though many diners deem the "waiters bringing the trays" of raw meat "out for you to admire" "just plain idiotic", said servers are "fun and nice."

Pamplemousse Grille *American/French* 27 22 25 E

Solana Beach | 514 Via de la Valle (I-5) | 858-792-9090 | www.pgrille.com

"If you win big at the racetrack" "across the street", "blow it" at this "elegant" Solana Beach "special-occasion" "splurge" where chef Jeffrey Strauss provides "dinner and a show" by first whipping up "amazing" American-French fare that displays "a great flair for the unusual", then "floating through the dining room" to "entertain guests" with his "amusing", "schmoozing" ways; P.S. lunch is served Friday only, and "what a way to end the week" it is!

Prado at Balboa Park *American* 22 26 22 M

Balboa Park | House of Hospitality | 1549 El Prado (Plaza de Panama) | 619-557-9441 | www.pradobalboa.com

"Top off a day" in "famously gorgeous" Balboa Park with this "special treat": "gracious" American dining in a "magical" "paradise", a vision of "pure loveliness" embodied by a "beautiful garden" and a "cool" "blown glass"-bedecked interior; the "divine dishes" "dazzle the eye and palate", while "silky smooth service" makes it a "great place to bring out-of-town guests" or the object of your affection.

Primavera Ristorante *Italian* 26 21 25 E

Coronado | 932 Orange Ave. (bet. 9th & 10th Sts.) | 619-435-0454 | www.primavera1st.com

It may be "under the radar", but this "tiny jewel" "in the heart of Coronado" "flies high", as "mouthwatering" Northern Italian cuisine "for the discerning palate" is purveyed by "superb" servers; also "top notch" is a wine list that's sufficiently "proper" for such an "intimate", "old-fashioned" "high-class" setting.

Roppongi *Asian Fusion* 25 22 21 E

La Jolla | 875 Prospect St. (Fay Ave.) | 858-551-5252 | www.roppongiusa.com

"Amazing Asian-fusion" small plates are "creatively crafted" and "presented as if every one were headed for the cover of *Gourmet* magazine" at this La Jolla "winner"; it's "elegant without being stuffy" inside, while the "beautiful outdoor fire-pit seating" gets the "stylish crowd" to engage in "excessive frivolity" (abetted by "a full selection of sake" no doubt); P.S. your "best bets" are the "half-price (yes, *half-price*) tapas and sushi 4-6 PM daily", so "order up a storm and share with friends."

Sammy's Woodfired Pizza *Pizza* 21 15 18 I

Del Mar | Del Mar Highlands | 12925 El Camino Real (Del Mar Heights Rd.) | 858-259-6600

Downtown | 770 Fourth Ave. (F St.) | 619-230-8888

Golden Triangle | Costa Verde Ctr. | 8650 Genesee Ave. (bet. La Jolla Village & Nobel Drs.) | 858-404-9898

(continued)

Sammy's Woodfired Pizza

La Jolla | 702 Pearl St. (Draper Ave.) | 858-456-5222
Mission Valley | Mission Valley Mall | 1620 Camino de la Reina (Mission Center Rd.) | 619-298-8222
Point Loma | Liberty Station | 2401 Truxton Rd., Ste. 102 (Womble Rd.) | 619-222-3111
San Marcos | 121 S. Las Posas Rd. (Grand Ave.) | 760-591-4222
Scripps Ranch | 10785 Scripps Poway Pkwy. (Springs Canyon Rd.) | 858-695-0900
www.sammyspizza.com

"Savvy restaurateur" Sammy Ladeki's homegrown chain is a "San Diego favorite" for "fresh and tasty" "West Coast pizza" with "innovative toppings" ("arugula and pear is a true wonder"), "massive", "addictive salads" and "yummy messy sundaes" for dessert ("be sure to scrape the glass, that's where all the caramel is!"); the staff of "surfers" sometimes "moves at a snail's pace", and with "a lot of kids" eating, they're "a bit on the noisy side", but the pies "never disappoint"; N.B. the currently closed Carlsbad outpost should open in spring '09.

Sushi Ota *Japanese* 28 | 12 | 19 | E

Pacific Beach | 4529 Mission Bay Dr. (Bunker Hill St.) | 858-270-5670

As "amazing" "as any place on the planet", this "pearl in a trashcan" conjures not only the "absolute best Japanese" in Pacific Beach but the No. 1 Food in San Diego courtesy of "genius" chef Yukito Ota and his "expert panel of sushi doctors" who assemble "silky" "treats" "so fresh, they almost evaporate on your tongue" ("sit at the bar" and let them "guide you"); its "oddball" setting in a strip mall is "lame", and you "need to book way too far in advance", so just "ignore everything but the taste" and "you'll have an experience you'll never forget."

Tapenade *French* 27 | 21 | 25 | E

La Jolla | 7612 Fay Ave. (bet. Kline & Pearl Sts.) | 858-551-7500 | www.tapenaderestaurant.com

"You're in for a great experience" when you venture "off-the-beaten" La Jolla path to this "close-to-ideal" New French "destination" where diners "trust" chef Jean-Michel Diot's "obvious commitment to quality ingredients" in creating "inventive" dishes that display "harmonious flavors and a counterplay of textures" (they're "well matched" by "extraordinary wines" too); it may be "a little stark" for being so "expensive", but it's "quiet and intimate", and "cordial" servers make sure everyone "goes home happy."

WineSellar & Brasserie S M *French* 28 | 20 | 27 | E

Golden Triangle | 9550 Waples St. (off Mira Mesa Blvd.) | 858-450-9557 | www.winesellar.com

It's "hard to find" in a "random" Golden Triangle "industrial zone", but this "tiny" "dream restaurant" is "well worth the hunt" for "imaginatively prepared", "beautifully presented" French fare; the "staggering" selection from the *vin* "warehouse" below is available upstairs at "minimal markups", the corkage fees are "nominal" and the "phenomenal", "informed" servers "recommend delicious pairings", all of which makes it "a must" for "wine dummies" and "oenophiles" alike.

FOOD | DECOR | SERVICE | COST

San Francisco Bay Area

TOP FOOD RANKING

	Restaurant	Cuisine
29	French Laundry	American/French
	Cyrus	French
28	Gary Danko	American
	Erna's Elderberry	Californian/French
	Kaygetsu	Japanese
	Quince	French/Italian
	La Fôret	Continental/French
	Ritz-Carlton	French
	Sushi Ran	Japanese
27	Chez Panisse	Californian/Mediterranean
	Masa's	French
	Acquerello	Italian
	Chapeau!	French
	Chez Panisse Café	Californian/Mediterranean
	Manresa	American
	Boulevard	American
	Michael Mina	American
	House	Asian Fusion
	Redd Restaurant	Californian

Acquerello S M *Italian* 27 | 24 | 27 | VE

Polk Gulch | 1722 Sacramento St. (bet. Polk St. & Van Ness Ave.) | San Francisco | 415-567-5432 | www.acquerello.com

When you want to be "pampered and catered to, to your heart's content", take yourself to this "saintly" "special-occasion" Italian set in a "charming old church" in Polk Gulch; "soft lights", a "hushed", "old-world atmosphere", namesake watercolors on the walls and "tuxedoed waiters" that proffer "exemplary" service and decant "perfect wine pairings" to complement "sublime" prix fixe menus (featuring "ephemeral pastas" among other offerings) prompt the "society-page" contingent to "count their blessings"; but a devilish few quip that the "somewhat fussy" setting "might feel more comfortable if I were in my 60s."

Boulevard *American* 27 | 25 | 25 | VE

Embarcadero | Audiffred Bldg. | 1 Mission St. (Steuart St.) | San Francisco | 415-543-6084 | www.boulevardrestaurant.com

"All hail chef Nancy" Oakes' "adventurous and divine" French-influenced New American fare "set against the beautiful backdrop of the Bay Bridge" at this "gorgeous" belle epoque brasserie on the Embarcadero that hits "the sweet spot between too stuffy and not serious enough"; the "knowledgeable" yet "down-to-earth" staff "continues to sparkle", treating everyone like "the celebrities eating at the next table", while a "mishmash of locals, tourists and biz-types" keeps it "perennially" packed; just bring along "two week's salary" and "it's all good."

Chapeau! ⓜ *French* 27 | 18 | 25 | E

Outer Richmond | 1408 Clement St. (15th Ave.) | San Francisco | 415-750-9787

"Hats off to the wonderful couple" who truly roll out the "Gallic" "welcome" mat at their "*très charmant*", "*très, très* convivial" Outer Richmond bistro that dishes out "blissful" fare that Francophiles tout as "four-star at two-star prices"; despite a hatbox of a setting so "tight" you can "eat off your neighbor's plate" and "jolly" chef-owner Philippe Gardelle now spending time at his new place, Clémentine, "loyal followers" swear they'd "go back at the drop of a chapeau."

Chez Panisse ⓢ *Californian/Mediterranean* 27 | 23 | 26 | VE

Berkeley | 1517 Shattuck Ave. (bet. Cedar & Vine Sts.) | 510-548-5525 | www.chezpanisse.com

Berkeley's "shrine continues to shine" as Alice Waters produces "garden-to-mouth" Cal-Med prix fixe dinners that "are not swayed by trend or innovation but by season" to "evoke the true taste" of "pedigreed organic" ingredients; the odd skeptic "might turn up his nose" at the "simple" "Craftsman decor" and "understated but perfect" service, but "every epicure must make the pilgrimage" to this "culinary landmark" "where the first shot in the Californian food revolution was fired", and perhaps "spy the demigoddess herself in the open kitchen."

Chez Panisse Café ⓢ *Californian/Mediterranean* 27 | 23 | 25 | E

Berkeley | 1517 Shattuck Ave. (bet. Cedar & Vine Sts.) | 510-548-5049 | www.chezpanisse.com

"It just doesn't get any better than this" "swoon" budget-watching Berkeleyites and "out-of-towners" eager to "sample Alice's" "deceptively simple" "source-oriented" Cal-Med "gastronomic delights" at lower à la carte prices and in an atmosphere with "less pomp and circumstance" than the "more formal restaurant downstairs"; "great wine" and "astonishingly good" pizzas, pastas and salads presented by an "attentive but not overwhelming" staff in "comfortable" Craftsman surroundings make this "gateway to mecca" a "delightful" experience.

Cyrus *French* 29 | 27 | 28 | VE

Healdsburg | Les Mars Hotel | 29 North St. (Healdsburg Ave.) | 707-433-3311 | www.cyrusrestaurant.com

Douglas Keane's "haute" New French "tour de force" with global influences is a "brilliant" "reason to go to" Healdsburg say those enraptured by his "almost flawless" "masterpieces" that include "opulent" and "stunning" "design-it-yourself" prix fixe and tasting menus that are "fit for royalty" and priced accordingly; "from the caviar and champagne cart" to "foie gras three ways" delivered by "pampering" "synchronized servers" beneath grand vaulted ceilings, it's all "pure theatrics" and "off the charts"; N.B. à la carte at the bar only.

Erna's Elderberry House *Californian/French* 28 | 27 | 28 | VE

Oakhurst | Château du Sureau | 48688 Victoria Ln. (Hwy. 41) | 559-683-6800 | www.elderberryhouse.com

"For a magical evening in a magical setting" attended by "first-class" service, it's "worth planning" your visit to Yosemite around a meal at this "enchanting" "Europe in Oakhurst" château-like dining room where "each amazing course" on the "leisurely" Cal-New French prix fixe menus (complemented by "great wines") "outshines the previous one"; "it's pricey" - especially if you book a room for the night - but the "gastronomic experience" "will be with you forever."

French Laundry, The *American/French* 29 | 26 | 28 | VE

Yountville | 6640 Washington St. (Creek St.) | 707-944-2380 | www.frenchlaundry.com

"Set your sights high and expect them to be exceeded" at Thomas Keller's "gustatory temple" in Yountville, a "once-in-a-lifetime gastronomic event" ("who can afford it twice?") that reclaims SF's No. 1 Food ranking for its "exhilarating" French-New American tasting menus that are "pure pleasure from the first bite to the last"; the "service is a seamless extension of the kitchen", "coddling and cosseting" foodies who've managed to "magically score a table" inside the "country manor house" setting, where the "complete experience" equals "four hours" of sheer "bliss."

Gary Danko *American* 28 | 27 | 28 | VE

Fisherman's Wharf | 800 N. Point St. (Hyde St.) | San Francisco | 415-749-2060 | www.garydanko.com

At Gary Danko's "luxurious" New American Wharf wunderkind - voted Most Popular in SF - diners are "treated like royalty" and "you might even see a Bay Area celebrity . . . if he comes out of the kitchen that night"; "sinfully rich" "build-your-own" tasting menus, a "first-rate cheese cart" and an "encyclopedic wine list" provide a "lifetime of cuisine memories" in the "upscale-fancy" but "not stuffy" space where "even the bathrooms are gorgeous", and locals know that those who can't nab an "impossible-to-get reservation" "can usually grab seats at the bar."

House, The *Asian Fusion* 27 | 15 | 21 | E

North Beach | 1230 Grant Ave. (bet. Columbus Ave. & Vallejo St.) | San Francisco | 415-986-8612 | www.thehse.com

"Hidden" in "Italian North Beach", this Asian fusion gem is a "very, very, very fine house", proffering "phenomenal", "exquisitely presented" spins on "iconic dishes" such as wasabi noodles and miso-marinated cod - with "no attitude" and at "about half the price of comparable places"; alas, its "simple" digs are in a "very, very, very small house", so "prepare to be packed in like sardines and use your voice as a bullhorn."

Kaygetsu Ⓜ *Japanese* 28 | 19 | 26 | VE

Menlo Park | Sharon Heights Shopping Ctr. | 325 Sharon Park Dr. (Sand Hill Rd.) | 650-234-1084 | www.kaygetsu.com

Behind the strip-mall facade of this Menlo Park Japanese "is a marvelous taste-bud adventure" featuring "meticulously prepared" "first-class" sushi "that would not be out of place in Tokyo", plus an "exquisite" "kaiseki menu" that's "like eating on an *Iron Chef* show"; devotees dismiss the "upscale prices" and "stark environment" and focus on the "excellent" service - and opportunity to "name-drop the Fortune 500 folks you've seen there"; N.B. now open for lunch.

La Forêt Ⓜ *Continental/French* 28 | 24 | 27 | VE

San Jose | 21747 Bertram Rd. (Almaden Rd.) | 408-997-3458 | www.laforetrestaurant.com

It's "definitely worth seeking out" this French-Continental "hidden jewel" in a "beautiful creekside setting" surrounded by woods in San

Jose that serves prix fixe and à la carte meals so "done to perfection" surveyors sigh "I want it all"; the "most romantic" ambiance, "fabulous wines" and "kind", "impeccably well-paced service" add to the "charm", so although "it will cost" you, it makes an "always superior", "wonderful place for a special event, date or getaway."

Manresa M *American* 27 | 24 | 26 | VE

Los Gatos | 320 Village Ln. (bet. N. Santa Cruz & University Aves.) | 408-354-4330 | www.manresarestaurant.com

"Leave your wallet and culinary prejudices at the door" and let "mad scientist" David Kinch "sweep your palate off to wonderland" at this "el Bulli-inspired" respite where "lucky diners" find themselves on "cloud 17" after indulging in wine-paired New American tasting dinners that "pay tribute to seasonality" with "humor" and "home-grown" "biodynamic" veggies; although the "non-highbrow setting" "hidden in the trees" of Los Gatos is nothing to write home about, the service is "superb" and the "mind-bending" experience "evokes smiles" "almost a year" later.

Masa's S M *French* 27 | 24 | 26 | VE

Downtown | Hotel Vintage Ct. | 648 Bush St. (bet. Powell & Stockton Sts.) | San Francisco | 415-989-7154 | www.masasrestaurant.com

Though it may be "less trendy" than some other top-tier restaurants, "you can always count on" this Downtown "classic" (since 1983) for "nonstop palate pleasure" and "polished professional" service; "believe everything you hear" about chef Gregory Short's "exquisite" six- and nine-course New French tasting menus and the "fabulous sommelier" "who works off an equally great wine list"; "gadzooks, it's very dear", but "worth every farthing" considering the "wonderful quiet atmosphere" that's sure to "impress that someone special"; N.B. jacket suggested.

Michael Mina *American* 27 | 24 | 26 | VE

Downtown | Westin St. Francis | 335 Powell St. (bet. Geary & Post Sts.) | San Francisco | 415-397-9222 | www.michaelmina.net

"If you want to impress or simply indulge", admirers say invest in this "extravagant" and "exceptional" New American in Downtown's Westin St. Francis, where prix fixe "trios of tastes" - "multiple presentations" of a single ingredient - "mean three times the enjoyment" and "great wines" complement the "culinary poetry"; "spot-on" servers strike "just the right balance of attention and privacy" as they work the "elegant", "neutrally toned" dining room, but downers declare the namesake chef's Mina-mal presence makes for "disappointing" and "overpriced" cuisine, which is served in a setting that's "loud" and "lacking in gravitas."

Quince *French/Italian* 28 | 24 | 26 | VE

Pacific Heights | 1701 Octavia St. (bet. Bush & Pine Sts.) | San Francisco | 415-775-8500 | www.quincerestaurant.com

"A tough table to get" and even "tougher to leave" swoon "true foodies" over this "sublime" "craftmanlike" New French-Italian Pacific Heights "jewel"; it's fast "gaining status" thanks to a menu of "glorious", daily changing fare that includes "pasta as you have never experienced it before" proffered by an "über-attentive staff" in an "intimate" setting that's "just shy of stuffy"; the "only drawback" is a "lack of space" - though an eventual move is planned.

	FOOD	DECOR	SERVICE	COST
Redd Restaurant *Californian*	27	22	24	VE

Yountville | 6480 Washington St. (California Dr.) | 707-944-2222 | www.reddnapavalley.com

A "modern Californian-cuisine genius", chef-owner Richard Reddington "aims to please" and hits his target at this "special place in a town full of special places", Yountville; "from fish to fowl to fillet", "every dish is a work of art" say Redd-blooded reviewers, who are "impressed with everything" from the "cutting-edge" menu and "ambitious" wine list to the "sophisticated" "minimalist" (some say "stark") setting; a "top-notch" sommelier and "gracious" servers even manage "to make the expensive tab seem reasonable."

	FOOD	DECOR	SERVICE	COST
Ritz-Carlton Dining Room *French*	28	27	28	VE

Nob Hill | Ritz-Carlton Hotel | 600 Stockton St. (bet. California & Pine Sts.) | San Francisco | 415-773-6198 | www.ritzcarltondiningroom.com

This "over-the-top" (complete with "formal", "Waspy decor") Nob Hill hotel dining room delivers all the "pomp and circumstance" desired by "dressed-to-the-nines" diners eager to "escape the trendy" spots for a "Fred-and-Ginger evening"; it's the "ultimate" "wallet-clearing" splurge, from "I-Ron chef" Siegel's "titillating" "sublime" Japanese-tinged New French prix fixe and tasting menus - the "courses and great surprises just keep coming" - to the "fantastic wines" and "pampering" service that's "so choreographed it should be set to music."

	FOOD	DECOR	SERVICE	COST
Slanted Door, The *Vietnamese*	25	22	21	E

Embarcadero | 1 Ferry Bldg. (Market St.) | San Francisco | 415-861-8032 | www.slanteddoor.com

"Make your rezzies far in advance" or plan to "squeeze yourself" into the "swank bar" at this Vietnamese in the Embarcadero's Ferry Building suggest "phans" of "genius" chef Charles Phan, who uses "absolutely the best ingredients" to "elevate" his cuisine to "otherworldly" heights; "local celebs" and "FiDi yuppies" pack the "sleek" (some say "far too loud") space with a "killer view" of the Bay, while a "tragically hip" staff provides "terrific" service.

	FOOD	DECOR	SERVICE	COST
Sushi Ran ◐ *Japanese*	28	19	22	E

Sausalito | 107 Caledonia St. (bet. Pine & Turney Sts.) | 415-332-3620 | www.sushiran.com

"Sushi to swoon for", a "spectacular sake list" and Japanese fusion entrees that show an "artist's touch" "set the standard by which other Japanese restaurants should be judged" at Sausalito's "inspired" temple to "incredibly fresh" fish; prepare to pay a "goodly sum" for this "world-class experience" that unfolds in a "calm" dining room that is "comfortable" rather than "beautiful"; when unable to land that "difficult-to-get prime-time reservation", devotees "line up early" for the adjacent wine bar.

FOOD | DECOR | SERVICE | COST

Seattle

TOP FOOD RANKING

	Restaurant	Cuisine
29	Herbfarm	Pacific NW
28	Rover's	French
	Cafe Juanita	Italian
	Sitka & Spruce	Eclectic
	Armandino's	Italian/Sandwiches
27	Paseo	Caribbean
	Kisaku Sushi	Japanese
	Inn at Langley	Pacific NW
	Nishino	Japanese
	Szechuan Chef*	Chinese
	Canlis	Pacific NW
	Phoenecia at Alki	Mediterranean
	Maneki	Japanese
	Restaurant Zoë	American
	Lark	American

Armandino's Salumi S M *Italian/Sandwiches* 28 | 11 | 20 | I

Pioneer Square | 309 Third Ave. S. (bet. Jackson & Main Sts.) | 206-621-8772 | www.salumicuredmeats.com

"Unforgettable" Italian sandwiches and salamis draw crowds and kudos to this Pioneer Square "hawg heaven" where the Batali family (yes, Mario's kin) cranks out "amazing" "homemade" cured meats in the back; the "shoebox"-size cafe is "cramped", the mood "fun" and the lines "out the door" as both regular folk and "every food luminary in the world" make the pilgrimage; N.B. it's open only Tuesday–Friday until 4 PM.

Cafe Juanita *Italian* 28 | 22 | 26 | E

Kirkland | 9702 NE 120th Pl. (97th St.) | 425-823-1505 | www.cafejuanita.com

Chef Holly Smith's Northern Italian cuisine is "consistently" "stunning" thanks to her "creative" touch with "impeccably" fresh local ingredients say the legions of satisfied suppers who've "battled traffic" to get to this "foodie" destination in Kirkland; its "deep" wine list features "lots" of "hard-to-finds" from The Boot, and "informed" servers add to the abundant "sense of competence and bonhomie" – so while it's "not cheap", it is "worth every penny."

Canlis S *Pacific NW* 27 | 27 | 27 | VE

Lake Union | 2576 Aurora Ave. N. (Halladay St., south of Aurora Bridge) | 206-283-3313 | www.canlis.com

"Spoil yourself" royally at this old-schooler that's been the city's "gold-standard" "special-event restaurant" for more than 50 years; the "world-class" Pacific NW food and wine are matched by "million-dollar" Lake Union views from a "chic", and some say "formal", mid-century modern room, and by the "gracious" "how-did-they-know"

* Indicates a tie with restaurant above

service that borders on magic; so leave your worries at home, but don't forget to "bring your platinum card"; N.B. new chef Jason Franey (ex NYC's Eleven Madison Park) took over in December 2008.

NEW Corson Building, The M *Eclectic* - | - | - | VE

Georgetown | 5609 Corson Ave. S. (Airport Way) | 206-762-3330 | www.thecorsonbuilding.com

Enthusiasts are clamoring for the Eclectic prix fixe locavore dinners at co-chef/co-owner Matt Dillon's new eatery situated in a 1910 Spanish-style building in an unlikely Georgetown locale beneath a freeway ramp; the set-menu, family-style meals (one seating per night) are served at communal tables in a cozy dining area that curves around a quaint fireplace; dinner runs $90 per person Thursday-Saturday, so $60 Sunday Suppers are a relative bargain.

Dahlia Lounge *Pacific NW* 25 | 24 | 23 | E

Downtown | 2001 Fourth Ave. (Virginia St.) | 206-682-4142 | www.tomdouglas.com

Tom Douglas' pricey flagship may be "not as exciting as it once was", but it remains an über-popular "perennial favorite" proffering "delightful" Pacific NW cuisine that riffs on Asian flavors, capped off by the "world's best coconut cream pie" (available to go at Douglas' bakery next door); there's "lots of space" between tables in the "whimsical", "gorgeous" Downtown room, so settle in for a "comfortable sit-down meal" served by a "thoughtful" staff.

Herbfarm, The M *Pacific NW* 29 | 26 | 28 | VE

Woodinville | 14590 NE 145th St. (Woodinville-Redmond Rd.) | 425-485-5300 | www.theherbfarm.com

A "once-in-a-lifetime dining experience", the "sublime" cuisine at this "over-the-top" "oasis" - ranked No. 1 for Food and Service - features "vibrant herbs" in a nine-course Pacific NW prix fixe menu (plus paired wines) that changes nightly, delivered by an "impeccable" staff; a "quick tour" of the garden is de rigueur before settling into the "lush" dining room in Woodinville's wine belt, and the bill, while "huge", covers four or five hours of "exquisite" eating; N.B. the verdict is still out on the chef change and overall experience following the departure of Jerry Traunfeld after 17 years at the stove.

Inn at Langley M *Pacific NW* 27 | 23 | 22 | VE

Langley | Inn at Langley | 400 First St. (Anthes Ave.) | 360-221-3033 | www.innatlangley.com

Not just a meal, an "experience" awaits Seattleites who ferry to this Whidbey Island inn for Matt Costello's "exquisite" and expensive six-course prix fixe of "fresh, honest" Pacific NW market finds; in the "intimate" kitchen/dining room, gourmands get a gander of the chef at work and may end up so sated they'll want to "stay the night"; N.B. open Thursday-Sunday in summer, and Friday-Sunday the rest of the year.

Kisaku Sushi *Japanese* 27 | 20 | 23 | M

Green Lake | 2101 N. 55th St. (Meridian Ave.) | 206-545-9050 | www.kisaku.com

"You cannot go wrong" when you "let the chef" choose your food at this Green Lake Japanese that sates with a "startling array" of "exceedingly fresh", "creative sushi"; serene decor and "reasonable prices" make this a "favorite", affordable haunt for locals who'd rather keep it their "secret"; N.B. closed Tuesdays.

Lark M *American* 27 | 23 | 25 | E

Capitol Hill | 926 12th Ave. (bet. E. Marion & Spring Sts.) | 206-323-5275 | www.larkseattle.com

Sybarites swoon for chef John Sundstrom's "bonanza" of New American small plates prepared with "stellar" "organic" ingredients - and a healthy dose of "love"; some say the "simple" "farmhouse" setting on Capitol Hill can be "uncomfortable" and quibble over tabs that are "too pricey by the ounce", but all agree on the "engaging", "gracious" service; N.B. there can be a line, which patrons wait out at the owners' bar next door.

Maneki M *Japanese* 27 | 17 | 21 | M

International District | 304 Sixth Ave. S. (bet. Jackson & Main Sts.) | 206-622-2631 | www.manekirestaurant.com

Seattle's "oldest" Japanese restaurant, this "authentic" hideaway tucked into an International District hillside offers "homestyle" "comfort food" alongside what fans consider the "best deal" for "top-quality sushi" in the city, plus a large sake selection; the vintage decor is sweet, but the secret's out, so get there early; N.B. reservations are required for a tatami room, but the dining room is waitlist-only.

Metropolitan Grill *Steak* 26 | 22 | 25 | E

Downtown | 820 Second Ave. (Marion St.) | 206-624-3287 | www.themetropolitangrill.com

Downtown's "old-fashioned" "power scene" is a "perennial favorite" thanks to its "absolutely outstanding" aged steaks (which could "make a cardiologist weep") and "colossal" lobsters; the "manly" 1940s-style dining room has a "classic" feel and the service is "near perfect", so most don't fret the "pricey" tabs - just "loosen your wallet" or "bring the corporate card", since it's "worth every penny and then some."

Nishino *Japanese* 27 | 21 | 24 | E

Madison Park | 3130 E. Madison St. (Lake Washington Blvd.) | 206-322-5800 | www.nishinorestaurant.com

For a "nirvanic" experience, sushistas and Seattle movers-and-shakers "let the chefs go crazy" in concocting "fabulous" "omakase" dinners at this "refined, if expensive", Madison Park Japanese; if it seems like "Nobu for half the price", that's because owner Tatsu Nishino is a Nobu Matsuhisa protégé, so it's little surprise that this "spectacular" spot is "the real deal."

Paseo S M ≠ *Caribbean* 27 | 7 | 13 | I

Fremont | 4225 Fremont Ave. N. (bet. 42nd & 43rd Sts.) | 206-545-7440

The "aroma will draw you in" to this "funky" Fremont "shack" proffering "generous" portions of "killer" Cuban sandwiches and Caribbean on the "cheap"; a "cramped" interior includes only a few seats (at the counter, where service is "friendly"), so it's best if you "don't plan on eating in" and opt for takeout; N.B. cash only, no liquor.

Phoenecia at Alki M *Mediterranean* 27 | 16 | 26 | M

West Seattle | 2716 Alki Ave. SW (bet. 60th & 61st Aves.) | 206-935-6550

"Relax, ignore the menu" and let owner Hussein Khazaal "make something very special just for you" at this "hidden" Med "treasure" that turns out "awesome" seafood, "spicy" chicken and "charred flatbreads"; though it can "get expensive", the trade-off is a "great location" on West Seattle's Alki Beach with "wonderful" Elliott Bay views.

Restaurant Zoë *American* 27 | 22 | 25 | E

Belltown | 2137 Second Ave. (Blanchard St.) | 206-256-2060 | www.restaurantzoe.com

There are "no zzzzzzs" at this zesty restaurant joke reviewers, since it's got a "cool beyond cool" Belltown vibe that's "bustling and fun" and the "flawless" New American cuisine boasts "knock-your-socks-off flavors" from "local, fresh ingredients"; "seating is tight" in the slightly "sterile" space, but "personable" "service makes up for it", as do the bar's "delicious" "twists on classic" cocktails.

Rover's [S] [M] *French* 28 | 24 | 27 | VE

Madison Valley | 2808 E. Madison St. (28th Ave.) | 206-325-7442 | www.rovers-seattle.com

Thierry Rautureau's "unparalleled" New French degustation menus (including a "stellar" vegetarian version) make this "elegant", "world-class" Madison Valley farmhouse a "haven" for appreciative locals and loads of visiting celebrities; service that "defines perfection" rounds out the "breathtakingly expensive" "experience"; N.B. à la carte options and Friday lunches can soften the wallet impact.

Sitka & Spruce [M] *Eclectic* 28 | 14 | 18 | M

Eastlake | 2238 Eastlake Ave. E. (bet. Boston & E. Lynn Sts.) | 206-324-0662 | www.sitkaandspruce.com

This "funky" "strip-mall" storefront in Eastlake is an "unbelievable surprise", turning out an "inventive" Eclectic menu filled with "plate-lickingly delicious" food featuring "local" ingredients "you've never tasted" before; the "tiny", "cramped" room "fills up fast", so expect "aggravatingly long waits", plus "shared tables" and service that "could use some polish" - none of which bothers the "haute"-minded foodies who flock here.

Szechuan Chef [S] *Chinese* 27 | 15 | 18 | I

Bellevue | Kelsey Creek Ctr. | 15015 Main St. (148th Ave.) | 425-746-9008 | www.szechuanchef.com

"So hot but worth the sweat" pant admirers of the "huge selection" of "fantastic", "fiery" Sichuan fare at this "always wonderful" Chinese "hole-in-the-wall"; it's "easy to miss" in a Bellevue "strip mall", so follow your nose toward the "aroma of deliciousness", and expect the "friendly" service to get the food out "fast."

Wild Ginger *Pacific Rim* 25 | 23 | 22 | E

Downtown | 1401 Third Ave. (Union St.) | 206-623-4450 | www.wildginger.net

It's "come a long way" since its start on Western Avenue 19 years ago say the legions who "love" this still-"buzzy", "beautiful" 350-seat Pacific Rim "hot spot" that's once again Seattle's Most Popular restaurant thanks to anthropologist-turned-restaurateur Rick Yoder's "sumptuous" menu of Asian curries, satays and spicy lahksa soups served by an "accommodating" staff; its Downtown digs are "noisy", "crowded" and "over-the-top" decry objectors, yet diners still can't get enough of it, so the lion's share of voters urge even "if you have to wait for a table, do it."

		FOOD	DECOR	SERVICE	COST

St. Louis

TOP FOOD RANKING

	Restaurant	Cuisine
28	Sidney Street Cafe	American
	Paul Manno's	Italian
27	Tony's	Italian
	Trattoria Marcella	Italian
	Niche	American
	Al's Restaurant	Seafood/Steak
	Dominic's	Italian
	Pomme	American/French
26	Crossing	American
	Annie Gunn's	American
	Atlas Restaurant	French/Italian
	Nippon Tei	Asian Fusion
	Grill at the Ritz-Carlton	American
	Giovanni's	Italian
	LoRusso's Cucina	Italian
	Chez Leon	French
25	Harvest	American

Al's Restaurant *Seafood/Steak* 27 | 18 | 26 | E

Downtown | 1200 N. First St. (Biddle St.) | 314-421-6399 | www.alsrestaurant.net

This "true St. Louis landmark" ("since 1925") remains "a trip back in time", an Italian-style Downtown chophouse featuring "fabulous steaks, veal" and seafood that are "worth" both "the dress code" (jackets required in fall and winter) and the "expense-account" prices; a post-Survey renovation should have improved the digs that aesthetes found so "tired."

Annie Gunn's *American* 26 | 21 | 23 | E

Chesterfield | 16806 Chesterfield Airport Rd. (Baxter Rd.) | 636-532-7684 | www.anniegunns.com

One of "the best West County has to offer" is this Traditional American that's "worth the trip" to Chesterfield for "superb steaks" and "top-notch seafood" from chef "Lou Rook, the genius in the kitchen"; it's "pricey, but you get what you pay for" – "terrific service", a "casual atmosphere" and a "fantastic wine list" – although a few warn that it's also "crowded", making reservations "a must"; P.S. don't forget to "fill your car up with goodies" from the attached Smoke House Market.

Atlas Restaurant *French/Italian* 26 | 20 | 25 | M

Forest Park | 5513 Pershing Ave. (bet. De Baliviere Ave. & Union Blvd.) | 314-367-6800 | www.atlasrestaurantstl.com

Regulars "hope nobody ever finds out about" Forest Park's "true Paris bistro without the jet lag", where the "honest, uncontrived, classic" French and Italian dishes are both "toe-curlingly good" and "a great value"; the seasonal fare (plus a "nice late-night dessert and coffee menu") is enhanced by "warm", "attentive owners", a "thoughtful" staff and a "simple", "roomy" interior.

Chez Leon M *French* 26 | 24 | 24 | E

Central West End | 4580 Laclede Ave. (Euclid Ave.) | 314-361-1589 | www.chezleon.com

"There's something about it that makes me happy" smile supporters of this "authentic" Central West End bistro where a "skillfully executed menu" is paired with "faithfully French decor" that's "so charming, you feel like you're in Paris"; the "lively, inviting atmosphere" comes complete with "fantastic service", sidewalk seating and a pianist on Fridays and Sundays, so "order the Grand Marnier soufflé" and "settle in for the evening"; P.S. the prix fixe menu is a "great value."

Crossing, The S *American* 26 | 20 | 24 | E

Clayton | 7823 Forsyth Blvd. (Central Ave.) | 314-721-7375 | www.thecrossingstl.com

Chef-owner Jim Fiala delivers one of "the finest dining experiences in St. Louis" at this Clayton New American offering a "continually updated" selection of "innovative, delicious" dishes "with French and Italian influences" ("the tasting menu with wine flights is the way to go"); "unmemorable decor" gives nitpickers pause, but most agree it's an "intimate", "charming environment" with "seamless" "service to match", hence fans "never come away with anything but a giant smile."

Dominic's S *Italian* 27 | 23 | 26 | E

The Hill | 5101 Wilson Ave. (Hereford St.) | 314-771-1632 | www.dominicsrestaurant.com

"Old-world charm meets fine Italian cuisine" at this "all-around wonderful", family-owned "classic" that's "a must on the Hill" for its "outstanding, authentic" fare and "extremely attentive", "personal tableside service"; entering the "dimly lit, romantic" space is "like stepping back in time", and its "elegant", "classy" decor makes it a "favorite" "for special occasions and business dinners."

1111 Mississippi S *Californian/Italian* 25 | 25 | 23 | M

Lafayette Square | 1111 Mississippi Ave. (Chouteau Ave.) | 314-241-9999 | www.1111-m.com

"A cornerstone in the Lafayette Square revival", this "trendy" spot set in a "renovated warehouse" offers an "interesting menu" of Tuscan-Californian cuisine "with an emphasis on fresh provisions", "variety and quality" but "without pretension"; the "multilevel interior" can get "noisy, but who cares" counter fans who focus instead on the "meticulous service", "superbly cultivated wine list" and patio seating; P.S. the "gooey butter cake is a must-try!"

Giovanni's on the Hill S *Italian* 26 | 22 | 25 | E

The Hill | 5201 Shaw Ave. (Marconi Ave.) | 314-772-5958 | www.giovannisonthehill.com

"Take a special someone" to this "remarkable" "institution" on the Hill that "deserves its reputation as one of the finest restaurants" in the area due to its "truly exceptional", "classic" Italian cuisine, "top-quality service" from a "tuxedoed" staff and "decor that reminds you of a palace"; it's an "excellent choice for a romantic night on the town" -

the "place to get engaged!" - but as much as the "food will amaze you, so will the bill."

Grill at the Ritz-Carlton, The *American* 26 | 26 | 27 | E

Clayton | Ritz-Carlton Hotel | 100 Carondelet Plaza (Hanley Rd.) | 314-863-6300 | www.ritz-carlton.com

"It's a Ritz, and it lives up to expectations" enthuse admirers of this hotel dining "oasis" where a "downright incredible" staff that's "second to none" "makes you feel important" as you indulge in "utterly sublime", "inventive" New American food; the "quiet", "beautiful" setting is "perfect for a special evening" or "business lunch", and while "the price will leave you shocked", it's "worth it."

Harvest M *American* 25 | 23 | 24 | E

Richmond Heights | 1059 S. Big Bend Blvd. (Clayton Rd.) | 314-645-3522 | www.harveststlouis.com

This "fabulous" Richmond Heights restaurant is "worth checking out every few months" for some of "the most creative cooking in St. Louis" courtesy of a "seasonally changing menu" that "incorporates regional, market-ready ingredients" into "adventurous takes on [New] American cuisine"; the "cozy", "rustic atmosphere" and "wonderful service" are "exceeded only by the wine list", although a few sweet tooths find "the bread pudding alone" reason enough to go.

LoRusso's Cucina M *Italian* 26 | 20 | 24 | M

The Hill | 3121 Watson Rd. (Arsenal St.) | 314-647-6222 | www.lorussos.com

"The snob appeal is low and the food appeal is high" at this "excellent" veteran Italian on "the edge of the Hill", where chef-owner "Rich LoRusso wins over a loyal clientele with his delicious" "menu that's authentic but still feels fresh" via a "range of standard pastas and innovative dishes" served in "ample portions"; "excellent service", a "welcoming" ambiance and a "decent wine list" complete the "well-rounded experience."

Niche *American* 27 | 25 | 24 | M

Benton Park | 1831 Sidney St. (I-55) | 314-773-7755 | www.nichestlouis.com

"Bringing great food and enjoyable ambiance together", this "welcome" New American in Benton Park offers a "short" "but top-notch" menu of "flawless", "cutting-edge" cuisine in a "sleek, modern" setting that "makes you feel chic"; meanwhile, "outstanding service" and a "fabulous value" three-course $35 prix fixe meal "make it a delight on every visit."

Nippon Tei M *Asian Fusion* 26 | 21 | 20 | M

Ballwin | 14025 Manchester Rd. (Weidmann Rd.) | 636-386-8999

Delivering "some of the best sushi in town" ("the fish is the freshest, or it's not served"), this Japanese-Asian fusion in suburban Ballwin also draws praise for its "excellent" entrees, including tableside sukiyaki and shabu-shabu; "don't be fooled by the strip-mall location" - it's actually "very elegant" - but do "take your time and enjoy" the "artistic presentations" and "well-trained" service; P.S. "make sure you have reservations", as it can "get crowded."

Paul Manno's S *Italian* 28 | 18 | 24 | M

Chesterfield | 75 Forum Shopping Ctr. (Woods Mill Rd.) | 314-878-1274

"Skip the Hill" and head to this veteran Italian "hidden" in a Chesterfield strip mall, where the "marvelous", "authentic" Sicilian fare is "just like mama used to make, because mama is still in the kitchen"; an "attentive staff" provides "impeccable service", while owner Paul Manno "loves to make his customers happy"; but a "small" dining room means you "sometimes have to wait" and then "eat elbow-to-elbow" - so do yourself a favor and "don't tell anyone."

Pomme *American/French* 27 | 22 | 25 | E

Clayton | 40 N. Central Ave. (bet. Forsyth Blvd. & Maryland Ave.) | 314-727-4141 | www.pommerestaurant.com

For "inventive cuisine that's always satisfying" and "executed with care", take a detour to this "intimate" Clayton venue where chef-owner Bryan Carr delivers "big flavor" via "fresh, innovative, seasonal" New French-New American cuisine that "uses only the best ingredients"; it's "great for a date or quiet dinner", with a "comfortable atmosphere" that's enhanced by "attentive service" and a "thoughtful wine list"; nevertheless, a handful harrumph about portions that are "modest given the prices."

Sidney Street Cafe [S][M] *American* 28 | 23 | 26 | E

Benton Park | 2000 Sidney St. (Salena St.) | 314-771-5777 | www.sidneystreetcafe.com

Rated No. 1 for Food and Popularity in St. Louis, this Benton Park "standard for others to follow" is a "perennial favorite" proffering a "superb", "inventive" array of "universally wonderful" New American cuisine; the "friendly", "knowledgeable" servers recite "from chalkboard menus" "with appetizing flair", while the "inviting" and "romantic atmosphere" proves "perfect for business, dates or special occasions"; nevertheless, "for such fine dining", regulars recommend "calling weeks in advance for a reservation."

Tony's [S] *Italian* 27 | 24 | 27 | E

Downtown | 410 Market St. (B'way) | 314-231-7007 | www.tonysstlouis.com

It's "still the best special-occasion restaurant in St. Louis" sigh supporters of this Downtown "treasure" that "lives up to its reputation" via "impeccable" Italian cuisine and "professional servers" who "anticipate your every need"; an "elegant ambiance" and "attention to detail" make this "a class act" for most, although modernists maintain it can be "a bit old-fashioned" (jackets are required Friday and Saturday) and cite "high prices."

Trattoria Marcella [S][M] *Italian* 27 | 20 | 25 | M

South City | 3600 Watson Rd. (Pernod Ave.) | 314-352-7706 | www.trattoriamarcella.com

"Sometimes the labor of love that goes into a restaurant is so palpable you can taste it in the food" fawn fans of this "vibrant", "convivial" South Side Italian where "always remarkable", "reasonably priced" fare ("risotto to dream about") is served by a "friendly, gracious staff"; since it "expanded" a few years ago, "you can get a seat" in the still-"cramped" space, although a nostalgic few feel it "lost a little of its ambiance" in the process.

FOOD | DECOR | SERVICE | COST

Washington, DC

TOP FOOD RANKING

	Restaurant	Cuisine
29	Makoto	Japanese
	Inn at Little Washington	American
28	Komi	American/Mediterranean
	L'Auberge Provençale	French
	CityZen	American
	Marcel's	Belgian/French
27	Citronelle	French
	Eve	American
	Obelisk	Italian
	L'Auberge Chez François	French
	Ray's The Steaks	Steak
	Prime Rib	Steak
	Le Paradou	French
	Palena	American
	Kinkead's	Seafood
26	Rasika	Indian
	Tosca	Italian

Central Michel Richard *American/French* 25 | 22 | 22 | E

Penn Quarter | 1001 Pennsylvania Ave. NW (11th St.) | 202-626-0015 | www.centralmichelrichard.com

At Penn Quarter's latest "'it'" spot, all-star chef Michel Richard (Citronelle) lends his "signature cheeky style" and "culinary chops" to "haute cuisine packaged for everyone" via a "mouthwatering" New American-French lineup that's billed as "comfort food gone upscale"; with its "informed" service and "smart" looks, it draws "daunting" crowds of bon vivants who exult in "vibrant" scenery, a "hot bar scene" and "super-high quality" that "doesn't break the bank."

Citronelle S M *French* 27 | 25 | 26 | VE

(aka Michel Richard's Citronelle)

Georgetown | Latham Hotel | 3000 M St. NW (30th St.) | 202-625-2150 | www.citronelledc.com

"The 'wow' factor" endures as gustatory "wizard" Michel Richard continues to "work magic" at the Most Popular restaurant in DC, this "world-class" Georgetown New French where the "endlessly inventive", "brilliantly executed" cuisine (paired with an "unmatched wine list") makes for "culinary theater"; "flawless service" and a "posh" setting with a "glassed-in kitchen" encourage a "joyous" "celebration", but be ready to "pay for perfection"; N.B. for a thriftier, if less flashy, sampler, try the lounge's menu.

CityZen S M *American* 28 | 27 | 27 | VE

SW | Mandarin Oriental | 1330 Maryland Ave. SW (12th St.) | 202-787-6006 | www.cityzenrestaurant.com

"Nothing is compromised" at this "luxurious" New American in the Mandarin Oriental, from the "magnificent", "nuanced" tasting menus to the "gracious", "unobtrusive service" to the "stunning" interior design that "defines modern elegance" with its "showcase open kitchen"; "amusing touches" like the "bite-size Parker House rolls" alone are "worth the trip" to "otherwise drab" SW, and it all comes together for a "phenomenal" "treat"; N.B. the prix fixe dinners start at $75 for three courses, and there's also a "bargain" bar menu.

Eve, Restaurant ☒ *American* 27 | 24 | 25 | VE

Old Town | 110 S. Pitt St. (bet. King & Prince Sts.) | Alexandria, VA | 703-706-0450 | www.restauranteve.com

A "Garden of Eden in Old Town", this "world-class" New American lets "brilliant" chef/co-owner Cathal Armstrong "spotlight whatever's in season" with "imaginative", "perfectly crafted" dishes served with "unstuffy" "charm" in a "stylish" bistro and fireplace lounge or "intimate" "special-occasion" tasting room; a "top-flight sommelier" makes "refreshingly unpretentious recommendations" from an "exceptional" list, and evangelists who "purr" over the "culinary epiphany" attest it's so "worth the price tag."

Inn at Little Washington *American* 29 | 28 | 29 | VE

Washington | Inn at Little Washington | 309 Middle St. (Main St.), VA | 540-675-3800 | www.theinnatlittlewashington.com

After 30 years, "Patrick O'Connell's slice of paradise" in rural VA still "beats every expectation" as the "ultimate" "theatrical experience" staged on a "sumptuous" set: its "exquisite" New American fare rivals "fine art", and it's rated No. 1 for Decor and Service in DC thanks to "over-the-top" "opulence" and staffers who work in "unobtrusive harmony" to "anticipate your every desire"; in short, it has inn-siders sighing "save up" - "this place is life-changing"; P.S. "stay overnight" in one of the "simply gorgeous" rooms.

Jaleo *Spanish* 23 | 19 | 19 | M

Penn Quarter | 480 Seventh St. NW (E St.) | 202-628-7949 ◐
Bethesda | 7271 Woodmont Ave. (Elm St.), MD | 301-913-0003
Crystal City | 2250A Crystal Dr. (23rd St. S.) | Arlington, VA | 703-413-8181
www.jaleo.com

Admirers say these "top" tapas "temples" from "celebrity chef" José Andrés rival "Madrid or Barcelona" with "tons" of "inventive" Spanish nibbles ("the bacon-wrapped dates are divine"), "knockout" sangria and a "colorful", "bustling" atmosphere that "makes a meal into a party"; though critics cite "spotty" service, "crowded" quarters and tabs that "add up quickly", most maintain it's "well worth it", especially when live music and flamenco dancing add to the "festive" feel.

Kinkead's *Seafood* 27 | 21 | 23 | E

Foggy Bottom | 2000 Pennsylvania Ave. NW (I St.) | 202-296-7700 | www.kinkead.com

Chef-owner Bob Kinkead "is always at the top of his game" at his "wonderful" Foggy Bottom seafood specialist, where his "superb touch" with fin fare "continues to impress" the "lobbyists, lawyers and politicians" who also enjoy the "comfortable" yet "sophisticated" quarters and "top-notch" service; those who find the staff "aloof" ("unless you're a regular") and say reservations are "hard to get" may want to try the "friendly" bar area, where nightly live jazz adds to the appeal.

FOOD | DECOR | SERVICE | COST

Komi *American/Mediterranean* 28 | 22 | 27 | VE

Dupont Circle | 1509 17th St. NW (P St.) | 202-332-9200 | www.komirestaurant.com

"It's not just good, it's revelatory" swoon admirers of "stunningly talented" chef-owner Johnny Monis' "exquisite" (and "expensive") Dupont Circle destination where the "delectable" prix fixe meals are "gastronomic journeys" featuring an "ingenious parade" of "intriguing" New American and "Med-inspired" bites that "just keep coming"; the "attentive" staff "makes you feel special" in the sleek yet very "small" interior, but the lengthy proceedings cause at least one surveyor to suggest that "three-hour dinners require much more forgiving furniture."

L'Auberge Chez François *French* 27 | 26 | 27 | VE

Great Falls | 332 Springvale Rd. (Beach Mill Rd.), VA | 703-759-3800 | www.laubergechezfrancois.com

It's "always a special treat to dine" at this "charming" French country inn near Great Falls, VA, where "wonderful" Alsatian cooking and "impeccable service" ("each staff member really wants you to have a marvelous" time) combine to make this the "quintessential" place to "celebrate anything"; so whether you sit by the fireplace in winter or out on the "beautiful" patio in spring, rest assured you'll have "one of the most pleasant experiences imaginable."

L'Auberge Provençale *French* 28 | 27 | 26 | VE

Boyce | L'Auberge Provençale | 13630 Lord Fairfax Hwy. (Rte. 50), VA | 540-837-1375 | www.laubergeprovencale.com

"Well worth the drive" to "Virginia wine country", this "adorable little inn" in Boyce serves "classic" French tasting menus ("always interesting and delicious") in a "lovely", antiques-filled "old manor house" that comes "complete with fireplace for winter and gardens for summer"; it's a "pampering" but "expensive" experience that makes "the perfect romantic getaway", particularly if you "spend the night" – after all, "breakfast is fantastic too!"

Le Paradou *French* 27 | 26 | 23 | VE

Penn Quarter | 678 Indiana Ave. NW (bet. 6th & 7th Sts.) | 202-347-6780 | www.leparadou.net

Those who "love exquisite, elevated [New] French cuisine" should "prepare to be wowed" at "talented" chef/co-owner Yannick Cam's "hushed", "modern" Penn Quarter dining room, an "elegant and rewarding extravaganza" featuring "beautiful presentations" of "heavenly" food; but while devotees laud the "well-spaced tables" and "professional service", others suggest the prices "can be more expensive than April 15th"; P.S. the prix fixe lunch is a "real bargain."

Makoto *Japanese* 29 | 20 | 26 | VE

Palisades | 4822 MacArthur Blvd. NW (U St.) | 202-298-6866

This "minimalist" Palisades Japanese achieves "perfection" in capturing "the feel of a Kyoto kaiseki" restaurant – "right down to the slippers", so "take off your shoes" when you enter – and it does the same with an "exceptional" eight- to 10-course chef's menu "that highlights the foods of the season" and earns the No. 1 Food ranking in DC; there's also "fresh, gorgeous" sushi from the bar plus "impeccable" service, so despite "uncomfortable seating", it's a truly "wonderful experience."

Marcel's *Belgian/French*

Food	Decor	Service	Cost
28	24	27	VE

West End | 2401 Pennsylvania Ave. NW (24th St.) | 202-296-1166 | www.marcelsdc.com

Chef Robert Wiedmaier "adds a 'Flemish flair' to decadent, sumptuous French cuisine" at his "elegantly festive" West End Belgian-Gallic destination where everything from his boudin blanc that's "like eating a cloud" to near-"perfect" service to "colorful" decor makes it a "great place for a celebration"; it also offers what some call the "best pre-theater prix fixe" around (free limo service to the Kennedy Center included), and while it's an "expensive" experience, most agree it's "worth every penny"; N.B. jackets required.

Obelisk [S] [M] *Italian*

Food	Decor	Service	Cost
27	20	26	VE

Dupont Circle | 2029 P St. NW (bet. 20th & 21st Sts.) | 202-872-1180

They've "still got it" cheer champions of this "top-flight" Dupont Circle "gem" where chef-owner Peter Pastan's "heavenly prix fixe" "embraces Italian rusticity" with an "unforgettable" daily changing "parade" of "exquisite" dishes and "well-paired wines"; "irreproachable service" helps make it "everything a special night should be", but the "unpretentious" townhouse space is "tiny", so be sure to make "reservations weeks in advance."

Palena [S] [M] *American*

Food	Decor	Service	Cost
27	21	22	E

Cleveland Park | 3529 Connecticut Ave. NW (bet. Ordway & Porter Sts.) | 202-537-9250 | www.palenarestaurant.com

"Chef's chef" Frank Ruta "is at the top of his game" at this Cleveland Park New American where his "meticulous" "made-from-scratch" methods yield "exciting, scrumptious" seasonal prix fixe menus that are served by "polished" staffers in an "intimate" back dining room; patrons without a reservation can still "squeeze" into the "informal" "walk-in" cafe/bar for the likes of "fabulous" "gourmet burgers" ("a total steal"), but "success has brought crowds" with it, so "plan to wait."

Prime Rib [S] *Steak*

Food	Decor	Service	Cost
27	24	26	VE

Golden Triangle | 2020 K St. NW (bet. 20th & 21st Sts.) | 202-466-8811 | www.theprimerib.com

"Indulge" in "a trip back to" "Sinatra-style" "class" at this steakhouse "institution" where "well-connected" types "splurge" on "phone book-sized slabs of perfect prime rib", "excellent crab" and "real gin martinis" served by "formal waiters" in "opulent", "dimly lit" digs; "piano-bass combos" "set the mood", and as there's "no bending to changeable fashion", "proper dress" is de rigueur.

Rasika [S] *Indian*

Food	Decor	Service	Cost
26	24	23	E

Penn Quarter | 633 D St. NW (bet. 6th & 7th Sts.) | 202-637-1222 | www.rasikarestaurant.com

"Success has not spoiled" this "most original" Penn Quarter "hot spot" that "redefines Indian cuisine" with "spectacular" dishes like street fare-inspired small plates and "insanely delicious" appetizers, all paired with a "superior wine" selection; with a "gorgeous" interior bathed in an "orange glow", it's a "chic place" that's also "surprisingly comfortable" thanks to "outstanding" service.

Ray's The Steaks *Steak* 27 | 10 | 19 | E

Courthouse | 2300 Wilson Blvd. (Wayne St.) | Arlington, VA | 703-841-7297

"A better deal does not exist" than at this Arlington "living legend" near the Courthouse metro that's rated the Top Steakhouse in DC for "incredible" house-butchered beef (plus "affordable wines" and sides "at no extra charge") that puts the "expensive chains to shame"; carnivores patiently endure the "rushed" service, "stark" space and "maddening no-reservations policy", 'cause "that's the shtick"; N.B. it moved to these roomier quarters post-Survey, which may affect the Decor score.

NEW **Source, The** ☒ *American* 25 | 26 | 23 | VE

Penn Quarter | Newseum | 575 Pennsylvania Ave. NW (6th St.) | 202-637-6100 | www.wolfgangpuck.com

Situated next to the Penn Quarter's blockbuster Newseum, Wolfgang Puck's New American "glam spot" is "hipper than the DC norm", delivering "style and substance in spades", especially when it comes to the "sublime" but "pricey" Asian-accented fare that's served in a "sophisticated" upstairs room where "everything shimmers"; a "fantastic" wine list and a "well-trained" staff also add to the experience, and more casual fare (e.g. "fabulous" sliders and his "famous" brick-oven pizzas) is doled out in the "chic" downstairs lounge.

Tosca ☒ *Italian* 26 | 23 | 25 | E

Penn Quarter | 1112 F St. NW (bet. 11th & 12th Sts.) | 202-367-1990 | www.toscadc.com

"*Magnifico!*" swoon surveyors whose "socks are knocked off" by the "superb, sophisticated" Italian cuisine at this Penn Quarter "class act", a "stalwart" in the local "power-lunch" rotation; add in a "gracious" staff, a "subdued" room and an "in-depth wine list", and Italophiles swear that while it's "not cheap", "you get every bit of what you pay for"; P.S. the "bargain" $35 pre-theater menu "steals the show."

Zaytinya ◐ *Mediterranean/Mideastern* 25 | 24 | 21 | E

Penn Quarter | Pepco Bldg. | 701 Ninth St. NW (G St.) | 202-638-0800 | www.zaytinya.com

"Magically blending both scene and substance (an accomplishment akin to achieving bipartisan cooperation on the Hill)", this Penn Quarter Med-Middle Eastern exudes "edgy class", letting patrons "snack it up big time" on "tantalizing" Greek, Turkish and Lebanese small plates served by a "courteous staff" in a "striking", "soaring" space; since everything from the "little pillows of fluffy hot bread" to the "unique" wines to the "affordable" tabs is a true "delight", you can expect both "crowds and noise", so "make a reservation."

Wine Vintage Chart

This chart, based on our 0 to 30 scale, is designed to help you select wine. The ratings (by **Howard Stravitz,** a law professor at the University of South Carolina) reflect the vintage quality and the wine's readiness to drink. We exclude the 1991–1993 vintages because they are not that good. A dash indicates the wine is either past its peak or too young to rate. Loire ratings are for dry white wines.

Whites	89	90	94	95	96	97	98	99	00	01	02	03	04	05	06	07
French:																
Alsace	24	25	24	23	23	22	25	23	25	26	22	21	24	25	24	-
Burgundy	23	22	-	27	26	23	21	25	25	24	27	23	26	27	25	23
Loire Valley	-	-	-	-	-	-	-	-	24	25	26	22	23	27	24	-
Champagne	26	29	-	26	27	24	23	24	24	22	26	21	-	-	-	-
Sauternes	25	28	-	21	23	25	23	24	24	29	25	24	21	26	23	27
California:																
Chardonnay	-	-	-	-	-	-	-	24	23	26	26	25	26	29	25	-
Sauvignon Blanc	-	-	-	-	-	-	-	-	-	-	-	26	27	26	27	26
Austrian:																
Grüner Velt./ Riesling	-	-	-	25	21	26	26	25	22	23	25	26	26	25	24	-
German:	26	27	24	23	26	25	26	23	21	29	27	24	26	28	24	-

Reds	89	90	94	95	96	97	98	99	00	01	02	03	04	05	06	07
French:																
Bordeaux	25	29	21	26	25	23	25	24	29	26	24	26	24	28	25	23
Burgundy	24	26	-	26	27	25	22	27	22	24	27	25	24	27	25	-
Rhône	28	28	23	26	22	24	27	26	27	26	-	26	24	27	25	-
Beaujolais	-	-	-	-	-	-	-	-	-	-	22	24	21	27	25	23
California:																
Cab./Merlot	-	28	29	27	25	28	23	26	-	27	26	25	24	26	23	-
Pinot Noir	-	-	-	-	-	-	-	24	23	25	28	26	27	25	24	-
Zinfandel	-	-	-	-	-	-	-	-	-	25	23	27	22	23	23	-
Oregon:																
Pinot Noir	-	-	-	-	-	-	-	-	-	-	27	25	26	27	26	-
Italian:																
Tuscany	-	25	23	24	20	29	24	27	24	27	-	25	27	25	24	-
Piedmont	27	27	-	-	26	27	26	25	28	27	-	24	23	26	25	24
Spanish:																
Rioja	-	-	26	26	24	25	-	25	24	27	-	24	25	26	24	-
Ribera del Duero/Priorat	-	-	26	26	27	25	24	25	24	27	20	24	27	26	24	-
Australian:																
Shiraz/Cab.	-	-	24	26	23	26	28	24	24	27	27	25	26	26	24	-
Chilean:	-	-	-	-	-	24	-	25	23	26	24	25	24	26	25	24

Zagat Products

Available wherever books are sold or at ZAGAT.com. To customize Zagat guides as gifts or marketing tools, call 800-540-9609.

RESTAURANTS & MAPS

America's Dining Deals
America's Top Restaurants
Atlanta
Beijing
Boston
Brooklyn
California Wine Country
Cape Cod & The Islands
Chicago
Chicago Dining Deals
Connecticut
Europe's Top Restaurants
Hamptons (incl. wineries)
Hawaii
Hong Kong
Las Vegas
London
Long Island (incl. wineries)
Los Angeles | So. California (guide & map)
Miami Beach
Miami | So. Florida
Montréal
New Jersey
New Jersey Shore
New Orleans
New York City (guide & map)
New York City Dining Deals
Palm Beach
Paris
Philadelphia
San Diego
San Francisco (guide & map)
San Francisco Dining Deals
Seattle
Shanghai
Texas
Tokyo
Toronto
Vancouver
Washington, DC | Baltimore
Washington, DC Dining Deals
Westchester | Hudson Valley
World's Top Restaurants

LIFESTYLE GUIDES

America's Top Golf Courses
Dating/Dumping Guide (NYC & LA)
Movie Guide
Music Guide
NYC Gourmet Shop./Entertaining
NYC Shopping

NIGHTLIFE GUIDES

Los Angeles
New York City
San Francisco

HOTEL & TRAVEL GUIDES

Beijing
Disneyland Resort Guide
Hawaii
Hong Kong
Las Vegas
London
Montréal
New Orleans
Shanghai
Top U.S. Hotels, Resorts & Spas
Toronto
Vancouver
Walt Disney World Insider's Guide
World's Top Hotels, Resorts & Spas

WEB & WIRELESS SERVICES

ZAGAT TO GO℠ for Smartphones
ZAGAT.com℠ • ZAGAT.mobi℠

7 20613 06146 4